26-7

Prison Treatment and Parole Survival:

An Empirical Assessment

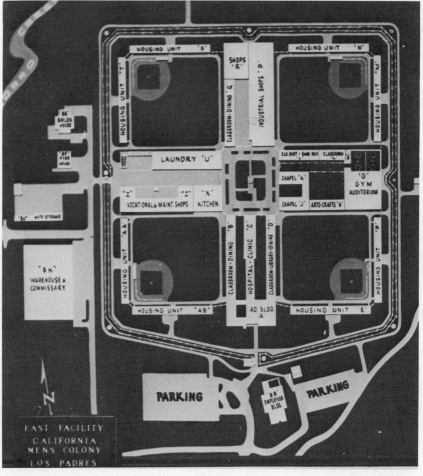

Prison Treatment and Parole Survival:

An Empirical Assessment

GENE KASSEBAUM

DAVID WARD

DANIEL WILNER

with chapter collaboration by
Renée Ward
and John Vincent

JOHN WILEY & SONS, INC.

New York · London · Sydney · Toronto

This study was supported by the United States Public Health Service through a grant from the National Institute of Mental Health (5-R11-MH89).

Photographs courtesy of the Department of Correction, State of California.

Library of Congress Catalog Card Number: 70-153082

ISBN 0-471-46000-1

Printed in the United States of America.

10 9 8 7 6 5 4 3 2 1

Preface

||||||||||||||||||||||||||||||||||||||||||||||||||||||||||||||||||||||||||||||||||||||||||||||||||||||||||||||||||||||||||||||||||||||||||||||||||||||||||||||||||||||||||||||

The research reported in this book is concerned with the systematic evaluation of certain short-run and long-run effects of participation in a correctional treatment program called "group counseling," which has been widely adopted in California. Group counseling, as defined by the former State Coordinator, Robert Harrison, ". . . is an effort to use the small group method to constructively increase the positive impact of correctional employees on inmates and parolees. It is an effort to develop more healthy communication and relationships within the prison. It is focused on conscious reality problems and feelings—past, present and future. The counselors include correctional officers, vocational teachers, shop foreman and others who have the greatest contact with inmates."[1] According to Walter Dunbar, the Director of the California Department of Corrections during the period of this study, group counseling ". . . attempts to reduce institutional tensions and incidents, encourage participation in correctional programs, and increase parole success."[2] But it is a truism that in the world of human affairs there are multiple versions of reality which, in part, result from the different positions men occupy in that world. Group counseling as viewed by some of its participants is exemplified by a poem, discovered in a man's cell following his escape from a California prison in 1959.

GROUP COUNCLING

The guard brought a duckett, on it it read—group
councling tomorrow.
Be their or you are dead.
The object of this meeting is as far as I can see.
Is to squeel on each other.

[1] Robert M. Harrison, "Mental Health Applications in the California Correctional System," a paper presented in Boston, June 1960.
[2] Robert M. Harrison and Paul F. C. Mueller, *Clue-Hunting About Group Counseling and Parole Outcome*, Research Report No. 11, Department of Corrections, State of California, May 1964.

The biggest fink goes free.

Thers one now telling his life as a boy according
to him it was all

Sorrow no joy.

His mother was a prostute his father was a drunk. And
his brother turned his sister out when he was just a punk

There are all tipes hear encluding a few queer.

Thers hypo Joe, and Clipto Pete and that two bit pimp
that I knew on the street

We are all hear to gether regardless of our crime

And you can bet your cottin picking ass were going to do
some time

So lets knock off this shit of talking to the Man, and
let him figure

It out for him self the best way he can.

Actually, many correctional staff members, including Harrison and Dunbar, were aware of the problems in developing and implementing an effective correctional treatment program; the interest of these men and others in locating deficiencies in old and new programs supplied part of the motivation for the Department of Corrections' cooperative attitude toward this study. Moreover, some inmates, perhaps even the writer of the poem, do become psychologically involved in group counseling sessions. But even taking this into account, it appears that the Department of Corrections perceives counseling somewhat differently—or, at least, ideally intends it to be different—than it often is viewed by the inmates, who are its ultimate recipients. The explanation of this disparity is inevitably part of our job of evaluation. Essentially this study reports on the extent to which the publicly expressed goals of group counseling, in fact, are achieved.

Many formidable problems are involved in conducting fair evaluation studies, and we discuss these difficulties in several chapters of this book. One problem is the task of putting the findings in a perspective that affords a view of the conclusions and their supporting data; a perspective that is neither so close to particulars that its general relevance is lost nor a perspective that takes in so wide a scope that generalizations become rootless. This task is particularly difficult when the programs of public institutions are being studied. Despite the premise that in a free society the workings of government are legitimately open to the scrutiny of citizens, the possibility always exists that conclusions critical of the program of a public agency will have the effect of reducing support for that program's goals.

Our purpose in writing this book is to describe accurately the group counseling program as it was carried out in California's newest prison, and to compare the behavior in prison and on parole of men who had counseling and men who did not have counseling, in an effort to determine whether participation had the effects that were expected.

Our perspective is that departments of correction are bureaucratic organizations that are charged with a number of responsibilities by the larger community. The most important of these directions relate to the contention, held by some, that law violators should be punished; the contention of others that law violators should be rehabilitated; and the contention of many that lawbreakers should be rehabilitated while they are kept away from the rest of the community in correctional institutions. The reconciliation of these mandates is difficult in day-to-day prison operations. Furthermore, it is difficult to determine the normative basis for actions that are taken in a prison or parole division. Despite public statements to the contrary, we maintain that prisons and parole divisions operate first and foremost to achieve the goal of social control. Peace and quiet are the first order of business in prison, and the detection of law violations or of signs of *impending* law violation is the first order of business of parole.

We begin our study with an expanded discussion of these points and return to them throughout the book. Chapter II describes the prison where the research was conducted and points up the social control aspects of prison management as manifested by the disciplinary machinery. Chapter III gives the design of the study and discusses the methodological problems encountered in evaluative research. Chapter IV is concerned with a special training program for prison counselors that was added to the training provided by the Department of Corrections. Chapter V describes group counseling sessions and gives the views of inmates who participated in the programs. Chapter VI examines the question of whether participation in the group program modified the attitudes of the inmates. Chapter VII applies our argument about the primacy of social control goals to the parole experiences of our study sample. Chapter VIII presents the research findings that are related to the effect of group counseling participation on parole survival, that is, adhering to the many conditions imposed by the parole contract and not being reported for new law violations. Chapter IX raises the question of what factors *in addition* to treatment status are related to parole survival. Chapter X presents a new view of the prison community as part of larger organizational stuctures, and also discusses the problems that evaluative research studies pose for administrators and treatment professionals in institutions.

It has not been our intention—nor did the Department of Corrections expect us—to make an overall study of the state's facilities or to make recommendations concerning how to run prisons. We spent much time talking to people who run prisons, and we are so convinced of the complexity of this task that we suggest no simple remedies. But the results of this and several other evaluations of correctional effectiveness have implications for both corrections and the social sciences, which we cannot ignore.

Much of the material for this study was obtained from conversations, planning sessions, and interviews with many men in the Department of Corrections. The list—too long to enumerate—runs from administrators like Richard McGee, and Walter Dunbar, to new correctional officers and helpful young ladies in records archives. The Superintendent of California Men's Colony, John H. Klinger (now retired), gave the project his support throughout. Those who know Klinger will understand that at California Men's Colony there was no question about who was running the prison, but Klinger never interpreted his responsibilities to include the running of the study. Unavoidably, the presence of outside researchers in the institution caused extra work for many of the staff (often for reasons that may not have been clear or agreeable), but the superintendent never attempted to ease his load by making our load heavier. We also spent many profitable hours in the office of Deputy Superintendent, Harold Field, who always accommodated one more change in the original plan for the daily operation of California Men's Colony. We express appreciation also to the then Program Administrators, Irving Abkin, Clement Swaggerty, and Howard McGarry for their cooperation and assistance.

We are particularly grateful for the support of J. Douglas Grant who was, during the early days of the study, Chief of Research, California Department of Corrections (CDC). His successors, John Conrad and Lawrence Bennett continued to make departmental resources available to us for our extended parole follow-up. The staff of the CDC Research Division also gave us much technical advice and information, particularly Paul Mueller and Miss Vida Ryan. Robert Harrison gave his constant support to the project.

Many persons contributed to the research. Carl Hopkins of the School of Public Health, U.C.L.A., helped to devise the initial statistical design, and in the early months of the project we drew heavily on his talents. The tireless service of Nancy Jorgensen during a year of often solitary work on the prison records is responsible for a body of data crucial to the entire enterprise. Will Kennedy was our resident sociologist at California Men's Colony (CMC) and, as the junior member of the field crew, often was left with the hard work of gathering data while others thought up still more questions to ask. Robert Martinson spent a year chasing both parolees and their records and set up a workable procedure for collecting parole agent reports throughout the state. John Vincent bridged the gap between the authors and the digital computer and usually was able to bring the computer more than halfway. He also is coauthor of Chapter Nine. Renée Ward worked on the parole follow-up phase of the study, made editorial contributions throughout the book and is coauthor of Chapter Seven. William C. Schutz conducted the supplemental training program for group leaders and is the author of Appendix C. Stephanie Glass provided editorial assistance in the first draft. We also are grateful for the help of the many secretaries who assisted us on the project. Our appreciation can be only collectively indicated to our anonymous respondents at the prison and on parole.

A number of very busy people spent much time reading an earlier draft of this manuscript. Their careful reviews and critiques were not only helpful but constituted an essential step in presenting the findings. They include our academic colleagues, Daniel Glaser, Donald Gottfredson, Sheldon Messinger, Jerome Rabow, Phillips Cutright, Irving Tallman, Donald MacTavish, Tony Cline, Ulla Bondeson, and several members of the California Department of Corrections, including Ernest Reimer, Lawrence Bennett, and Irving Abkin.

None of the ultimate responsibility for the final form of this book rests on any of these persons. That belongs to us.

Gene G. Kassebaum
David A. Ward
Daniel M. Wilner

Contents

Prison Treatment and Parole Survival:

An Empirical Assessment

Correctional agencies and social control: prisons gowned in hospital whites

The cells in the medium security prison where this study took place are painted in a variety of pastel colors. Each inmate has a key to his own "room." Recreational activities include outdoor bowling, tennis, handball, and shuffleboard. One inmate received a disciplinary report for breaking a window when he hit a golf ball with too much vigor on the miniature golf course. Another inmate tried to sue the superintendent for causing him to become overweight because the prison fare included "too much fried chicken, strawberry shortcake, and other rich food." Major components of the treatment program included: group counseling, "community living" (a version of the therapeutic community approach), alcoholics anonymous, formal education through high school, and vocational training. Limited individual psychotherapy was available from the prison's clinical staff. An effort was made in one of the prison's four separate 600-man living units to address inmates as "Mr. —."

These features of California Men's Colony—East are among the most visible indicators of the burgeoning influence of the treatment philosophy in American penology. But multicolored rooms are still cells, inmate keys do not work when the master cell lock switch is thrown, one cannot go home when the bowling match is over, full participation in all aspects of the treatment program does not guarantee release, and the violation of any of a detailed list of inmate regulations may be punished by up to 29 days in an isolation cell (not "room"). One of the contentions of inmates at California Men's Colony—East and an important question for this study was whether an elaborate treatment program and some new amenities for inmates and parolees were only disguises for a correctional organization whose real interests were in running a peaceful prison and in maintaining

1

surveillance over parolees. Students of penology and prison and parole workers have emphasized for more than a decade the "dual mandate" of corrections: treatment and punishment. It has been further argued that these goals are to a large extent contradictory and that the primacy of one has negative implications for satisfying the other. Actually, arguments about the raison d'etre for prisons also include contentions that imprisonment serves a deterrent function for other would-be law breakers, that prisons, at least, remove criminals from the community, and that penal confinement serves a retributive function. There have been shifts in public support for these several functions. But prisons have a tendency to continue to operate in a fairly uniform manner despite these shifts and despite the interest of various groups in coming up with new approaches to cope with "the crime problem." Prisons are parts of bureaucratic organizations and, as such, they come to have lives of their own. Thus, issues of organizational survival (enhancement if possible) and the personal careers of members of the organization are factors that have a major bearing on the manner in which popular mandates are discharged.

In the pages that follow we describe a prison treatment program and report the results of a study of the effects of participation in this program on the attitudes and behavior of men in a California prison and on their chances for surviving parole after their release into the community. But our study of "group counseling" cannot be presented without also describing the context within which the program was implemented. California Men's Colony—East, the site of the research, is a *medium security* prison, which means that it clearly has the "dual mandate" to provide both treatment and custody. Furthermore, the prison is part of a larger bureaucratic organization and, hence, maintains exchange relationships with other parts of the system and is subject to policies set for the entire system.

Thus, in addition to describing the group treatment program and to measuring its impact on inmates, we also describe the system for maintaining control of the inmates and order in the prison and the system for maintaining control over men paroled to the community. When we have finished, we shall have reported not only the effects of participation in a prison treatment program but also shall have shed light on the contention of some men in the prison that group counseling was really not a treatment program but, instead, was a new custodial device.

Deviance and social control

Given our commitment to consider control issues as well as treatment issues in a correctional system, we appropriately begin with a discussion of the general significance of an institutional arrangement for the control of behavior. In a very broad sense, the workings of societies may be viewed as a dialectic between two sets of forces: one tending to sustain a degree of order, continuity, and structure, and the other producing change and departures from the expected.[1] Deviant behavior is behavior that departs from normative expectations to the extent that some response from the community is evoked. That response may range from social ostracism and warnings to legal prohibitions and formal countermeasures taken against "lawbreakers." As a result of shifts in public opinion, definitions of deviant behavior change from time to time, and the label of "deviance" includes acts that were once regarded as violations of the law but because of changes in the law are no longer "illegal," acts that some people or groups contend should be legally prohibited, thereby making them criminal, and acts that are presently prohibited by the substantive criminal law. It is in response to acts that fall into this last category that formal mechanisms of social control are activated.

Federal, state, and local governments are organizations of social power that operate on a basis of less than 100 percent popular support and have at their disposal a variety of mechanisms to control the incidence of illegal behavior.[2] But, as the definitions of illegal behavior have varied over time and from place to place, so have the methods of dealing with lawbreakers. In addition to execution, branding, and physical torture, societies have sought to segregate criminals or enemies of the State by means of exile and by confinement in penal colonies, galley ships, dungeons, asylums, workhouses, labor camps, farms, and mines. Although contemporary penal policy still involves the segregation of lawbreakers in special institutions, namely prisons, much has changed. Older forms of incarceration were explicitly harsh in theory as well as in practice, and programs to promote the reintegration of the prisoner into society were not a matter of concern. In most of the United States at the present time, imprisonment still involves a variety of deprivations, but prisons also operate according to an ideology phrased in terms of the modification of criminal behavior patterns and the eventual reintegration of their inmates into the larger community. Foremost among the means devised to accomplish the goal of "rehabilitation" are a variety of "treatment programs."

The interest in correctional treatment is of recent origin, having strongly

[1] See Don Martindale, *The Nature and Types of Sociological Theory*, Boston: Houghton Mifflin, 1960, pp. 127–210; and Ralf Dahrendorf, *Class and Class Conflict in Industrial Society*, Stanford: Stanford University Press, 1959.

[2] See C. N. Cassanelli, *The Politics of Freedom*, Seattle: University of Washington Press, 1961, where government is defined as "an organization consisting of many sub-organizations and possessing a near monopoly of the means of violence within a society. It determines and executes formal public policy and it maintains an implicit but constant threat to make use of means of violence in case it is not obeyed," p. 6.

emerged only during the past several decades, due in part to humanitarian concerns but also as a result of the realization that confinement in even the harshest prison was not deterring ex-inmates from continuing their criminal careers after release. A third factor accounting for the emergence of the treatment philosophy has been the rapid growth and development of the behavioral sciences and of the related professions of social work, clinical psychology, and psychiatry.

Penal policy based on the notion of deterrence by punishment has been modified to include concepts based on the premise that criminal behavior derives from faulty personality development and from impaired social and economic conditions which can be altered only by providing the opportunities for correcting and improving these impairments. Confinement has come to be justified as providing the setting within which rehabilitation takes place through participation in programs such as individual psychotherapy, group counseling, academic education, and vocational training. But penal philosophy is changing, not changed, and despite the new language, the new physical settings, and the new program, the question is: To what extent do treatment considerations influence the day-to-day operations of prisons and parole agencies? Phrased in another way, the question is whether, at California Men's Colony—East, we are studying patients or prisoners.

Patients or prisoners?

When confronted with some of the published reports of treatment programs in correctional institutions, it is easy to forget that one is not reading about a clinic or a hospital. The old terms of "guard," "convict," "cell," and "prison" have been replaced by "correctional officer," "resident," "room," and "institution" in all but the maximum security prisons in most departments of correction. Undoubtedly, this reflects more than a mere change in nomenclature. Even so, security fences and locks remain, and it is only realistic to keep them in mind so that the discussion of treatment does not become too rarified for the everyday world of prison confinement.

The distinctive aspect of life at California Men's Colony is not the fact that inmates are participating in a psychologically based treatment program. Criminal behavior has increasingly become subject to psychiatric interpretations, and in this regard the prison inmate does not differ from many of his peers in the free world.[3] In recent decades the rapid expansion

[3] Estimates of the extent of mental and emotional disturbance in the United States vary, and the subject is too complex to detain us here. For example, the "Midtown

of psychologically based techniques of influence, persuasion, and manipulation of behavior has occurred throughout American society. They include motivation research in advertising, the "human relations" movement in industry, and a wide range of psychological and quasi-therapeutic aids that are available for the distressed individual, the lonely crowd, and the tarnished corporate image. Tranquilizing and energizing drugs are widely prescribed, and some prepaid medical care plans now include psychotherapy.

Now, it is also the case that treatment programs are directed toward persons who are not voluntary participants. Most important among them are the programs in public mental hospitals and prisons. Correctional treatment is to be distinguished from treatment in medicine and psychiatry in terms of intake and release procedures.[4] In medicine the patient places himself in the conditional and limited care of the physician whose task is to alleviate his distress. The right of the patient to initiate treatment or to withdraw from it is rarely questioned except in the case of highly contagious disease. Patients in a custodial psychiatric facility have been "committed" and are not permitted to leave the grounds as an expression of refusing or withdrawing from treatment. (They can remain "unreceptive." Unfortunately, a stance of this kind quickly encourages the diagnostic label of "chronic" and may result in nearly permanent incarceration or until such time as the patient becomes "receptive" to treatment and may then be regarded as able to function in free society.) In psychiatric treatment the patient's felt distress, symptoms, anxieties, and feelings are examined; if psychosis is suspected (or more accurately, in some cases if a person's relatives are attempting to get him committed to a mental institution because of suspected psychosis) an effort is made to determine the kind of treatment best suited to the disorder.

In the case of criminals, however, the offender or his family seldom seek treatment through judicial intervention, and the primary concern of law enforcement agencies is, in most cases, not with the state of the offender's psyche. The law is behavioristic: a proven illegal act can lead to imprisonment and, hence, to "treatment" whether or not it is associated with diagnosed personality disturbance.

Because the ends of medicine and law are different, their procedures are different. The initial distinction is clear, even in phraseology. Thus,

Manhattan Study," classified 23.4 per cent of a sample of 1,660 non-institutionalized in-residence New Yorkers as mentally impaired. See Leo Srole, Thomas S. Langner, Stanley T. Michael, Marvin K. Opler, and Thomas A. C. Rennie, *Mental Health in the Metropolis*, New York: McGraw-Hill Book Company, 1962, p. 138.

[4] See Erving Goffman's essay, "The Medical Model and Mental Hospitalization," in *Asylums*, Garden City: Anchor Books, 1961, pp. 321–386.

in medicine the patient is said to have a "presenting complaint"; in criminal law the State has a complaint. In medicine the first task is to arrive at a diagnosis; in law it is to establish that an illegal act was committed by the accused. In medicinal procedure the treatment follows from the diagnosis and may involve confinement; in criminal procedure the treatment is a consequence of conviction and involves a diagnosis only to the extent that probation departments may recommend probation in lieu of imprisonment. In medicine the patient seeks treatment for relief from the symptoms; in prison the inmate typically seeks release from the treatment.

Lawbreakers may be sent to prison for "treatment" or to be "rehabilitated," but there is a question as to whether participation in any or all elements of the prison's treatment program for periods of many months or even years has any real relevance to the decision to release the inmate from "treatment." Parole decisions also are based on the concerns of the public about releasing certain types of offenders "too soon" and on the kind of "adjustment" the inmate has made in prison. Aubert and Messinger, in differentiating the sick role and criminal behavior, have drawn attention to the nominal status of the notion of "recovery" of the criminal:

> The most convincing argument for the irrelevance of recovery predictions in the criminal law is that the law so readily substitutes fines for imprisonment, and that some modern systems of criminal law authorize imprisonment for periods far in excess of the life expectancy of any human being. In fines there is obviously no complication about the predicted time of recovery. Further, the idea of punishing people in terms of time-serving is a relatively new one; most systems of criminal law have done without sanctions meted out in time periods. The criminal law draws upon the future merely because under modern conditions time is one of the dimensions along which sanctions can be ordered.[5]

The recent perspective adopted by correctional treatment specialists considers as a given the nonconformity of the persons delivered into their charge; and, under new indeterminant sentence laws, staff members no longer have to regard the expiration of a given span of time in prison as the signal for release of the prisoner. What is required now is the imposition of incarceration, plus treatment, plus some "signs of change" in the prisoner's behavior and attitudes. To drastically oversimplify: formerly

---

[5] Vilhelm Aubert and Sheldon Messinger, "The Criminal and the Sick," *Inquiry*, 1 (1958), pp. 137–160. See also, Vilhelm Aubert, "Legal Justice and Mental Health," in *The Hidden Society*, Totowa, New Jersey: The Bedminster Press, 1965, pp. 55–82.

a fixed span of time was subtracted from the criminal's free life as the price of his crime; today, treatment is imposed on him until such time as he is adjudged by a releasing authority to be relatively safe for a return to the larger community.[6]

Once inside prison, treatment is available to inmates both on a self-referral basis and, in an increasing number of cases, as a mandatory obligation, based on staff opinion that participation in a certain program will benefit them. In many correctional systems, for instance, in California, the initial period of confinement includes a review of the background characteristics of each inmate, and a program is recommended for the inmate by a diagnostic and classification committee. This recommended program, however, is subject to influence by the availability of facilities (types of school and vocational training programs), the length of the waiting lists to get into various jobs and programs, the inmate's custody classification, and the operational needs of the prison. (For example, are inmates needed to work in the kitchen or in the powerhouse?) Also, despite the administration of batteries of psychological tests, there are few empirical studies or even theoretical formuli that link a profile of scores with either performance in or probable response to treatment programs.[7] In California,

---

[6] A good example of enforced confinement specifically for the sake of "rehabilitation" is provided by California's civil commitment of persons addicted to narcotics or "in imminent danger of becoming addicted to narcotics." Persons convicted of felonies or misdemeanors (not necessarily related to drug use) may have criminal proceedings suspended prior to the imposition of sentence and be referred for new separate civil commitment proceedings. The superior court ". . . may commit the persons to the custody of the Director of Corrections for confinement in the California Rehabilitation Center. When the rehabilitation commitment has been complied with, *or on the completion of seven years* (italics ours), the individual is returned to the committing court . . . and the proceedings which were suspended after the conviction of a felony (misdemeanor) are again activated." Civil commitment proceedings may also be initiated by other persons including family members, and even in these cases, persons are committed for treatment until such time as ". . . the Director of Corrections and the Narcotic Addict Evaluation Authority believe the individual has recovered from his addiction, or at the end of seven years. . . ." Even voluntary commitments to the California Rehabilitation Center are ". . . for a definite period of two and one-half years even though he initially requested the treatment." *Civil Commitment Program for Narcotics Addicts 1961 through 1966: Summary Statistics*, Administrative Statistics Section, Research Division, Department of Corrections, Sacramento, California, December 1966, pp. 2–3.

[7] For an exceptional case see Marguerite Q. Grant, "Interaction Between Kinds of Treatments and Kinds of Delinquents, A Current Trend in Correctional Research," *Inquiries Concerning Kinds of Treatment for Kinds of Delinquents*, Monograph No. 2, Sacramento, California: Board of Corrections, July, 1961, pp. 5–14 and Marguerite Q. Warren, "The Community Treatment Project: History and Prospects," in S. A. Yefsky (ed.) *Law Enforcement Science and Technology*, Washington, D.C.: Thompson Book Co., 1967, pp. 191–200.

for example, group counseling is recommended for virtually all offenders of all ages and educational levels in all types of institutions. Although there exists a belief among staff members that not everyone will profit from the counseling experience, there is no procedure for screening inmates for assignment to the group programs. In those institutions where participation in group counseling or community living programs is compulsory, there is again no distinction between inmates who might benefit from, or be receptive to, such treatment and those who will probably not benefit or who are resistant.

Prison classification committees also generally recommend to all inmates that they enroll in vocational training, academic education, religious and recreational programs; but active participation in every program offered in the prison does not guarantee release. This curious situation seems to reflect the lack of generalized support for any explicit theory of crime causation by correctional administrations and parole board members. Without explicit linkages between presumed causes of deviance and countermeasures related to those causes, adherence to vague and conflicting standards will continue to characterize correctional decision making.

The points with respect to crime causation that are of key importance to correctional treatment programming are: (1) whether there are theories of crime causation for which there is supporting empirical evidence; (2) whether there are treatment programs based on these causal explanations; and (3) whether there is evidence that the treatment is effective in modifying criminal behavior. Our study here deals with the second and third of these points.

There are several other features of correctional treatment that must be included in this discussion. First, the prison inmate should be viewed as occupying a unique position in a treatment setting in that he is required to assist in the day-to-day maintenance and operation of the organization. Work, for example, is referred to by some staff members as a "privilege," but inmates who do not avail themselves of this "privilege" may be subject to disciplinary action. Although some patients in mental hospitals may be incapacitated in one way or another, all patients can be excused from work because there is a paid civilian staff to operate the institution. Prison inmates are required to work because the punitive aspect of confinement is still a reality, because it is argued that order and control are enhanced when inmates are busily occupied, and because work is asserted to be "character building" (that is, it serves a rehabilitative function).

A final distinction between medical and correctional treatment is that the post-release status of the prison inmate differs fundamentally from the released patient of a medical or mental institution. The post-release status of a recovering patient is one that typically entitles him to certain exemptions from his normal role obligations and to more dependence on other persons; the illness can even qualify him for insurance and unemployment benefits. On the other hand, as will be discussed in Chapter VII, the parolee not only reenters the community without exemptions from role obligations but has, in fact, additional obligations that exceed the ones of free citizens. The parolee, for example, has an obligation to find a job and to keep it, and some actions that are legal for free citizens, for instance, the right to leave the city or the state, to open a charge account, and to get married, are subject to official approval. Moreover, the increased surveillance to which he is subject, combined with the greater variety of his activities that are subject to official action and the limits of his civil rights, makes detection of any further illegal behavior more likely for him than for free citizens.

The point here is not to debate the wisdom of these measures, but to underscore some of the salient features of the treatment program examined in this study. Any discussion of correctional treatment programs and techniques must take into account the legal status of the offender in prison and on parole, as well as the institutional context in which the treatment takes place.

Treatment in the prison setting

In formulating a design for the assessment of the effects of group counseling on prison inmates, we took as a point of departure the question of how a large-scale treatment program could be implemented in an institutional setting that is traditionally authoritarian by intention, and deprivational in effect. It is worth repeating that the rise of the treatment movement in penology has not been accompanied by the disappearance of custodial interests. Treatment programs have represented an additional function for prisons instead of a replacement for custodial practices. In California, the job of the correctional officer has slowly but surely come to include the participation in treatment activities in addition to his traditional responsibility for the safekeeping of the prisoner, which has been the primary business of prison guards since the first turnkey in the first gaol. Directly relevant to this study is the fact that during the past decade correctional officers have come to play a key role in the group counseling and community living programs.

CONTRADICTORY DIRECTIVES IN CORRECTIONS[8]

The part of the "dual mandate" of corrections that relates to treatment goals is based on an assumption of continuity in behavior and personality between therapist and patient. This philosophy has been implemented in the California Department of Corrections by techniques that, to varying degrees, employ permissiveness, nondirection, and personal acceptance of the inmate. For example, a departmental manual on group counseling states:

> The first requirement (of group counseling) is the development of the group setting necessary for clients to feel free to discuss with security their own and others' feelings and attitudes toward the situation in which they find themselves. The second requirement . . . is a condition of mutual acceptance among those in the group . . . not only must the group feel free to discuss their problems, but the general atmosphere in which they do so must be supportive.
>
> In general, the procedures and techniques used . . . are secondary to the warm and accepting attitudes and the freedom of the client to make choices and respond spontaneously in the treatment situation.[9]

At the same time, another departmental directive warns that undue familiarity is prohibited:

> Employees shall not indulge in undue familiarity with inmates nor shall they permit undue familiarity on the part of inmates toward themselves. Whenever there is reason for an employee to discuss the prisoner's problems with him, the employee shall maintain a helpful but professional attitude toward the prisoner. The employee shall not discuss his own personal affairs with the prisoner nor shall any employee engage in any game, contest or sport with any inmate.[10]

The rules also clearly define the subordinate status of any inmate vis-à-vis the staff:

> All inmates shall promptly and politely obey orders or instructions given them by employees of the institution or by employees of other agencies in charge of inmates.[11]

---

[8] See Donald R. Cressey, "Contradictory Directives in Complex Organizations," *Administrative Science Quarterly*, **4** (June, 1959) pp. 1–19.

[9] Norman Fenton, *Group Counseling: A Preface to its Use in Correctional and Welfare Agencies*, Sacramento, California: The Institute for the Study of Crime and Delinquency, 1961, pp. 46–50.

[10] *Rules of the Director of Corrections*, Department of Corrections, California, 1960.

[11] *Ibid.*

Custodial ends require that inmates be induced to conform to a set of regulations that maximizes the visibility, predictability, orderliness, and docility of the institutional population. The efficiency of a given custodial staff is assessed in terms of the extent to which it obtains inmate compliance with regulations, and its ability to prevent disturbances and quell resistance, whether this is accomplished through coercion and manipulation or by persuasion and incentives. The problem of integrating these two sets of imperatives—the custodial end of conformity and order and the treatment end of free expression and permissiveness—has received much attention in the literature, but it remains an administrative problem of considerable proportions.[12]

A second, separate problem in fulfilling the rehabilitation mandate is the limited number of professional clinical personnel who can be induced to implement treatment programs as they are ideally visualized. The supply of psychiatrists, clinical psychologists, and psychiatric social workers is not considered adequate to the program needs of the inmate population even in the few correctional institutions for inmates legally defined as criminally insane or severely disturbed. Thus, a treatment program that requires staff members with high levels of formal education and training is available to only a select few of the inmate population.[13]

[12] A study of an experimental treatment program that emphasizes the role custodial interests play in determining the extent to which treatment considerations really prevail in the day-to-day operation of a correctional institution is Elliot Studt, Sheldon L. Messinger, Thomas P. Wilson, *C-Unit: Search for Community in Prison*, New York: Russell Sage Foundation, 1968. See also Donald R. Cressey, "Limitations on Organization of the Prison," in *Theoretical Studies in Social Organization of the Prison*, New York: Social Science Research Council, Pamphlet No. 15, 1960, pp. 78–110; Richard A. Cloward, "Social Control in the Prison," *ibid.*, pp. 20–48; Lloyd E. Ohlin, "Conflicting Interests in Correctional Objectives," *ibid.*, pp. 111–129; Richard A. Korn and Lloyd W. McCorkle, *Criminology and Penology*, New York: Henry Holt and Company, 1959, pp. 441–447; 495–506.

[13] The group counseling program may be seen as another of the efforts to establish, within prisons, so-called "therapeutic communities." The California Department of Corrections has been particularly interested in this approach and has been much influenced by the work of Maxwell Jones. Dr. Jones worked as a consultant to the Department and supervised the establishment of a therapeutic community-type program at the California Institution for Men. For descriptions of this approach, see Maxwell Jones, *The Therapeutic Community*, New York: Basic Books, Inc., 1953. It is to be noted that the concepts of social psychiatry are difficult to apply in prison. Jones writes:

It would . . . be fascinating to know what success a numerous staff of psychoanalysts would have with a selected group of prison inmates. However, it has proved impossible to attract psychiatrists (including non-analysts) in sufficient numbers to assess in any large-scale experiment what they have to contribute. It is doubtful if they could function adequately in a prison setting unless the anti-therapeutic factors in the social organization

The pressure on correctional personnel to rehabilitate criminals on a mass scale, coupled with the small numbers of clinically trained personnel, has provided a major impetus for the development of group treatment programs that utilize all categories of prison staff members including, most importantly, correctional officers. (Group counseling thus is to be distinguished from *group therapy* in which the groups are led by clinical personnel.) Hence, the largest treatment program in the California Department of Corrections is carried out almost entirely by persons who are from the standpoint of clinical specialty, nonprofessional.[14]

THE TRADITIONAL PRISON

One aspect of prison treatment that must be considered is the argument that prison experience in and of itself is an inducement to further illicit and illegal activity.[15] This condition is believed to arise as a consequence of the following circumstances:

(a) Imprisonment provides an opportunity for new or younger inmates to learn about criminal activities and opportunities from more sophisticated inmates with whom they are in close and sustained contact.

(b) The psychological deprivations imposed by imprisonment provide inmates with retroactive justifications for their crimes.

(c) The material deprivations imposed by imprisonment together with the density of population, result in the exploitation or involvement of many inmates in a system of subterfuge, and manipulation in the pursuit of valued goods and services.

(d) The dehumanizing element of prison life, most important, the lack of opportunity for individual decision making, does not develop the self-confidence and the sense of responsibility that inmates will need in the free world.[16]

of the prison could at the same time be modified. It is of course equally important that psychiatrists should become fully conversant with the prison culture and particularly with the very real difficulties of the custodial staff. *ibid.*, p. 86.

Also see Jones, *Social Psychiatry in Practice*, Baltimore: Penguin Books, 1968.

[14] For a history of the development of programs utilizing nonprofessional staff members as treatment personnel, see Joseph W. Eaton, *Stone Walls Not a Prison Make*, Springfield, Illinois: Charles C Thomas, 1962.

[15] See Donald Clemmer, "Imprisonment as a Source of Criminality," *Journal of Criminal Law, Criminology and Police Science*, 41 (Sept.–Oct., 1950), pp. 311–319. An opposing view is given by Donald L. Garrity, "The Prison as a Rehabilitative Agency," in Donald R. Cressey (ed.), *The Prison*, New York: Holt, Rinehart and Winston, 1961, pp. 358–380.

[16] Two of the best descriptions of the "pains of imprisonment" in institutions for

Many studies have reported that, given these conditions, a complex and pervasive inmate social structure develops that fosters the evasion of official norms and is ideologically opposed to the values held by prison staff members—the values on which treatment programs are based.

The prison community thus is to be viewed as consisting of a formal administrative structure and an informal inmate social system which are interdependent.[17]

Taking these factors into account, the hallmark of the traditional prison can be considered as a "cadre" of strategically placed inmates who structure communications within the prison, invoke sanctions, and promulgate norms prescribing and proscribing conduct for the inmate community. Under these conditions, the task of the incoming prisoner is to internalize the norms, become sophisticated with regard to the patterns of allegiance and behavior, and learn to manipulate both guards and inmates in competition for material advantages and ego support in an environment in which both are in short supply. This learning process has been termed "prisonization."

The traditional prison, with its inmate code and folklore, thus is organized to produce great resistance to any therapeutic program that is merely grafted onto its social system. This resistance has been recognized, and an attempt to deal with it can be seen in the recent efforts that view treatment programs as modifying both formal and informal social arrangements in the prison community. It is contended that treatment programs such as group counseling alter the social system in which treatment takes place by broadening the basis of interaction and communication between staff members and inmates. These new relationships inveigh against, that is, weaken the endorsement of, the norms of the traditional inmate community, and strengthen the endorsement of staff (conventional values), which in turn should promote positive changes in inmate behavior. Treatment is thus asserted to achieve its ends directly through the group counseling experience, and indirectly by altering the prisonization process.

Whether the norms of the inmate community are really different from the norms of the conventional community, whether the inmates at California Men's Colony endorsed a distinctive set of inmate norms, and whether the group treatment programs affected the degree of endorsement of inmate norms are issues that we shall examine in detail in this book. At present we only wish to point out that the descriptions of traditional inmate

men are to be found in Gresham M. Sykes, *The Society of Captives*, Princeton: Princeton University Press, 1958; and Erving Goffman, *Asylums, op. cit.*

[17] Two collections of papers already cited contain most of the best known studies of formal and informal prison organization. See *Theoretical Studies in Social Organization of the Prison, op. cit.*; and Cressey, *The Prison, op. cit.*

communities in the sociological literature are, for the most part, studies conducted in states where most of the adult felons were housed in one maximum security prison and most of the younger felons were housed in a reformatory. Our study, however, has been conducted in one prison of a department of corrections that is comprised of, at least, ten separate major institutions. We found that the fact that the prison we studied was part of a larger system of prisons has such important implications for the social structure of the inmate community, and thus for treatment programming, that a new and different view of the prison community is called for. Chapter X of this book is devoted to a presentation of the empirical evidence and theoretical considerations from which this revised view emerged.

PAROLE PERFORMANCE AS THE MEASURE OF TREATMENT OUTCOME

It is necessary to extend the consideration of correctional treatment and social control issues to the topic of postrelease behavior. We were not able in this study to measure the impact of group counseling apart from the context in which it operated. That is, we did not measure group treatment applied to convicted felons in the setting of a community treatment center or through the facilities of an outpatient clinic; we measured the impact of prison group treatment. The prison setting necessarily clouds the issue of whether any changes in the attitudes or behavior of Men's Colony—East inmates were the result of imprisonment or whether the changes would have occurred if the men had remained in the free world. However, we were able to examine the attitudes and the behavior, over time, of men who participated in the group treatment programs and men who did not.

Our outcome criteria were the ones cited by Department of Corrections staff members to be the consequences of group counseling participation: lessened endorsement of the inmate code (positive attitude change), fewer prison disciplinary reports, and a lower likelihood of being returned to prison. Two of these measures—prison disciplinary reports and recidivism—reflect social control issues. It was necessary for us to describe prison disciplinary procedures and problems in order to understand why prison rules violations are taken to be measures of inmate "adjustment." The use of recidivism as a criterion of outcome poses more difficult problems. The comparison of the recidivism rate of parolees to the criminal behavior of free citizens is extremely questionable when so little is known about the implications of the status of "parolee" and about the many specific regulations, conditions of surveillance, and possibilities of reimprisonment by administrative rather than court action, to which parolees are subject. In a later chapter, we raise the question of whether formal parole dispositions reflect parolee behavior accurately enough to be useful in ferreting out possible changes in behavior that result from exposure to the various treatment programs.

At the present time, however, these rates can be used if the outcome behavior is regarded as a measure of parole conformity rather than recidivism, and if this behavior is explicitly regarded, at least in part, as a function of administrative and procedural factors in the parole division.

For the purpose of this research we define the post-release goal of treatment as the increase of the probability of a successful parole. Data will be presented concerning aspects of the parolee status, as well as a discussion of the parole agent's perception of the parolee, but the internal organization of the parole division will not be analyzed in this study. Our attention will be devoted mostly to the question of whether there is a difference in parole conformity between treatment and control subjects.

SUMMARY

In setting up a study design to assess the efficacy of a prison treatment technique—group counseling—the following have been taken into account:

1. That the distinctive feature of correctional group treatment compared to psychotherapeutic treatment in the free world is the involuntary nature of the recruitment of subjects.
2. That the treatment program is operated within a setting that contains sources of strong resistance to the program; one of these sources is the inmates, another is the custody staff members, and another is the nature of the system itself.
3. That the prison setting itself is imbedded in a complex and far-flung organization so that changes in one part of the system have implications for the other parts.
4. That the principal measures of treatment impact are the differences in the degree to which treatment and control subjects conform to prison and parole regulations.

The purpose of this book is to report a study of how men convicted of felonious conduct were dealt with by one state's Department of Corrections. This study examines the effects of participation in a program that is designed to modify criminal behavior within the context of the formal organization of the prison and the parole division. The issue will become self-evident in the chapters that follow: namely, is there reason to expect that even the newest prison programs with the "richest" staffing can counter the negative consequences of imprisonment? Can participation in these programs provide new skills and change the personalities and perspectives of inmates so that there is less probability of return to prison?

Doing time in a pastel prison

Well, gee, you expect us to do handsprings here because these televisions are here? What does a television set mean when you've got a guy's heart whipped out? Do you expect me to be the apotheosis of joy because you have given me a key that leads to no place, when you can lock me in at any whim? I don't need this key, take the key and take this television set if you want it . . . it's a lie anyway, the way you're using it. I'm not knocking television, but I'm just saying, the way it's used . . . it's given to you by this omnipotent, omniscient author whom you never see . . . this guy running this whole show. He's gonna let you watch the TV— big deal, and you're dying. Besides, who cares about the TV . . . and the guys that watch it—they wouldn't watch it if there was anything else to do. TV is a good way to avoid what is. If you watch the TV you might not think.

CMCE Inmate

California Men's Colony—East (CMCE), the site of this study, is a medium security prison that was opened in 1961. It is part of a larger system of correctional institutions which have been constructed over the years and because of changes in prison architecture, have come to house different types of offenders. The Department of Corrections maintains two high walled maximum security prisons to hold men with extensive criminal records or with long sentences for crimes of violence, and to hold men who represent serious escape risks or institutional "adjustment" problems. For these reasons the men in maximum security prisons generally are regarded as poorer prospects for treatment. The department operates several minimum security facilities to house younger offenders (regarded as good treatment prospects) and older inmates who are serving a first term for nonviolent crimes, and to house men with limited criminal careers and men close to release. In all cases they must also be well behaved in terms of institutional adjustment. The two medium security prisons, of which Men's Colony—East is one, contain prisoners who are deemed to need secure but not close confinement. Men's Colony inmates generally are not experiencing penal confinement for the first time: at the time of our study, seven out of eight CMCE inmates had histories of prior commitment to jails, reformatories, minimum security prisons, or other medium security prisons. A small number of men began their terms in the maximum security prisons and were transferred to CMCE after a period of good behavior. Other men were transferred to CMCE after a period of bad behavior in institutions lower on the security scale.[1] Men's Colony—East also receives new commitments who are facing long prison terms for crimes such as robbery or selling narcotics. These men are housed in a medium security setting until their "adjustment" indicates whether maximum or medium facilities are appropriate. Men's Colony—East was thus designed with a particular type of inmate population in mind, and its physical plant, staffing, and program reflects its place midway on the treatment-potential/security-requirements ranking system used by the California Department of Corrections.[2]

PHYSICAL PLANT

Men's Colony—East is bounded by two cyclone fences 16 feet high, interspaced by eight concrete gun towers 35 feet high. Four of the towers are routinely manned. As is shown in Figure 2.1, it is divided into four quadrangles, each housing 600 men.

---

[1] The good and bad behavior designations here are determined almost entirely by two measures: whether or not the inmate tried to escape, and whether or not he violated prison rules. The point is that men can work their way down to CMCE by good behavior at maximum security prisons, or they can work their way up to CMCE by bad behavior at minimum security prisons. A small number of inmates may be received in transfer from the other medium security prisons, generally, to separate the members of cliques or enemies.

[2] Men's Colony—East is the larger of two institutions which are located on the same grounds at San Luis Obispo on the California coast, midway between San Francisco and Los Angeles. The other facility, California Men's Colony—West, is a barracks-type institution which houses approximately 1400 minimum custody men, 95 percent of whom are over age 40. (At the time of this study, the medium age at CMCW was 53.1 years compared to 30.6 at CMCE.) One superintendent rules both institutions, but he is the only person with such joint responsibilities. The transfers of staff or inmates between West and East facilities require the same formal processing as do transfers between CMCE and prisons located elsewhere in the state. The study reported in this volume included only the East facility.

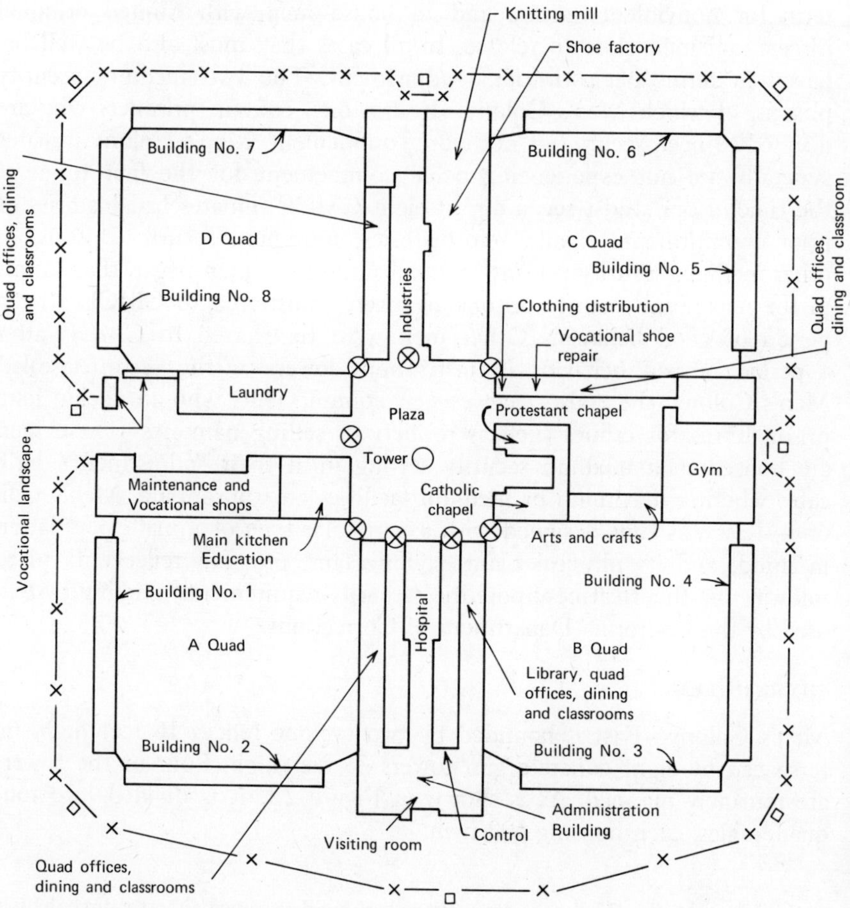

figure 2.1   (The ⊗ indicates electronically controlled plaza turnstiles.)

Construction was based in part on the argument that smaller prisons reduce management and control problems and provide more appropriate settings for treatment; it also was based on a realistic appraisal of the department's chances for getting funds to build four new separate small prisons from the state legislature. Men's Colony—East thus represents an interesting new type of prison architecture that incorporates the features of small institutions (given United States standards) with the economy of building and maintaining one large physical plant. The original plan called for each of the four 600-man units of Men's Colony (the "quads") to be run, insofar as possible, as a semiautonomous institution. Each of the four quads was designed to house its population in two 300-man buildings subdivided into six sections containing 50 men, with each man having a single cell. The 50-man sections include a dayroom where cards and other games are played, a television room, and a shower room. Cells or "rooms" are of the "over-under" type of construction in which the bunk space for one cell is built into the upper half of one wall and the bunk space of the adjoining cell is built into the bottom half of the wall. A narrow floor-to-cell area is left for walking, sitting at a table attached to the wall, and for toilet facilities. This type of construction was designed to prevent the inevitable effort to house more inmates in the prison than the number for which it was intended, and it permits the construction of four cells in the space needed for three conventional prison cells. Besides the bed, each room contains a toilet, a sink with hot and cold running water, and three shelves for storing clothes. Earphones for listening to the programs of two radio stations piped from a control sound center also are provided. Ventilation is provided by a circulating air system that also supplies heat, and by an outside window in each cell. (That is, all cells are built against the outside walls; there are no interior cell blocks.) The cells or "rooms" have fluorescent lighting and are painted in alternating green, gray, and beige colors. Cell doors are solid was a small window, and each inmate has a key to his own door, a feature designed to reduce the problem of pilfering and the "planting" of items in open cells, and to reduce the amount of time that correctional officers must devote to locking and unlocking doors as inmates enter or leave their cells. During night hours all cells are "deadlocked" through a central locking device that overrides inmate keys, and men can be released from the rooms only by the use of a special staff key.

The quadrangles are the basic sleeping, eating, recreational, and social units of the prison. In addition, each quad has its own elementary school. The quads are arranged around a separate central core that includes the administrative offices, the visiting areas, the central kitchen that serves the four separate air conditioned dining rooms, the high school classrooms, the vocational training shops, the hobby shops, the laundry, the maintenance shops, the chapels, and the gymnasium.

Entrance to the quadrangles can only be gained through turnstiles from the central plaza. (These turnstiles are really large revolving doors made of closely spaced bars, similar to subway exits in New York.) Each inmate carries a laminated identification card with his picture and a designation of his residence in A, B, C, or D quad. Traffic through the turnstiles is controlled through a central tower that uses closed circuit television to view inmates and their identification card before permitting the turnstile to turn. The ease of control that was the intention of the design of the turnstile system, however, has never actually been achieved. Daily ebbs and flows of traffic make the control of 18 turnstiles by the tower officers impossible, and other correctional officers must go to the turnstiles to personally control traffic during the rush hours. At other times, staff members as well as inmates often have to stand in line waiting for the tower officer to switch his monitor over to their turnstile.

This system provided an obvious challenge to the ingenuity of the more seasoned inmates at Men's Colony, and they soon found ways to "beat the system." For example, the men are required to have written permission in order to move from one quad to another, but passes are difficult to read on the television receivers. The tower control officer can do little more than check to determine if the man has the right quad identification letter on his ID card. But the inmates also have learned that the television camera cannot distinguish between a quad letter that is under a laminated surface and one that is temporarily pasted over another letter on the surface of the card. Inmates have found that when a man goes into a quad other than his own, although he is supposed to report in at the quad office, unless an officer stops him there is nothing to keep him from getting "lost" in the other quads. The problem of ironing out the kinks in a new system is summed up in a wry remark of the associate superintendent: "This system of a central tower using TV cameras to control inmate traffic was designed by an idiot . . . and that idiot was me!"

Although the traffic between quads has been controlled to a considerable degree through the use of the turnstile system supplemented by prison personnel, the inmates in any quad cannot be said to be isolated from the other quads. The centralization of some important staff services and certain work assignments—coupled with some movement between quads for less official purposes—has prevented the complete separation of men in the four quadrangles. The centralization of quadrangle and institution operations also has the effect of making it difficult for the quad administrators to achieve a high degree of autonomy for their unit.

QUADRANGLE CENTRAL STAFF ORGANIZATION

Despite the separate duties of the quad and central administrations some important business at Men's Colony is conducted on both the institutional and quadrangle levels. Major disciplinary problems are handled, for example, by an institutional committee made up of the heads of the quadrangles, called "program administrators," and the representatives of the central staff. Minor rule infractions are handled by quad committees comprised of the program administrator, the senior correctional counselor (caseworker), and the day-shift lieutenant. Inmate classification functions (initial job assignment, custody classification, and the like) are organized on the same basis, with cases first discussed by an institutional committee and with the quad committees' handling the business of reclassification when it does not involve questions of transfer to another institution or pertain to changes in institutional policies or procedures.

What these divisions of responsibilities clearly indicate is that the most important decisions for inmates and staff are made at the institution, not the quad, level. The formal structure that underlies these allocations of responsibility and authority are shown in Figures 2.2, 2.3 and 2.4.

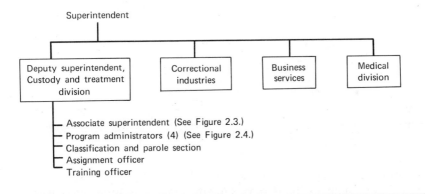

figure 2.2   The formal organization of California Men's Colony—East.

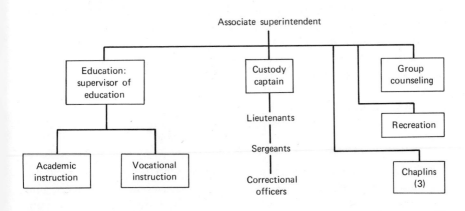

figure 2.3   The associate services.

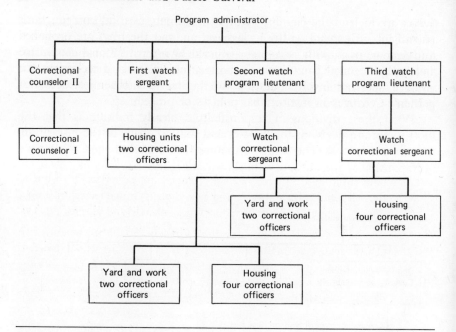

figure 2.4   The quads (four).

Formally, the program administrators (PA) of each quadrangle are directly responsible to the deputy superintendent. As is the case with the deputy superintendent position, the PA position is a combination of both treatment and custody supervisory functions. Notice that among the centralized services under the authority of the associate superintendent, who also reports to the deputy superintendent, are the educational, vocational, recreational, religious, and group counseling programs. The associate superintendent is thus in a position of control over both custodial staff members and the heads of the treatment services throughout the institution. This particular allocation of responsibility has made it difficult for the program administrators to be the "junior wardens" as originally planned. The staff members with power at Men's Colony are the ones who have control over institution-wide knowledge and responsibilities.

CENTRALIZED SERVICES AND PROGRAMS

Men's Colony inmates eat, sleep, go to grade school, participate in group counseling sessions, and have recreational activities in their quads, and they spend most of their time there. But when they enroll in certain programs, hold certain jobs, or need certain services, they leave the quads and participate in centralized activities. The most important of these activities are high school courses, vocational training, medical services, work assignments in industry, religious services, and the meetings of Alcoholics Anonymous. In addition, some men join the handicraft program, some use the library and the gym, and most men attend all-institution events, for instance, special shows and movies. Briefly described, the major activities at Men's Colony are as follows:

1. *Recreation.* The usual team sports (baseball, basketball) are available plus weight-lifting, boxing, outdoor bowling, bocce ball, miniature golf, tennis, handball, croquet, horseshoes, and shuffleboard. There are both intra- and interquad games. Inmates are permitted to listen to the radio until 12 midnight and television is available until 10 P.M. during the week and 11 P.M. on the weekends and before holidays.

2. *Academic and vocational education.* Grades 1 to 12 are taught, with eighth grade and high school diplomas given. The school program runs concurrently with that of the local schools in San Luis Obispo, and the staff is comprised of instructors from the community schools whose time was paid for by the Department of Corrections. It is accredited as are other public schools, and diplomas are issued by the regular public school district in which the prison is situated. In addition, inmates who completed high school can take correspondence courses offered by the University of California.

   Vocational training is offered in the following fields: electronics, machine shop, arts and crafts, landscaping, mill and cabinet, auto shop, sheet metal, paint shop, plumbing, welding, bakery, drafting, shoe shop, and dry cleaning.

3. *Medical.* The medical staff consists of four physicians, three dentists, a psychiatrist, and about 20 ancillary personnel. In addition, approximately 80 inmates work in the hospital as clerks, janitors, and ward attendants. The psychiatrist spends between 60 and 70 percent of his time writing up reports for the parole board on special cases (for example, the ones involving violence and sexual assaults). Most of the remaining time is spent, as the psychiatrist phrased it, "cooling down" inmates at the request of the staff, giving advice on men being considered for transfer, and seeing severely disturbed inmates. The psychiatrist and the chief medical officer are also members of the institution disciplinary committee.

   The hospital contains five rooms, three of which are soundproof (located next to the segregation unit) and which are referred to as "strip cells." These rooms are designed for psychotic inmates but can be used by custody for particularly violent or noisy inmates (whom the staff call "acter-outers").

4. *Industries.* The principal industries at Men's Colony are a shoe factory and a knitting mill. According to the industries' supervisor, qualifications for the several hundred inmates who work on these jobs are "a willingness to work harder than on other inmate jobs," and a need for money and a need for some educational and vocational training. Thus men employed in the factory and the mill are somewhat older than the average in the prison population. Inmates also work throughout the institution as clerks and typists, cooks, janitors, groundskeepers, maintenance men, and laundry workers.

5. *Religious activities and Alcoholics Anonymous.* About 200 men attend Mass on Sundays and about 300 attend Protestant services. Besides conducting the usual religious services, the chaplains help some inmates with family problems and, occasionally, with problems in finding jobs prior to release. Both Protestant and Catholic chaplains report that men often come to them when they feel that their correctional counselors are either unwilling or unable to help them. One of the chaplains estimated that about 25 percent of the men attending services are "shucking it," that is, going to church to impress the Adult Authority (parole board). This does not appear to be undue cynicism. There are sign-up sheets at church to record attendance. Formerly the sheets were passed out at the start of services and men would come in, sign their names, and leave before the services began. This procedure has been revised to take attendance after services.

The prison chapter of Alcoholics Anonymous meets weekly. To join this group, an inmate need only say that he was an alcoholic. There were two sponsors: one staff member and one man from a nearby community. Membership averages about 100.

6. *Mail and visiting.* Inmates can visit and correspond with up to ten approved persons. (A married couple living in the same household is considered as one person.) In addition, inmates can write to former or prospective employers. Letters cannot exceed one sheet written on both sides, and no more than one per day can be sent. All mail is subject to censorship.

Men's Colony thus may be viewed as having all of the usual institutional programs in addition to some unique recreational features.

COMMISSARY PRIVILEGES

Compared to prisons around the country, another somewhat unusual feature of Men's Colony is the amount and variety of personal property that inmates may have. A variety of privately owned items are permitted, including the following: a sweater, sweat shirts, suspenders, house slippers, bathrobe, shoes (black or brown only), necktie (solid color, conservative hues), a wallet, a watch (not to exceed $10 in value), a pen-and-pencil set (black and blue ink only), a wedding band, photographs (shall not include any scantily clad individuals), a photograph album, a cigarette lighter (not to exceed $1.50 in value), an athletic supporter, an electric shaver, a typewriter, musical instruments, a chess set (value limited to $10), a tennis racquet, and approved magazines, newspapers, and books (by mail only, direct from publisher or vendor). The majority of these items can be obtained through the prison canteen along with soap, candies, popcorn, cigars, greeting cards, ice cream, and the like. Even though the availability of these amenities may seem trivial, these items assume considerable importance in prison settings and may evoke notices in the inmate newspaper such as: "Yes, the Eastside Canteen has Sugar Daddies and Jaw Breakers . . . Sugar Daddies . . . a new taste treat in candy . . . are five cents each and come in assorted colors." And "Roses are Red, the Thorns are Green/Valentine Cards are at the Canteen."

The nature of the request made by the Inmate Advisory Council (IAC) is illuminating in this regard, since the requests put to the superintendent are modest indeed. This reflects not only the importance that seemingly petty items may assume in an institutional environment but also the very limited power of the inmate council at Men's Colony.[3] The following examples are taken from the reports of inmate requests and the superintendent's subsequent action, which were published in the prison newspaper.

> *IAC Request:* Syrups and Juices: A motion was made that on pancake and French toast days a morning fruit be served (containing juices) that could be used to add to the meager supply of hot syrup served on these occasions. Seconded and carried.

---

[3] The IAC was disbanded by the superintendent after a food and work strike that occurred shortly after the prison opened. The men stayed away from work and meals for approximately two days. A large number of men alleged to be actively involved were transported from CMCE to other prisons in the middle of the night. A show of armed force from the staff and the absence of a thorough organization among inmates led to the collapse of the effort. The inmates in one quad did not participate but were not criticized by the other inmates because they were viewed as "nuts" and, therefore, could not be held accountable for their "deviant" behavior. Little property damage occurred during the strike, but some personal assaults on inmates by other inmates were reported. The Inmate Council was reinstated several months later but as four separate bodies, one for each quadrangle.

Superintendent's Action: Request approved. Canned fruits which provide sweet syrup will be served on mornings when there are hot cakes.

IAC Request: Regarding the possibility of providing boxes to cover the fire extinguishers, thus to prevent them from being squirted.

Superintendent's Action: Request approved. We shall try out this plan in D Quad only for the present.

IAC Request: Regarding the possibility of instituting a watch repair service through the canteen with the work to be done by a qualified inmate.

Superintendent's Action: Request not approved. Such a plan has been tried out on a number of occasions in the past. There appears to be no way, in the absence of an instructor in watch repair, to prevent abuse of this type of privilege and the illicit dealings that develop in connection with it.

RECREATION AS A CUSTODIAL DEVICE

There are many deprivations in prison, and outsiders can easily minimize or be ignorant of the distress that can revolve around seemingly trivial features of institutional life. Nonetheless, it is not inaccurate to state that physical hardship, fatigue, food shortages, and unsanitary and unhealthy living condition are not among the burdens imposed on men at CMCE. The salubrious climate encourages, and regulations permit, inmates to sunbathe on free time. And, many inmates have a good deal of the latter. Inmates playing bongo drums, guitars, and other musical instruments may be heard from the yard of each quadrangle. Although the sight of several inmates practicing chip shots with golf clubs may evoke accusations that the prison is a country club, it should be pointed out that the recreational program does provide, at least, a range of activities that occupy time; the latter being a matter of serious concern to prison administrators because of the limits of the industries program and the amount of housekeeping work that can be assigned. For many Men's Colony inmates the assignment of a job means work for only a few hours a day, often on make-work, cleaning, and groundskeeping assignments.

An hour-by-hour recapitulation of the activities covering the previous 24-hour period by 51 of the inmates that we interviewed provided an indication of the amount of free time that many of the men had. Twenty-nine percent did not work at all, 35 percent worked less than 5 hours, and 37 percent said that they went to school (3 to 4 hours in class per day). Recreation (television, cards, sports, and the like) was mentioned as occupying 2 to 6 hours of the day by 51 percent of the men, and as occupying more than 6 hours for another 20 percent.

An elaborate and varied recreation program of team and individual activities thus is viewed as serving the function of reducing idleness which, in turn, is thought to be conducive to "troublemaking."

In addition, recreational privileges can be used to enforce conformity or docility because of the possibility of withdrawing them as a punishment. Although inmates during our stay were written up for such minor rule violations as the unauthorized flying of a kite and the destruction of state property by knocking a golf ball through a window, it should be pointed out that the wider variety of privileges means also that there are some additional rules to break at Men's Colony and that a wider variety of disciplinary sanctions are available to the staff by means of removal or denial of the privileges.

The programs and policies of Men's Colony—East are, for the most part, like those of other California prisons; differences between Men's Colony and prisons elsewhere in the United States are more a reflection of differences between the California Department of Corrections and the other state penal systems than they are an indication of the distinctive features of Men's Colony.

THE MEN'S COLONY INMATES

Before we consider the characteristics of men in this prison and how they compare with men in other California institutions, we must bear in mind that prison confinement is the end result of complex legal processes that involve the police, prosecuting attorneys, and the courts. Actions taken in the name of the state reflect a wide variety of social factors that are not systematically examined in this study. Here we can only point out that criminal laws are not applied to all persons in the same way, nor is any given law enforced with equal strength. Police interest, zeal, and efficiency in moving against different categories of offenders varies over time and between the communities within the same state. Furthermore, studies of the "mortality" rate of those cases in which persons are arrested on criminal charges reveal that only about one in ten persons arrested on *felony* charges are ultimately convicted and confined in prison.[4] It is also the case in California and in all other jurisdictions that a disproportionate

---

[4] A report by the President's Commission on Law Enforcement and the Administration of Justice indicates that there were 2,780,140 "index crimes" (willful homicide, forcible rape, aggravated assault, robbery, burglary, theft of $50 or over, motor vehicle theft) reported to the FBI in 1965. 727,000 arrests were made for these crimes for which 63,000 persons were sentenced to prison. Another 21,000 persons ultimately reached prison after violating the conditions of probation. Of the total number of persons arrested then, approximately 11.5 percent were imprisoned. See *The Challenge of Crime in a Free Society*, Washington, D.C.: U.S. Government Printing Office, 1967, pp. 262–263.

number of the persons that are processed by the criminal justice system are poor, young, male, and the members of minority groups. The inmates at Men's Colony—East represent a good sample of the lawbreakers who are in prisons; they are not a representative sample of those who break laws.

With this general caveat in mind, it is important to indicate that the men at CMCE were similar to other California prisoners in terms of a number of characteristics (see *Appendix B*). For example, the proportions of inmates of white-Anglo, Black, and Mexican descent at CMCE mirror the ethnic distribution of these groups in the state's total prison population. (The Black and Mexican share is disproportionately high in all prisons, relative to the proportions that these groups represent in the total population of the state.) Compared to all male prisoners in California, a slightly smaller proportion of CMCE inmates were committed for forgery and grand theft, and a slightly larger proportion were committed for sex offenses and narcotics. The CMCE population was somewhat younger than the departmental average, had fewer parole violators, and included a smaller share of men with prior prison experience; the proportion of men who had tried to escape from custody was close to the proportion in the total prison population. By using these criteria, which the Department of Corrections uses to characterize the populations of its prisons, the Men's Colony—East inmates are fairly typical California prisoners.

A more detailed description of the Men's Colony population depends on data gathered by our own research staff. These data, taken from the records of our follow-up sample of 968 inmates indicate that nearly all CMCE inmates had some type of police record. Six percent had records of arrests or fines; 3 percent had received probation; and most of the remainder (87 percent) were known to have been confined in a juvenile facility or a jail. Only 4 percent had no police record. About one half (49 percent) were serving their first prison term, 31 percent their second, and 20 percent their third, fourth, or more. Nearly two thirds of the inmates were arrested first as juveniles: 26 percent by age fourteen, 19 percent by age sixteen, and another 18 percent by age eighteen.

Most CMCE inmates (68 percent) came from metropolitan areas; an additional 12 percent came from cities of 50,000 to 100,000 population. As is true of most prisoners in most prisons, they came from lower or working class backgrounds.[5] Of those who knew their father's occupation

[5] Occupational and educational background was reflected in the responses to an item given in our 50 percent questionnaire sample: "In civilian life, if you were asked one of these four names for your social class, in which would you say you were a member?" Seventy-six percent said either "lower" or "working" class.

(833 of 968), only 14 percent specified a white collar job. The men themselves worked (if at all) at unskilled heavy labor (18 percent), driving or delivery work (7 percent), or some other type of unskilled or semiskilled work (39 percent). Experience in a skilled trade was claimed by 22 percent; the remainder worked at clerical or sales jobs. Only four men reported managerial or professional backgrounds.

By the time they were released from CMCE, about one half (48 percent) of the men had less than an eighth-grade education. (This includes men who had taken elementary school courses in prison.) Only 14 percent of the men had finished high school and 6 percent had attended college for, at least, one year.

These, then, are the characteristics of the prison population under study: nearly one half are members of minority groups (Blacks and Mexicans), they are poorly educated, have unstable employment records and, when the men worked, they were employed at unskilled jobs. Men in this prison population have histories of early arrest and penal confinement, and they have been, in the main, convicted on forgery and bad checks charges, burglary, and narcotics use or sale. They represent an intermediate group of prison inmates: a sprinkling of well-behaved and well-institutionalized old cons, a fair number of men never confined before, and a large number of men who have already done enough jail and prison time to move about easily in the prison environment, but who have not yet done so much time as to be thoroughly institutionalized. In the following chapters we shall discuss the relationship of these demographic characteristics to the in-prison adjustment and to the post-release success of our study sample.

CMCE INMATES DESCRIBE HOW IT IS

Most of the data about inmates that we report in this study were obtained through the use of questionnaires or through the examination of prison records. In this way large samples could be studied, and a relatively large number of variables could be included. However, the use of survey methods limits the feedback possible with the more direct and unstructured personal communication with subjects. We wanted freer communication with inmates in order to obtain information about life and doing time at CMCE which would permit us to construct instruments that would tap meaningful issues for the large survey sample population. A second reason for conducting personal interviews with inmates was that the quantitative data that make up the bulk of the empirical evidence about group treatment cannot provide the reader (or the researcher) with a sense of what life was like for CMCE inmates.

For these reasons, we initiated a series of 76 interviews early in the life of the project, with the selection made on a random basis. A second series of 40 interviews involved men who were ready to be released on parole.[6] Using these two samples, we can offer a view of life at Men's Colony—East as described by those who lived there.

The first interview series was made up of nine open-end questions. Two of the questions were concerned with eliciting complaints: "What are the hardest things to adjust to at CMCE?" and "What is the most annoying thing about doing time at CMCE?" The replies to both were pooled and subsumed under one set of categories. One half (50 percent) of the men said *other inmates* were the most problematic aspect of prison; of the men thus answering, one out of four mentioned homosexuals, specifically, as the annoyance. The next most frequently mentioned categories were "rules and regulations" and "loss of freedom," followed by "the indeterminate sentence," "broken contact with families," and "petty things done by officers." About one fourth of all men replied "nothing—adjustment is not particularly hard."[7]

To the query, "What's the best way to get along with other inmates?" the traditional norm of "do your own time" accounted for 67 percent of the responses. The rest of the replies were classified into many categories, with none accounting for more than a few cases each.

When asked, "What's the most important thing that would help you get paroled?" One out of every four inmates said that he did not know

---

[6] The first series of interviews were organized around nine general questions, which were posed in the same sequence to each subject. The questions were general and open-ended. Brief notes were made during the interview with the interviewer dictating a summary into a tape recorder after the session. In a few cases when English was not the inmate's most comfortable idiom, the interviews were conducted in Spanish. The replies were transcribed and classified in subject-matter categories. Based on our experience with these early interviews, it was decided that we should obtain verbatim transcriptions (in preference to notes) because of the heavy use of argot by the respondents. Accordingly, each interview was tape recorded with the permission of the respondent, who was assured of anonymity. From these prerelease interviews, many of the attitudes expressed in the first interview series were elaborated. Several of the extended comments reported in this section are taken from these sessions with the prerelease group of interviewees, but the content analysis of general inmate descriptions of life and times at CMCE was done with the responses of the first group of 76 men.

[7] Comment is necessary here because of a disparity between the interview replies and the responses to the same questions when they were included in a questionnaire with structured alternative answers. In the survey, the alternatives most frequently checked were (1) absence of home and family and (2) the indeterminate sentence. These distributions are as follows:

because parole was based on the peculiarities of individual cases, or the whims and caprice of parole board members. An additional 25 percent of the interview sample said that serving "enough" time was of primary importance and that a man's institutional behavior or the activities (programs) in which he participated either did not affect parole or were only secondary considerations. However, one half of the interviewees reported that the most important thing in getting paroled was to show improvement through participation in institutional programs and to stay out of trouble. That is, enroll in as many programs and activities as possible to demonstrate a positive motivation. Several inmates emphasized the need to gain insight into one's problems. Of particular interest to us was the finding that was based on the interviews conducted with men in prison

What aspect of prison life do you find most difficult to adjust to?

		Percent
_____	Absence of home and family	37
_____	Absence of social life and friends outside	17
_____	Lack of sex with women	10
_____	Other inmates	9
_____	Custodial Officials	4
_____	Lack of privacy	4
_____	Rules and regulations	3
_____	Nothing, adjustment easy	4
_____	Other or more than one answer	12
		100

What is the most annoying thing about doing time here?

_____	The never-knowing system of the indeterminant sentencing law.	52
_____	Being treated by staff as though you were a child.	12
_____	You can't get a straight answer from a staff member without buck-passing.	9
_____	Staff tries to give impression they are never wrong.	8
_____	New and inexperienced staff who try to be too friendly with inmates.	2
_____	Nothing particularly annoys me here.	5
_____	Others or more than one answer.	12
		100
		(849)[a]

[a] Twenty-two "No response" excluded from analysis.

We feel that by providing answers that included phenomena outside of the prison itself, we broadened the frame of reference to this question. In the interviews, however, the focus was on prison life, and we believe that the respondents defined the question in terms of prison activities in most cases instead of the broader concerns with the law or with persons left behind in the outside world.

and on parole, that the most consistently expressed view of group counseling was that its value was chiefly in satisfying the Adult Authority at parole hearings. Like class attendance in some universities, inmates felt that a participation in group counseling might not be a major factor in getting paroled, but a lack of participation was likely to be regarded negatively by the Adult Authority.

Aside from a few mild criticisms about the food, complaints about doing time at CMCE generally reflected the problems of getting along with others in a crowded, overmanipulative environment. For example, one inmate responded to the question "What's the hardest thing about doing time here?" in terms of the problem of having to put up with other inmates:

> The noise—the inmates themselves. For example listen to those bongos and horns [points to the yard outside the window where various musical instruments could be heard]. Instead of talking in conversational tones, yelling at a guy. To put it bluntly, inmates have no respect for the other man's feelings. [What is the best way to get along with other inmates?] I avoid them. There's about three guys I associate with. This is a hell of a thing for an inmate to say. [Why?] It shows we can't even get along with each other.

Another man spoke in similar terms:

> You are confined in such a small area, you confront so many people all the time. There's no privacy, even in the room [cell]. [Could you give an example of agitation and harassment?] Loaning cigarettes and coffee is one thing. I only loan out or really give out what I can afford to lose.

The prison staff, particularly the younger and newer officers hired when the new prison opened, were criticized by many interviewees who had done time elsewhere or who were older. One inmate, who felt that "the officers" were the hardest thing to adjust to at CMCE, commented:

> The institution is fine, but the officers! I did my first 18 months at San Quentin; they seem to have a different kind of officer there, they don't badger you so much. There they let you do your own time; here you have to help them . . . you not only have to do your own time at CMC, but you have to help the officers do their time too. Not all, but so many overdo their job. It seems they think you are trying to beat them and so you try to beat them more than you would otherwise. For example, going into your room every week for a shakedown, or you go to the hospital— you get shook down when you go in and when you go out again; they

seem to think everybody is a nut. They [the staff] seem to have some kind of narcotic fetish here because they're always worrying about and looking for narcotics.[8]

Several men talked of tough, even brutal, treatment that they had experienced in the other prisons, but they did not necessarily endorse the program or the institutional atmosphere at CMCE:

[Do you think there's a convict code? . . . Rights and Wrongs, Do's and Don'ts?] Yeah . . . there should be, but this State's pretty flexible. I mean, back where I came from . . . I done eight months in a County Jail in (a Midwestern City) and it was more a prison style—big walls, gun towers, the guards punch you in the stomach, knock you down, kick your brains out and put you in a hospital . . . back there they'd kill a fink in a minute, but out here I don't know, I think half this place is snitches. I don't trust nobody in it.

Another inmate reacted to the contrast between Men's Colony and another California prison, San Quentin:

[Well, what is the thing you find hardest to adjust to here?] Outside of just loss of freedom, little petty bullshit you run into here from both officers and inmates. The regimentation. Living by bells and so forth is too much. [How does it compare with other prisons you've been in?] The inmates here are more docile compared to San Quentin. There's more tension up there. A lot of killings and so forth up there.

They have nice facilities here. When they handed me my key [to his cell] when I got here, I almost fell over. . . . Officers here are overly petty about things. Of course, they [the administration] tell officers to go in the cells [referring to periodic shakedowns of the cells to search for contraband]. At San Quentin, there's so many guys [inmates], they [staff] don't have time to be on you. They [the staff] want to talk to you here, that's almost unknown in the joint. [The subject refers to San Quentin or Folsom as a "joint"—he does not consider CMCE a "joint"] A couple of [staff] want to be buddy-buddy and all that. That ain't right. Business is business. Don't be talking about no broads or cutting up touches [reminiscing; comparing notes] about the streets [with the staff]. But I guess

---

[8] What this man refers to as a "narcotics fetish" on the part of prison staff was not completely unfounded. More than a fifth of the inmate population were sentenced for narcotics sale or possession, an even larger proportion of inmates had a history of drug use, and at one time during the project a large supply of drugs stored for the prison hospital was stolen and distributed through inmate merchandising channels.

it's part of the program here. They're going to carry this care and treatment to extremes.

Although 25 percent of the men claimed they had no particular problems of adjustment, several exhibited a certain degree of overaccommodation to life at CMCE. As one man put it:

> I got my time, no complaints. They said "one to life." Well, life [sentence] is pretty hard to look at, but I got my [parole] date now so no worry . . . Main thing, gotta do your own time. [What is the hardest thing to adjust to?] Nothing. [Shrugs] I think if the people would let me go out on weekends, I'd spend the rest of my life in here.

Another respondent stressed the difficulty of adjusting to the leisure time available:

> [What is CMCE like as a prison?] It's a rest home, to tell you the honest truth. Because in other penitentiaries, from what I hear and what I've seen is . . . at three o'clock you're locked up, and don't go out no more. [At Men's Colony] you go out, walk the yard until ten o'clock, do anything you want and on weekends you get to stay until eleven o'clock. But it's just like a rest home—you get three squares a day, you go to work, you get paid for working—most joints do anyhow—and you can lay out here in the sun, give you a pair of shorts to wear if you want them . . . cut the levi pants . . . and it's more of a rest home than anything else. You leave here and people swear to God that you was out on a vacation somewhere because you come back with a nice tan.

Men's Colony inmates thus regarded the institution as a relatively easy place to do time or, at worst, regarded it as an exasperating place because the inmate body lacked the solidarity found in more traditionally run prisons. There were, however, two aspects of prison life not peculiar to CMCE that bothered almost all inmates and most staff members: race relations and homosexuality.

RACE PROBLEMS

For the most part, racial problems in prisons are similar to and spring directly from racial conflict in the country at large, but the conditions of prison life often aggravate the problems.

As we have stated the Men's Colony population was slightly more than one half (55 percent) white, with the rest divided between blacks (23 percent), Mexican-Americans (18 percent), and men of American Indian and Oriental ancestry. The first three were viewed as significant social groupings by our inmate respondents, the only variation being the preference of the particular respondent. Thus the following response is typical:

[If you had to describe the inmate community or society here, are there any particular groups that stand out in your mind?] Two, not because I'm white, but your Mexican group and colored groups are bad, both. [You have the Mexican, white and colored—that's the big thing? Now, do you thing that's the most important division?] Well, as far as I'm concerned it's not, because I'm not a prejudiced person. I have colored in here come to me with their problems, the Mexicans come to me with their problems, but as far as the attitudes of the two groups are concerned, I think your most troublesome group, actually, is the Mexican group. They're loud and they're looking for some sort of status or something. I don't know what they're after. They holler about the spooks [Negroes] looking for recognition. But who is after more recognition than [the] Mexican, after screeching like a Comanche? You walk into a TV room, you'll see the colored sitting there with their mouth shut, and in the back five or six Mexicans carrying on a conversation so loud you can't hear.

Many whites remarked that they resented living with nonwhites in close proximity. Throughout the study periods we heard, were told, or observed that queuing up for meals and seating arrangements were subject to informal understandings within and between racial groups. The institution rule was that men were to walk to meals in a free fashion, but that once in line, seats at the four-man tables were to be filled in sequence with no table-hopping or seat-saving. Inmates who objected to sitting with men of another race or ethnic group tried to counter this procedure by hanging back until others of their choosing got in line, but the supervising correctional officers were supposed to make sure that the incoming inmates lined up without such delays.[9] However, there were strong informal pressures on the officers as well as inmates not to force integration, since the self-selected grouping stabilized a tense situation. This "detante" was described as follows by a white inmate:

Race here—this has astounded me, and this is the first time I've ever been anywhere where there's this majority of mixture that there's no

9 Both San Quentin and Folsom formerly maintained racially segregated food lines, but both had discontinued them at the time of the interview. To our knowledge there were no officially sanctioned Jim Crow practices or facilities in the Department of Corrections. The prisons of California were the first integrated communities in the personal experience of most of the inmates and, for that matter, in that of most of the staff as well.

tension. You know, we had that food demonstration—the colored stayed on their side of the line, we stayed on ours, if we had any beefs with any white guys we handled our beefs, they handled theirs. Everybody got along fine; nobody wanted to break this deal, or break over the line. And the same with eating together. Now you'll see them—like if you see a bunch of colored guys going up the stairs, the white guys'll hang back, some of them won't eat with them—the guys from Folsom, San Quentin, and some other places don't have to do it there.

Another respondent also spoke of the groups whose separate but co-ordinated activities were behind the united front of inmates during the food strike and work stoppage that occurred during the early days of our study. The interviewer asked whether there had been any difficulties between the racial subdivisions of the inmates during this strike.

No, because we broke into groups. Now, I'll tell you something funny about that—the first time I ever saw that happen. The whites took care of the whites, the colored took care of the colored, the Mexicans took care of the Mexicans. They disciplined their own groups—like this one colored guy went to work and a bunch of white guys were going to jump him—and the colored guys said, well, they would take care of him—and they took care of him.

Despite the efforts of all of the groups to stabilize relations between racial and ethnic groupings in the prison, there were enough violations or alleged violations of the agreements and arrangements to threaten the status quo and keep race relations a matter of continuing concern to everyone in the institution.

HOMOSEXUALITY

The homosexuality issue differs from race problems to the extent to which it may be ascribed to the factors of imprisonment. These factors include prolonged, intense personal relations, the loss of ego support, the loss of affection from family and friends, and the absence of women.

Homosexuality was alleged by some of our interviewees to be widely prevalent in the prison. The best evidence we had on this point was provided by a questionnaire that we administered to a random sample of inmates ($N=871$). Twenty-one percent of the respondents were of the opinion that, at least, one half of the men had or would have had a homosexual affair at some time while they were in prison. An additional 25 percent thought that the incidence of homosexuality was more like three out of ten.

Conflicts and anxieties about race issues and homosexuality were often exacerbated when they were combined into interracial homosexual relationships:

> There are queens [effeminate homosexuals] in the general [inmate] population. You sit in the TV room—now this is in my quad—I have just seen a man pull about a yard of dick out of her jaws and she'll sit there with a white boy—she's as black as the ace of spades—drinking his coffee out of his cup. And he'll reach over and play with her and she'd kiss him [Interviewer: Right there?]. Yes, there's no shame in them . . . Another thing, you walk into the dining room and you sit across the table and you look at that and you know what it is and you look at your cup—did that sonofabitch have this cup this morning? And that's not right.

Although a variety of collective and individual problems may be observed in the social relations of inmates, the issues pertaining to race and homosexual behavior seem to constitute primary foci of conflict and tension in the prison. Attention to these matters is justified at this point in our discussion not merely because they are part of the prison experience of Men's Colony inmates but also because feelings and attitudes concerning homosexuality and relations between different races are important topics in the lives of citizens in the outside community, and for this reason they are represented in the attitudes of the prison staff. Because staff members have their own strong personal feelings about these issues, it is difficult to keep these feelings disengaged when the issues arise in their work. And, there were several recurring situations where staff members had to deal with the problems posed by racial conflict and homosexuality. In group counseling sessions, for example, these issues were supposed to be discussed in general terms as well as in specific terms when the issue pertained to a member of the group. How group leaders, who are supposed to conduct discussions of how one might reduce feelings of prejudice, psychosexual ambivalence, and interpersonal conflict, feel about these issues is a matter of some importance and will be dealt with in Chapter IV.

Another place where these issues are dealt with, at least on a surface level, is at the meetings of the Prison Disciplinary Committee. The fact that a disciplinary committee exists at all suggests that the serious problems inmates encounter are *not* resolved through discussions in group counseling sessions. The functions of the Prison Disciplinary Committee are so important to all members of the prison community that they should be described before we proceed to the business of discussing the treatment program we studied at Men's Colony-East.

The control of "troublemaking" in prison

Prison life may be distinguished, in degree if not in kind, from other communal forms by the extent to which conduct is prescribed and proscribed by the authorities. Goffman has taken this feature as a component of his definition of the total institution:

> [In the total institution] all aspects of life are conducted in the same place and under the same single authority. Second, each phase of the member's daily activity is carried on in the immediate company of a large batch of others, all of whom are treated alike and required to do the same thing together. Third, all phases of the day's activities are tightly scheduled with one activity leading into the next at a prearranged time, the whole sequence of activities being imposed from above by a system of explicit formal rulings and a body of officials. Finally, the various imposed activities are brought together into a single rational plan purportedly designed to fulfill the official aims of the institution.[10]

Elsewhere in the same volume, Goffman links both punishment and institutional privilege as part of the organization's sanction system and emphasizes its abnormal character in comparison with civil society.

> Punishments and privileges are themselves modes of organization peculiar to total institutions. Whatever their severity, punishments are largely known in the inmate's home world as something applied to animals and children; this conditioning, behavioristic model is not widely applied to adults, since failure to maintain required standards typically leads to indirect disadvantageous consequences and not to specific immediate punishment at all. And privileges in the total institutions . . . are not the same as perquisites, indulgences, or values, but merely the absence of deprivations one ordinarily expects not to have to sustain.[11]

There are several sources of the canons of conduct that govern inmate behavior. One of them is the list of departmental and prison regulations covering actions and activities expected or forbidden in the prison. A second set of rules consists of all the laws that normally apply to residents of the state. (For example, anything that is a felony in the state of California is also a felony in a California prison, and a person so charged may be prosecuted by the district attorney of the county in which the prison is located.)

---

[10] Erving Goffman, *Asylums*, op. cit., p. 6.
[11] Ibid., p. 51.

But prisons are not unlike military bases, hospitals, monasteries, universities, and other organizations that have rules of their own to apply to those who come under their jurisdiction. Prisons have perhaps fewer privileges (and, thus, fewer punishments due to the removal or denial of privileges) and those who misbehave in a prison tend to be kept longer instead of being rejected from the organization. (Transfer of troublesome inmates to another prison is often used, as will be shown, for example, in case No. 4 below.) However, it is the overriding concern about "trouble" within the organization that differentiates prisons from other total institutions. Although it is the case that men in prison have committed serious and often repeated violations of the laws of the larger society, it is also the case that most of the men are not reported for violating prison rules. What happens, according to custodial administrators, is that "five percent of the inmates continually make trouble, and they spoil it for the rest."[12] The argument further extended is that a small proportion of the inmates in any prison are consistently involved in rule-breaking behavior that must be punished not only to try to stop the misbehavior of the individual involved but, more important, to prevent other inmates from gaining the impression that they can "get away with things." The latter point is important because it presumes that there is a predisposition on the part of most inmates to violate rules either because they are being held in an unpleasant place against their will, or because they are members of groups which, because of age, race, IQ test score, psychiatric diagnosis, or some other criteria, are always ready to resist "legal authority."

The argument in short is: (1) most inmates are troublemakers—or will be if given an opportunity; (2) little rules violations lead to big rules violations; and (3) if an inmate is not punished for breaking the rules, others will think that they can break the rules with impunity. The policy implications of these assumptions is that *all* behavior should be governed by rules and *any* violations of the rules should result in punishment, swift and sure. There is a model of behavior assumed in this argument, and the compatibility of treatment and custodial ends in prison depends in large part on the degree to which this model also underlies the treatment policies and programs.

We consider next a description of how the social control mandate was implemented at Men's Colony—East and at the end of the discussion

[12] In a study of rule enforcement policies and practices in a medium security federal prison, Ward reported that 45 percent of the disciplinary reports during a given period were contributed by 5 percent of the inmate population. David A. Ward, *Prison Rule Enforcement and Changing Organizational Goals*, unpublished Ph.D. dissertation, University of Illinois, 1960.

return to a comparison of the custodial model of behavior and the model on which the group counseling program is based.

RECONCILING ORGANIZATIONAL INTERESTS IN THE DISCIPLINARY COMMITTEE

Outside of the duties of the parole board, there is no other decision-making activity more difficult for prison staff members than the attempt to find appropriate methods to deal with inmates who have violated institutional rules.[13] The members of the Disciplinary Committee have to reconcile in each case their own conflicting views and concerns about individualized treatment and social control with the implications of their actions for the inmate population at large, and on the morale of the custodial staff, all within the context of established departmental policy, and the policies and traditions peculiar to the individual prison. The Disciplinary Committee, like the outside criminal court and the parole board, is in the position of having to make difficult decisions about the efficacy of certain punitive sanctions and/or treatment techniques as a means of controlling those who violate laws and rules. The Disciplinary Committee in prison has, with the exception of fines, the same alternatives as the criminal court in the outside community: warnings, suspended sentences (probation), referral to psychiatric treatment, and confinement. In addition, the committee, like the parole board, must seek to determine whether the release of an inmate from punitive confinement is warranted. In the

---

[13] Some of the better discussions of social control mechanisms in prisons include: Richard A. Cloward, "Social Control in the Prison," *op. cit.*, pp. 20–48; Gresham Sykes, *The Society of Captives*, op. cit.; Richard R. Korn and Lloyd W. McCorkle, *Criminology and Penology*, op. cit.; pp. 471–477; Allen Cook, Norman Fenton, Robert Heinze, "Methods of Handling the Severely Recalcitrant Inmate," *Proceedings of the American Correctional Association*, 1955; Donald R. Cressey, "Rehabilitation Theory and Reality II, Organization and Freedom," *California Youth Authority Quarterly*, 10, Summer, 1957, pp. 40–47; Vernon Fox, "Analysis of Prison Disciplinary Problems," *Journal of Criminal Law, Criminology and Police Science*, 49, November–December, 1958, pp. 321–326; Richard W. Nice, "The Adjustment Committee: Adversary or Adjunct to Treatment," *American Journal of Corrections*, 22, November–December, 1960, pp. 26–30; Daniel Glaser, *The Effectiveness of a Prison and Parole System*, Indianapolis: The Bobbs-Merrill Company, Inc., 1964, pp. 172–184; see also the discussions of prison discipline in *The Manual of Correctional Standards* and *Task Force Report: Corrections*, The President's Commission on Law Enforcement and Administration of Justice, Washington, D.C., U.S. Government Printing Office, 1967, pp. 50–51, 84–85; Frank J. Remington, Donald J. Newman, Edward L. Kimball, Melli Marygold, Herman Goldstein, "The Objective of Maintaining Order [In Prison]," *Criminal Justice Administration: Materials and Cases*, Indianapolis: The Bobbs-Merrill Company, Inc., 1969, pp. 817–851; Howard Mittman, "Punishment and Discipline in Prisons," *American Journal of Corrections*, 32, May–June, 1970, pp. 10–17.

first case, the release from segregation/isolation is involved; in the second, it is release from the prison.

Reports of rule violations and appearances before a disciplinary committee are matters of concern to inmates and matters of interest to the staff and to the parole board. The principal reason for this is that those reports are deemed to be measures of inmate "adjustment." In this case, the adjustment is always presumed to be negative. Records of disciplinary infractions are taken into account by the staff in recommending housing, job, program, and custody changes, and the reports also are used by the parole board in considering the prospects of parole success. In a situation where the indicators of personality or attitude change are ambiguous, the disciplinary report provides an indicator that is explicit and measurable.[14] Disciplinary reports and appearances before the Disciplinary Committee are then important matters to inmates—important enough to provide a good many of the reasons that explain why inmates become frustrated and concerned about the procedures and decisions of the committee.

In addition to its meaning for inmates, the committee represents, as indicated earlier, a meeting ground of custodial and treatment interests. No longer is prison discipline a matter of exclusive concern to the lieutenants, captains, and associate wardens of the custody staff. At Men's Colony—East, the Disciplinary Committee members included a variety of treatment specialists: senior caseworkers, a psychiatrist, and the chief medical officer. The influence of the treatment philosophy is evident not only in the consideration of a variety of social and psychological factors in the deliberations surrounding many cases but also in the committee decisions. Certain rebellious or "disturbed" inmates may be referred to the care of the psychiatrist instead of being sent to the segregation unit; evidence of psychosis in a man appearing before the committee may be the basis for a recommendation that he be transferred to a medical facility better equipped to handle such cases; the committee may "recommend" to an inmate that he participate in institutional programs such as group counseling or that he increase the degree to which he participates in

---

[14] Correctional decision-making groups also tend to rely on indicators such as the number or variety of programs in which an inmate has participated as measures of change for the better or worse. In this respect, several inmates at Men's Colony reported, not altogether facetiously, the old prisoners nostrum for obtaining parole: a man who wishes to show that he has been rehabilitated should, "raise hell at first, nothing serious like assaulting an officer or anything like that, but you don't sign up for anything and your attitude is poor, then you make a startling change and go along with the program." The dramatic turnabout makes it possible for caseworkers, disciplinary committees, or parole boards to see "evidence" that the inmate has changed for the better. The inmate who is always a troublemaker or always a model prisoner is hard pressed to present evidence that he is a different—and improved—version of the man who started his sentence.

group counseling sessions. The discussion of cases increasingly involves an "understanding" of the inmate's background and a knowledge of his prior institutional behavior, including behavior other than prior breaches of rules of conduct in the prison. The big question for the Disciplinary Committee is: Are decisions to be made to serve the best interests of the inmate or to serve the best interests of the organization?

THE ADMINISTRATION OF JUSTICE IN THE PRISON COMMUNITY

Disciplinary action at Men's Colony—East was taken on two levels: the handling of minor infractions on the quad level, and the handling of major infractions on the institution level. This discussion is devoted to an analysis of the latter, since this kind of rule-breaking behavior is of more serious consequence to both staff and inmates. Major rule infractions include fighting, attempted escape, homosexuality, disrespect and disobedience to an officer, possessing or dealing in contraband, gambling, the destruction of state property, the violation of rules pertaining to mail and visiting privileges, stealing, and the misuse of stimulants or sedatives.[15] For these violations a number of dispositions were available: confinement (up to 29 days) in the segregation unit, the restriction of privileges, warning and reprimand, a change of housing unit, job or custody classification, suspension of any of the foregoing, referral to the psychiatrist, or a transfer to another institution. There could be any combination of these dispositions or no action at all.

Action on the institution level took place at least twice each week. The members of the committee included the associate superintendent (and occasionally, the deputy superintendent) who served as chairman, the program administrators, captain, psychiatrist, chief medical officer, classification and parole representative, and a lieutenant. Uniformed correctional officers acted as court officers. Hearings generally began with informal comments about the number of men to be seen, about the more interesting or serious violations, and about the return of familiar names among the cases. Formal business began with a brief review of the charges brought against the first inmate to be seen, a procedure repeated before each inmate entered the hearing room.

Committee members were seated behind a long conference table in upholstered armchairs. The inmate was seated on a straight-backed wooden chair, with a correctional officer standing close behind his right shoulder. (Inmates on less serious charges sometimes were brought directly

---

[15] Minor rule infractions that are handled by quadrangle staff disciplinary committees include: being out of bounds, the violations of clothing, safety, and sanitation regulations, poor work reports, and inconsequential altercations between inmates.

from their regular living quarters or work assignments, but others were brought from the segregation unit where they had been held pending the appearance before the committee. These men were dressed in white coveralls and slippers.) The charges were read to the inmate at which time he was asked whether he was "guilty" or "not guilty" or sometimes more informally: "What have you got to say for yourself?" With this background the best way to describe the conduct of the disciplinary proceedings at Men's Colony is to use the examples of specific cases that we observed or that were reported by our on-site research staff member from his routine attendance at the committee meetings.[16] The cases cover a variety of prison sins and neither the cases nor the methods of dealing with them, in our experience in other prisons, are distinctive to Men's Colony—East.

The facts of the following case (Case No. 1) were excerpted from a report by the reporting correctional officer; the appearance of the inmates before the Disciplinary Committee is recounted by our research staff observer. (All other case descriptions were taken from the reports made by the UCLA project staff.)

---

case 1   Inmates S and G were leaving C Quad and returning to their respective Quads at approximately 8:55 P.M. After playing bridge on an approved pass, they were passing through the control plaza and were stopped for a routine search. While searching Inmate S, Officer P found a love letter which S was carrying to an inmate in B Quad from an inmate who lived in A Quad. Inmate stated during an interview with the writer that he "was only the horse between the two."

During a similar routine search of Inmate G, Officer C found a love letter in G's personal effects addressed to another inmate; upon seeing that Officer C was going to inspect the letter, he grabbed it from the Officer's hands, tore it up and stated it was private property

---

[16] Since it was our intention to study the treatment varieties within the settings in which they were applied, the research staff devoted considerable time to activities that were not obviously related to the group treatment program. Our extended discussions with inmates, some of whom were not enrolled in the group counseling program, and the routine attendance of our on-site research assistant at the meetings of the institutional disciplinary committee evoked some questions and a certain amount of concern from prison staff members. It was necessary in the case of the latter to provide prison officials with reminders that this key aspect of institutional life might be affected by the presence of a group treatment program, and to point out that our survey of all group counseling leaders in the Department of Corrections had indicated that a majority felt that group counseling participation reduced the incidence of prison rule violations. The need to justify this research interest was dramatized by a short-lived rumor that our research assistant was really an undercover magazine reporter.

and that the Officer had no business reading it. At this point Inmate G became extremely emotional. He began crying and grabbing his stomach, stating he had stomach cramps and asked that he be taken to the hospital for medication. The MTA [medical department official on duty] stated that [G's] emotional state was of such a nature that he had to administer a sedative.

During an interview with the writer, G professed everlasting love for Inmate T and stated that his only concern was the possibility of this relationship being broken up. He also stated that he had contacted his father and requested that his father secure employment for T. He also stated that upon release he intended to live with T and continue this relationship. During the interview, G was crying and at times almost hysterical. This was *after* the administering of the sedative by MTA.

After the interviews with Inmates S and G, Inmate T was escorted to the Lieutenant's Office and interviewed by Sergeant E . . . and the writer; he admitted having written to and received love letters of an immoral nature from G. He also stated that he realized he and G had placed themselves in a compromising position but asserted that no sexual acts had been committed. Inmate T stated he had strong feelings for G. Inmate T was highly disturbed during the interview. He attempted to take all the blame for the involvement of the other two inmates (S and G).

The fact that there was emotional instability involved to such an extent that medical attention was required, the Officer of the Day was contacted and permission was granted for the placement of the aforementioned inmates on Administrative Segregation status, which was accomplished without incident. It is the opinion of the writer that, as all three inmates involved work in Correctional Industries, an evaluation should be made before permitting these inmates to work in "close proximity."

The resolution of the case as reported by our observer:

Inmate G admitted guilt and said little before leaving. (He had a date to appear before the Adult Authority.) He was given a warning and reprimand, partially because of the fact that the medical officer's recommendation gave the opinion that the inmate, although an "emotional homosexual," could "adjust well" and should be released as soon as possible. It was also in G's favor that the note was not regarded as obscene. G has had a clean record and is considered a good inmate. He said he had had no other homosexual relationships at CMCE, and committee discussion indicated that the members believed this assertion to be true. G's program administrator had argued for leniency. (After the discussion of this case, he left commenting, "well, the defense lawyer is leaving now.")

T was called in, and said only that he was good friends with G. He is not noted as an overt homosexual by the staff, although his record contained the allegation that he had had homosexual relations with his brother and a four-year-old boy.

S then came in and in a matter-of-fact manner admitted that he and G were homosexual, said he didn't know about T. He said little more.

Among the committee, three types of reactions could be observed. One program administrator expressed tolerance. He raised questions pertaining to what might be done to "help" the men. Another member of the committee regarded homosexual affairs as inevitable in prison and expressed the attitude that if inmates get involved they should conduct their affairs "so they don't bother anybody and do not get themselves in trouble." At one point he remarked about the note: "How are we going to teach these guys not to put it in writing?" Another custodial representative expressed principal concern about the need to support the correctional officers (take punitive action to back up the officer's report). It was decided that all three inmates were to be warned against future note passing. No further punitive action was taken.

Disciplinary committees spend their time not only in handling violations of the rules but in trying to deal with rather complex instances of bizarre behavior, as is illustrated by the following cases.

---

case 2   Inmate R was charged with using offensive language and disobeying orders. The inmate wrote a letter to a prison official saying: "Roses are red, violets are blue, if I were a prick, I would be you." Inmate R entered, and the charges against him were reviewed. R pled guilty, explaining that he was emotionally upset and that he had to "strike out at authority," and that he doesn't even know the officer to whom he sent the letter. Another charge against him, that of disobeying orders, was lodged because he had put a piece of newspaper in his cell window and refused to remove it when ordered by another officer. R asserted that he was doing nothing, but that other inmates were looking at him through the window. At the hearing he stated he was under a strain because of "water constantly dripping in his toilet." He then said he had committed two irrational acts, and he supposed he'd "have time to think it over." An officer said: "Aren't you anticipating a little about your [parole] date?" R said: "I think it safe to assume I'll lose it." Another staff member said: "Sounds like you want to lose it." R replied: "I don't." The committee also reminded R of his previous demands for medical attention, and that "all six liver tests were negative." R said: "I'm a hypochondriac with all the rest of my problems." R was sentenced to 30 days' loss of privileges for each offense, with the sentences to run concurrently. After he left the room, the ranking committee official turned to a program administrator and said: "Can't the lieutenant in your quad find something better to do than fool around with lunatics like this?"

case 3   Inmate C had been involved in a fight with another inmate. C was a "protection" case and was classified as a "psychotic in partial remission suffering from severe paranoia." C, with tears in his eyes, began his appearance before the committee by complaining that he had been trying to see the superintendent "about these guys who call me a snitch and say they're going to kill snitches. It's an awful situation to have to call on the institution to protect you from these guys. You should keep these psychopaths from jumping on me— these extremely violent punks who are running the institution— people who are supposed to be running it aren't. It sickens me, and I'm extremely incensed." C then related a story of how he had trouble with some inmates and was threatened by them in an area where a correctional officer could overhear them, but the officer did nothing about it. C went to the sergeant and told him that, "the staff can't have inmates forming groups and running the institution like they do." He told the sergeant that it was cowardice on the part of the officials in denying a situation that actually exists. He complained that, "all that happened was that the sergeant chewed me out for being a coward. As far as I know, I'm living exemplarily. What am I supposed to do? I don't know how I could act more intelligently. I don't know what I could do."

Inmate H, charged with fighting with C, said that he had been sitting in the TV room and that C had sneezed on him. H turned around and asked him to cover his mouth. C said, "fuck you," and "what are you trying to do, run things around here," and the fight started. During committee discussions, comments were made that C could not be turned loose in the quad, although some of what he said may be true, "he brings it on himself." Dr. P (a physician) said that to be consistent with another case of fighting the committee should release C as the victim of an attack. Dr. P also argued that C should be considered on the instant offense and not on how much trouble he makes for the staff. Another committee member said facetiously of C: "I'd like to execute him, execute them both, especially C. They give me too much trouble in the quad." Dr. P asked: "Where's the evidence?" The chairman told the Dr. to "remember that this is not a court, and we're not bound to rules of evidence." Another member said he agreed with the doctor that, "we have to have some standards to go by," and that the committee had to have some evidence.

The penalties suggested were a two weekend lockup and a five weekend lockup. One committee member said he did not think that there was any alternative but to let C go because it was not a good case. The officer had not included in his report enough of the actual words exchanged by the inmates, and the fight actually had not taken place in the TV room. The senior custody staff member was asked why the officers did not quote the inmates. He replied that, "the officers have other duties."

H was given two weekend lockups. The chairman told H that C was a hard person to put up with and probably had done the most to cause the fight, but that the committee did not have much evidence of that. C was called in and told that he would be released. C declared that, "this should have been done before and when are you guys going to start running the institution?" The chairman became irritated and told C that he was causing his own trouble by going around telling people "where to get off," when he should tend to his own business, and that he was "darn lucky not to get anything" (in the way of punitive action).

Transfer to another institution was an administrative tool used by the committee. In some cases transfer was desired by an inmate, as evidenced in the following instance, in which the security of the institution was threatened by the presence of a man with a grievance to settle.

---

case 4   Inmate L was charged with possession of contraband—a pair of scissors had been found in his room. The inmate stated that it was for the purpose of killing three inmates who had raped him. L would not tell where he got the shears, or who he planned to kill or who raped him, or indeed anything else; he said that he, "had a score to settle, and that was it." The committee chairman asked him to tell, "to save trouble." L replied that he was brought up, "not to tell no names." He said that the attack took place in the gym and that, "Negroes did it" (L is white). He then said: "I never go to the law for no one—I take care of myself." The chairman said: "Cut me in on this one; otherwise you force me to lock you up—I'm not going to have any killings here." L refused and was taken from the room. The chairman made the comment: "We'll have to transfer him. If I let him out in the yard again after he said this, I'd be a damn fool. We're not going to have any killings here." Final disposition of the case was 29 days isolation and administrative segregation pending transfer to another prison.

In addition to citations involving inmate behavior toward staff and toward other inmates, many prison rule infractions involve property regulations. These cases are reminders of the degree to which behavior is regulated in a prison setting.

---

case 5   Inmate P had two cans of shoe polish that only could have come from the shoeshine stand (for staff). P stated that he had gotten the cans from a parolee who had left the institution. P was given three weekend lockups.

The following case is taken verbatim from the inmate's file.

---

case 6   "At approximately 12:25 P.M., this date, while supervising the feeding of inmates in the quad dining room, the writer observed Inmate V approach the cookie tray from the back side of the serving table and remove two (2) cookies from it. V surrendered the cookies and headed for the scullery. A few minutes later, when the line backer [man who stands behind the food line] was removing the cookie tray from the serving table, V walked over to the tray and removed another cookie and headed back into the scullery area. V was receptive to counseling and was informed of this report." This violation pertained to rule D-1601, "proper use of food." V was, "held guilty. One weekend lockup, suspended for three months clear conduct" [probation].

Other cases are compounded by assessments of inmate behavior, in which a trivial property offense becomes aggravated by the nature of the inmate's reaction to the officer making the citation.

---

case 7   An inmate had taken two apples instead of one from the dining room food line, and when stopped by an officer, he warned the officer not to take anything from him. There were two supplemental reports stating that the inmate was disrespectful to the officer, using "hand gestures and making asides" to bystanding inmates. A member of the disciplinary committee (his program administrator) said that the inmate makes the staff nervous because of his reputation as a difficult behavior problem and "possible psychotic." He said part of the problem is that the inmate, "acts and looks like a tough guy." In his appearance before the committee, the inmate said he had "a control problem about my hostility." The chairman asked him what he would like to do; the inmate asked if he could work in the dining room on clean up. After talking a while, the inmate was not "defiant," a fact which was pointed out to him. He was told that the staff in the quad wanted the inmate transferred, but that he would be given a second chance—after ten days isolation—and that he would not be transferred out of the quad.

When the evidence regarding possession of contraband property was lacking, occasionally a case was dropped. Usually, however, general inferences were regarded as sufficient to establish that an offense had taken place and that there was a sufficient basis for committee action.

---

case 8   Inmate M was accused of taking "stimulants or sedatives." It was charged that he had taken some medication bought from another inmate. An inmate had informed one of the staff members about the transaction. Inmate M had been found "wandering about, sick at his stomach." M pleaded "not guilty." The medical officer asked what made him sick. Inmate M said: "I don't know, I think it was the evening meal. I didn't take anything." The doctor said: "Did you fake being sick?" Inmate: "No." After he left, one of the committee suggested the charges be dismissed because there was no proof that the inmate had acquired contraband drugs. The medical evidence was ambiguous. The doctor, however, was of the opinion that the inmate had taken "something" and suggested five days isolation. The rest agreed that the man was guilty, and he was given a sentence of five days.

---

case 9   Inmates D, K, and Y were charged with stealing typewriter ribbons and pens for sale in the quad. Another inmate, N, said that D got the goods from the warehouse and had given him some to sell. N had sold two typewriter ribbons. D denied everything. K admitted buying a ribbon and nothing else. Y, an inmate clerk, was reputed to be a "wheeler and dealer" and a "3 for 1" loan shark. He complained that his room had been robbed of ten packs of cigarettes and five jars of coffee. His comments, with all present assuming he was a dealer, made the committee break into laughter several times; when asked how all the contraband got into his room, he replied: "OK, I'm a

crook, but that doesn't mean they should be able to rob my cell."
N was given ten days in segregation, Y five days, and D was found
"not guilty." N and Y were told not to be upset that D was "getting
off." It was just that the committee had no evidence against him,
although they were sure he was involved. N was told to stay away
from inmates like D because, "it will always wind up with you taking
the rap." K was given five days and told it might help him to lose
weight. When D entered the room to hear the disposition, he started
a story not realizing he was to be released because of lack of evidence.
The chairman told him that they had some doubt that he was
involved because it wasn't his "M.O." but that, "perhaps you're
going into more petty stuff now that you are getting old." D was
told he was not guilty at which point he stopped talking.

The meetings of the Disciplinary Committee most often brought staff
members into frequent contact with that minority of the inmate population who gave them most of their "trouble." In some of these cases the
committee hearings assumed a ceremonial function with both staff members and inmate making no effort to hide the fact that the committee's
action would have no real influence on the inmate's future behavior. The
committee members and the inmate accepted the fact that for other reasons, such as "backing" officers, penalties had to be imposed.

---

case 10   Inmate O was charged with being intoxicated. O admitted that he
had been drinking "Pruno" (a fermented mixture of sugar, water,
oranges or grapes). He said he was trying to shape up—he found
that he "can't win against the system," and even though it looked
bad to be called before the committee so soon after his arrival from
San Quentin, he was going to try. O said he had no excuse for his
actions, and only the future would show his good intentions. Some
bookie forms had been found in O's cell, and he was asked about
them. He said he "was holding them for someone else," and was
told, "that isn't a good way to stay out of trouble." O had not been
charged with possessing the slips, and there was no further discussion of this issue. However, in addition to drinking "Pruno," he had
been charged with putting a piece of broken glass on a seat. He
said in regard to this that a jar had been broken and in picking up
pieces he had "absent-mindedly" put a piece of glass on the seat
next to him in the gymnasium. The chairman noted that O was a
"special interest case" because he had been received at CMCE from
San Quentin. He had worked his way up to the latter through the
segregation units of other prisons. O was reported to be a "gunsel"
(tough) when he was a young inmate, but he had grown into a

"con." The chairman characterized O's presentation as the "all-American boy type who is putting out the line that he is going to change." The committee noted, however, that O's straightforward story was not "his usual way of operating." The chairman also remarked that if O had wanted a weapon, "he wouldn't have chosen a piece of glass—he would have gotten a man-sized spike or something." O was told that his straightforwardness was appreciated and that the committee hoped he was really straightening up. The chairman said: "You are getting ten days [in segregation]—you can do it standing on your head—let's see what you do when you get out."

THE INMATE VIEW OF DISCIPLINARY COMMITTEE PROCEDURES

The Prison Disciplinary Committee is not bound by the rules of constitutional due process, which include the right to be represented by counsel, the right to be tried by a jury of peers, and the right to appeal decisions to a higher court. But the committee appears to inmates to have, at least, a quasi-judicial character, which means that it is seen as having some commitment to the legal rules of procedure. The problem is that inmates do not understand that the committee, like the criminal court, is one part of a system that deals with rule breakers. The remarks made by the Disciplinary Committee members that inmates do not hear often indicate prejudgment of cases before the inmates are formally seen. Comments such as: "How long do we want to keep him locked?" suggest the high degree of reliance the committee has placed on the prehearing investigations conducted by the sergeants and lieutenants as the means of sifting the cases of clear violations from the ones involving mistakes in judgment by correctional officers. Unlike the criminal court, when the accused stands before the Prison Disciplinary Committee, he generally is presumed to be guilty unless he can prove himself innocent. The decision as to an inmate's guilt really is made when a correctional officer decides to report the inmate's rule violation. The only cases that are screened out through the review of disciplinary reports by the officer's immediate supervisor are the ones in which the infractions involve mistakes in interpretation of policy by the officer, cases in which the issue can be resolved by the officer and inmate or, in rare cases, when the officer's judgment was very bad. *Thus the committee is most accurately viewed as a body that is concerned primarily with making decisions about what to do with guilty inmates.* (Inmate complaints of "unfair" treatment rarely refer to the steps by which the inmate's rule violation was reported or the subsequent investigation of the circumstances surrounding the violation. We did not hear one inmate complain that his "rights" or even the rules of "fair play" were violated during the prehearing investigation. The entire focus of concern was on the procedures and activities of the Disciplinary Committee.)[17]

[17] The authority of prison officials to utilize whatever disciplinary procedures and devices they deemed necessary to maintain control over "recalcitrant" inmates is no longer being taken for granted. In her review of the issues involved in the development of a "humane standard" of prison discipline, Betty Friedlander summarizes the trend of recent court decisions in cases that involve complaints by inmates:

> Until recently, the federal courts refused to review charges which arose as a result of state prison disciplinary procedures. The aggrieved prisoners, therefore, could only pursue whatever remedies, if any, were available to them in state courts. But given the virtually unanimous and marked reluctance of state and federal courts to review the internal management of the prison system, such directed pursuits were almost invariably doomed to futility.
>
> A number of recent United States Supreme Court decisions, however, have undermined the rationale which formerly supported the federal courts' refusal to take jurisdiction in these matters. *Robinson v. California,* 370 U.S. 660 (1962), established that the Eighth Amendment, which prohibits cruel and unusual punishment, the basis of most complaints involving prison discipline, was applicable to the states through the Fourteenth Amendment. *Cooper v. Pate,* 378 U.S. 546 (1964), settled the question that persons confined in state prisons were within the protection of the Civil Rights Act, and in *Monroe v. Pape,* 365 U.S. 167 (1961) the court held that in an action under the Civil Rights Act, federal court jurisdiction was not dependent upon a previous exhaustion of state court remedies. The court reaffirmed this doctrine in *McNeese v. Board of Education,* 373 U.S. 668 (1963). Finally, the federal courts, while still appearing to prefer their long-standing policy of non-interference in state prison administration, have recently evidenced a somewhat greater willingness to intervene, especially in cases alleging brutal and extreme excesses in prison discipline.
>
> A significant decision emerging from the backdrop of these cases, and the concomitantly developing judicial stance and attitudes, is *Wright v. McMann,* 387 F. 2nd 519 (2nd Cir. 1967). Wright, a New York State prisoner, instituted an action under the Civil Rights Act, 42 U.S.C. 1981, 1983, 1985 (3) against the Warden of Clinton State Prison. Alleging that his constitutional rights (under the First, Fifth and Eighth Amendments) were violated by the administration of disciplinary punishment, Wright sought both money damages and injunctive relief. The District Court dismissed the complaint without a hearing on defendant's motion. The court held that the complaint did not sufficiently show the denial of plaintiff's constitutional rights and that the plaintiff's remedy, if any, lay in the state courts, *Wright v. McMann,* 257 F. Supp. 739 (N.D.N.Y. 1966). The Circuit Court reversed and remanded the case, holding that under the circumstances presented the plaintiff was not required to exhaust his state remedies. More importantly, the court held that the plaintiff was entitled to a state hearing on his Eighth Amendment claim that the discipline imposed constituted cruel and unusual punishment.

Betty Friedlander, "*Wright v. McMann* and Cruel and Unusual Punishment," *The Prison Journal,* XLVIII, Spring–Summer, 1968, pp. 40–41. The entire issue is devoted to articles dealing with the "Rights of Prisoners in Confinement in the United States."

The erroneous notion that the committee is in the business of trying accused persons to establish guilt or innocence lies behind the frequently expressed requests of inmates that they be permitted to have counsel, call their own witnesses, or require that the reporting officer be present at the hearing. We sought to determine the chances an inmate had to be exonerated by the committee by relating the pleas and dispositions in 303 cases that were processed by the Disciplinary Committee during the course of our study; as Table 2.1 shows, those chances were about two in ten.

table 2.1   Pleas and Dispositions in CMC Disciplinary Committee

Committee Final Disposition	Inmate Plea		Total
	Guilty	Not Guilty	
Guilty	100 percent (205)	78 percent (76)	93 percent (281)
Not guilty	(0)	22 percent (22)	7 percent (22)
Total	68 percent (205)	32 percent (98)	(303)

The fact that disciplinary committees find few inmates "not guilty" is not surprising when one is reminded that the members of the court consist of the senior staff members in the administrative hierarchy. The actions these men take are highly visible to all persons in the institution. The court can rarely afford to find inmates innocent because such a ruling implies that the reporting staff member was wrong. For the morale of the rank-and-file correctional officers, such inferences cannot be permitted.

Disciplinary committee decisions are made on the basis of the written information at hand which concerns the inmate's background and personal history: the reports of staff members, and the verbal testimony from other inmates that has been collected by investigating staff members. The review of the circumstances surrounding the rule violation and the arguments and pleas of innocence are a ritual permitted the inmate that satisfies a feeling by the staff that justice has been served when the offender has been permitted to "speak his piece" and "have his day in court." The frustration of inmates in these hearings becomes evident in their actions and statements as the session progresses. Slowly the inmate becomes aware that what he says carries no weight, and that the veracity of reporting staff members' judgment will not be an issue. He then may become angry and may accuse the staff of refusing to listen to him, of malfeasance, and of being prejudiced or unfair. Only the inmate who has been through this experience many times before is the wiser for it. He does not argue, he admits guilt, and he asserts that there is not any point to arguing, since he will not be believed anyway. He is prepared before he comes into the room to receive the sentencing action that is the real purpose of the whole procedure.

If it is understood that the attention of disciplinary committees is directed to the issues of what to do with *convicted* rule breakers, we can better understand the problems faced by the staff members and how they attempt to resolve them. Is it possible to recommend psychotherapy for one man caught fighting while giving the other combatant a sentence of ten days in segregation? Is it possible to refer two men found in bed together to the psychiatrist and not subject them to any punitive sanctions? Is it possible for the court to refer a chronic rule violator to a group counseling program and to take away the privileges of a first offender when the same rule infraction is involved? In other contexts these decisions, which impose different sanctions for the same offense according to characteristics of the offender, may be common, but they are not in the context of the total institution. These decisions inevitably evoke cries—from correctional officers and inmates—that favoritism or prejudice was the basis of differing dispositions or that inmates were able to "con" the committee. These complaints are generated mainly because the basis for the Disciplinary Committee decisions are not made "public," thus neither officers nor inmates know what evidence and circumstances have been considered by the court. Even the inmate appearing before the committee does not know the factors considered in his case, since these deliberations have taken place while he waited outside the hearing room.

The Disciplinary Committee is aware of the image it presents as the representative of institutional policy. Its members well know that their decisions will be criticized if they are out of line with the expectations of the various interest groups in the prison community. For example, in our review of inmate files, we encountered complaints made by Adult Authority members about Disciplinary Committee dispositions. One such report stated that the AA (Adult Authority) "wondered what the reasons are that the committee used for such decisions." The complaining, and to some extent the badgering, that the committee members receive from the Adult Authority, the custodial and treatment personnel they supervise, and from the inmates produces strong pressures for standard penalties. On the other hand, a standard penalties system is difficult to implement as long as "individualized treatment" is a policy matter and the decisions are made in executive sessions.

THE CUSTODIAL AND GROUP TREATMENT MODELS OF BEHAVIOR

Disciplinary Committee action is, quite obviously, not a typical instance of staff-inmate interaction. But the Disciplinary Committee underscores (precisely because of its unusual character) the ultimate realities of the prison situation. The senior staff holds the correctional officers responsible for making decisions and for using discretion concerning rule enforcement; but once an inmate is officially cited (accused) of misconduct, the guilt of the inmate is not subject to further serious debate. The fact that very few cases appearing before the Disciplinary Committee do not receive punishment and that the committee may impose punishment for "policy reasons," even when it is in doubt about the inmate's precise fault (for example, to be consistent or to show firmness), drives home the point that the activity of the committee is to impose sanctions, not to ascertain guilt or innocence. The ultimate consequence of getting caught in violations of prison regulations is to experience punishment. The punishment is imposed by the senior staff, in the light of the definitions of the behavior in question provided by the line staff. It is assumed that the inmates know the rules of the institution and that punishment has a deterrent value, at least for other inmates, if not for the man in question.

The relevance of the prison's disciplinary machinery to its treatment program lies in the model of behavior that is assumed by both treatment and custodial norms, and in the nature of the means exerted to induce desired behavior in the prison. To the extent that the assumptions concerning behavior and the modes of manipulation of behavior in disciplinary and treatment arrangements are congruent, one may expect less conflict between these organizational functions. On the other hand, to the extent that these arrangements are incongruent, or are perceived by inmates as incongruent, it is likely that the organization will experience greater conflict. One of the difficulties that besets prison treatment programs like group counseling is the disparity between traditional custodial practices, implemented through disciplinary committees, and the treatment norms and objectives pursued in counseling sessions.

In the latter, for instance, inmates are supposed to openly express criticism of each other—and of the institution—and conduct is understood in terms of psychic and environmental determinants. Since all the members of the Disciplinary Committee, with one exception, were leaders of counseling groups or community living units, the disparity of these two views of human behavior is apparent as a role difference. The participation of the group leader on the Disciplinary Committee blurs his image as a permissive auditor of members' problems in group counseling sessions. The penalties imposed by the Disciplinary Committee settle any inmate doubts about the presumption by the staff of the value of obedience and of docility for inmates. Stated another way, what would happen if the presumed freedom of inmates to have candid discussions and differences of opinion with their group counseling leaders was extended beyond the time and locale of the group meeting?

The Disciplinary Committee is charged with dealing with recurrent problems of social control in the prison. To accomplish this goal, it uses routine police methods: surveillance, informers, and interrogation. After assembling information, it imposes penalties of a punitive nature. Counseling groups also attempt to deal with or, at least, to discuss recurrent problems. Here the men are urged to talk freely with confidence that the general content will "remain in the group." Inmates regard candor in counseling sessions as potentially dangerous to their self-interest. They wonder whether it is realistic to assume that the information derived during counseling will be disregarded in future appraisals of their conduct or in considering the circumstances surrounding the violation of prison rules.

The staff, too, of course, experienced problems in adapting a therapeutic view in a job context characterized by custodial imperatives. These problems are graphically expressed in the lengthy and somewhat unusual training sessions for counseling leaders discussed in Chapter IV. Now, however, we describe the design of our study and examine, among other things, why a special training program for group leaders was developed for this project. We shall return to the subject of social control in correctional systems at various points in the succeeding chapters.

A design for assessing group treatment effects

Any correctional agency not using a prediction procedure to study the effectiveness of its decisions and operations is perpetrating a crime against the taxpayer.

J. Douglas Grant

The statement quoted above was made by the Chief of the Research Division of the California Department of Corrections at the time that this project was initiated. Grant had seen a wide variety of new treatment programs presented to the Department of Corrections, most of which were billed as the long-sought solution to the problem of recidivism. He also was aware that the recidivism rates tabulated each year by the Research Division were unchanged. It became apparent that more was needed than assertions about treatment effects, no matter how earnestly made. Grant's concerns prompted his paper, "It's Time to Start Counting," in which he made the following points:

1. Experience is not a sufficient basis for decision making.
2. Correctional agencies are spending too much money collecting information that has little influence on the decisions that are made.
3. Systematic study can develop prediction devices that are useful.
4. Current prison programs do not help many men who participate in them and are wasted on men who are good risks to begin with.
5. Decisions made subjectively should not be excused from accountability.[1]

[1] J. Douglas Grant, "It's Time to Start Counting," *Crime and Delinquency*, vol. 8, no. 3, July 1962, pp. 259–264.

Although these principles elicit widespread endorsement, the actual carrying out of such evaluative research raises a number of issues. They are somewhat analogous to the problems of evaluating treatment effects in psychotherapy. With respect to these problems, Hans Eysenck has commented:

> To judge by their writings, some advocates of psychotherapy appear to take an attitude similar to that adopted by Galen, the father of modern medicine, in his advocacy of the wondrous powers of Samian clay: "All who drink this remedy recover in a short time, except those whom it does not help, who all die and have no relief from any other medicine. Therefore it is obvious that it fails only in incurable cases." There are three main differences between Galen's hypothesis and that maintained by modern psychotherapists. In the first place, we have the question of *definition*. There is no disagreement about the nature of Samian clay, but as regards psychotherapy, *quot homines, tot sententiae*. In the second place there is the question of the *criterion of cure*. In Galen's case this was survival, which is easy to observe; in the case of psychotherapy, the criterion itself is in doubt, and its measurement fraught with difficulties. In the third place there is the *time factor*. Those who partook of Galen's remedy "recovered in a short time," so that the effects were easily observed; psychotherapy, particularly that of the psychoanalytic type, may go on for as many as twenty years or more, so that considerable difficulties arise in allocating responsibility for any recovery.[2]

In this section our task is to deal with these issues as they pertained and were dealt with in this study. First, we are concerned with the problem of defining group counseling, then with the criteria by which its impact might be judged and, finally, with the time factor. After a brief review of other studies of correctional group treatment, we give a detailed description of the design used in this study.

Group counseling: its definition and aims

WHAT IS GROUP COUNSELING?

In one sense our task of evaluating group counseling is less problematic than that of evaluating psychotherapy because in the California Department of Corrections (CDC) it is primarily based on the precepts and procedures articulated by one man, Dr. Norman Fenton. Fenton intro-

---

[2] Hans J. Eysenck, "The Effects of Psychotherapy," *International Journal of Psychiatry*, vol. 1, no. 1, 1965, p. 102.

duced group counseling into the department at San Quentin's Reception-Diagnostic Center in 1944, and his book is the department's training manual for group counselors.[3] For these reasons, conflicting definitions and techniques have plagued our research less than they have plagued the research efforts described by Eysenck. Nonetheless, Fenton's description of the interactional processes of the sessions (what goes on between group members and between group members and the leader) is couched in very general terms, and the theoretical bases on which group counseling is built are not clearly spelled out. The aims of group counseling are not easily operationalized, nor is it described in terms that lend themselves to the precise analysis of group structure or process.

Essentially, we are told that a therapeutic technique called group counseling, involving periodic meetings of staff and inmates to talk over matters of concern, has certain consequences for the participants—consequences that have rehabilitative effects. But we are not sure just what it is about the group sessions that promote changes in attitudes and behavior. This limitation in conceptional precision, however, does not prevent us from studying the effects of group counseling participation when an appropriate research design is employed.

Operationally, group counseling means that ten or twelve inmates meet one or two hours a week under the guidance of a lay group leader. Some leaders are administrative personnel, caseworkers, teachers, guards, or clerical and technical staff workers; others are therapeutic specialists (physicians, social workers, and psychologists). Nonprofessional personnel in group leader roles, to some extent, are trained and supervised by the group counseling supervisor in each prison. In most cases, these supervisors hold B.A. degrees and have received graduate training in social work. Participation in group counseling is normally voluntary for inmates.

The key proposition underlying the operation of these groups is the assertion that a given group can affect a member's attitudes and behavior.[4] Fenton states that if a group is to positively influence a group member's behavior, two basic requirements must be met.

The first requirement is the *development of the group setting necessary for clients to feel free to discuss with security their own and each other's feelings and attitudes toward the situation in which they find themselves.* The group members must perceive the leader as someone who accepts

---

[3] The following material is abstracted from Norman Fenton, Group Counseling: A Preface to Its Use in Correctional and Welfare Agencies, op. cit., pp. 7–12. See also, Norman Fenton, "Mental Health Applications in the California Correctional System," paper presented at the conference on "Mental Health Aspects of Corrections," Chatham Bars Inn, Massachusetts, June 4, 1960.

[4] Ibid., p. 46.

them as persons in whom he has a sincere interest and about whose welfare he is genuinely concerned. Members will then ". . . feel free to say what is on their minds or in their hearts" and the group will be able to offer to its members ". . . a kind of sanctuary or refuge from the callous environment of the prison yard."[5]

The second requirement for effective group counseling is a *condition of mutual acceptance among those in the group.* The atmosphere of the group must be supportive if members are to help each other and be helped by the leader. "This is especially true in the treatment of those in conflict with the law, because rejection, the poisonous opposite of acceptance, so often seems to have played a significant role in the explanation of the origin of the symptoms of criminality."

Fenton asserts that in the early life of the criminal, rejection by other people, notably parents or others in authority, has been a significant factor in arousing and establishing feelings of hostility or resentment. These feelings are expressed later in life in theft, robbery, or assaultive behavior.[6]

These two requirements work to promote a "mutually trustful understanding between the group leader and the client." Fenton refers to statements by Carl Rogers that the procedures and techniques used in counseling are of secondary importance to warm and accepting attitudes and to the freedom of the client to make choices and to respond spontaneously in the treatment situation.[7]

When the above requirements are met, the goals of group counseling may be successfully pursued.[8] They are:

1. To help prisoners adjust to the frustrations that are an unalterable part of life in an institution and in society.
2. To enable the clients to recognize the significance of emotional conflicts as underlying criminality.
3. To provide the opportunity for the client to learn from his peers about the social aspects of his personality.
4. To make possible a better understanding of make-believe, of phantasy, and of how costly may be behavioral responses to the antisocial content of daydreams.
5. [To improve] the emotional climate of the institution.

Group counseling, as defined by Fenton, thus involves the use of techniques with which the leader can counsel a group of individuals and

[5] Ibid., p. 46.
[6] Ibid., p. 49.
[7] Ibid., pp. 49–50.
[8] Ibid., pp. 51–55.

can direct or facilitate constructive interpersonal relationships. The leader seeks to promote a situation in which the interaction of the group members themselves have favorable effects on those in attendance.[9]

This group program seems to be based essentially on certain tenets of Freudian psychology, Roger's nondirective counseling, group psychotherapy, social casework practice, and sociological studies of the social organization of the inmate community.[10] Group counseling is viewed as a therapeutic device that attempts to provide the warm, supportive relationship with authority figures that inmates were denied as youngsters and that underlies their criminality. The group leader is to regard outbursts against the prison, its officials, or himself as evidence of the immaturity of clients who are really reacting to father figures. An atmosphere of interest and support by the leader and other group members will help the inmate mature (resolve his emotional problems). His relationships with others will improve, and the likelihood of his returning to patterns of criminal behavior will be reduced. Although the group leader should be as nondirective as possible, it should be remembered that the techniques for conducting the session are of lesser importance than the general atmosphere that prevails in the group.

Fenton's perspective can be observed in the descriptions of the purposes of the group counseling program that were expressed to us in numerous interviews and conversations with CDC employees. A general

[9] Ibid., p. 101.

[10] A comparison of Fenton's group counseling with Eysenck's "middle-of-the-road" definition of psychotherapy indicates considerable similarity:

1. There is an interpersonal relationship of a prolonged kind between two or more people.
2. One of the participants has had special experience and/or has received special training in the handling of human relationships.
3. One or more of the participants have entered the relationship because of a felt dissatisfaction with their emotional and/or interpersonal adjustment.
4. The methods used are of a psychological nature, that is, involve such mechanisms as explanation, suggestion, persuasion and so forth.
5. The procedure of the therapist is based upon some formal theory regarding mental disorder in general, and the specific disorder of the patient in particular.
6. The aim of the process is the amelioration of the difficulties which cause the patient to seek the help of the therapist.

Eysenck, op. cit., p. 103. The major differences between individual psychotherapy and group counseling are: (1) the lesser degree to which "felt dissatisfaction" motivates some inmates to join groups, (2) the lesser degree to which group leaders have received professional training in the theory and method of treatment, and (3) the degree of importance attached to the group as a factor in modifying attitudes and behavior. Group therapy combines the elements of both approaches.

agreement existed that group counseling was supposed to provide an opportunity for the following.

1. The psychological ventilation through the expression of feelings toward society, the judicial system, the prison, and prison personnel.
2. A self-understanding on the part of inmates, derived from guided group discussion, from witnessing the expression of feelings by other inmates, and from the interpretation of these feelings by other inmates, and by the group leader.
3. A ventilation and self-understanding on the part of the group leaders.

The latter point is an extension of Fenton's approach and is based on the feeling of many group leaders that they have developed a better understanding of individual inmates, of inmate perspectives, and of inmate life through their group sessions. In fact, when discussing group counseling, the most frequently used word by staff and inmates is "understanding."

One other program development should be mentioned at this point because it has evolved out of group counseling and embodies many of its features. That program is called "community living"; it combines group counseling with some of the features of the therapeutic community programs developed by Maxwell Jones and Harry Wilmer.[11] The California Department of Corrections carries out this somewhat more complex form of treatment by housing inmates in organized groups of 50 to 100 men. with many routine prison activities centered on the housing unit. The community living unit holds daily general assemblies of all its members under the leadership of the treatment, custodial, and administrative personnel who are responsible for the men in the unit. At Men's Colony these units consisted of 50 inmates and three staff members, generally, including a caseworker, a correctional officer, and a treatment or custodial staff administrator.

It is not really accurate to call community living the CDC's version of the therapeutic community because the theory and practices of Jones and Wilmer are not employed. Instead, community living is to be regarded as an extension of group counseling, but with bigger groups and more frequent meetings. The leaders of community living groups receive the same training and instructional materials as the ones given to the regular group counseling leaders.[12] The content and character of the dis-

---

[11] Maxwell Jones, *The Therapeutic Community*, op cit.; Harry A. Wilmer, *Social Psychiatry in Action*, op. cit. See also, Fenton's paper, op. cit.

[12] Group counseling and community living units throughout the California Department of Corrections are directed by a "Group Counseling Supervisor," whose headquarters are at Sacramento. During the course of our study this position was held by Robert M. Harrison, a psychiatric social worker.

cussions in the community living sessions are identical to those of the smaller groups.

In this study we do not attempt to discuss the validity of all of Fenton's contentions about the etiology of criminal behavior nor do we discuss some of his specific statements, for instance, the assertion that group counseling sessions are "a haven" for the inmate. Whether this is true, or whether, as some inmates have implied, the yard is the only haven from nosy and interfering treatment staff members, is not a major issue. Other issues—such as whether an inmate's group discussions with a staff member and other inmates, in fact, can be free and unlimited; whether staff members will regard inmate criticism of them as childish outbursts; whether the probability of future criminal behavior can be modified by a warm relationship with an authority figure once or twice a week; whether, in fact, warm supportive relationships prevail in prison group sessions; whether inmate attitudes and behavior change for the better as a result of group treatment—are closely related to the purpose of this study and are discussed in subsequent chapters. But our main purpose is to evaluate the effects of the counseling program.

In the pages that follow, it thus should be kept in mind that this program was not developed by the writers or by the administrators of the prison studied. It is one application of a program used throughout the California Department of Corrections.

THE MEASUREMENT OF TREATMENT OUTCOME

The intended effects of the group counseling program are not explicit in the writings of Fenton though they may be implied. These may include fewer disciplinary reports, perhaps, certain shifts in personality test scores, less hostile views of inmates expressed by other inmates and by staff members, and fewer inmates returning to prison after treatment. During the early phases of our study, these aims were the ones most often suggested by staff members.

Opinions on the degree to which these aims were realized varied throughout the Department of Corrections, as evidenced by a survey we conducted in 1961.[13] The table below indicates the views of 4062 corrections employees who were divided into two groups—those involved in doing group counseling activities and noncounselors.

Counselors expressed the most favorable views, but even within this group only 4 out of 10 thought group counseling induced personality

---

[13] Gene G. Kassebaum, David A. Ward, and Daniel M. Wilner, *Group Treatment by Correctional Personnel: A Survey of the California Department of Corrections,* Monograph no. 3, Sacramento: Board of Corrections, January 1963, p. 18.

table 3.1   Percent of Group Counselors and Noncounselors Expressing Optimism and Pessimism About Effects of Group Counseling on Inmates[a]

Questionnaire Statement		True	Uncertain	False
"Inmates from group counseling break fewer rules."	Group Counselors	64	22	12
	Noncounselors	45	35	17
"Group counseling induces personality change."	Group Counselors	40	36	22
	Noncounselors	40	38	20
"Inmates from group counseling violate parole less."	Group Counselors	30	49	19
	Noncounselors	28	45	24

[a] Total number of staff engaged in group counseling, 827; total number of noncounseling staff, 3235; and percentage of nonresponse never exceeded 3 percent.

change, and only 3 out of 10 thought it would definitely reduce parole violation rates (see Table 3.1).

Clearly, there is less optimism about the reduction of recidivism through group treatment participation than there is for the reduction of rule violations. We did not know, for example, whether group members should be expected to receive no disciplinary reports, one or two reports, one or two instead of four or five, or fewer violations of the most important prison rules. It was also unclear whether improved inmate-staff relations meant that staff and inmates should come to enjoy each other's company or whether it meant that they more often spoke to each other in a civil manner. It was not clear whether reduced recidivism should be taken to imply that none of the participants came back or that "one man was saved," or whether reduced recidivism meant that participants were returned to prison in the same frequency but committed fewer or less serious crimes.

The vagueness of the organizational aims of the group counseling program thus posed a problem for evaluative research in another area that Jahoda and Barnitz illustrate as follows: [the investigator] ". . . will want to know whether raising the level of literacy means teaching the people to read the classics or sign their names."[14] Our task, then, was to try to

[14] Marie Jahoda, and E. Barnitz, "The Nature of Evaluation," *International Social Sciences Bulletin,* **7,** 1955, p. 353. Watson identified "upwards of a hundred criteria used singly or in combination" to evaluate psychotherapy. Robert I. Watson, "Measuring the Effectiveness of Psychotherapy: Problems for Investigation," *Journal of Clinical*

delimit the effects of treatment outcome to certain expressed goals and to specify criteria to accomplish this task. In the following pages it will be observed that we have used four of the five measures that Eysenck says can be applied in studies of treatment outcome: (1) introspective reports by participants obtained through interviews and questionnaires; (2) personality test results; (3) social action effects defined as certain actions taken by society in regard to the persons under treatment, for example, arrests, parole revocation, and prison disciplinary reports; and (4) experimental investigations designed to test specific hypotheses.[15]

These measurement techniques, however, did not satisfy the concerns of some treatment staff members who believed that the tools of behavioral science research were not sophisticated enough to measure "what really goes on in a group." It was argued, for example, that "numbers mean nothing"; that it would be impossible to measure "what happens in here" (pointing to the heart) or to measure the "feelings" that inmates and leaders experience in the group sessions. From this perspective, then, this evaluation was doomed to failure from the start, since we could not investigate every possible consequence of group counseling.

These comments should be kept in mind because critical responses to the evaluations of treatment generally involve the post facto specification of outcome criteria or the degree of change to be expected in the program. It was only in the light of negative findings that staff who originally had contended that participants in counseling were less likely to break prison rules and return to prison began to specify the degree of change or improvement expected or the other criteria that should have been used. Examples of these post facto outcome criteria include the following statements: "The program was a success because the behavior of one man had changed for the better" or "Maybe they come back to prison, but they get along better with their families." A somewhat different criterion involved the morale of correctional officers, which it was asserted had improved because of participation in the counseling program. We shall have more to say in Chapter X about the use by treatment staff members of shifting criteria of treatment outcome.

Psychology, **8**, 1952, pp. 60–64. At least one investigator argues that there is so much disagreement over what constitutes organizational effectiveness and he makes "no attempt to say what 'effectiveness' is, except to describe the precise procedure by which we divide the groups for study." Andrew L. Comrey, "A Research Plan for the Study of Organizational Effectiveness" in Albert H. Rubenstein and Chadwick J. Haberstroh (eds.), *Some Theories of Organization*, Homewood, Illinois: The Dorsey Press, Inc., 1960, p. 362.

[15] Eysenck, op. cit., pp. 104–106.

TIME AS A METHODOLOGICAL ISSUE

How much exposure to group treatment is required before changes in attitude and behavior should be observable? The answer usually given is that it takes different times for different people. It is difficult to establish minimal periods of exposure to treatment and follow-up that satisfy all staff members. Our decisions about the length of exposure and follow-up were based on these factors: (1) the average term served at Men's Colony and the average parole term had to be considered; (2) other studies that involved parole follow-up provided guidelines; (3) the prison and the Department of Corrections would not consent to the indefinite disturbance of institutional routine posed by the project. Our data indicate quite clearly that the periods of exposure to treatment and follow-up were sufficiently long to permit a fair test of the group program at Men's Colony.

Assessments of group treatment in California

Early in the life of the Men's Colony project, we examined what had been published on the outcome of correctional treatment programs.[16] This task was facilitated by the materials gathered by Walter Bailey in his evaluation of 100 studies of correctional treatment, published between 1940 and 1960.[17] Bailey concluded that almost all of the reports em-

---

[16] In addition to the sources mentioned below, we found the following valuable: Edward A. Suchman, "A Model for Research and Evaluation on Rehabilitation" in Marvin B. Sussman (ed.), *Sociology and Rehabilitation*, American Sociological Association, 1966, pp. 52–70; Donald R. Cressey, "The Nature and Effectiveness of Correctional Techniques," *Law and Contemporary Problems*, School of Law, Duke University, vol. 23, no. 4, 1958, pp. 754–771; Daniel Glaser, "Correctional Research: An Elusive Paradise," *The Journal of Research in Crime and Delinquency*, vol. 2, no. 1, January 1965, pp. 1–11; Leslie T. Wilkins, *Social Deviance: Social Policy, Action and Research*, Englewood Cliffs, New Jersey: Prentice-Hall, Inc., 1964; Paul E. Meehl, *Clinical Versus Statistical Prediction*, Minneapolis: University of Minnesota Press, 1954; Theodore Volsky, Jr., Thomas M. Magoon, Warren T. Norman, Donald P. Hoyt, *The Outcomes of Counseling and Psychotherapy*, Minneapolis: University of Minnesota Press, 1965; Herbert H. Hyman, Charles R. Wright and Terence K. Hopkins, *Applications of Methods of Evaluation*, Berkeley: University of California Press, 1962, especially Part I; Elizabeth Herzog, *Some Guidelines for Evaluative Research: Assessing Psychosocial Change in Individuals*, United States Department of Health, Education and Welfare, Social Security Administration, Children's Bureau, publication no. 375, Washington, D.C., 1959, pp. 64–71; *International Social Science Bulletin*, **VII**, 1955, whole issue devoted to problems of evaluative research.

[17] Walter C. Bailey, "Correctional Outcome: An Evaluation of 100 Reports," School of Social Welfare, University of California, Los Angeles, 1961 (mimeographed).

ployed questionable research designs and that, in most of the cases, where positive results were attributed to a treatment program, poor methodology compromised the findings.[18] We paid careful attention to the methodological problems encountered in the projects reviewed by Bailey and in several later reports that had become available in preliminary or published form.[19] We now briefly describe three projects involving group treatment in California. The first two, conducted by the Department of Corrections, focus on aspects of the group counseling experience, whereas the third, not a departmental project, varies the characteristics of the participants.

Fowler compared the parole experiences of 1968 adult male felons who had been in Intensive Treatment Units in two prisons with 1433 inmates who were randomly selected from a pool of treatment eligibles.[20] Treatment consisted of one individual and one group treatment session per week for each subject for a period of 12 months. Parole failure was defined as a return to a California prison, or a suspension of parole for 90 days or more. Discharge from parole constituted success. If at the end of 2 years a man was neither returned to prison nor discharged from parole, he was put into the success category; a man under suspension was considered a failure. The treatment cases did better on parole than the controls—39 percent successfully discharged compared to 34 percent—a difference significant at the .05 level. The explanation of greater success because of participation in Intensive Treatment Units is suspect when a careful multivariate analysis reveals that the treatment subjects have a significantly higher pretreatment probability of success as measured by parole prediction scores.

Paul Mueller of the CDC's Research Division conducted a series of retrospective studies that compared participation in "stable" and "unstable" counseling groups.[21] (The former was defined as, at least, one year with one leader.) For men released from three minimum security prisons, participation in "stable" groups was significantly associated with

---

[18] Ibid., p. 11.

[19] See also Eric K. Clarke, "Group Therapy in Rehabilitation," *Federal Probation*, **16**, December 1952, pp. 28–33; Robert D. Wirt and J. L. Jacobson, *Experimental Studies in Group Psychotherapy with Prisoners*, Minnesota Department of Social Welfare, Minnesota State Prison, 1958 (mimeographed); H. Ashley Weeks, *Youthful Offenders at Highfields*, Ann Arbor: The University of Michigan Press, 1958; Robert B. Levinson and Howard L. Kitchener, *Demonstration Counseling Project*, Parts I and II, undated (mimeographed).

[20] R. E. Fowler, "Multivariate Analysis of the Intensive Treatment Program," California Department of Corrections, 1963 (mimeographed).

[21] Paul F. Mueller, *Summary of Parole Outcome Findings in Stable Group Counseling*, California Department of Corrections, Research Division, 1964.

more favorable parole outcome. Trends were similar for men released from the state's maximum security prison, Folsom, but differences were not statistically significant. An overall conclusion was hard to draw because the findings varied between institutions. For example: Folsom Prison releasees who had been members of any type of counseling group did significantly better on parole than did Folsom men who had had no group counseling; however, there were no significant differences in parole outcome between those who had and those who had no group counseling among Deuel Vocational Institution releasees (young men) from 1958 to 1961. In spite of an inconsistency over time or institution, these clue-hunting investigations indicated that parolees who had had more stable group experiences in prison tended to fare better on parole than did men with less stable, or no group counseling experiences. These inquiries dealt only with *inmates who voluntarily* enrolled in group counseling; they did not attempt to examine the impact of the group program on men who were required to participate in it either by parole board "recommendation" or by order of the institutional staff. Whether the volunteers were more likely to succeed on parole, even without the program, is not known.

The differentiation of subjects according to variables other than treatment exposure was the explicit focus of a study by Grant and Grant.[22] The theory underlying the program, called "Living Groups," is that most delinquents are "acting-out personalities" whose behavior can best be changed by placing them in confined settings where they must continually face their own problems. These problems are manifested in their interpersonal relationships with other group members. Groups were small closed communities of 20 men each, established for 6- or 9-week periods. A sample of 511 men volunteered from a United States Navy prison located in California.

> The twenty men, with three supervisors, lived together in the same barracks, ate together, worked on a farm as a unit, held classes together, participated as a team in recreational activities. The group was "closed" not only in the sense that no new members were admitted nor old members dismissed, but also in the sense that great effort was made to eliminate interpersonal dealings with anyone outside the group. The attempt was made to establish close continuing interpersonal relationships within the group—with no way out.[23]

There were 27 Living Groups, each run by three Marine noncommissioned

[22] J. Douglas Grant, and Marguerite Q. Grant, "A Group Dynamics Approach to the Treatment of Nonconformists in the Navy," *Annals of American Academy of Social Sciences*, **322**, March 1959, pp. 126–135.

[23] Ibid., p. 130.

officers and a psychologist consultant. The latter's main assignment was to conduct daily 90-minute, group therapy sessions attended by the 20 men and the supervisors. The groups varied in: the predicted success of supervisory teams in reducing delinquency-prone attitude; the level of interpersonal social maturity of group members; and the duration at the supervisor-group relationship. Measures of treatment impact included an evaluation by subjects, peers, supervisors, and the psychologist. There was a 6-month follow-up after a return to duty. All subjects participated in some type of program—that is, there was no control group. The findings were that "high maturity" subjects did significantly better when returned to duty than did low maturity subjects. Success was not affected by the maturity characteristics of the subject's group, by the duration of the supervisor-group relationships, or by the predicted supervisory effectiveness of the leaders. The relationships between the maturity of the subject and the predicted supervisory effectiveness, however, was significant. The Grants concluded: high maturity inmates have a high potential for improved restoration behavior if they are subjected to an attitude-change program under effective supervision. The study does not support a closed Living Group program for low maturity inmates and, in fact, suggests that at least some aspects of an effective program for high maturity inmates can be detrimental to low maturity inmates.[24]

Because of the Grants' experiment we considered the need to obtain data on participant potential for group treatment. Reluctantly, we decided that it would not be feasible to set up groups on the basis of a classification of "psychological maturity," given the realities of the prison situation. A design using a series of tests or ratings that involved the individual clinical assessment of participants (necessary in order to classify and reclassify subjects) would have required a large clinical staff. Since there were only two clinical psychologists at Men's Colony, it would have been impossible to have more than two living groups at any one time. In addition, the architecture of the prison did not permit the establishment of closed groups. We were able to approximate a maturity classification by using scores from the California Psychological Inventory. These data are presented in Appendix D.

Formulating the study design

Early studies of treatment outcome and the general literature on methodological problems of evaluation provided us with guidelines for making

---

[24] Ibid., p. 134.

research decisions. A fundamental decision was to impose an experimental design on the existing program. That is, not to set up a specially staffed and temporarily, heavily subsidized program that could reach only a small number of inmates and would be unrealistic in terms of departmental and prison budgets. Underlying this decision was one assumption of the group counseling program, namely that nonprofessional group leaders could elicit attitude and behavioral changes in inmates.

A longitudinal design was selected in preference to a cross-sectional one. The principle issues here concerned the initial comparability of inmates who did and did not have counseling experience, the precision of the description of the counseling experience, and the identification of factors that accounted for individual differences in response to treatment. Although the techniques of partial correlation used in cross-sectional analyses might clarify the comparability problem, we believed that more conclusive evaluation could be obtained by a longitudinal experiment in which initially comparable groups of men were assigned to treatment or to control conditions (with other aspects of imprisonment kept as constant as possible) and in which subjects were studied over time.

At least six characteristics of longitudinal experimental designs are required to accomplish the aims of an evaluation study like this one:

1. An adequate control group.
2. The controlled selection and assignment of subjects to the treatment and control conditions to ensure initial comparability.
3. The spatial separation of subjects in the different treatment settings to minimize contamination of the independent variable.
4. A range of types of persons to permit the generalization of findings.
5. A uniform follow-up of all experimental and control subjects after release.
6. The instruments for observation and measurement of independent and dependent variables.

Our efforts to meet these requirements follow the specification of hypotheses to be tested.

THE FORMAL STRUCTURE OF THEORY TO BE TESTED

Our review of the literature dealing with group treatment and our discussions with prison staff members led us to establish several hypotheses based on the assumed importance of group counseling in facilitating communications between inmates and staff. Communication should be, according to the theoretical basis of the program, subject to fewer conventional restrictions and should encourage confrontations and disclosures between leaders and group members which are tabooed by those tenets of the inmate code that value the withholding of information. The virtue of inmate solidarity should be called into question by inviting inmates' criticism of other inmates in the counseling session. In these terms, what was anticipated was not depth psychology, but the lessened endorsement of values that sanction further antisocial behavior. We thus were led to suppose that if adherence to the inmate code were weakened, there would be less resistance to the acceptance of conventional alternatives to post-release crime.

The twofold notion that treatment might effect inmate values, and that this in turn might result in the lessened sanction of illegal behavior, was phrased as testable hypotheses.

First, it is argued that participation in group counseling changes attitudes, specifically that it alters allegiance to inmate norms.

---

hypothesis 1   Participation in treatment results in lessened endorsement of the inmate code.

But it is said that more occurs than just a shift in inmate values. (For example, staff-inmate communication is facilitated, and there is more of it.) And, hence, participation and all that it implies results in lowered *resistance* to accepting conventional alternatives to illegal or antisocial behavior (which, in turn, affects the incidence of the behavior itself). Treatment, then, affects not only attitudes but also affects acts. Although the link between them might seem causal (attitude changes make a change in behavior possible) apparently one is not a necessary antecedent of the other according to Fenton. He merely suggests that they are two consequences of group counseling.

Proponents assert that behavioral changes are both short- and long-term, and thus we have separated immediate from postrelease effects. Both are operationalized in negative terms, that is, positive impact is defined as the absence of certain behaviors (trouble with authorities) not the presence of certain acts. More specifically:

---

hypothesis 2   Inmates who participated in the group counseling program will receive fewer prison disciplinary reports.

hypothesis 3   Parolees who participated in the prison group counseling program will have lower recidivism rates than controls.

The independent variable is differential exposure to the treatment program (group counseling); dependent variables are attitudinal and behavioral and reflect short- and long-term effects. Measures of in-prison response to treatment are the endorsement of inmate norms and the breaking prison rules. End result measures are postrelease behavior—conformity to parole regulations and recidivism. These criteria were selected to empirically support one of the following eight outcome possibilities:

Outcome	Accept	Reject
I	1, 2, 3	
II		1, 2, 3
III	1, 2	3
IV	1, 3	2
V	1	2, 3
VI	2, 3	1
VII	3	1, 2
VIII	2	1, 3

THE SELECTION OF A SITE

It was apparent from the earliest discussions of this project that the research operation could not be statewide. The ten prisons, which comprised the Department of Corrections in 1961, differed too greatly in terms of the architectural design, the size and makeup of inmate population, the size and makeup of staff, and the industrial, work, and treatment programs to allow the simple summing of information from all facilities. Also, because of the size of the state, repeated visits to monitor widely dispersed study operations were prohibitively costly.

Even the selection of several institutions from the department posed problems. Two of the ten prisons were classified as maximum security, two as medium security, two as minimum security, one housed aged inmates, another contained only youth offenders, another was for men with medical and psychiatric problems, and the tenth prison was for women. Eliminating the last four as special purpose institutions, we were left with six possibilities. The difficulty with four of these prisons was in the ability to generalize from findings based on the extreme populations of inmates in the maximum and minimum security settings. Custodial and security considerations dominated institutional life at the maximum security prisons, whereas the most elaborate treatment programs in the Department of Corrections characterized the minimum security institutions.

We thus decided to focus our study on the impact of group treatment on men in a medium security prison setting. Studies focused on this population permitted a greater power of generalization because of the more equal distribution of custodial and treatment concerns in institutional operations. Second, although it is true that only about 30 percent of the men in California prisons are housed in medium security prisons at any one time, a figure of upward of 40 percent represents the real proportion of California prisoners who have been confined in medium security prisons during their terms. Some of the inmates who end up at San Quentin and Folsom were management problems at medium security prisons. Many inmates who end up at medium and minimum security facilities earned their transfers after a period of testing their institutional adjustment at a prison higher in the security ratings. Other men, originally committed to minimum security institutions, are transferred to medium security prisons after demonstrating their inability to "go along with the program."

A third reason for selecting a medium security prison population is that a better representation of offenders is found in these institutions. A disproportionate number of men convicted of crimes of violence are housed in maximum security prisons, but men who have committed property offenses (nonsufficient funds checks, larceny, fraud, embezzlement, and the like) are overrepresented in minimum security facilities. Inmates of maximum security prisons have the most extensive criminal careers; inmates of minimum security institutions have the least extensive. A mixture of all types of offenders and careers is found in the medium security prison population.

At the time our study was to be initiated, there was one medium security prison in operation and another under construction. The selection was made following the inspection of the prison site at San Luis Obispo. (Inspection is, perhaps, too serious a term. Superintendent John Klinger and Dr. Kassebaum floundered through the mud and looked into the still bare concrete and steel shell of the partially completed California Men's Colony—East Facility.) Most of the initial information about the new prison came from Mr. Klinger, who was to administer both the East Facility and California Men's Colony—West (known throughout the department as "the old men's home"). The new prison was to house 2400 men in a medium security setting containing the most recent innovations in architectural design and institutional operation. Housing, recreation, and dining facilities were organized on a quadrangle basis, with each quad being a semiautonomous unit of 600 men. It was apparent that the total number of inmates and staff would be sufficient for adequate statistical analysis; furthermore, the structure of the physical plant would permit the operation of several different treatment conditions. The random assignment of inmates to the four quads would result in four samples more comparable in both population characteristics and prison environment than would be possible if the samples were drawn from separate prisons in the state. Finally, because at the time of planning, the institution had not yet been opened, the introduction of special assignment procedures and treatment and research operations would pose fewer problems than at long established institutions.

PROBLEMS POSED FOR INSTITUTIONAL OPERATIONS

A research design was drawn up that capitalized on the flexibility inherent in the fact that CMCE was a new prison. Initially it called for a control group and three varieties of group counseling, to be distributed among the four quads. To achieve comparable subsamples, the random assignment of inmates to each was necessary. In addition, large samples of the prison population would take questionnaires and tests and would be interviewed. Background data would have to be gathered from inmate records, and the access to group sessions and important institutional committee meetings would be required.

All of this implied extensive interference in the programming of the institution, and strongly suggested the advisability of joint planning with the staff prior to the opening of the prison to its first inmates. Accordingly, several planning sessions were held at the prison before a final design was decided on.

The first formal meeting on the design took place in February 1961 at the prison with representatives of the Department of Corrections, including J. Douglas Grant, Chief of the Research Division and the Men's Colony—East administration. After hearing about the preliminary plans, the institution staff raised these questions:

1. Would the research plan be adversely affected by constant and even rapid turnover if Men's Colony inmates were sent out to a new minimum security facility at Susanville, which also was nearing completion?

2. Would it be possible to maintain a completely undifferentiated type of population distribution in the four quadrangles, inasmuch as a recent departmental decision had been made to place in one of the quadrangles a number of psychotic inmates in the stage of "partial remission," some aged inmates with arson histories (which prevented their being housed in the wooden barracks of Men's Colony—West), some young "management problems," and some particularly troublesome homosexuals?

3. Would the integrity of the design be compromised by the prison administration's need to transfer men from one quadrangle to another for security and control reasons?

The first question was resolved by the department's agreement to our request that transfers to fill the new Susanville facility be temporarily suspended at Men's Colony until data collection at the prison was completed. We might note that the Men's Colony staff found the research project to be an advantage to them in, at least, this regard, because "good" inmates would be kept at the institution instead of continually being transferred. The department did not draw on the study population to fill fire camp or conservation assignments during the first year of the study and only to a minimal degree during the second year, selecting only those men whose date of entry into the program or parole eligibility obviated their being included in the follow-up sample.

Second, in the light of the institution's need to house "special" categories of inmates in one quad, we decided to restrict our study population to three of the four quadrangles (A, B, and C) rather than sacrifice random assignment. (Notice that designations of "special" were made in departmental headquarters, not at CMCE.) This was the most important modification of the research design made for the benefit of institutional needs. It should be noted that not all "problem" inmates were assigned to D Quad. For example, inmates transferred to Men's Colony because they were management problems elsewhere became part of the regular prison population and, thus, were eligible for participation in the study.

The third question was not easily answered. To persuade the Adult Authority that it was warranted to deny group counseling to a sizable number of inmates was not a simple task. At that time, about 12,000 inmates and hundreds of staff members were involved in group counseling programs, and the Adult Authority, and to some extent the department, had become convinced during the preceding years of the soundness of the program. This, despite the fact that there was no systematically collected evidence that such participation, in fact, had changed in-prison or post-prison behavior. Our argument was that only through maintaining a control group for a specified period of time would it be possible to assess the impact of group counseling on inmate attitudes and parolee behavior. We pointed out that there was only one prison in California where all inmates were enrolled in counseling, and, after some discussion, the advantages of the control group feature of the design were seen to outweigh the disadvantages of the denial on a random basis of any program that might benefit an inmate. Finally, it was noted that if group counseling was found to make for positive changes in inmates, then, perhaps, all inmates should be enrolled in the program.

In regard to the problem that was posed by the transfers within the institution, it was agreed that the administrator of each of the quadrangles could, at his discretion, reassign to a different program group or housing assignment up to five men out of one hundred. Thus, if the initial assignment procedure resulted in the placement of an uncooperative person in mandatory group counseling, the administrator could transfer the inmate to the voluntary program assignment if, in his judgment, this would clearly be more beneficial to the inmate and to the other members of the group to which he originally was assigned. Those transfers could be made only *from* compulsory group treatment programs and only *to* voluntary programs. The superintendent could make transfers at his discretion without limitation or restrictions. In view of the implications of transfers for the research effort, however, the superintendent agreed to try to limit transfers between the quadrangles or out of prison to cases in which the transfer necessity clearly overrode the implications of the move for the research design.

In May 1961, a second meeting was held. Its purpose was to set forth a reasonably detailed statement of the inmate assignment plan, the definition of the varieties of treatment, and the staffing required. This plan was designed to meet research requirements within the limits of prison staffing and program capabilities.

VARIETIES OF TREATMENT AND CONTROL

It was agreed that the group treatment varieties would constitute additions to the usual programs of religion, recreation, academic schooling, and vocational training. Three conditions of group counseling and two control groups were established as follows:

---

condition 1   *Voluntary Small Group Counseling.* This condition consisted of small groups of men (10 to 12) who met weekly for an hour. Inmate participation was voluntary. Group leaders represented all segments of the staff and had the usual training provided by the department for all group counselors. This option created a second self-selected control group (see Condition 5).

condition 2   *Mandatory Small Group Counseling.* In Condition 2, group counseling was required for all inmates in one building of one quadrangle. As in Condition 1, groups were small and not necessarily based on common housing units. Groups met more often than in Condition 1—twice weekly, each meeting was one hour. Group leaders were correctional counselors (caseworkers), lieutenants, and correctional officers. One other element that distinguished this variety from Condition 1 was that all group leaders received supplementary training in group counseling techniques (provided by research funds). This training was supplementary to the training some leaders had received in their formal education in social work and to the training that all leaders had received from the Department of Corrections.

The reasons for the provision of this extra training is discussed later in this chapter and is described in detail in Chapter IV.

condition 3   *Mandatory Large Group Counseling.* This variety of group treatment, which centered around men from a common living unit, such as a hall or wing of a cell house, was referred to as Community Living. At Men's Colony the physical layout of the prison divided the men into groups of 50—each quadrangle had two buildings each housing 300 men, with each building comprised of three floors of 100 men, divided again into two groups of 50 by means of a central control area. Each 50-man section had its own dayroom, and it was in these rooms that the entire group was required to meet four times each week for one-hour sessions. The three leaders were members of the custodial and treatment staff attached to that unit, at least one of whom was required to be a senior administrative official, such as the quadrangle's administrator, or a senior custodial officer or a treatment specialist, such as the senior caseworker with group counseling experience. In addition to daily meetings, on the fifth day the large group split into three smaller groups, each with one group leader. Each of these group leaders received the supplementary training in group counseling methods described above for the leaders of mandatory small group counseling.

condition 4   *Mandatory Controls.* The only difference between the mandatory controls (men in C Quad) and the other treatment conditions was that participation in any type of organized group counseling was not part of the total quad program. All other elements of the institutional program were available.

condition 5   *Voluntary Controls.* By implication, the units of A and B Quads, in which group counseling was voluntary, also had a self-selected (voluntary) control sample.

Implementing the design

STAFFING OF THE GROUP TREATMENT PROGRAM

The Men's Colony staff believed that they could cope with the requirements of time, effort, and manpower involved in the operation of all of the programs except the one in the community living units. The extra burden imposed on institution resources by mandatory counseling was

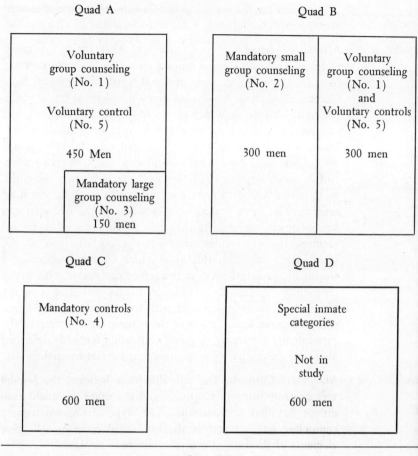

figure 3.1

met through the addition to the prison staff of two additional counseling specialists (caseworkers who had had graduate training in social work and counseling experience) paid for from UCLA project funds. In addition to leading a counseling group in a community living unit, both of these extra staff members were: (1) to substitute for leaders who might be unable to meet with their groups because of illness, vacations, or other reasons, (2) to be available to assist any group leader who was having problems in conducting his group, (3) to assist other caseworkers in their normal duties and (4) to keep daily logs of events and issues that occurred in their counseling sessions. The men selected to fill these positions were recruited for work at CMCE through the usual selection procedures.

Here we also must point out another important decision in regard to staffing that had been made earlier as a result of discussions with representatives of the National Institute of Mental Health, who posed the question of whether a project that evaluated group counseling as it was operated in the department was really a fair test of this counseling. If the outcome was negative, it might be argued that the group programs would have shown positive results "if only they had been run the way they should be run," that is, with more highly trained leaders. Hence, we revised an earlier decision to only evaluate an ongoing program by establishing variations of the group counseling program whose leaders participated in an intensive training program. Thus, we raised the level of training for some group leaders above the limits of departmental funding.

Briefly, leaders were selected from the mandatory group counseling conditions and met in two groups of 16 each for a three-day workshop at a site away from the prison. Nine follow-up sessions were held biweekly in a recreation center on the grounds of CMC—West Facility. This supplementary training was directed by William C. Schutz, a psychologist with considerable experience in similar training efforts. The details of these training sessions are given in Chapter IV.

INMATE ASSIGNMENT PROCEDURE

With the cooperation of the superintendent and his staff, an inmate assignment procedure was developed that was unambiguous to the officers making assignment decisions, and that assured unbiased election to the treatment and control conditions. Because the quadrangles were sequentially activated—first A Quad, then B, then C—housing was assigned to incoming inmates as the quads were readied for occupancy. The procedure is described and diagramed below (see Figure 3.2).

Two categories of inmates had to be identified and then assigned to housing units on a somewhat different basis than the study eligibles. These were "special" category cases and men who were ineligible for the parole follow-up study. The research team had agreed to the institution's request that men sent to CMCE who were designated "special" would be assigned directly to D Quad. This designation was made by departmental headquarters not by CMCE staff and included postpsychotic cases, aged, arsonists, transients, and the so-called management cases. This does not mean that all "troublemakers" were sent to D Quad.

The other category (men who were not eligible for parole follow-up) were assigned to voluntary counseling units. Ineligibility was defined as not being in the prison long enough to meet the minimum criterion for treatment exposure (six months), or having no chance of parole prior to the cutoff date for institutional data collection, or being over the age of 65

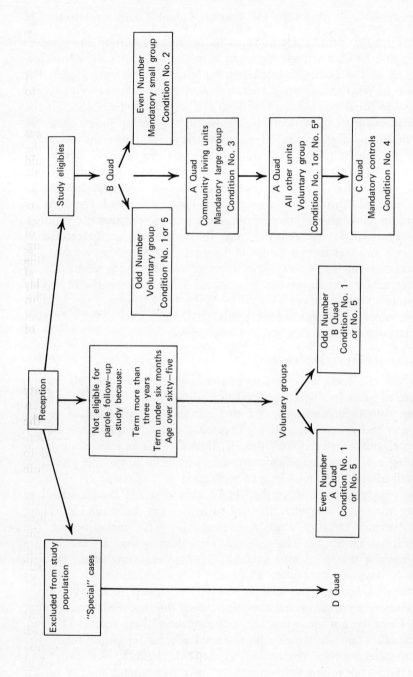

figure 3.2   The inmate assignment procedure. ([a] Depending on inmate's choice.)

80

at admission. In other words, men whose terms had been set by the parole board and had less than six months remaining to be served in the prison and men who would not be eligible for parole for at least three years were part of all phases of the study, except the parole follow-up. Housing assignment was based on the last digit of their departmental serial number: if it was even, they went to A Quad, if odd, to B Quad.

All incoming inmates who did not fall into one or the other of the two above categories were assigned to one of the treatment conditions on a random basis without further consideration of individual characteristics. Since new inmates arrive in groups, it first was necessary to specify a systematic way to list them for the assignment procedure. This was done by ranking the men in each group in order of the last two digits of their departmental serial number—men then were assigned to the first vacancy in accord with the following plan.

1. The first assignment was to B Quad. If the last digit of the inmate's serial number was even, he was assigned to one of the units where counseling was mandatory (Condition No. 2). If his number was odd he went to housing units in which counseling was voluntary. That is, he became part of either condition No. 1 or No. 5, whichever he elected.

2. Next came the assignment to the Community Living Units of A Quad, where he became part of Condition No. 3 (mandatory large group counseling).

3. Then came assignment to the units with voluntary counseling in A Quad. Depending upon the inmate's choice he became part of Condition No. 1 or No. 5.

4. Next was the assignment to Condition No. 4—Mandatory Controls in C Quad.

As was observed earlier in this chapter, treatment effect often has been obscured by either the lack of, or biased assignment to, a control group. At this point it is useful to consider data on how well the assignment system worked in producing comparable treatment and control groups.

An examination of five variables—type of primary offense, prior commitment, race, base expectancy, and intelligence quotient—shows no significant differences between our treatment and control groups. The first four were selected because they were known to be related to parole success, and we believed that IQ might effect the desire or ability to participate in the treatment program. These data are presented in Appendix A.

Base Expectancy (discussed at length in Chapter IX) is of special interest because it represents the sum of the best indicators of parole violation, weighted to maximize the correlation between a set of presentence variables and relative weights are listed as Table 6 in Appendix A. This index was developed via multiple regression analysis by Don M. Gottfredson, formerly of the Department of Corrections. Its use provides strong evidence that the randomization procedure did result in exposing to treatment and in releasing to parole groups of men who do not differ from one another on variables established to be related to parole success.

DATA COLLECTION AT MEN'S COLONY

Project funds provided for a full-time sociologist and a half-time research assistant to reside at the study site. In addition, we and other project staff from UCLA made biweekly trips of several days each. During the 18 months of the institutional phase, many kinds of data were collected from hundreds of inmates using a number of different techniques. These instruments are summarized below; they include: an abstract of prison records prepared for every inmate released to parole supervision; questionnaires dealing with inmate values, the first of which was given to a 50 percent random sample of inmates and the second of which was administered six months later to all men who had taken the first; a questionnaire dealing with group counseling that was given to participants in the program; and a psychological inventory that was given to a sample of men who were about to be paroled. In addition, interviews were conducted with 75 inmates selected on a random basis.

Since at the time that these instruments were administered we were not able to identify which inmates would be released to parole, that is, who would become part of the parole follow-up cohort, we therefore do not have all data possible on every parolee. For example: some men who ultimately became part of the parole cohort had not taken the inmate attitude questionnaire, or the group counseling questionnaire. In the summary that follows the extent of the overlap for the parole cohort will be detailed descriptions of instruments, and their analyses make up the bulk of the remaining chapters.

1. *Prison Record Abstract.* An abstract from official records of 59 items was prepared for 968 inmates who met study requirements for inclusion in the follow-up study. Coded information was gathered about treatment exposure, criminal career, personal and family background, psychiatric diagnosis, prison activities, prison rule violations, and release plans. Additional written commentaries supplied illustrative and anecdotal materials. The bulk of these data are presented in Chapter IX.

    In connection with an analysis of inmate types, presented in Chapter VI, a shortened version was completed for an additional 217 inmates.

2. *Inmate Values Questionnaire.* This questionnaire contained measures of inmate code endorsement, several standardized scales, and many items related to group counseling. It was administered to a 50 percent random sample of all inmates (1800) in the three study quadrangles. This resulted in a total of 871 usable forms. To assess change over time, there was a second administration six months later to all men remaining from the original sample. Five hundred and sixty-seven usable forms were obtained. These data are discussed in Chapter VI.

Two hundred and eighty-seven men in the parole cohort took the first questionnaire, and 150 were still in the prison for the second.

3. *The Group Counseling Questionnaire.* This questionnaire, referred to as the "Group Opinion Inventory" (GOI), was administered only to participants in group counseling. Data derived from the 490 usable forms appears in Chapter V. (The same inventory also was administered to all group leaders.)

Because of the fact that this inventory was given late in the institutional phase of the study, only 96 men in the parole cohort had taken it.

4. *California Psychological Inventory.* A 40 percent sample of men ready for release were given the CPI. These data are discussed in Appendix D.

5. *Interviews.* Seventy-five interviews were conducted with a randomly selected sample of inmates on a variety of topics that ranged from inmate adjustment to feelings about the treatment program. Excerpts appear in Chapter II.

PAROLE FOLLOW-UP

Following a large number of subjects for several years is a difficult, time-consuming, and costly proposition. Our decision to have a three-year follow-up for nearly 1000 subjects was possible only because of California law and departmental operations. Attrition is a major issue in any longitudinal design, but in our study this problem was minimized because the penal code provides indeterminate sentences for all offenders and because the policy of the State Board of Corrections is to release all inmates to parole supervision. That is, the flexibility of the sentencing law gives the paroling body (the Adult Authority) the opportunity to impose fairly long periods of parole, during which regular reporting of whereabouts, job, and the like, is required.

In addition, we were able to obtain arrest data and Adult Authority actions for all subjects from two correctional data collection operations: the California Bureau of Criminal Identification and Investigations runs an efficient centralized arrest reporting system and the Research Division of the Department of Corrections conducts a well-organized follow-up system.

CONCLUSION

A delay in final funding arrangements was responsible for a corresponding delay in the full implementation of the design until June 1962. During the interim period, however, the prison assigned incoming inmates to housing and treatment programs in accordance with the research formula. It was an indication of the strength of commitment of Superintendent Klinger and the Sacramento Central Office that, during a period of several months of uncertainty about ultimate funding, the prison maintained the scheduled program. After funding was definite, a final meeting was held with the members of the prison staff, the Department headquarters staff, and the Adult Authority. The principal issues were again concerns about "the denial of treatment" (group counseling) to men in C Quad and the rumored plans for shifts in prison populations throughout the department, which would affect the population at CMCE. Of additional concern, was the need to obtain the cooperation of the Adult Authority in not giving preferential treatment in parole decisions to men participating in the group treatment programs. At the conclusion of this meeting, the Adult Authority, the department, and the institution reaffirmed their support of the study as originally planned. The Adult Authority also agreed to omit discussion of group treatment participation with prospective parolees and, in the granting of paroles, to try not to discriminate against men in control samples.

The essential phases of the study can be summarized as follows.

June, 1961 to December, 1961. The prison opened, and the assignment of inmates to housing units was made according to the research design. There was no group treatment plan in operation.

January to August 1962. The regular group counseling program began, as did the regular institutional training program for group leaders. Although one community living unit and the mandatory group counseling programs had begun, the supplemental training for group leaders was not yet in operation. (During this period, funds were not in hand to enable either supplemental training for group leaders or for an increment of staff.) Operation of C Quad was the same as the other quadrangles, with the exception of a group counseling program. The institution staff maintained the procedures for the random assignment of incoming men to housing and treatment and control varieties.

September 1962. Enabling funds permitted the start of the supplemental training program, the establishment of two additional community living units, the increment in prison staff, and the assignment of research project personnel to resident status on the site.

July 1962 to December 31, 1963. The release of study subjects on parole.

October 1962 to December 1963. Institutional data collection phase (including data on men released since July), and the operation of the experimental programs as designed.

March 1963 to December 1965. Data collection from parolees and parole agent records.

December 31, 1966 to June 1967. Last date for the inclusion of arrest and disposition data on men in follow-up, providing a minimum of 36 months follow-up on all cases. Approximately five months additional time was required for the CDC Research Division to receive parole agents' reports and to gather arrest data from the Bureau of Criminal Identification.

July 1967 to August 1969. The analysis of masses of data collected over the preceding five years, the critique of analysis and manuscript drafts by the California Department of Corrections personnel, the staff members at Men's Colony—East, and our colleagues in sociology and psychology.

Despite a delay in getting the research design underway and the loss of one quadrangle from the original study plan, the Men's Colony project approximates more closely the requisite conditions for an experimental longitudinal study of correctional treatment outcome than do most of the earlier studies that came to our attention.

||||||||||||||||||||||||||||||||||||||||||||||||||||||||||||||||||||||||||||||||||||||||||||||||||||||||||||||||||||||||||||||||||||||||||

The training of group counselors

Two training programs for group counselors were conducted at Men's Colony—East. During the first year and one half of the institution's operation the in-service training of group counselors was provided through a series of one-hour monthly lectures by the supervisor of group counseling. In addition, sessions were scheduled in which group leaders raised specific questions that arose from problems in conducting their groups. These meetings were poorly attended, and it was our impression that many of the men who did come seemed to be apathetic and disinterested.

A new program was initiated in early 1963 by the counseling supervisor. It became mandatory that each group leader attend a one-half day training session every three months. No in-service training credit was given for attending these sessions, but credit was given toward a senior or an advanced counselor rating in the Department of Corrections.

The first compulsory training program consisted of a lecture on Norman Fenton's book on group counseling by the counseling supervisor, a talk by the prison psychiatrist about the principles of clinical group counseling on a professional level, and a movie on counseling produced by the Menninger Clinic.

The second training session was conducted by the Department of Corrections coordinator of group counseling, who divided the assembly into small groups, each of which discussed problems the leaders were experiencing in conducting their inmate groups. These problems then were referred to the coordinator who proceeded to conduct a "model" demonstration group composed of inmates who had been selected for their verbal skills, and who had been instructed to be very active participants in the coordinator's group.

The third group meeting was conducted by the Men's Colony counseling supervisor and by a clinical psychologist also on the staff. They reviewed 55 questions submitted by the counselors and asked the assembly to comment on each.

In addition to participation in the quarterly meetings, new group leaders (except correctional counselors) were given a copy of the departmental manual on group counseling. The new men received instruction on what the Department of Corrections was attempting to do in its counseling program and were assigned to observe several sessions of ongoing inmate groups. The group counseling coordinator accompanied the new counselor to the first meeting of his group and acted as co-leader for the first session.

Correctional Counselors (CC's) did not go through this initial training, either because they had had group counseling training elsewhere in the Department of Corrections or because they had university training as social workers. The CC's did attend the quarterly sessions, however.

During the study period the counseling coordinator was seldom consulted by the new group leaders. Although a small library of books on counseling and therapy was housed in the coordinator's office, it was little used at the time of the study. No list of available titles had been distributed to group leaders.

It was our view that at the time the study began the instruction given to correctional personnel in counseling techniques was limited and was generally not regarded as very helpful to the leaders. It should be kept in mind that CMCE had just opened, and many of its staff were men entirely new to corrections. In-service training time was in short supply and heavily committed to the more immediate tasks of operating a new prison.

Nevertheless, the training situation elsewhere in the Department of Corrections did not appear markedly different. A study by Alfred Katz based on interviews of 58 group counselors at two California prisons (San Quentin and CIM at Chino) in 1959 to 1960 concluded that in-service training received by the respondents was minimal:

> Despite the strong emphasis of the department's manual, and Dr. Fenton's own stress upon it, we found that only a small minority of the counselors reported they had received any specific in-service preparation or training as group leaders. Furthermore, [although] 33% reported receiving supervision in groups and 17% received individual supervision half of the counselors reported that they received neither. When supervision was received it was reported to vary greatly in intensity, regularity and effectiveness. These facts are undoubtedly related to the rapid growth and the scale of the California program. The California Corrections insti-

tutions have a large number of functioning groups and group counselors but only one or two counseling co-ordinators in each facility.[1]

To provide a stronger test of group treatment we decided to provide supplementary training for staff leaders which would exceed the departmental training program. The research budget thus included funds to hire a psychologist with extensive experience in group leader training, Dr. William Schutz of the University of California, Berkeley.[2] A training program was planned to extend for approximately nine months, to be attended by the leaders of all large and small mandatory groups. A total of 31 men comprised this special training group: one third were correctional officers, one third were correctional counselors, and one third were custody staff administrators.

Several program administrators and the correctional counselors in the program had formal education that included college degrees and, in several cases, advanced degrees in social work. The formal education of the custodial staff members consisted, in most cases, of a high school diploma. The men also differed widely on the amount of previous group counseling experience they had had prior to the training seminar. About one third had more than 100 hours of this experience, another one third had from a few hours to 99 hours in groups, and the rest had no previous experience.

THE SUPPLEMENTARY GROUP LEADERS TRAINING PROGRAM

For the training program the 31 group counselors were divided into two groups. Each group was given an intensive three-day training period at a local hotel (the "Inn"), followed by nine one-half day sessions spaced approximately two weeks apart. These sessions were held in a recreation building, outside the main complex of prison buildings but still on the prison grounds.

It was reported to us that the common experience of in-service training programs was that attendance was often irregular unless either sanctions or inducements accompanied the program. It thus was decided to give participants in our three-day workshop overtime pay and, for the majority of participants who did not hold administrative positions, the overtime pay continued through the follow-up sessions. These costs were absorbed by the research project and, perhaps, the provision of these funds helps to explain the very low rate of tardiness or absence that prevailed during our training program.

The first three-day period was designed to give the counselors the

[1] Katz, Alfred, "Lay Group Counseling," *Crime and Delinquency*, July 1963, pp. 282–289.

[2] Dr. Schutz is now at the Esalen Institute, Big Sur, California.

personal experience of being in a counseling group. The trainer (Schutz) acted as the group leader for the group of counselors during the three-day period. In addition to trying to make the experience a personally intensive one, attention was given to the theory of counseling, and there was considerable focus on behavior of the group leader, since he served as one model of a counselor.

The subsequent meetings continued in the format of a counseling group, but they also emphasized specific problems that the counselors encountered in their own groups. Occasionally, the meetings involved role-playing an inmate group with various people acting as counselors.

The research-sponsored training program thus differed from the in-service training in frequency and in mode of operation; it met more often and it focused on group dynamics instead of more didactic instruction.

The latter point should be stressed. In the supplemental, research-sponsored training program, the group experience itself was the means of instruction. The trainees learned about group process from their own experience as group members, and they learned about leadership style from their observation of the trainer-leader. Perhaps, it is more accurate to say that training consisted of the interaction between the trainees' experience as group members and the trainer's role as leader both directly perceived and explicitly commented on by the trainer.

The three-day sessions at the Inn served in several ways to set the UCLA funded training apart from that provided by the Department of Corrections. First, the decor and accommodations of the suite of rooms engaged were relatively luxurious and were a considerable departure from the usual institution setting for meetings. Members sat in easy chairs and sofas around a large fireplace; there was a cocktail hour at the end of each day. Participants wore casual clothing, a fact particularly significant for uniformed personnel, who were not clearly labeled as to status. The use of titles was discouraged within the group, and the use of first names was encouraged. (Although a considerable increase in informality was thus gained, the members never entirely abandoned titles of address, continuing throughout the sessions to refer to the trainer as "Doc" or "Dr. Schutz" rather than "Bill.") Scheduled meetings on evenings and Sundays, and after-dinner discussions likewise reinforced the general conception that the program was one that was connected with the UCLA project instead of with the Department of Corrections.

At some of the training meetings that followed the three-day workshop, one of the senior research staff[3] was present as a nonparticipating member. After these sessions, discussions were held with the trainer to

[3] Kassebaum.

compare impressions and conclusions about the character of the meeting. During two meetings, with the approval of the participants, complete sound recordings were made of the discussions. The tape recorder did not appear to alter the content or style of the discussion in the opinion of both observers.

The transcripts of these discussions provide many illustrations of the techniques employed by the trainer and of the reactions of the trainees. The following excerpts from notes made by the trainer immediately after the Inn meetings indicate the range of topics discussed by this particular group:

[The training meetings at the Inn] were very good overall. . . . The beginning was difficult as usual, with a demand for structure but deference to authority. The group was somewhat too large. . . General topics discussed were as follows:

1. *Power and Authority.* This was a discussion of differences between quads and quad leaders (Program Administrators). The PA's were confronted directly and they were able to express their feelings directly to each other in front of the groups. This seemed extremely valuable to them. The reaction of their subordinates was mixed, with some members feeling very uneasy. However, the next day the feeling was expressed that some men—to their surprise—now had more respect for the PA's after seeing them informally. It also gave the subordinates more confidence since they realized that even the higher-ups had problems and feelings of insecurity similar to their own.

2. *Homosexuality.* This was a discussion of the problem in prison and the feelings of the group counselors themselves about this issue. This seemed very valuable because it permitted a more realistic and less moralistic view of the issue, including the notion that these tendencies exist in virtually all men to some degree.

3. *Custody versus Treatment.* This issue seemed to underlie philosophies of prison behavior. Discussion seemed to evolve into the need to examine the situations in which treatment was appropriate, and in which custody was necessary. It seemed agreed that treatment was the preferable approach at all times, but there were situations in which custodial measures were required.

4. *Group Counseling.* The view was presented that the group leader does only what is necessary for the group to function effectively, leaving as much as possible to the group. The point was stressed that his job is to create an atmosphere in which the group members can be open and honest in expressing their feelings. This involves a variety of leader behaviors, as appropriate, including "uncorking" people, challeng-

ing and supporting them, expressing his own feelings, serving as a model, handling problem members that the group cannot manage, and being quiet. This theory was presented behaviorally as well as by lecture. The meeting was run from the beginning as a counseling session so that the trainer exhibited the behavior he felt most effective.

In the sessions that followed, these topics recurred as well as a variety of other issues. For example, the members frequently expressed impatience with the group-centered approach of the training, and they asserted that a lecture approach would be superior, or that they failed to learn anything from the group. The following is an exchange between the trainer and Green, the most outspoken, aggressive, and popular man in one of the groups:

SCHUTZ.   Did anyone read any of those books we talked about last time?

FARMER.   I read one, but I didn't recall any of the particular points. (Great laughter.)

SCHUTZ.   Did you read it?

GREEN.   No, I didn't. I read that homosexuality thing about four months ago. I found out today, though, that it was on men, so I figure I missed the point. But there are so many that I haven't gotten to . . . but as long as nobody else read their's. . . .

SCHUTZ.   Yes, you see I have a funny feeling about this group, and about what I'm doing because I think of all the people in the group, the one person that seems to have picked up a number of things that I've said from time to time, and seems to have incorporated it into his own approach, most obviously to me, I think, is Green.

GREEN.   Doctor, you're sick! (General laughter.) I deliberately avoid doing all these things, because it wouldn't be comfortable.

SCHUTZ.   Let's take Taylor's point, for example (referring to a previous discussion). When you talked about the importance of confronting a man with his own problem, that is, not letting him just blow off in the groups but talk directly to him—that's something that I would certainly agree with, and I think I've said a number of times in the past here.

GREEN.   Yeah, you may have, but this is something I've always felt. I don't think it's anything I've gained here. I've always had this feeling. This thing is serving no purpose.

SCHUTZ.   Well, you know, I might be wrong, but—

FARMER.   Oh, you are! (Laughter.) Shattering! Ego shattering!

SCHUTZ.   Well, this has been my impression. I am caught up short every once in a while when I hear coming out of your mouths the things that I have said. And I wouldn't say, well, that it's impossible that you have been saying this for a long time and it just so happens that our approaches are really the same, but I don't think so. Just like now. You say when you came here you expected to get something out of it, but as I recall that's not what you said when you came here. (Laughter.)

GREEN.   No... I don't know really what I was looking for, except that I guess more from a lecturer, or a, you know, a classroom-type of approach. And I didn't feel that being a member of a group was going to help me any when I came into this, and I still don't think it has. But some of the things said I have to agree with. But my feelings on this group, or what I participate in it, never gave me any different view on group counseling. But some of the things you've said or other people have said, have soaked in. And some of them I've rejected.

SCHUTZ.   Well, just another feeling along this line I've had is that when I've said something and tried to make a point, that I've had the feeling that you've grasped the point as well as anybody else in the group. And you're with it, and understand what's happening.

GREEN.   Now in the Community Living group they tell me they've helped me, and now you tell me you've helped me, and . . . I hope my superiors recognize it. (Laughter.)

SCHUTZ.   What?

GREEN.   That I've improved.

THOMAS.   Where else could you go? (Laughter.)

SCHUTZ.   I guess it's really hard to say to somebody you've helped him.

GREEN.   Well, I don't think I've grown alone. I've been helped by a lot of people. But I would have gotten more, and would have expected more if this had been a lecture type, and I've long planned for some type of lecture to train new counseling leaders, if they're going to force everybody to get into this kind of stuff. Park is an example. These people come to work for the department and they're here for six months and they go into group counseling. These people aren't trained. They blunder through for two or three years, and after two or three years you've learned something—you've got to . . . about the people you're dealing with. You say there are no clear-cut answers, and I agree with this, but there sure as hell should be something presented in lecture form.

One of the aims of the training program was to prompt the leaders to frankly express their own feelings about topics that are of serious concern in prison. The assumption was that if the group leaders were ambivalent about controversial matters in the institution, they would not be comfortable in expressing their feelings and would be unable to lead effectively the inmate groups in considering these topics.

In all prisons, no more troublesome problems exist than the ones involving homosexuality and race relations. In several training sessions both of these topics were discussed. A considerable amount of prejudice, especially toward Negroes, was revealed and discussed along with its possible effect on the correctional officers' treatment of inmates. It seemed very valuable, although quite disturbing, to some members to have these attitudes aired. The purpose of the following lengthy excerpt is to give an idea of the manner in which the training sessions were conducted and, specifically, to demonstrate the manner in which the trainer attempted to continually focus the group members' attention on their own feelings about sensitive matters like homosexuality and race prejudice. These issues, it will be shown, were difficult topics for the counselors to handle:

BALLIN. (Start of the training seminar.) I had an interesting experience in my group about a week ago. There's been a little bit of a problem in our quad regarding these homosexuals, and just to start this group of mine—it's been running, oh, relatively normal let's say for about a year and a half that I've had it—I asked them pointedly if they wanted to discuss homosexuality and just sat there and listened, and we had one of the best in terms of participation, best groups we've had yet. It was interesting, we had one little youngster —well, not youngster—but one young member of the group who got physically ill about three-quarters of the way through it, because of the general topic and his feelings about this type of thing. I'm quite anxious to get back this week and see if they, by themselves, have carried this on. There's been comment that this group has a tendency to steer clear of the topic of homosexuality that most groups will eventually get into.

SCHUTZ. How far did they get?

BALLIN. The group displayed their feelings about eating with the homosexuals, which is what our problem is centered on at the time in the quad. They were pretty outspoken in the initial phases of the group. They were very outspoken about the fact that they had to sit with these people, and that the vocabulary that was used, and the expressions at the dinner table were such that it made them ill to sit there and listen to these homosexuals talk about making love and, "honey, I'll see you at the shower," or "I'll see you over at the gym," and this and that. So they were really pretty outspoken about it. We had a new member who was just visiting my group. I'd invited him to visit; if he wants to enter, this will be up to him. The first half hour or so of this hour and fifteen minutes that we've used, they were really outspoken and this man didn't say anything. As a matter of fact, he came in late after my initial question, and listened to this and then made the statement, "Well, I am a homosexual and have been fighting this problem for a long time, and I wonder if you have guts enough to help me with it." Which threw it right back in the lap of the rest of the group. They'd been making some pretty wild statements about how their personal feelings were against homosexuals per se, and here was one challenging them to help him. We didn't get that problem resolved, but we sure got it out on the table. It'll be an interesting group.

ODAKA.   I had the opposite reaction. When they found out that one of the new fellows that was going to come in was homosexual, they let out such a big whoop that I asked (the group counseling coordinator) not to let him in because these guys threatened not to come to class.

BALLIN.   They threatened not to come to class because a homosexual was involved in it?

ODAKA.   Was *going* to come in.

BALLIN.   Was *going* to come in. It's a rather difficult topic to handle in any group, either as a leader or as a participant, because we all have such feelings about this subject. But it was rather fortunate the way the group just happened to fall in place that time. I've been accused of setting up the whole thing prematurely, which I did not do. But this again, I'm not worried about, as far as my leadership of the group. Might even be a comfortable feeling for them to believe I can do this kind of manipulation.

SCHUTZ.   What was your participation in it? Did you say how you felt about homosexuals as well?

BALLIN.   No, it never got around to my own feelings about it.

SCHUTZ.   Do you think you'd be willing to, if it was appropriate?

BALLIN.   If it were appropriate. I have no—I know of no qualms on my part regarding this topic. But I was sitting here thinking, I believe that you yourself made this comment about how this group has managed to avoid reference to that topic altogether, and this other —my own group worked out so beautifully in terms of participation.

Now there are going to be some problems on the part of these people. They went out with problems, they went out with some real anxieties. I wonder what's happened in the past week, either to allay these fears or enhance their interest so they'll come out and talk about it.

SCHUTZ. How did they react to this homosexual when he made his statement?

BALLIN. Their initial impression was to direct it toward me, but not directly to me. From this angle—they were looking to me as "Do we have to talk about this?" I didn't react. So then he challenged them directly. He took the ball back and challenged them. Said, "Well, do you really want to help me, or if I'm out of place you go ahead and tell me and I'll leave." Then, of course, this was a challenge that they couldn't very well back away from, so they took it. I had a very nice time, just sitting back and every once in awhile just prompting one of the members to try to get him back into the discussion. About 15 minutes before the session ended, one youngster in the group expressed the fact that all of this was making him ill, and he asked to be excused. The group themselves challenged him about his own feelings, and maybe his anxieties about homosexuality. The reason that he couldn't take this is probably that he has a problem in the area.

MERTON. I know we have a pretty active homosexual in a community living group. He's quite effeminate in his behavior, isn't he? Has anything ever come up in the group in connection with him?

LITTLE. He's admitted that he's homosexual. We never seem to stay on the subject very long.

HERMANN. What is his approach to them? "I am, so what?"

LITTLE. Yeah. I think that's where the large group is at a disadvantage with the small group. We could keep this going more when he brought it up.

TRACY. You can't keep it going in a large group, is that what you think?

LITTLE. Yes, because of those that don't want to participate. Oh, by snickers and other impressions that he gets, make him reluctant to talk about it. In other words, with a volunteer group smaller, where they're already interested in it, it would be easier to keep the subject going.

SCHUTZ. Well, what do you see as your role in trying to keep it going?

LITTLE. Well, that's our role, it's true, but I think it's a very difficult role in such large groups.

SCHUTZ. What kind of things do you do? To try to keep it going?

LITTLE. Well, questions, and asking the other members of the group how they feel about it. Get a pretty negative reaction from the other group members.

SCHUTZ. What else do you think can be done? Anyone have any ideas? (Long pause.)

MERTON. I had a fellow that we transferred to another quad that kept painting his eyebrows and stuff like that, and I was trying to use a real nice approach to him. You know, okay, we'll let you grow your eyebrows out, we'll give you a week or something. And I formed such a nice relationship with this guy that the next time he came into the office, he sort of tickled me in the ribs as he walked through the doorway (embarrassed laugh). I thought, "oh boy!" you know? "I got this guy involved." And immediately after that, though, when we had to discipline him on some other things, he became extremely belligerent and hysterical, and then he wound up in another quad. One of the thoughts I had is that if you get too chummy with one of these guys, you see, and you're too nice to them, and then they get some feelings, you know, that this is a real friendly relationship, and then it's like a woman scorned sort of thing. Then when you have to be strict with them about something, they'll react like hell.

SCHUTZ. This problem of homosexuality is such an important[4] topic, as it obviously is for the inmate group, maybe it would be worthwhile trying to talk about it right here and now, among ourselves.

STRONG. Probably good timing as far as my quad is concerned. We've got a growing problem of homosexuals in our quad. . . .

(Here a 15-minute digression followed on the growing problem of the control of homosexuality in the prison. After about 15 minutes, Schutz tried to refocus the group on members' feelings instead of on institution policy.)

SCHUTZ. Well, how do you feel about homosexuals, say a Negro and a white. What feeling do you have about it? Not as officers, just your own personal feelings about it.

GROGGIN. Well, just seeing them together, I don't think much about it. But I had the . . . misfortune, or whatever you want to call it, of walking in on two of them in bed, and this . . . really shook me up.

---

[4] Leader encourages topic of homosexuality, but urges the focus on members' feelings.

SCHUTZ. How do you mean, shook you up?

GROGGIN. Well, it just seemed kind of revolting, two grown men in bed. I key-locked the door and called for help. Then I talked to Officer Jones, and he said this occasion had happened to him, he did the same thing, so that's probably the way most of the officers feel about it.

SCHUTZ. Is that the way most of the officers feel about it?

FIRTH. It's a very revolting situation. I have never found myself, as he was saying he did, or Mr. ————. I was on duty with Mr.———— the night he was there, not in the building at the time, but I'm afraid I would find it very revolting if I ever walked in on anything like that. I couldn't sanction it at all. I can't see how we could go any easier on them or be as easy as we are on them, as far as I'm concerned.

ODAKA. Would it make any difference to you if one was white and one was Negro?

FIRTH. How do you mean?

ODAKA. I mean, worse?

FIRTH. (Long pause.) Oh, I don't know if it would be any worse. It's just as bad any way you want to look at it.

MERTON. I think if I were honest in my feelings, it would seem I think even though I profess no prejudice and that sort of thing, I think if I would see a white with a Negro, a white woman with a Negro man, or vice versa, I think I would have to admit some emotional reaction. I think I would also have somewhat additional reaction to this in a homosexual relationship. Even though rationally I think myself that it shouldn't matter, emotionally, I think I feel . . . well, that this is a little extra, you know?

FIRTH. That's a disgusting situation, but what are you personally going to do about it? I'll go along with you there, you see a white man with a colored woman or vice versa. . . .

MERTON. I didn't say it was disgusting.

FIRTH. Oh.

MERTON. No, I don't . . . I didn't say that. I said I have to admit that I get some kind of a reaction, but I—

FIRTH. What was your reaction when the queen tickled you and all that? Did you have any feeling?

MERTON. Well, I was a little surprised, and then I think amusement, in order to, of course, cope with it, but . . . .

FIRTH.   Did you say anything?

MERTON.   I don't remember saying anything.

FIRTH.   Wasn't a colored inmate was it?

MERTON.   No.

FIRTH.   Oh.

MERTON.   You are disgusted with it?

FIRTH.   With homosexuality?

MERTON.   No, with whites and Negroes . . . woman and man.

FIRTH.   I would be, yes. In other words, you're saying that I'm prejudiced.

MERTON.   (Laughs) Well, this would lead to it, I think. If you were disgusted this would show some prejudice.

SCHUTZ.   Well, I'm not quite so interested in labeling you as in finding out what people feel about it. You don't think it should be. . . .

FIRTH.   This is the way I—whether I'm prejudiced or not, I don't believe there should be any interrace relationship that way.

SCHUTZ.   Why is that?

FIRTH.   I don't know.

SCHUTZ.   Well, suppose you had to give two answers, and the first was, "I don't know." What would the second one be?[5]

FIRTH.   I got to think about it a minute.

ODAKA.   Where would you draw the line? Would the line be just Negro and white, or would the line be farther down, maybe Mexican, or. . . .

FIRTH.   As you started to ask the question, I guess maybe that is where I arrived at this . . . is that I know of a case of a white person marrying a Spanish or Mexican and the children weren't Spanish color, or white . . . they were blotchy. And they grew up that way. I know the boys are full-grown men, and I don't think that this is right for the children. Something like that, and I think that this is where I had arrived at this feeling.

ODAKA.   So you don't draw the line just on Negroes?

FIRTH.   No.

ODAKA.   What part of the country do you come from?

FIRTH.   California.

---

[5] This is a technique for not allowing the participant to withdraw when a discussion is becoming focused uncomfortably for him.

SCHUTZ. What if they don't have children, then it's okay?

FIRTH. No, it isn't.

SCHUTZ. Then there must be other. . . .

FIRTH. I can't think of any.

SCHUTZ. See, I'm using you, but actually I'm sure that everybody has some kind of feeling. . . .

FIRTH. Oh, I realize that. But no, I can't think of any other reason. The sergeant brought that out, and as he was asking it, I was thinking of this one example, and you said possibly there would be two reasons and this came to mind and I thought it was very unfair. For the man and woman themselves, it may be all right, but I guess living close to the school I know how the children were treated as they were growing up.

SCHUTZ. Well, let me ask you this. How do you feel about Negroes?

FIRTH. How do I feel about them? They got as much right to live as anybody else. There's just as smart Negroes as there is white people.

SCHUTZ. You mean there's no difference between Negroes and whites?

FIRTH. Other than color, no.

SCHUTZ. Everybody agree with that?

SWOPES. I'm from Texas. (General laughter.)

ODAKA. You cut one, they bleed red just the same as anybody else.

SWOPES. I can't accept the . . . theory he was saying that Negroes are equal to whites. I'm from the South and I understand that I've got to accept that, and I've tried, but I just can't do it.

SCHUTZ. How do you feel about it?

SWOPES. Oh, I don't dislike them, I just can't accept them as equals.

SCHUTZ. What are they like?[6]

SWOPES. Oh, they all seem sort of dull to me.

SCHUTZ. You mean stupid?

SWOPES. Uh . . . less intelligent than white people.

SCHUTZ. Is there anything else about them that's different?

SWOPES. Pattern of social life. (Pause.) Well, they . . . I'm not talking about them all, but . . . the race doesn't seem to have as high moral standards as the Caucasian and other races have.

SCHUTZ. Could you be more specific?

[6] This intervention and the ones immediately following are an attempt to elicit and to examine stereotypes held by the members.

SWOPES. Well, in the army I've seen them argue over their own food, and . . . they seem to do more stealing than their share. For instance, in Washington, D.C., 54% Negro population, they commit 84% of the crimes.

SCHUTZ. And what does this show?

SWOPES. It shows that their moral standards aren't as high as the white people.

SCHUTZ. By moral standards, you mean stealing and things like that?

SWOPES. Stealing and . . . just their overall standards. Even cleanliness.

SCHUTZ. They're dirty?

SWOPES. Not all of them, but I think they tend to live a little dirtier than most white people . . . the ones I've come in contact with.

SCHUTZ. Is there anything else?

SWOPES. In '54 I attended a college that had been Negro up to that year, and about 100 of us white people there and about 1500 Negroes— West Virginia State College . . . and most of the Negroes there were what you would call the cream of the crops for Negroes, most of them were from the North, New York and other northern states, well-to-do families, and they didn't impress me too much. I think they had the same opportunities as the whites to learn, I believe their education was as good as the whites, but the majority of them didn't seem to be able to catch on in more technical subjects. They were very good at art, music and the Arts, but take ROTC for instance, most of them were out in left field they couldn't seem to progress.

SCHUTZ. How do you feel? How does this affect you?

NEVINS. I didn't say how I felt.

SCHUTZ. That's why I asked you.

NEVINS. No, I don't really think that I feel that they're below us. I accept them as individuals. Some of them are below us, and some of them are possibly above us. I treat them as individuals.

SCHUTZ. So you have no prejudice?

NEVINS. Oh, to some degree I would say that I do have, but I wouldn't say that I'm prejudiced. I do take a little care to judge them as individuals. I evaluate them and then make my decisions. Like I said, I feel that some of them are quite low in their standards and what not, and I think that in my dealings with them I am aware of the possibility that I am prejudiced to a degree, and I go a step farther to be a little more lenient with a colored person than I normally would be, because I am aware that I am possibly prejudiced to some degree, and I don't want this to influence my actions.

STRONG. I think that Swopes' statements brought up a very interesting point in that he says that Negroes don't seem to catch on as fast as white people in a lot of things. . . . Do you think that white people have anything to do with this?

SWOPES. No.

STRONG. You don't think it has to do with environment or social life or. . .

SWOPES. I can't see where white people can affect the Negro ability to learn. You're born with that.

STRONG. Well, isn't it true that the colored people have been kept out of schools in the South for generations?

SWOPES. Keeping them out wouldn't affect their I.Q. They still have ability to learn.

NEVINS. Well, I don't think they've been kept out of school, they've just been segregated and had to attend their own schools, which were just as high level schools as the white schools.

SCHUTZ. Well, Swopes was also talking about a group who had obviously had more equal opportunity than the Southern group, because they were in a school . . . he classed them I think, as a higher group of colored people than you would normally find down there. (Turning to a member who has just muttered something unintelligible.) Did you say how you feel about Negroes?

TANNER. Yes, I could. I have some prejudiced feelings about the general population of Negroes, and again, I think it's a culturally related thing.

SCHUTZ. What are they like, and how are they different from whites?

TANNER. As a group, I think they've had less opportunity, and I think that the ones we run into particularly are ones who are using their minority group status to a disadvantage both to themselves and to us. And I react to this very strongly. I don't care for a colored man who will use, say, the NAACP for personal gain, and I think that too many of them do. It's like a labor union who will use their lobbyists for particular aims against the general good.

SCHUTZ. How do you feel about Negroes?

TANNER. Prejudiced to a degree.

SCHUTZ.   Well, now that's sort of a general word.[7] What are they like?

TANNER.   It's a difficult subject, as everyone in here knows, and to pinpoint it as you're asking us to do, is a pretty difficult thing. I'm going to tend to clarify my answers and give them categories. I don't want to live closely with Negroes, again, because I think that it breeds a lower class of people than I want to place myself in, or see myself in, and for that reason I feel resentful to them. And I think that probably describes my prejudice.

SCHUTZ.   Could you describe lower class? What do they do that's lower than whites?

TANNER.   Let's put it the other way. Let's say that I would like to place myself above them, rather than degrading them I would like to see myself as upper-middle or whatever. . .

SCHUTZ.   This often means you have certain stereotypes about them.

TANNER.   Right. Do you want me to describe my stereotypes? Generally as has been expressed, a feeling that as a group, they are less educated, more prone to act in an aggressive manner, than with the finesse that we would like to think that we act with, and a little bit more aggressive and obnoxious. I would tend to use either word in discussing my dealings with them. It seems that they would take advantage with less concern for the consequences in any particular situation, than say, a Caucasian or Oriental, or even for that matter, a Mexican.

MERTON.   Wouldn't that make the Negro that we get . . . we get a higher percentage of the young years . . . a more healthy person than the check writers?

SCHUTZ.   In what respect, Merton?

MERTON.   Well, his aggressions are still pretty healthy, his drives. . . .

MILLER.   I can't know exactly how you mean this.

MERTON.   Well, to me, I see the check-writer as rather a more pathetic, sicker guy, but. . . .

MILLER.   Are there any things you admire about Negroes?

MERTON.   Well, they got real good sexual equipment (laughs) . . . better than whites.

MILLER.   I noticed that nobody had mentioned this here.

---

[7] Again, an attempt to encourage specific expressions of feeling, avoiding generalities such as "prejudice."

MERTON.   I believe it. Well, I have not made a detailed study of it, but, from casual observation it's pretty obvious to me.

SCHUTZ.   Is that true? You all verify this?

WILSON.   After two years in the medics, I'll verify it.

MERTON.   I feel well-disposed toward the Negroes. I like them. But I like Mexicans, too. . . .

SCHUTZ.   Well now, you didn't avoid the question. That's one important area, but how do you feel about their sexual equipment?

MERTON.   I'm jealous, myself . . . sometimes.

SHERMAN.   When I see a white girl with a colored man, I always want to go over and punch him in the nose, but . . . I saw several colored girls that I might have gone out with, but I figured I'd get caught, you know, somebody might see me, and I'd feel awful guilty about it.

SCHUTZ.   Why would you punch him in the nose?

SHERMAN.   I don't know. I just see red. I mean, who does the sonofabitch think he is?

MERTON.   But you've been attracted to a colored girl?

SHERMAN.   Yeah. Very light ones.

STRONG.   Well, when you see this colored guy with this white girl, do you think of his big black dick going in there, is that part of the thing involved?

SHERMAN.   No, I just thought he was getting out of his place. I believe these people just do it, just to show the white people they can.

WILLIAMS.   What were your feelings toward the white girl?

SHERMAN.   I wouldn't go out with her. I mean, after all, she's been out with Negroes, so I wouldn't. . . (all laugh)

MERTON.   I'd suffer by comparison.

WILLIAMS.   I don't think so . . . just the idea. . . .

STRONG.   You could never satisfy her after. . . Seems he's stepping out of his place or something. We don't like the niggers to go out with a white girl, and here he is with one.

SCHUTZ.   What's that got to do with your not going out with her?

SHERMAN.   Well, I just don't think I would.

STRONG.   She's tainted after that.

SHERMAN.   Well, you know, I think we're overlooking one important point in discussing the Negro race and their place in this country.

I wonder what would happen if they had've shipped 10,000 whites over to Africa 400 years ago. . . .

SCHUTZ. Well, pardon me, before we get sociological, but I wonder if we could continue this, because the feelings about sexual problems and so forth might be very basic feelings towards Negroes. There's probably a need for it in here.[8]

SHERMAN. A Negro told me one time—said the reason that the white people hated them was because they were jealous of their sexual powers. I didn't go along with the idea, the theory. I don't think that's why most Southerners don't like them.

SCHUTZ. Well, I wonder if we could try to be honest, and find out how many people in here believe this. That they have some superiority in this area.

SHERMAN. (After a long silence) I doubt it. I think they probably lack finesse. They probably don't have the technique, it's more like . . . more like a couple of dogs. You know, they just go after it.

BALLIN. I still have strong feelings about this. I think the one thing that I resent as a group, is again, it boils down to the aggressiveness they show in their dealings with the whites and among themselves. You see, they don't keep their hostilities and their inhibitions bottled up. They release them regardless of what the consequences are. And they make no bones about it. Whereas our—at least my own upbringing has been to avoid any type of arrest or aggression or fighting or screwing around if I thought I'd be caught. And I don't do it if I thought I'd be caught. Whereas I figure, I have a general feeling that the colored aren't going to be this restrictive. Now I may be wrong, but this is one of the things that I think make me react to them as a group. Not as individuals.

STRONG. Well, this is part of the problem. We feel that they are freer with sex, or promiscuous, and it just doesn't bother them. While we are the other way, with a puritanical background, and maybe we're jealous of this.

WILSON. Well, we're talking about bringing up. I still maintain that you have to ask yourself what the hell would your bringing up be if your parents had been slaves? You can't overlook this point, whether you want to or not.

SHERMAN. I think they were probably better off as slaves than they were as savages in the jungle.

---

[8] This is another forceful attempt to keep the discussion focused on their basic attitudes, a difficult area to discuss, instead of retreating to intellectualism.

MERTON. There's a lot of evidence that indicates that their social structure and their way of life in native areas was not necessarily savage. They had their system of behavior, their customs and mores and so forth, which in some ways might have been healthier.

BALLIN. When you speak of health, and you have a couple of times, you're talking about the mental health of the individual. You're talking about his own feelings about himself. Is that right?

MERTON. Oh, I suppose so.

SCHUTZ. We seem to again be off on a sociological kick.

MERTON. Yeah . . . Although it's an interesting bit of incidental intelligence that the percentage of Negroes in the old man's institution . . . whereas in the young Negroes it's about the average in the state, in the older man's institution, the percentage of Negroes to the percentage in the state drops way below in contrast to the Caucasian.

ADLER. Is this related to the sexual problem?

MERTON. Yes. Well, I think that it's related in that we have very few sexual offenders among older Negroes, whereas you have a lot of sexual offenders among the Caucasian. And I think it has something to do with the fact that their system of moral values, whatever they are, permit them more expression of their basic needs.

DEXTER. Why, as a general rule, do the whites as we brought out here, place themselves above the Negro, yet on your homosexual relations, where there's mixed races, Negro-white the white about 90 to 95% of the time plays the feminine role, and the Negro the male role? Why is this, I wonder?

MERTON. It might be related to the same thing.

SCHUTZ. I wonder if you became homosexuals, let's say, would you rather have a Negro or a white partner? It's hard to imagine the problem. . . .[9]

ODAKA. If you get bad off, you take anything.

STRONG. I think probably most of us would take a white partner.

MERTON. Yeah, I don't feel especially that it would be a Negro partner.

STRONG. Depends on your feeling about it, I think. I think the same

[9] This is an attempt to take a step further in their examination of their feelings about both homosexuality and race. It is a strong step because the imagery aroused makes the issue very real.

prejudice would enter into that as our normal thinking. If we were homosexual, this wouldn't change our prejudice.

(Long pause)

FRANK.   I've seen some pretty bad incidents caused from this homosexual relationship, association between races like that. Guy got knifed, cut, because you don't have an affair with Negroes . . . that's a white homosexual I'm quoting . . . so some of the white boys did him in.

MERTON.   I had one little feminine Negro—a swisher, you know—who said he was in trouble, under pressure from the whites because he said that he was prejudiced, and they said he should share with the whites as well as with the Negroes. Some time these things take some peculiar forms.

SCHUTZ.   See, it looks like two of the most emotionally powerful topics that come up among the inmates are homosexuality and racial questions. And I think the more we can get into our own feelings about this and understand them, probably the better able we'll be to cope with them when they come up. That is, we can stay talking about and try to avoid sociology and abstractions . . . I think it will be more valuable. (Silence.) I suppose it is very important to fill out those slips.[10]

FRANK.   I'm still worried about what you did, Merton, when this guy tickled you in the ribs. I mean, this bothered me because I was approached once myself and . . . .

MERTON.   I don't think I had too much of a reaction. I really believe I handled it casually, with a little bit of amusement. I must have had a little touch of concern, because I mentioned it to some of my staff, you know, I think this guy must like me, you know. And then he winked at me one time. But I think I have enough concern . . . that I had to mention it to somebody . . . talk about it.

SCHUTZ.   Twice.

MERTON.   Who?

SCHUTZ.   Twice. You've mentioned it twice. You mentioned it before.

MERTON.   Well, does that satisfy you?

FRANK.   You didn't say anything to the man, then?

MERTON.   No, he went by real fast. I don't think I said anything.

FRANK.   You didn't talk to him later?

---

[10] The trainer was reacting to the overtime pay slips that were being passed around among the members on this day.

MERTON.   Well, yes I did, but I didn't mention it, no. I think I accepted his . . . my not talking to him about it . . . I mean I can understand him having some feeling like this, so why should I discuss it with him especially.

FRANK.   I had a queen in Soledad, and maybe it's something wrong with me, but they had to boot him out of the institution almost. It almost got out of hand.

SCHUTZ.   How did it make you feel?

FRANK.   Uh . . . Sick.

SCHUTZ.   Is that all?

FRANK.   Uh . . . almost nauseated.

SCHUTZ.   Was there any good part of the feeling?

FRANK.   No. None at all.

SCHUTZ.   How would you feel about another guard who had this happen to him fairly often?

FRANK.   How would I feel about another guard?

SCHUTZ.   If this happened fairly often, if he had queens falling in love with him?

FRANK.   Well, I don't know. This only happened to me once. I was working in the house where this queen lived, and well, it started, the queen lived down toward the end of the building, and at night there was quite a group of men congregated around the queen's room, watching her in there shaving her legs and various other things. So I moved her up to the cell right next to my desk. Well, she kind of accepted this as maybe an act on my part to move her up where she'd be mine (giggle), you know, and it got pretty open. She thought I was moving her up to keep her away from the boys because I wanted her for myself.

SCHUTZ.   Well, what about that?

FRANK.   Well, actually I didn't. (All laugh.)

STRONG.   As a result of this experience, did you feel differently when you operated with queens?

FRANK.   Do I feel any different?

STRONG.   Did you change your way of operating with queens after this?

FRANK.   Well, I couldn't accept them before and I can't now. So there's been no change there.

STRONG.   What do you mean, you can't accept them?

FRANK.   Well, they're pretty sickening to me. Disgusting.

MERTON.   Are you fearful?

FRANK.   No, I'm not fearful. I know what you're probing at, and I'm not going to let you get me in that corner.

MERTON.   No, I mean would it make you fearful that you'd get involved in a relationship. . . .

FRANK.   No, no . . . it's just that. . . .

MERTON.   You know, something strange, foreign, something you really don't want. Does it make you fearful in that sense?

FRANK.   No, it's just that . . . well, I don't know how to explain it. It's disgusting. A man, a human. . . .

STRONG.   At some point in your life, if you had a homosexual experience that was distasteful to you, or someone approached you. . . .

FRANK.   No, you see, I was pretty young when I started with the department and I haven't been in the army or anything. Well, I started Soledad when I was twenty. Well, I didn't know anything about homosexuals, you see, I was just as green as could be. Course, I went to a small school there in Nogales and was not too exposed to it in any way in school or anything, so my first idea was when I went to work at Soledad and I didn't know what to think. It was something else. I walked down the corridor and here's some man with his eyebrows painted up and hair fixed real fancy, swishing his ass down the corridor, and I just had to stand . . . and I mean I just didn't know what to think. I mean, this was my first experience. Completely. I was just a kid.

SCHUTZ.   Charles, both you and Tom use the word "disgusted," or "revolted," or something of this type. I wonder if you could say what other things in life disgust you or revolt you.

(The discussion continued with comments relating to how "disgusting" or "revolting" homosexuality was to the group members and then turned back to the reaction of members to homosexual "queens.")

PLUNKET.   We got a couple of queens over there in my building that disgust me in that same way. Now the rest of them, no trouble whatsoever. Have no feelings one way or the other. These two, they seem to go out of their way to be obnoxious about it. When I see those two, I . . . . disgusting!

FRANK.   Well, it was difficult for me at first, but after a while, I learned to more or less accept them because I learned that I had to, and I do now. I don't accept them but I mean, I can work with them. I can sit a queen down right in front of me and talk to him all afternoon, see. I have no feelings one way or another, but this is something I had to adjust to. I wasn't in the army, I didn't have them to contend with.

JACKSON.   The case of these queens that kind of flaunt it . . . Does this disgust you anymore than say, some gal sitting up on a bar stool with her legs up?

FRANK.   Well, that would depend on what she looked like. Some girls yes, some girls, no. (General laughter.)

JACKSON.   This wouldn't disgust you, where a queen flaunting her sexuality would.

WILLIAMS.   It isn't the person exactly then that disgusts you, as it is the act itself. This is the way I found it. Like the example of the man taking his shoes off and putting his feet on the table. It isn't the person himself, it's the act that disgusts you.

STRONG.   Are you saying that when you see a queen, you think about what this queen does, such as sucking dicks, or taking it in the rear end, when you see queens, you think of this and . . . this disgusts you?

FRANK.   I think this is the way I feel about it.

PLUNKET.   Well, I don't feel that way. Because there's one queen, she serves in the dining hall, said one time, "Oh, how I wish I could have a great big old peter pushed up my butt," and something like that. And now that is disgusting to me. Whereas the rest of them, well, I don't care if they get caught in the act . . . as long as they don't. . . .

SCHUTZ.   I don't know if other people feel this way, but when you say I don't like to think about it, partly for me, there's a little fascination, I think, in this possibility. I don't know whether others of you feel this way too, but it's not a completely unconflicted reaction.

PLUNKET.   You think I'm fascinated with these queens, is that what you're saying?

SCHUTZ.   Well, when Strong mentioned the long, black dick for example, I must admit that, you know, there was a little. . . .

FRANK.   Well, I think that was a little exaggeration. The only time we've actually seen these long, black dicks is in the showers where there's white butts around. I think that's the reason we think of them being as large as they are, because of these white butts around . . . The (unclear) Negroes have been screwing them for years. (Laughter)

MERTON.   There's an erotic element in there.

SCHUTZ.   Like I like to look at it or see or something, but I can feel the fascination part as well as the negative. I don't want to do that, I just want to watch it. I wonder if this is just unique to me, or if some of the rest of you feel it too.

STRONG.   No, I don't think it's unique with you, I think I feel some of the same thing. I think we probably all do. I think it's a reaction to this, how we react to our own feelings about this thing, this fascination.

ODAKA.   I notice some of the conversation is about queens. But there's the aggressive type too, you know. How about that?

STRONG.   How do you feel about it?

ODAKA.   I can understand the reason for the homosexuality, but I don't want any aggressiveness on my shift. Like I say, if you do it in Hollywood, it's okay with me, but you do it around here, you're going to eventually end up with a knifing.

SCHUTZ.   What were you going to say?

MERTON.   Well, I was wondering about this fascination. . . .

(Loss of about one minute of discussion due to changing tape reels.)

SCHUTZ.   You think of it in terms of how it would be gratifying to a woman?

MERTON.   Yeah. How it . . . sort of feminine, and the receptive process, you know.

SWOPES.   Then there might be something to it (unintelligible) . . . is that what you're saying?

SCHUTZ.   Yeah. Well, the rest of you aren't saying. Is this just a characteristic of program directors, this feeling? Do the rest of you have these feelings, or are you not willing to talk about them, or what?

(Long pause.)

SWOPES.   Well, I know myself, I've never given it any thought, so I . . . don't know how you can bring any subject into it unless you've given it some thought . . . special thought. Wonder thought. I've never even wondered about it.

STRONG.   Have you ever thought of a homosexual grabbing you by the prick and maybe sucking on it a little bit for you?

SWOPES.   Well, I go along with Steve and say that when I was in the service I had one approach me, and I never did (laugh) let it get any farther than that, let me tell you that. So, I mean. . . .

MERTON.   No, I wouldn't either. Let it get any farther in actual practice. But I wasn't referring to that with regard to me.

SWOPES.   What do you mean, actual practice?

MERTON.   Well, I wouldn't let any one approach me. If they tickled my ribs that's as far as they would get.

SWOPES.   That's getting pretty far.

SCHUTZ.   That's different from part of the feeling I might have about it. I mean, it doesn't mean that you're going to do anything about it, but what I'm trying to explore is whether part of your feeling is this fascination, or however else it's said, because. . . .

FIRTH.   Getting back to this word, "disgust." This is the thing that . . . it disgusted me at the time and it still does.

FRANK.   Why this disgust? What's so disgusting about it?

FIRTH.   Well, it just isn't socially accepted.

FRANK.   There's a lot of things that aren't socially accepted that aren't disgusting.

FIRTH.   You've never seen two grown men in bed together in your life. What the hell's going on here . . . get outta here.

SCHUTZ.   You want to run away?

FIRTH.   Well, I suppose I didn't actually run away, but I. . . .

MERTON.   What did you want to run away from—your thoughts?

FIRTH.   The surprise, I suppose.

MERTON.   Well, when someone gives you a surprise birthday party, is the first thing you want to do is run away?

FIRTH.   Well, if it was that type, I probably would run away! (Laughter.)

MERTON.   Okay, that's not what I had in mind, but I. . . .

FIRTH.   Well, a birthday party and this is two different things. . . .

MERTON.   Yeah, but I'm just trying to say that maybe it's more than surprise. Because I don't think you'd react to any surprise by trying to get away from it.

FIRTH.   Well, I think that any officer who works in a unit has, like he says, conditioned himself to a certain extent to expect this. But then, all of a sudden, there it is. Shocks you. Actually the two people involved, I never even suspected of being homosexuals. And one of them I knew pretty well, I mean we were speaking acquaintances.

JACKSON.   Okay. In other words, this makes you feel that maybe all people are capable of this, even you, and maybe this is something to run away from.

FIRTH.   Possibly. Actually, I didn't run away. I key-locked the door then ran and got help.

JACKSON.   But you didn't stand and watch them.

FIRTH.   That's right.

SCHUTZ.   You didn't look at all? You didn't take any quick glance?

FIRTH.   I did, yes. They had a sheet up in front of the bed. And the one boy raised it up. I could see the other one in back. Maybe there was some element of safety, too, in leaving the room—after all, you don't know what they were going to do. They were surprised, too. But as actually an act going on, I don't know what they were doing. . . .

SCHUTZ.   Were you curious, or would you be curious? Would you like to take a look and see how they do it? (Pause.) No interest?

FIRTH.   Well, I was a bit surprised, and I was revolted. It made me . . . uh . . . think a little against the human race a little bit. In other words, myself.

JACKSON.   This thing on the standpoint of fascination. I was thinking back to the navy, all the joking and so forth done about this thing, but actually, I never observed a homosexual act taking place aboard ship. And yet you have this constant . . . thing in, you know, in the shower. It's your turn in the barrel, and I'll take you down and show you the golden rivet and all this sort of stuff. If it indicates a preoccupation or a kind of fascination necessarily . . . I never thought of it before.

PLUNKET.   You should have been on that transport I was on. Hád colored troops on there, and one night this old colored boy, he was taking them all on. And all the crew on board that ship was lined up about . . . He was saying, "Oh, I love you sailors—next! Oh, you sailors is so good!"

JACKSON.   This is a different thing that I'm talking about, though. This is a thing that seemed to involve about everybody, but yet there was no carry-through. There was something kind of a preoccupation, but no carry-through. Everybody talked.

NELSON.   You sound disappointed.

JACKSON.   Do I really? Well, I never . . . they all carried on, but I never had any feeling, any homosexual feeling, any desire to fuck anybody in the ass that I remember. Never had any inclination to suck anybody's peter.

NELSON. Sounds like you were part of an in-group. You could joke about this, but never let (unintelligible).

PLUNKET. Well, I know of cases . . . I've heard of cases of this taking place on the ship, but I never observed it. But every place I went, like I said, they always joke about it. But up until the time you see it happen, the way I seen it happen, you are quite surprised to see how many of these guys that were joking about it would actually fall in line. I mean, there was a *long* line.

JACKSON. Where were you? Where were you in the line? (General good-humoured uproar.) You had to be someplace where you could observe.

WILLIAMS. Yeah, you knew the length of the line, and what they were saying and everything.

STRONG. He walked it once.

WILLIAMS. See, you just left yourself wide open there. You knew every word the guy said. (Laughter.)

PLUNKET. Well, in my work as an officer, I've looked up a lot of asses, and I haven't seen one that fascinated me yet. (*Note:* Member is referring to skin searches of inmates, which include rectal examination to detect hidden contraband.)

STRONG. Probably say the same thing if you'd looked up a lot of snatches, too.

PLUNKET. Oh, I don't know about that.

(Long Pause.)

SCHUTZ. Shall we take a break?

(Cut. After a coffee break, the session resumes)

JACKSON. I was just thinking about this homosexuality, and this thing in the service where you had this constant preoccupation with it. It's probably some of the same elements that causes it in prison. Probably some of the people in the prison who participate in homosexuality there wouldn't participate in it on the street. And I wonder if it also doesn't have some connection with the person who is homosexual in the street. In other words, in the service, why undoubtedly it's got something to do with them being starved for sexual relationships. You know there's nothing there, nothing else, so you try to fill the gap somehow. And maybe with the homosexual, because of the inability to relate with the female, they find their outlet where they can . . . find another outlet.

SCHUTZ.[11]   I had a few feelings about what we just started, and one is, as I mentioned, I think contact with what we talked about is very important, and the more we can get into it and explore how each of us feels about it I think the more effectively you can deal with it when you run into it in the inmates. And the second thing, as I think of it, we didn't really go enough into . . . the racial problem. We hit at it, but then we got off of it a little bit. I think it would probably be useful to talk more about it. And another thing is that, initially, how you get a group to talk about it, and maybe part of what I was trying to do was demonstrate how you do do it. It's a tough topic, and that means that as the group leader, you have to take a lot of initiative because people aren't going to do it otherwise, and I think what you have to do is ask specific people particular questions. Questions that might be a little shocking, like, "Imagine yourself a homosexual—which would you choose?" and so forth. Which is, on the whole, pretty strong medicine to give a group because these are very emotionally loaded kinds of things. But in an area like this, I think often you have to do this. And finally, if people aren't really coming clean, then to express your own feelings about it, as I did with the fascination and so forth, which I might have even done earlier, can be helpful. Because if you do it yourself, it usually makes it easier for other people to do it. Especially if it is something not easy to acknowledge—that you may have feelings that are positive about this kind of an act. Even though you don't really do it, maybe there are some feelings. This almost has to be true with virtually everybody, if you let yourself in on it. So these are some methods that I think you can use. Another point that occurred to me is that in understanding, if the immediate reaction you have is one of revulsion or disgust and no desire to explore what happens, then I think that this might indicate that you have a hard time understanding what's going on. If the initial reaction you have had to a homosexual act is to withdraw from it, then you might not ever understand how they are feeling and why they are doing it, and thereby get a more effective way of handling the problem. In other words, your own reluctance to explore the area of homosexuality might mean that the only way you can deal with it is strong-arm methods. And you know they're not working. The thing goes

[11] This is an example of introducing more didactic material on group counseling methods by using experiences that occurred in the group.

on and on. And this really isn't too effective. So that maybe the more open you can be to understanding and acknowledging your own feelings, the more able you are to really begin to understand what they are doing and why they are doing it. Then perhaps you'll be able to deal more effectively with the whole situation. These are some of the problems that occurred to me.

MERTON. You mean to direct the group in that direction and then. . . .

SCHUTZ. Yeah. I think the one thing we saw here is that there is a tremendous tendency to get away from the subject. It's almost like a bucking bronco. You start out, but all of a sudden you get flung in a direction that's way away from it. Remember the sociological talk, the psychological explanations and speculations about it? And you really have to almost hold a tight rein on the group and not let them do that, or else very quickly you'll be off in some other direction. I think on any topic that's very emotionally loaded like that you really have to pretty much step in and become more active than you'd have to in a different kind of a problem. Otherwise, you'll just never get anywhere. Because as soon as somebody gets uncomfortable, they'll take it somewhere else and everybody will get all involved in this other topic. Not because it's so interesting, but because that allows them to stay away from the topic that's really difficult. (Pause.) You know, like the history topic. We could have gone on for hours on the history of the American Negro and it would have been interesting, but also, you know, diversionary.

The impact of the training sessions may be gauged in part by the increasing level of candor and emotional intensity that characterized each successive session, culminating in the final meeting. This final session of one group, by common agreement, was the most expressive of the series.

The meeting began with a presentation by the trainer of the results of a battery of psychological tests that had been taken during the previous two weeks by the members. This was accompanied by some guessing by members about how the various members scored on the tests. The men guessed fairly accurately about how others filled out the tests.

A pause occurred, and then followed a prolonged discussion of the child-rearing practices of several of the members. To the observer, the striking feature of the discussion was the extent to which many of the men admitted employing severe techniques of punishment. In the early sessions it is unlikely that anyone would have admitted to anything but very permissive, nonpunitive behavior with children, in line with their conceptions of the nondirective ideals of counseling. In this session, however, Farmer led off by saying that he expects from his two children unquestioning obedience, which he had produced by means of periodic beatings when he felt that they were necessary. Another member asked how Farmer himself was raised. Farmer replied that *his* father had beaten him with plow reins regularly. The first member said that although plow reins were pretty tough, his own father had beaten him with a four-foot quirt studded with rosettes. He recalled the whip would wrap around a couple of times, each rosette leaving a raised welt. Farmer stated that even with plow reins you could raise welts "big as wienies," and again boasted that with his marine belt he could reduce his children "to hamburger, if need be." The men appeared to be exaggerating the severity of their parents' child rearing as if some kind of manhood were involved. Several disagreed, other persons spoke ruefully, and some spoke enthusiastically in agreement with the need for corporal punishment in the socialization of children and accepted the use of straps, whips, and boards as implements for administering beatings. It was clearly implied that preschool children received whippings. There was a difference of opinion expressed about whether an adolescent child should continue to receive beatings.

It seemed from the discussion that the men were, perhaps, talking much tougher than they actually behaved, and their remarks were, perhaps, not to be taken as an indication of the real severity of their child rearing. It was evident, however, that some disposition toward corporal punishment existed. At no time was any suggestion made that physical punishment was or should be employed on prison inmates.

The use of collective punishment was discussed. Several men agreed that when the guilt of one child could not be established, *their* fathers would have usually beaten all children. Schutz asked if this meant that it was better to punish some innocent persons in order to get a guilty one. The members who endorsed corporal punishment of children agreed, although some said that an investigation to determine guilt should be made. Schutz asked if this held true for inmates too, and several said "yes," but others disagreed.

In the final phase of the meeting, Wills, who had been silent at the start of these meetings and rather hostile to the group, began to speak concerning his own upbringing, which he credited with causing him rather serious personal problems in the expression of affection. His recent marriage was evidently not going well, and he stated that his wife periodically left him until they could both "feel up to getting together again." He stated that he felt his own difficulties stemmed from never having experienced real continuous affection in his childhood. He described himself as defensive, intellectual, and brittle. Jackson, who had earlier opposed the notion of child beating by saying that his own children were not being raised in this manner, spoke about a group psychotherapy service (in a nearby mental health center), to which he and his wife were going. Wills said he would look into it. Merton offered to put him in touch with therapists there. Several members spoke supportingly of Wills and said they could like him much better now that he had disclosed these facts about himself. Interaction was exceedingly emotional and affect laden at this point, and a usually silent man spoke about a woman in some trouble whom he had met, comforted, and with whom he had had sexual intercourse the previous night. He said he probably enjoyed the comforting as much as the sex and de-emphasized the element of conquest typically embroidering such accounts. There was no jesting from the others during this account.

Somewhere, interleafed in the disclosures of the final phase, were the remarks of an officer who was leaving the prison to resume his previous civilian work. Several other staff men sighed enviously. One asked him if he would give him a job. Another said he envied him because he wanted to go back to graduate school but did not have the guts to quit his secure job and face the grind of school studies. Another officer said he had had many years experience at a skilled trade in the military and would like to quit prison work to open up a similar business, but he was afraid to give up the security of a state job. About one half of the group were deeply moved at the thought of someone leaving and striking off on his own. The last few moments were very emotional, with several people saying unfavorable or self-critical things about themselves and with others expressing solidarity with the group. The observer had never seen the group so emotional. Schutz expressed his gratitude to the group for having provided many stimulating hours and bade them farewell. The group disbanded with expressions of solidarity and camaraderie.

The content of the last session illustrates one of the main features of this training philosophy. Very little of the discussion dealt explicitly with leading counseling groups. Almost everything that was said referred to the personalities and behavior of the members. The emotional tone and the extent of the frank disclosure of feelings such as the confessing of marital problems were on a level of emotional candor not expressed at the beginning of the seminar. On the other hand, the open admission of authoritarian modes of child rearing appear to be difficult to reconcile with the role of nondirective counselor.

Inmate views of group counseling

At the time our study was set for full operation at Men's Colony—East, 76 counseling groups had been established in the three quads under study. Twenty-three of the groups involved mandatory participation in small groups and 53 involved groups made up of voluntary participants. In addition, there were three community living groups made up of 50 men each, in which participation was mandatory. In this chapter we describe the character and intent of the counseling groups at Men's Colony, relying mainly on our own observations and those of inmates, the logs of community living group leaders, and questionnaire data.

The task of description is not an easy one because of the considerable diversity in leadership and member behavior. There were differing levels of formal education, prison job assignments, years of prison service, and formal training of the group leaders; some groups were run by experienced counselors and social workers with graduate degrees, although other groups were run by guards who had worked at the prison for less than one year and who had had high school educations. The composition of the inmate groups also varied. A few included inmates with several years experience at doing time together at San Quentin or some other prison; other groups were composed entirely of men who were strangers to each other and who were serving their first term in prison. Most groups were mixtures of these extremes.

At the beginning of the study, plans were made for the systematic observation of the counseling groups, but several features of the field situation made it unfeasible. Most important were the problems encountered when members of the research team attended group meetings. The presence of one or more of the senior research staff was generally a stimulus to the group to ask questions about the project, the prison in general, and parole. We were appealed to as authorities on correctional treatment issues, and frequently inmates tried to use a researcher's status as a Ph.D. to set up invidious comparisons with the prison staff member who was the group leader. Inmates would often ask what we thought of the intent or the method of group counseling. Since we disclaimed any affiliation with the Department of Corrections or any interest other than in evaluation, we were frequently asked what we thought of the program. Occasionally, our presence prompted inmates to ask us questions that were, in fact, deprecating remarks, ostensibly directed to the researcher but intended for the leader, such as "Don't you think a group leader should be qualified or have special training?" "Can a bullshit group like this do anything for anybody?" and "What good is a program that makes you sit in silence for an hour every day?" Nonresponse was interpreted as unwillingness by us to make critical remarks before a staff member.

On other occasions, however, our presence was welcomed by leaders who were hard pressed to explain the need for groups with compulsory attendance, control groups, and the random assignment of inmates to the various quads. Inmates frustrated with the conduct of some counseling and community living groups expressed considerable resentment and hostility toward the mandatory attendance aspect of the program, and the presence of a research staff member provided an opportunity for the group members to displace hostility onto that aspect of the research project.

Sometimes specific questions about the research were directed to the visitor. In these instances, the leader generally tried to answer inmate questions about the research design, questions about which he was either improperly or incompletely informed. On some of these occasions, the leader's replies were so erroneous or misleading as to require immediate rectification (that is, participation in the group discussion) by the researcher.

Intervention was most frequently occasioned by mistaken or inappropriate references to the feature of the project that involved a "follow-up" of the inmates on release from prison. We found it necessary to explain that our follow-up was largely a statistical procedure utilizing Department of Corrections records and not a program involving a special surveillance or restrictive supervision of parolees. These commentaries tended to take the role of discussion leader from the hands of the prison staff member and place it on the researcher.

In addition, when senior research staff members sat in on the groups, it then was impossible to remain nonparticipating visitors in most of the groups.

Remote observation also had to be ruled out for several reasons. Group meetings were held in rooms not equipped with one-way glass. Nor could filming and recording equipment be set up on any permanent basis because the rooms were in use before and after the meetings. The use of a tape recorder without visual observation posed the problems of distinguishing voices and of disentangling one comment from another when many group members talked at one time and of missing the nonverbal and inaudible communication that occurred during the long periods of silence (snickers, grunts, laughs, facial expressions, whispers, and hand and body movements).

The task of tape recording or notating group activity was further confounded when, during the project, several other prisons in California began keeping records on the degree and quality of inmate participation in counseling sessions and then began including this information in inmate files for review by institution officials and the parole board. Rumors that Men's Colony would follow suit made note-taking and tape recording by us so threatening to inmates that it affected their conduct in the group meetings.

For these reasons an extensive schedule of group observation, however valuable, could not be undertaken. In order to get a feel for the range of group activities, we made a number of unannounced visits to groups in addition to visiting some groups for consecutive meetings. The following cases illustrate what we observed to be the nature of group sessions.

GROUP NO. 1 (MANDATORY SMALL GROUP)

When the observer arrived, the members of the group were seated in chairs arranged around three walls of a classroom. After a short time, the group gradually fell silent. The officer said nothing for a few minutes and then asked whether there was some residual feeling from the previous week's discussion. There was no direct reply to this, but one of the inmates asked what the counseling leaders had done at the UCLA sponsored training workshop held at a nearby inn. The leader said that this was not relevant to the group and declined further comment.

The leader then asked the group what they thought of him. Several inmates answered that if they did think something bad of the leader they would not say so since, as one put it, "even if you were the greatest guy alive, I think it would still be human nature that if I got in trouble you might be prone to be more hard on me because [I criticized you]."

Another inmate stated that, although he thought the leader was a good guy as a person, the inmate did not like him because of his badge, and that there would always be an "ill feeling" because the officer is a symbol of the authority keeping him there. Still another member countered by making a comment defending the officer's fairness in dealing with the inmates.

A member then mentioned that men in the quad were surprised to find that the leader was "OK" because his reputation at another California prison had been that of "a bastard." There then followed a discussion of whether the leader had changed, or whether the situation was different between the two prisons. The leader said little except to ask "do you think it is possible for a person to change that much?"

In the final minutes an inmate made a short speech, directed to the group as a whole, in which he stated that he thought that the leader was a nice guy but that he "had his doubts" about anyone who would take a job locking people up and being a "zoo-keeper." The inmate said he just couldn't do that to people and he wondered about the personality and motivations of anyone who could. The leader said he had not thought of it in that way, but declined further comment.

After the meeting, the leader commented that allowing the men to talk critically about the staff, "blows off steam and makes the Quad easier to handle."

GROUP NO. 2 (VOLUNTARY SMALL GROUP)

The observer attended several successive sessions of a group conducted by a sergeant. On the second occasion the group leader was not able to meet the group and had not notified the members nor arranged for an alternate leader. For the previous several weeks, a correctional officer also had been attending the group as part of his training. The new man was apparently unclear about his role as substitute leader in the absence of the regular leader, and this feeling was reflected by the members as well.

The group began with several small, low-voiced conversations that continued for nearly 25 minutes. The officer looked mildly embarrassed and stared out the door. Finally, he took the role of leader without explicitly announcing that he was doing so. He asked a very vocal inmate who had been the center of attention the previous week why he "felt the way he did."

This was a stimulus to the inmate to start a type of monologue that had characterized his behavior in previous sessions. It seemed likely that the officer was counting on an articulate, amusing, and lengthy story to get the group going on its discussion.

The monologue took the form of the inmate representing all the world as a collection of purely selfish hedonists; the thesis was that nobody cares for anybody, and least of all did the inmate care for anybody. He spoke at great length, warming to his subject, and eliciting laughter, agreement, and other responses that indicated attention from the other men. The inmate sketched a series of paradoxes, continually posing puzzles and contradictions to the group, all on the theme that events and people are not what they seem. For example, the inmate attacked the police and the courts as an unreasoning and intemperate force unequally applied to the disadvantaged and the minorities. But when another member agreed and cited harsh laws against narcotics, the inmate demonstrated that the evils resulting from narcotics usage made it very plausible that an extremely restrictive set of laws would pass, or argued against persons who supported him in the discussion. The acting leader did not further intervene, and the meeting closed at the end of the inmate's long recitation.

GROUP NO. 3 (MANDATORY SMALL GROUP)

This group was supervised by a correctional officer who was an unusually skillful group leader. Like No. 2, the group discussion was usually organized around one inmate, although not necessarily the same inmate at each session. In one session of this group the observer was sitting in the room before the counseling hour. Several inmates were seated around the room. One was reading a comic book, and another had a mason jar of coffee and wore a white cap, identifying him as a kitchen worker. An inmate entered the room and stepped quickly to the blackboard. Taking a piece of chalk, he drew a cartoon showing a man flying a kite while being observed by another cartoon figure representing a furious guard. After this quick sketch he sat down.

The group leader arrived and said "Buenos dias" to several Mexican inmates who answered in Spanish. (Such verbal familiarity was rare in our experience in the prison.) After a few moments when the individual conversations gradually subsided, the inmate who had made the drawing began to speak. He asked directly if it had been the leader who had written him up on a disciplinary infraction on the previous day. The leader answered equally directly that, yes, it had been. In the quick exchange that followed the meaning of the cartoon became clear: the inmate had constructed a kite out of paper and thin wood strips from the hobby shop. He had flown it from the quad where it attracted much attention. When it was noticed, an officer in the yard (the group leader) called to him and ordered him to pull the kite in. The inmate did not comply, and he was given a citation to appear before the Disciplinary Committee. The charge was the misuse of state property, since the string had been purloined from an industrial shop (also because the prison had no formal regulation outlawing kite-flying). The leader defended his action without apology stating that the inmate, by his refusal to pull the kite in, had given him no choice.

At this point another inmate intervened and subjected the first inmate to a critical examination. "Of course, the write-up was chicken," he said, "and the state can afford the string, but the important thing here is how you looked when [the group leader] told you to pull the kite in. You was running around all wild and excited, and I could see you looking at the other guys and you couldn't stand pulling the kite down in front of the other cons. They egged you on and you fell right in. That's what's going to happen to you on the street [on parole]. You have to look big in front of the others."

The ensuing discussion, not of the kite and not of the write-up but about the alleged effect of the pressures exerted by the other inmates in the yard, seemed to illustrate the possibilities of something other than mere conversation taking place in group counseling. The criticism of the first inmate led the second to discuss details of his own arrest, and some of his own dependence on an image as a tough guy from the Youth Authority institutions in which he had spent many years.

These three sessions are typical of many that were informally observed. Our observations and discussions with staff and inmates led us to conclude that the small groups frequently were beset with the following problems.

1. A tendency for superficiality, a lack of emotional involvement, and evidence of insincerity.

2. A tendency for talkative members to monopolize the discussion to the exclusion and boredom of others.

3. A feeling of frustration and a lack of confidence in the leaders' or members' ability to "do the job" without professional supervision.

4. A tendency to focus on stories and personal accounts that were not further analyzed or used for discussion but were used to provide competition for another inmate's account of his preprison experiences or exploits.

5. A tendency for staff members to permit periods of silence up to the length of the entire session because of their misinterpretation of "nondirective counseling" or their own inability to elicit discussion instead of personal narratives and storytelling. In some cases this may reflect inadequate training, in other cases it reflects inadequate counselors.

However, as in the case of Group No. 3, some groups exhibited behavior which was, in the opinion of the observers, similar to therapy groups in noncorrectional settings where the leader is unobstrusive but in command of the situation, and his manner suggested relaxed self-confidence. The members spoke critically and spontaneously and gave evidence of trusting the leader and one another. Based on feedback from inmate interviews (which we consider later in this chapter), conversations with staff members, and the reports of the on-site research staff, there were some, but not many, groups (like No. 3) in which the conduct of the sessions approximated the goals of counseling set forth in the departmental training manual.

THE COMMUNITY LIVING UNIT GROUP MEETINGS

To describe the daily 50-man group counseling sessions in the Community Living Units, we have combined material taken from special daily logs kept by the two staff members whose positions were supported by our project, with our own observations and those of inmate participants.

From the outset, silence and nonparticipation of a majority of the group members plagued the Mandatory Large Group sessions. Its larger size made silence more useful as a mode of resistance than was the case in the small groups. Entries in the staff logs record examples:

> Thirty-seven group members present. The meeting quieted down around 8:10 A.M. From 8:10 to 9:00 A.M. there remained complete silence. As (inmate) B. was walking out of the room he said, "there isn't a man in here," or something to that effect.

> The group settled down quickly but long period of silence followed; however, some nonverbal exchange in the way of smiles and other facial gestures were noted by staff during the silence. Silence was broken by Mr. B. (staff member) who commented on the silence which was followed by another period of silence. Mr. B. then asked the group if the silence was part of a conspiracy by the group or just a consequence of it being Monday morning. This led to some defensive comment to the effect that the group did not know what was appropriate to discuss since they had been left with the impression that only a discussion of personal feelings was meaningful. Mr. B. pointed out that this was not the case that anything could be discussed but the group should be mindful of the feeling behind the discussion, or lack of it, since it was revealing of the personalities and problems of the people involved.

The silence appeared at times to represent a general lack of cooperation and an expression of resentment concerning the compulsory program. At other times, it appeared motivated by a distrust in the purpose of the meetings.

> About a ten minute's silence was broken by Mr. B. who asked Inmate D. why he was smiling. Inmate D. said that he thought it was a very ridiculous situation. There was some more silence. Someone asked Inmate D. why he thought it was ridiculous. This led to some discussion about what the group could talk about. Inmate M. stated that maybe every man in committing his crime had done the best he could under the circumstances. This led to a round of discussion. There was another episode in which Inmate R. again asked what did Mr. B. mean by asking what were the feelings behind a news item (discussed at a previous session). Mr. B. was quite active . . . explaining that what was impor-

tant were feelings that a person had in connection with a thing that he read or saw or heard that might relate to feelings that were involved in his getting into difficulty. Towards the end of the hour the group did shift into some pretty serious levels about what they could talk about and how intimate they could get. When a group of three were challenged by Mr. B. in the corner for talking on the side, one of them came out with some real feelings with regard to the group being "a lot of asinine shit." This was a real manifestation of feelings and some effect was made to demonstrate that such feelings were not unacceptable and in fact they were the meat of good productive sessions. But again the group dwelt a great deal on whether or not they were safe in expressing real feelings.

A year later, entries such as the following were still being made:

The entire hour was spent in silence with the exception of a side conversation between (inmate) R. and M.

And still later:

Staff members present were Mr. N., Mr. E., and a relief officer. The group formed slowly and 11 members were absent (of the 50 inmates who were supposed to attend). They were silent for the first several minutes, then Mr. N. began a discussion with Inmate A. The discussion had to do with the fact that Inmate A. read a book during the meetings and generally did not participate. After a brief interchange, Inmate M. commented that Inmate A. was merely sparring with Mr. N. and was not interested in opening up or revealing anything about himself. Inmate A. was asking what the group wanted to know about him. This discussion ended between Inmates M. and A., and Mr. N. again brought it back to Inmate A., beginning another discussion. Other members of the group joined in the discussion and began talking about the group—the silent members of the group, and the fact that some of the members were reading books and coming in late or not attending at all. The late-comers, the book-readers, the nonattenders all having a hampering effect on the group, as well as the people who do not express their opinions at any time. (Right inmates) were all active in the discussion as to whether the group meetings were a bunch of small talk, or whether they were useful and meaningful to the members. There was considerable indication from several members that they wanted to create good conditions for an active, meaningful group.

In the post-meeting staff discussion, it was felt that this was a useful meeting in which considerable group feeling was expressed and that there was considerable evidence of group cohesiveness. Several of the usually nonspeakers were drawn out in this group, particularly Inmate A.

Various procedures were suggested by inmates for coping with the problem of silence. One session produced the plan of designating one member as the target for attention at each session . . . the so-called "hot seat."

> Inmate B took lead in the discussion, thinking about how they might better use the group. He suggested the "hot seat" technique and indicated that he would prefer going down the roster so that everyone had an opportunity to take the hot seat. The group responded well to this idea, and the general feeling seemed to be that each one of them would be willing to take the hot seat if they were sure that others would do the same. There was a great deal of interest generated in this particular discussion, wide participation and a serious air among the whole group.

These efforts failed to materialize into a formal technique, but frequently when topics arose that were of immediate rather than remote or academic concern, the group not only discussed the issues throughout a session, but continued the discussion for several sessions.

An example of this sustained interest is to be found in the log of one of the Community Living Units for four meetings. Inmate B. voiced a complaint that an officer who was attending the group discussion had unfairly written him up for taking food from the dining room. After a discussion of several minutes, a second inmate, Inmate L., commented that he thought Inmate B.'s principal concern was that he felt the officer was prejudiced against him on racial grounds. Inmate B. agreed. (Both Inmates B. and L. were Negro; the officer was white.) The officer denied prejudice. The correctional counselor's notes state:

> With staff encouragement, there was some recognition by several members in the group that most people have some feelings of prejudice and that this might be on racial, religious, or other grounds. The discussion was continuing actively at the end of the meeting in this vein and the group did not break up readily. (Afterward) the discussion continued out in the hall.

The discussion continued the following day, as the same counselor's notes describe:

> After initial pause, Mr. N. recalled the discussion of the previous day and observed that the discussion had not been finished and suggested that there were still some more things to discuss. Inmate B. made the statement that he felt it is preferable to bring out the feelings of one's own

prejudice toward other minority groups and also to bring out the feelings of prejudice that one has from others. Inmate B. still does not believe that there was no prejudice involved in the officer's "beefing" him, but he did experience some reduction in his irritation about the fact of the officer's prejudice. Inmate G. expressed some prejudice that he feels has reduced in intensity in recent years, and gave an example of such a feeling by stating if a Mexican or Negro forces himself into the line ahead of him at Mess Hall he feels differently than if it's a white person. Later he got some criticism about the expression of this feeling from three inmates. He got pretty heated about the criticism and tended to withdraw from the discussion. Another inmate came to his support saying that the rest of the group should be more inclined to recognize their feelings of prejudice and he doubted that they were being perfectly honest when they said that they had no prejudiced feelings at all. Following this there were some attempts to distinguish between "acted out" prejudice and "felt" prejudice. Somehow the feeling of prejudice was reasonably acceptable, whereas any prejudiced action against another person was not acceptable.

The discussion was completed with a Mexican inmate's becoming impatient at the (white) staff's refusal to agree that ethnic or racial discrimination was at times an adequate explanation of life difficulties.

Inmate L. made comments about the article which was about a 19-year-old Mexican boy who had become involved in considerable criminal activity in the Los Angeles area. It reported the boy's history of YA (Youth Authority) and other institutions. Inmate L. spoke very heatedly about the prejudice that Mexicans experience in Los Angeles, from the police and other authorities, and from citizens generally. There was the idea presented, and supported by Inmate H., that prejudice and racial bias against an individual can cause him to become involved in criminal behavior. The frustrations are so great for the minority person and the situation is so hopeless for him that he has no ready alternative to advance himself. Inmate H. became quite irritated with Mr. N. when Mr. N. attempted to point out the importance of how the individual responds to pressure, such as racial prejudice, and that the individual still remains responsible for his own behavior.

Besides such personally relevant problems as race, the Community Living Units sometimes aired problems of institutional living. A lengthy account, again in the words of the correctional counselor, shows how he was effective in confronting an inmate in an argument in the presence of the group.

[I] asked [an inmate who had recently been given a parole date] if the favorable Board appearance hadn't affected him, to which [the inmate] answered that he wasn't thinking about that, that he was thinking about many other things. Then, after a few moments of silence, [I] inquired as to what things he might be thinking about the *low blow* he had received at the Board. He then very emotionally explained that he had received word that his mother was dying, and that the Board had a letter to this effect from other people and the doctor and when he mentioned this to the Board that he would like to get out and help her while he could, [a Board member] said to him that it might be better if they kept him in prison until she died. This was followed by a long discourse about the lack of feeling or understanding that the Board had for the "convicts" they dealt with, that they obviously just couldn't understand how a man could be close to and love his mother as he did, etc., and during this discourse it became obvious that he was quite angry with the Board for giving him a release date four months off, and ignoring his and other relatives' appeals for his earlier release on the basis of the mother's illness. [I] inquired if anyone might have differently interpreted the message that [the Board member] was endeavoring to convey to Inmate G. Inmate P. responded to the effect that [Board member] probably recognized Inmate G. as being a mama's boy and that maybe he meant that if mama was no longer there, that Inmate G. could act like a man. Inmate G. was quite defensive in his retort, giving a quite different interpretation to what the Board member had said. Inmate G. had made reference to a letter from a doctor to the effect that his mother was dying, and since [I] inquired of Inmate G. as to whether or not he had seen such a letter or if the Board had read such a letter to him. At this point, he became very evasive, stating that any such letter wouldn't be read to him, since it was considered confidential, etc., but that he had in fact a letter from a friend of his mother, who had stated that she was very ill, that he had wanted to take it in and present it to the Board but the officer wouldn't allow him to do this; however, he had told the Board of her condition, etc., and they had ignored this by giving him a parole date four months off, and that in his mother's extremely weakened condition, she would in all probability die while he was in prison.

At this point, [I] said that to the best of [my] knowledge, no letter had been received from a doctor giving a professional terminal prognosis. At this point, Inmate G. became very defensive again and pointed out to me that he had mentioned a letter from the doctor that was received prior to his August appearance. [I] stated that a letter had been received from a physician at that time stating that his mother suffered from a chronic illness, however, that both he and [I] knew that she had been suffering from this illness for many years. At this point, Inmate G. became very emotional and advised [me] that he would bring a letter in, got up and left the room, shortly returning with a letter from a relative who stated that she had been to see his mother—that they had tried to talk her into going to the hospital where she would get proper care but that she had refused, preferring to remain alone in her apartment. Apparently that visit had taken place on the preceding day and she stated she planned to again visit his mother on the date of the letter and would add a postscript after she had seen her. In the postscript she stated the mother appeared to be feeling considerably better. [I] inquired as to whether or not he wanted this letter read to the group, and he said, "Yes, read it to the group." After reading the letter, [I] commented that this woman had stated his mother was feeling better on the day it had been mailed, to which Inmate G. responded that she had taken a considerable turn for the worse, and that he had received word that for the last three or four days she had been in a coma and she was alone in her apartment, with none of her elderly neighbors able to take care of her. This was a terrible situation to have exist and again reflected on the Adult Authority preventing him from going out to help her. The letter had been returned to Inmate G. advising it had been written on the eighteenth. [I] then pointed out the inconsistency of what he was saying: that she had been in a coma for three or four days when the letter had been sent to him only three days previously, and that surely she couldn't remain in a coma for three or four days without adequate medical care, that she would require intravenous feeding etc. This brought some laughter from the group to which Inmate G. became very defensive and commented on the group snickering, etc., on something that was so serious and unfunny that he didn't see how people could laugh about a situation like this, that it could only come from men who had absolutely no regard for their mothers, etc.

The group's reaction to Inmate G.'s chastisement was either disinterest or possible chagrin, as there was no verbal response. Inmate A. then spoke up expressing that the Board had, in fact, given Inmate G. a pretty *cold shot* in not allowing him to go on parole immediately in view of the mother's condition, etc.; however, Inmate B. expressed the feeling that the Board was trying to act in Inmate G.'s best interest in view of the fact that he hadn't really tried to help his mother when he had the opportunity to do so (while) on parole. To [me] it was apparent that Inmate G. was utilizing the same defenses he always used which consists of rationalization and projection, skillfully avoiding acceptance of any of the responsibility for things that happen to him. It is [my] impression that the group is becoming more and more aware of Inmate G.'s defenses and the extremes he will go to, to project blame away from himself, even to the point of complete distortion of the facts.

Although resistance and reticence are normal properties of discussion of therapy groups in all settings, prison inmates seem to be particularly suspicious of the motives of the staff in encouraging them to participate in the counseling program. As was the case in the training sessions, in the inmate counseling groups, the staff and inmates were concerned with whether a given situation or action was to be interpreted as an effort to control and to maintain surveillance or as an effort to rehabilitate and to treat. Moreover, the utility of group discussion to inmates and to the organization was sometimes regarded differently by the staff and the inmates.

Group counseling sessions frequently were efforts of the leader and the members to get each other to accept one of two contrasting definitions of the situation. The leaders regarded the defensive reactions of the inmates as resistance, and the inmates regarded staff leadership difficulties (nondirection) as evidence of insincerity and covert custodialism. Inmate resistance frequently took the form of denying that the sessions had even the intent of treatment. The fact that the power of the prison administration stood behind the program and that sanctions could be employed to deal with noncompliance was cited by inmates as an indication that counseling was concerned not with helping them work through interpersonal problems, but with legitimizing their incarceration.

Many inmates felt that group counseling was a device of the prison staff that gave the appearance of a treatment program while it actually gathered information from the inmates for the purposes of surveillance and control. This distrust, which applied to other aspects of the treatment program as well as to group counseling, was articulated as follows when an inmate was asked, "What do you think the word rehabilitation means as the word is used by correctional authorities?"

> This is the wrong word. It means reform. A better word for what they [Adult Authority] mean is *retribution*. We are paying now for committing crime. If we commit more crime, then we will have to pay more. Everyone knows the Authorities use fancy words like "rehabilitation" to fool the public into thinking that the old system is no longer in effect. In reality, punishment and retribution is still the only method of handling felons. If there were such a program as "rehabilitation," we would never hear [from the parole board], "you just haven't brought us enough *time*."

Finally, inmates frequently were constrained from speaking by fears of disapproval, ridicule, or because of other inmates. Previously we mentioned the problems of confidentiality of reports, here the issue of confidentiality was that of revealing to nongroup members what goes on in the group. The men worried about whether what was said in the counseling group would be discussed outside the group. The matter was of greatest concern to participants in the small groups, most of whose cell and work neighbors were not in their groups. In one session, the group leader recorded an inmate commentary on this issue:

> Inmate M. introduced the subject of the inmate code and discussed this in terms of the work of the large group. He made some observations on the hierarchical structure of the inmate culture and stated that since the inmates wanted to maintain this structure they could not interact freely and openly in large groups. By so doing, they would reshuffle the balance of the hierarchy, and this would be too threatening. Nobody wants to develop the name for being a sniveler or a snitch, and they fear this may very well happen if they discuss freely in the group.

INMATE INTERVIEWS

Interviews conveyed the strong impression that relatively few inmates entered group counseling with the conviction that they were participating in a meaningful treatment program. The usual advice new inmates received from others was to the effect that counseling was not adequately nor honestly run, but that participation looked good to the Adult Authority, and, in fact, counseling was one of the measurable items of an inmate's experience in prison (like school attendance, trade training, and disciplinary reports) that could be considered. Although participation may not help inmates to make parole, its absence, generally noticed by the Adult Authority, is often interpreted as a lack of interest in helping oneself and getting involved in the treatment program. For the Adult Authority, the record of length of participation in group counseling is a useful index of prisoner experience because it joins that relatively small list of activities that can be quantified and used in plus-or-minus fashion in determining parole eligibility.

Regardless of what they may have been told prior to their experience with the counseling program, some inmates did accept the official statement of the aim and the effect of group counseling. They felt that counseling could help a man to understand himself and others. Other inmates accepted the aim but felt that the inadequacies of staff leadership or of the inmate members or of both prevented the program from having the intended positive effects. Many inmates rejected the official aim, but they participated because it would look good on their records at parole hearing time. Finally, others rejected the program and would not participate; they regarded counseling as another tool of custody to obtain information from unwary inmates.

Each of these four views are illustrated by excerpts from interviews.[1] First, a favorably disposed prisoner:

> I will very seldom see my own faults, whereas you could see them a lot clearer than I could. And in a group where you have 12 or 13 people sitting around in a circle talking, usually you would hit on something which has an effect on other persons. Maybe a problem which he has had and which he has been able to solve and that he might be able to pass this information on to you. I've seen people sitting in group and I knew they were *bullshitting*, I knew that they were *shucking* [insincere]. And maybe I wouldn't say anything for three or four weeks, but eventually they would hit me on the wrong day and I would say something. Then . . . sometimes they get pretty hot . . . the groups at the *joint* [prison] . . . I know that this has happened to me . . . some people would hit on some of my shortcomings and I'd get extremely indignant, but the moment I'd go back to my cell and I'd sit there—you can't help but think about it when somebody's insulted you or something like that—and the majority of times the individual is right in what he said. So I might not go back and tell him that he's right, but if I have any kind of forethought at all I'll try and correct it, or I'll start working on it.

There was frequent criticism of the capabilities of most group leaders, either because of personality, formal training, or status in the prison's organizational hierarchy. (Of course, some staff members were regarded as effective leaders on precisely the same grounds.)

Most leaders are rank-and-file custodial officers who have neither professional standing nor high organizational status. The lack of both of these means of legitimizing leadership was believed to be a serious limitation by many group leaders, and it constituted a major criticism of counseling as viewed by the inmates. That is, it is difficult to separate the effect of the leader's behavior in the group from his out-of-group status. An important authority figure in the institution, such as associate warden, captain, program administrator, or lieutenant, brings to the group an attribute that provides assistance in maintaining control over the direction of group discussion and in minimizing overt inmate resistance to the program. High organizational status is a factor in legitimizing group leader status. Group counselors who are treatment professionals, for

[1] Our interview procedure is described in Chapter II.

instance, psychologists or psychiatrists, can legitimate their leader status by an appeal to their formal training and technical competence.

Despite limited leader authority, several correctional officers were able to use leadership styles or techniques that were helpful in gaining the interest of the group members. In the following quotation, an inmate describes one device used to make the sessions more meaningful.

> This is a pretty good group I'm in. It wasn't at first because no one knew anyone. At first it was just getting acquainted. It was one of those typical things where everybody . . . bullshitted, told a few lies, avoided the truth pretty well. The [sessions] I liked was where we identified a lot of problems previous to the one before we *fell* [were arrested], things that turned us into crooks, problems we're gonna face when we get out . . . they'll be similar situations . . . and how we're gonna handle them . . . this has been good. Oh, and another thing that's new with me anyhow, the officers have been bringing a few *jackets* [records] to the group . . . central files, summaries of a fellow, evaluations of them by correctional counselors, their rap sheets, etc. How they're evaluating them and how the fellows in the group see them—that was really good. They just *pulled the covers off* a lot of guys, the truth came out—it was pretty good.

Although inmate record files can be a useful aid, it should be noted that the use of this file material poses problems in terms of maintaining the confidentiality of staff reports, evaluations, and personal history information. A correctional officer must exercise great care that he does not divulge materials from inmate files that will violate confidences to clinical or to custodial staff members or that will incense an inmate against a caseworker for writing an unfavorable report to the parole board. This restraint is difficult because these evaluations by clinicians, caseworkers, and family members may be precisely the kind of material an officer would find useful in "pulling the covers off" an inmate.

The third and fourth views of counseling were undeniably negative in that both rejected the authenticity and efficacy of the treatment program. Many men felt that participation in group counseling was regarded by the staff as a measure of their (inmates) receptivity to treatment and as evidence of their willingness to change. Some of them participated; others did not. One of the former put it this way: "I don't particularly care for counseling. I more or less took it for appearance sake—you know, take it to the Board [parole board]; it looks good." Often those who did not participate thought the disadvantages for parole eligibility outweighed the advantages. The following remarks reflect the fourth viewpoint.

> If you say anything [in group counseling] that isn't too good, it will get in your jacket and go to the parole board. And that's what got a lot of

guys in here where they don't trust them group counseling classes. Because you want to be honest . . . but you're worried about what the parole board is gonna hear too, you know. So that scares them.

In the interviews we asked about problems that had been particularly troublesome during the present prison term. After the problem was mentioned, the interviewer asked whether "group counseling had been helpful in regard to this problem?" The question was not relevant for C quad men or for men in A or B who were not in counseling groups ($N=22$); of the remaining 54 men (those with counseling experience), 31 (57 percent) said they would not or had not brought up a personal problem in their group. Only 7 of the 20 who had introduced their problem in groups found this helpful. Three gave replies that were difficult to classify.

If counseling was not regarded as much of an aid to problem solving, it also was low on the list of "most valuable" prison programs and was high among the ones regarded as being "least valuable." Academic education was felt to be most valuable by 42 percent of the respondents, closely followed in popularity by vocational training (34 percent). The recreation program, chapel, and prison jobs together accounted for another 12 percent. Group counseling was mentioned by only 9 percent of the respondents. When asked for the least valuable, almost two thirds (63 percent) had nothing to say, but 18 percent said "group counseling," 15 percent named vocational training, and 4 percent mentioned Alcoholics Anonymous and religious programs.

Client reactions through survey data

The first survey, called the Inmate Questionnaire, contained items related to inmate values, prison experience, and preprison background. A 50 percent random sample of the inmate population was selected. (D Quad was excluded.) Another questionnaire, called the Group Opinion Inventory, was comprised of a set of items that were intended to measure the extent of inmate participation in group activity as well as the sources of satisfaction and dissatisfaction with the group experience. Unlike respondents for the Inmate Questionnaire, some of whom were participants in counseling, some of whom were not, respondents for the Group Opinion Inventory were only participants.

In this section, selected data from both these questionnaires will be offered to describe the inmates' reactions to participation in the counseling program. The next chapter discusses the normative orientation of Men's Colony inmates and whether that orientation was influenced by participation in group treatment.

THE INMATE QUESTIONNAIRE: TIME 1

Respondents for the Inmate Questionnaire were selected by taking every other name on an alphabetical roster, each quad starting with the first or second name according to a coin toss. Groups of 85 men were requested to come to one of three questionnaire sessions that were conducted simultaneously. The survey was completed in two days, nine sessions per day, all within the normal working hours of the inmate (that is, we were able to avoid asking men to fill out questionnaires during the "prime" evening hours when many recreational activities competed). All administration sessions were held either in the classroom or in the chapel area of the associated services section of the institution. News announcements of the time and purpose of the survey appeared in the prison newspaper prior to its administration.

The sessions were conducted only by UCLA project personnel who prefaced each administration with a statement of the purpose of the survey. We reminded the respondents that we had been in the prison for several months during which many of them had been interviewed, and that if our assurances of confidentiality in these earlier cases had not been good, they would have heard about it. The inmates also were reminded that the institutional personnel had no knowledge of the specific content of the questionnaire prior to its administration. They were told to answer all questions but to omit an answer rather than to give one that was not genuine. To match the responses obtained on this questionnaire with other study data, we asked the men to sign their names to the forms, place them in an envelope, seal it, and place the envelope in a carton with many other forms in the front of the room. After each day, the cartons of completed questionnaires were carried out of the institution only by UCLA project personnel and were placed in a University of California station wagon, a fact observed and commented on by many inmates. (For example, we found that in turning down the friendly offer of a staff member to assist us in carrying the cartons out of the prison, we made a wise decision, since many of the inmates might have seen what would have appeared to have been the prison staff "taking the questionnaires away.") It is our impression that these evidences of efforts to insure confidentiality of answers, as well as our affiliation with an outside agency with a reputation for neutrality, were useful in our effort to promote candor.

Out of a maximum of 900 cases (50 percent of the 3 quads' potential population) 871 usable forms were obtained from the men in this sample.

Approximately one third of the completed questionnaires were drawn from each of three quads: 32 percent from A Quad, 35 percent from B

Quad, and 33 percent from C quad. Fifteen percent of the respondents had been at CMCE 6 months; 32 percent had been there between 6 and 12 months; and the remainder (53 percent) had been there more than one year. Of the 70 items, there were one dozen structured questions pertaining to counseling and one open-end question. Data presented here will deal only with reactions to these items.

The forced-choice questions dealt with specific issues raised in interviews such as whether or not men could speak frankly during counseling sessions, whether disputes should be brought to the group for discussion, whether the leaders were competent, and so forth. Respondents were asked to agree or disagree, usually on a 4-point scale. In addition, inmates were asked whether they agreed or disagreed with the outcomes of counseling that we were using as measures of effectiveness, namely the violations of prison and parole rules. Last, they were asked to complete in their own words the following statement: "My main criticism of the group counseling program is —————————."

Answers to the structured items give an indication of the range of support and rejection of the group counseling program. Four out of five of the men disagreed with the statement that asserted counseling was a waste of time for the inmate. Two thirds agreed that correctional officers were not competent to run groups.

Perhaps, the most significant issue for the effectiveness of the program would be the extent to which men are candid and feel secure about discussing themselves (their problems, conflicts, or feelings). We asked four related questions that distinguished between the fact of candor (or lack of it), the desirability of candor, and its effects. There was agreement that men did not talk frankly (four out of five), and one half of the respondents agreed that if too much was revealed it would be used against them. Apparently it was felt that men did not involve themselves for reasons that were in addition to a sense of distrust of the staff—perhaps, a distrust of the inmates or the belief that "men" do not talk about feelings or discomfort or the inability to do so. However, three out of four disagreed that counseling in fact provided information for the staff to use against the inmates. In the light of the other items we would interpret this response to suggest that, since the inmates did not provide much personal information, the staff did not have much to use against them— but that if information was given, it might very well be used by staff in a way that was detrimental to the men.

Opinions about the propriety of using the counseling group to air interpersonal difficulties were tapped by this item:

> Inmates Anderson and Baker, members of the same counseling group, have a serious dispute outside the group. Other group members notice the bad feeling between them and during a session ask Anderson what is

wrong. Anderson says there is nothing wrong because he believes that if he tells the reason for the trouble at a group counseling session, it would be ratting on Baker.

Forty-nine percent of the men agreed with Anderson, and 62 percent believed that "most inmates" would agree with Anderson. That is, men felt that their fellow inmates would perceive such a situation—bringing a dispute to the group for consideration—as disloyalty (ratting) more often than they themselves would. The effect of this pluralistic ignorance would be a reluctance on the part of a sizable number of men to discuss the issues that counseling is supposed to deal with.

When asked about the main criticism that they had of the counseling program, one half of the sample (433) did not respond at all, or gave an unintelligible or uncodable or incomplete answer. The fact that the no response category for the structured questions discussed above was never more than five percent (generally three or four percent) suggests that (1) a low level of education may have been a handicap for many; (2) that there was limited motivation to think about, and then to express in writing, their thoughts about a counseling program in which some may have had no interest and/or did not participate; and (3) that in the hands of prison staff criticism could be taken as evidence of "poor adjustment" and, thus, they were reluctant to respond. Of the 438 completed answers, eighteen percent gave no criticism and, instead, volunteered a positive or accepting statement. The most common category of criticism dealt with the lack of qualified group leaders (27 percent). Twenty-three percent stressed the fact that members did not speak candidly whether from fear of staff recriminations or from a need to enhance their images with fellow inmates; 18 percent focused on the lack of direction in the sessions ("they are bull sessions"). The remaining 14 percent expressed the view that the intent of the program was control, not therapy. (These data are presented in Table 5.1.)

Here are some of their complaints in their own words:

> The counseling leader is usually an incompetent member of the staff. Especially when dealing with socially maladjusted people.

> Lack of qualified psychiatrists to get into the deeper emotional problems.

Some respondents tempered their criticism by stating that with proper leaders, counseling would be useful:

> There are no qualified personnel to lead these groups, consequently the majority of the groups are nothing very beneficial to anyone. With proper leadership, I believe Group Counseling could help a lot of people inside or out of prison.

table 5.1   Coding Open-End Item on "Main Criticism of Counseling"

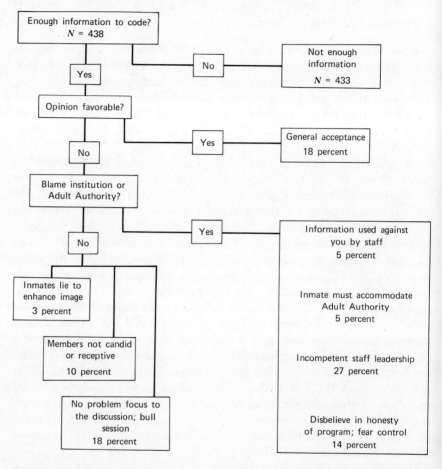

Responses that combined questions of leader competence with the criticism that the sessions had no problem focus, but seemed to stress group session focus were coded in the "bull session" category.

Availability of leaders (adequate) for such widespread activity is limited. More professional personnel is necessary. Groups as they stand don't have leadership to prod inmates toward areas requiring attention. Consequently many hours are spent just bitching about this bull [correctional officer] or that bull, and nothing concrete is really established.

They are not run as they should be. They help keep pressures down within the institution, but deal very little with outside problems. They are mostly bull sessions on the latest prison gossip, ball games, etc.

Too much straying from basic problems and discussing things which have no bearing on why one is here or what he can do in the future to avoid being here.

Sometimes just sit in room with no one talking, makes the hour very long.

Too much crying over spilt milk.

In 18 months of group counseling, I only learned more ways to commit crimes—Heard all about other inmates' crimes and all they had—new cars, etc.—and yet they bummed cigarettes—It's just a process of wasting time and attempted brainwashing.

I don't wish to converse with a correctional officer or staff member.

After certain length of time it becomes boring and does more bad than good. I also consider it a legal form of brainwashing.

In summary, this questionnaire contained a variety of items that specifically posed the issues which were raised in the interviews and which were manifest in the response to the open-end item. The answers to these structured items give an indication of the range of support and rejection of the program. About one fourth of the men agreed that group counseling was mostly a waste of time for the inmate and that group counseling provided a lot of information to the staff that was used against the inmate. About one half of the men agreed that if a man revealed too much about himself to any staff member, the information would probably be used against him. Sixty-five percent of the respondents agreed that, generally speaking, correctional officers were not competent to lead group counseling sessions; four fifths of the sample agreed with the statement, "Most men I know do not talk frankly and openly of their personal problems in group counseling."

Slightly more inmates thought that the program had a positive impact on prison behavior than on parole. Fifty-five percent agreed that, "Offenders in group counseling tend to break fewer prison rules than those who do not participate." Forty-seven percent of the sample agreed that, "Inmates in group counseling are less likely to violate parole than those who do not participate."

THE INMATE QUESTIONNAIRE: TIME 2

In order to determine the consistency with which these views were held, we gave a second administration of the Inmate Questionnaire six months later to all men who took the first and were still in the prison.

table 5.2   Inmate Opinions Regarding Group Counseling (as Expressed at Two Points in Time)

	Percent Agree		
	Time 1	Time 2	Significance Levels
Group counseling a waste of time	21	17	p < .02
Correctional officers not competent to run groups	65	60	p < .01
Most men do not talk frankly in counseling	81	75	p < .01
If you reveal too much the information is used against you	51	40	p < .01
Counseling provides information to staff which is used against inmate	23	22	n.s.
Anderson and Baker should *not* bring their dispute to group discussion:			
Respondents opinion	49	52	n.s.
Guess "most inmates"	62	64	n.s.
Men in counseling break fewer prison rules	55	49	p < .01
Men from counseling violate parole less	47	49	n.s.
	(871)	(567)	

Five hundred and sixty-seven usable forms were obtained. Table 5.2 presents data for both administrations. *Note.* A significantly small proportion of time 2 respondents held critical views at the second administration. However, our discussion of whether this shift is a function of treatment exposure or something else must wait until Chapter VI.

‖‖

The inmate code and attitude change

‖‖

INMATE. Now you must understand a convict society is very demanding. . . . A convict society lives by two sets of laws. A convict code means in essence, in convict terminology, that you will "do your own number." You will not see anything that doesn't concern you, you will have consideration for your fellows, and they will have consideration for you. In this institution, they have the people who have a habit of attempting to live more than one number, finaglers, people who will give information to the point of false information and false imputation for personal gain, which is really more reminiscent of the free world.

INTERVIEWER. What happens to those people?

INMATE. In this institution not much happens, except they get paroled earlier.

INTERVIEWER. The snitch, you mean, gets advantages. . . .

INMATE. Yes, he does.

INTERVIEWER. Well, let me ask you this question: About two weeks ago, there was a fellow who got leaned on pretty heavily right in the middle of the quad. He ended up in the hospital. I'm not interested in the names. . . .

INMATE: This young man is unfortunate. [He] would be arrested with the type of life he leads in the free world, merely because it's an irresponsible way of living, and he was harmed here and probably in any prison that he happens to go to will be harmed further. Because he violates the basic precepts of good living. The basic precepts, I might say, since we're in a crowded little civilization here, are consideration for your fellow man, do not borrow that which you can't repay, don't play with homosexuals. If you do, join their

141

society and leave the others alone. Don't attempt to do another man's number and concentrate on forming for yourself a better tomorrow than were your yesterdays.

INTERVIEWER.   And he broke . . . one or all of these?

INMATE.   He broke possibly three of the rules without going too far. This is unfortunate, I don't mean to condone what was done to him—it was wrong. I think that in a way, or one way or another, that the man who did this, or the men who were responsible for this, will pay. But this is not my domain. I am, by circumstances, a convict under the convict code. It's unfortunate, but that's what happened.

(Conversation with CMC inmate)

INTRODUCTION

Treatment programs, whether in prisons or elsewhere, operate within a social context. In this study, that context is the formal and informal social organization of the prison. Behavior in the treatment program has implications for the wider context; the individual's position in the informal social organization may have implications for his participation in, and reaction to, many aspects of institutional programs, including the treatment program. In particular, the possibility that reactions to treatment might vary according to inmate type has such potential importance to the evaluation of outcome that we must take it into account.

In previous chapters we showed that inmates' apprehensions concerning custodial surveillance and the kind of appearance they make to the parole board exert an influence on the way group counseling is perceived and evaluated. In the present chapter, we examine the degree to which differences exist in roles in inmate society, and the extent to which endorsement of norms may change as a result of treatment exposure.

STUDIES OF INMATE TYPES

The problem of assessing a given inmate's position in the prison requires first that a conception of the structure (set of positions or roles) be adopted and, second, that a means of measurement is available. In the criminological literature there are many studies that deal, in one way or another, with this problem. A very brief review of some of them will be useful in discussing our own procedure.

It might be said that the principal preoccupation of sociologists in studying prisons has been with distinguishing the culture of the so-called prison "community" and with the configuration of roles which constitute the structure of that community. Some efforts have been made to relate inmate types to receptivity to treatment programs and to treatment outcome, but, in the main, studies of inmate types are efforts at the description of an ongoing social system.

Clemmer's study, *The Prison Community*, which was the first major effort at typing prisoners, did not make an effort to account for the development of the prisoner community but was concerned with describing the social life of prisoners at the time of the study.[1] Later examinations have found inmate types similar to Clemmer's *stools, wolves, right guys, politicians,* and *hoosiers,* but later concern also has been directed to the process by which inmate types evolved.

Sykes and Messinger, for example, describe the value system of prisoners—the inmate code—as a collection of normative imperatives that are "held forth as guides for the behavior of the inmate in his relations with fellow prisoners and custodians."[2] The core of this value system is the ideal of inmate solidarity; those inmates who adhere most strongly to these norms are accorded high prestige in the prisoner community.

Sykes and Messinger view the functional significance of the inmate code as a response to the deprivations and frustrations of prison life to which the inmate population must adapt itself. That is, the inmate code is a collection of normative prescriptions and maxims that guide the inmate in efforts to deal with the pains of imprisonment. Inmates conform to some degree, and at one time or another, to the various components of the inmate code. Thus, there is the *right guy* who is the model of loyalty to all aspects of the code; there is the *rat* who betrays his fellow prisoners; there is the *tough* who "quarrels easily and fights without cause"; the *merchant* exploits his fellow inmates not by force or violence but by manipulation and trickery; the *weakling* is unable to stand the rigors of penal confinement; the *wolf* or *fag* is either unable to endure prolonged heterosexual deprivation or finds the prison a good setting in which to pursue a long held homosexual way of life; and the *square John* allies himself with the values of the prison staff and the conventional community and considers himself in the prison but not "of" it.[3]

Sykes and Messinger further assert that: "The actual behavior of prisoners ranges from full adherence to the norms of the inmate world to deviance of various types. These behavioral patterns, recognized and labeled by prisoners . . . form a collection of social roles, which with their interrelationships, constitute the inmate social system."[4]

Another view that emphasizes the efforts of inmates to come to terms

---

[1] Donald Clemmer, *The Prison Community*, New York: Rinehart & Co., Inc., 1940.

[2] Sykes and Messinger, "The Inmate Social System," in *Theoretical Studies in Social Organization of the Prison*, op. cit., pp. 5–19.

[3] Ibid., pp. 9–15.

[4] Ibid., p. 11.

with the material, social, and psychological pains of imprisonment is set forth by Richard Cloward.[5] The inmate social system is seen as a response to the experience of "status degradation"—as an effort by some inmates to restore status to those dispossessed of roles and identities held in the free world:

> Although the bulk of inmate behavior is characterized by passivity and docility, by defeatism and resignation, there are some prisoners who refuse or are unable to lower their aspirations and to accept their degraded position. Disillusioned and frustrated, they seek means of escaping degradation.[6]

These prisoners who resist the encroachment of penal confinement on their self-definition represent a potential threat to the official (that is, custodial) system that is countered by permitting inmates access to higher status by illegitimate means. That is, ". . . the official system accommodates to the inmate system in ways that have the consequence of creating *illegitimate opportunity structures.*"[7] The staff, because their formal means of control are limited (for example, reporting every violation of prison rules would embroil the staff in unending efforts at adjudication), permit certain kinds of informal accommodation. Some inmates—*merchants* or *peddlers*—are permitted differential access by deviant means to material goods and services, the *politician* or *fixer* has differential access by deviant means to information and custodial personnel; and the *real man* or *right guy* has differential access by deviant means to status (for example, permitting an inmate to evade prison rules).[8] The merchants, politicians, and right guys act as the bridge that binds the inmate system and the formal system together.

Cloward (as well as Sykes and Messinger, Goffman,[9] Korn and McCorkle,[10] and others) views the social structure of the inmate community as representing the articulation of different kinds of adjustments, accommodations, or adaptations to the pains of imprisonment. This theoretical perspective of the prison has been criticized by Irwin and Cressey who have contended ". . . that the 'functional' or 'indigenous origin'

---

[5] Richard Cloward, "Social Control in the Prison," in *Theoretical Studies in Social Organization of the Prison,* op. cit., pp. 20–48.

[6] *Ibid.,* p. 32. For further discussion of this concept, see Harold Garfinkel, "Conditions of Successful Degradation Ceremonies," *American Journal of Sociology,* 61 (March 1960), pp. 421–422.

[7] Ibid., p. 33.

[8] *Ibid.,* pp. 36–41.

[9] Erving Goffman, *Asylums,* Garden City, New York: Doubleday & Co., Inc., 1961.

[10] Richard Korn and Lloyd McCorkle, *Criminology and Penology,* op. cit., pp. 515–530.

notion has been over-emphasized and that observers have overlooked the dramatic effect that external behavior patterns have on the conduct of inmates in any given prison."[11] Irwin and Cressey have urged consideration of the effects on prison behavior of preprison factors such as latent culture, latent identities, and history of prior penal confinement.

The relevance of preprison backgrounds and experiences to in-prison behavior has been considered by Clarence Schrag and by many of his students. Schrag views the prisoner community as consisting of a set of role alternatives that deal primarily with issues involving social relations among inmates, contacts with staff members, and access to the civilian world.[12] The set includes four major configurations, to which are attached the prison labels "square John," "right guy," "con politician," and outlaw."

Schrag shifted from argot labels to "a more neutral terminology" to emphasize the relationship of these role configurations to other social or cultural aspects of the prison community.[13] Taking into account distinguishing factors such as criminal record, family and community experiences, and attitudes toward crime and society, the following social types were generalized from the argot role terms:[14]

Major Argot Role Configurations	*Social Types*
Square John	Prosocial
Right guy	Antisocial
Con-politician	Pseudosocial
Outlaw	Asocial

Using Schrag's social types as a basis, a number of investigations have focused further attention on issues such as the relationship between inmate types and prison program participation,[15] socialization or prisonization,[16] and parole performance.[17] Our initial thinking about the possible

[11] John Irwin, and Donald R. Cressey, "Thieves, Convicts and the Inmate Culture," *Social Problems* **10** (Fall 1962), pp. 145–155.

[12] Clarence Schrag, "A Preliminary Criminal Typology," *Pacific Sociological Review* **4** (Spring 1961).

[13] Ibid., pp. 11–12. See also Clarence Schrag, "Some Foundations for a Theory of Corrections," in Donald R. Cressey (ed.), *The Prison,* op. cit., pp. 346–356.

[14] Ibid., pp. 348–350.

[15] See Peter Garabedian, "Western Penitentiary: A Study in Social Organization," unpublished Ph.D. Dissertation, University of Washington, 1959.

[16] See Peter Garabedian, "Socialization in the Prison Community," *Social Problems,* **11** (Fall 1963), pp. 139–152; and Stanton Wheeler, "Socialization in Correctional Communities," *American Sociological Review,* **26** (October 1961), pp. 706–711.

[17] Donald L. Garrity, "The Effects of Length of Incarceration Upon Parole Adjust-

effects of prison group counseling led us to expect a positive change in attitudes and behavior as a result of group counseling participation only if treatment exposure weakened the endorsement of the norms of the inmate community. Thus our effort to measure inmate values stemmed from the specific interest in the impact of prison culture on inmate attitude change (prisonization) and the parole performance of various types of inmates.

The first problem we encountered in investigating these questions was the difficulty of defining the inmate types in operational terms. Since we were attempting first to empirically establish the existence of inmate types as described by Schrag and his colleagues, we used as a beginning guide the operational definitions of Schrag's types as they were developed by Donald Garrity. Garrity's definitions of the role types, and the attributes required to comprise each, are indicated in Figure 6.1.

Employing inmate record data from the Washington Reformatory and Washington State Penitentiary, Garrity first classified the *square Johns*, then he classified, following in order, the *right guys* and *outlaws*, and finally the *politicians* and *dings*. Although Garrity sought to estimate the optimum sentence for each type, it is our purpose here to discover how successfully he was able to isolate and identify the categories.

An adjustment was indicated for the three categories of *square John*, *right guy*, and *politician* to embrace those individuals who lacked but one of the defining characteristics. A resulting set of three *quasi* categories was established which, in the case of the *quasi-right guy* in the reformatory, resulted in a 40 percent increase in identification when it was coupled with the category *right guy*. Further adaptation was made in expanding the *ding* category to specify the mentally deficient, the psychotic, the homosexual, and the *rapo*. In the reformatory, Garrity failed to classify approximately 27 percent of the inmates; in the pentitentiary, approximately 36 percent could not be classified.

We gathered prison file data for 1180 Men's Colony inmates which included most of the role attributes used by Garrity. These items included psychiatric diagnosis, prison rules violations, the involvement in prison programs, the type of offense, criminality in family, education, the age at first arrest, the prior penal commitments (type and number), community background, mental status (IQ), and marital history. By using a few key variables, we attempted a classification which is outlined in Figure 6.2.

ment and Estimation of Optimum Sentence: Washington State Correctional Institutions," unpublished Ph.D. Dissertation, University of Washington, 1956. See also Donald L. Garrity, "The Prison as a Rehabilitative Agency," in Donald R. Cressey (ed.), *The Prison*, op. cit., pp. 375–378.

In addition to the criteria listed in Figure 6.2, we attempted to establish the following corroborative data for each type.

Outlaw should have:
1. One or more disciplinary reports.
2. Record of a commitment offense of an assaultive nature (assault, rape, attempted murder, etc.)

Square John should have:
1. No reported criminality in family.
2. No commitment for narcotics use, possession, or sale.
3. No arrest before the age of 24.

Politician-Merchant should have:
1. Average or above average intelligence (IQ).
2. Formal education at the high school level or higher.

Right Guy should have:
1. Reported criminality in family.
2. First arrest at an early age.

However, the gross typology outlined in Figure 6.2 was not tested, since we were unable to classify three fourths of the sample population even according to these few attributes. It was possible to identify 47 outlaws, 57 square Johns, 27 politician-merchants, and 110 right guys. To this an additional 118 men were clinically diagnosed as manifesting psychotic traits and could be categorized as dings. Thus, we were able to classify 339 men out of 1180 (34 percent) by using Garrity's operational definition of inmate types.

The difficulty of applying this scheme to the Men's Colony population is fourfold. First, there is a major offense category that is neglected. In the state of Washington at the time of Garrity's study, narcotics offenses were only a small fraction of the prison population; in California at the present time, narcotics users form a considerable proportion of the prison census. To exclude narcotics offenders in our typology, would be a serious omission.

A second problem is that Garrity presents an incomplete logical scheme. That is to say, the criterial attributes for one type are not relevant to another type; they do not have to be present or absent in all cases. For example, age at first arrest is a relevant attribute for *right guy*, but not for *politician* or *outlaw*.

A third problem is that a great leap is required to go from the description of the roles as *behavior* and *outlook* to the defining indicators in

figure 6.1

Attributes

Role Type and Number of Attributes Required for Classification	A Previous Criminal Record	B Behavior Disorder	C Institutional Conduct	D Use of Prison Time	E Type of Offense	F Employment Record	G Family Background
Square John E, F, G (2 out of 3)	None	None	None or less than 1 minor per year	Constructive	Against person or property; sex against adult	Regular	Average or below, no delinquency
Right Guy A, J, K, L, D (3 out of 5)	Several misdemeanors, previous felonies or combination	—	—	Average	Person, property, PV, auto theft	—	Below average, no delinquency; average and delinquency; below average with delinquency
Politician G, L, C, D (2 out of 4)	—	—	None or less than 1 minor per year	Constructive or average	Property or forgery	—	Above average or average with no delinquency
Outlaw F, N, O (2 out of 3)	—	Psychopathic w/o sex disorder, neurotic et al.	Less than one major per year, 1 or more minor, combination	Unconstructive	Person, property, PV, auto, sex against adult	Casual	—
Ding Mentally Deficient D, F (1 out of 2)	—	—	One or more minor, less than 1 major, combination	Average or unconstructive	—	Casual	—
Square John E, F, G (2 out of 3)	—	—	—	—	—	—	—

148

figure 6.1 (continued)

Attributes

Role Type and Number of Attributes Required for Classification	H Education	I Age First Arrest	J Type of Criminal Career	K Prior Penal Commitments	L Community Background	M IQ	N Marital Status	O Family Interests
Right Guy A, J, K, L, D (3 out of 5)	Some high school or less	19 or less	Property or combination	Training school, reformatory, pen., or combination	Urban or transient	—	—	—
Politician G, L, C, D (2 out of 4)	Some high school or more	—	—	—	Urban	Average or above	—	—
Outlaw F, N, O (2 out of 3)	—	—	—	—	—	—	Single or divorced	—
Ding Mentally Deficient D, F (1 out of 2)	Grammar school or less	—	—	—	—	Low or inferior	—	—

Psychotic Ding ALL
⎧ Psychiatric report: psychotic, pre-psychotic, psychopath with sex disorder
⎪ Institution conduct: 1 or more minor, no more than 1 major, or combination
⎨ Use of prison time: Average or unconstructive
⎩ Employment: Casual

Homosexual Ding ALL
⎧ Psychiatric report: Homosexual
⎨ Institution conduct: 1 or more minor, no more than 1 major, or combination
⎩ Previous criminal record: 1 or more misdemeanors, 1 or more felonies, or combination

Rapo Ding ALL
⎧ Offense: Sex against a child
⎪ Previous crime: 1 or more misdemeanors, 1 or more felonies, or combination
⎨ Type criminal career: Sex offenses
⎩ Prison time: Constructive

Is there a psychiatric diagnosis of psychopath
(including antisocial, emotionally unstable,
low frustration tolerance, and weak superego)?

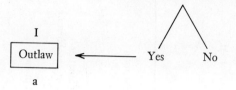

I

| Outlaw |

a

Yes   No

II

| Square
John |

b

Are there disciplinary infractions?

No   Yes

Is there a prior commitment to
youth or adult penal institutions?

No   Yes

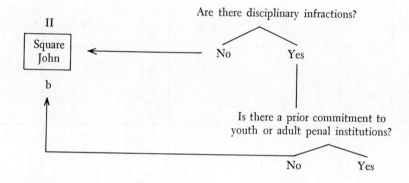

Is the offense grand theft
(excluding auto), forgery,
or property offense?

III

| Politician-
Merchant |

c

Yes

IV

| Right Guy |

d

No

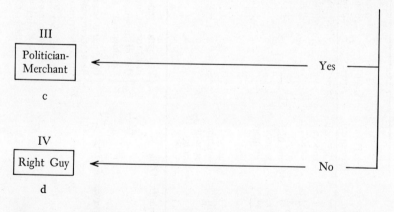

figure 6.2   Procedure for establishing inmate types from inmate record data: No. 1

terms of record about information such as offense, age, family, background, and the like. Even the ease of access to the latter does not settle the doubt about whether a close fit is likely between a typology of such attributes and the theoretical conception of inmate roles. Of course, it is very difficult to find in prison records adequate indicators of theoretical attributes. For example, merchants may be running contraband rackets, but, like the narcotics distributors in the community, personal risk is minimized by the echelons of middlemen and peddlers that exist between the racket boss and law enforcement. Even if an inmate is apprehended, the question a prison disciplinary report usually cannot answer is whether the inmate was merchandising contraband or whether he was a customer. Just as arrest records are poor indicators of criminal sophistication, disciplinary reports are poor indicators of prisoner sophistication. The better the merchant, the fewer times he is reported for violating prison rules. Reliable operational criteria for key attributes of this kind are difficult to find in prison records.

Moreover, the problem of measuring inmate values by construction of a typology led us to consider the possibility that the setting at CMCE might not resemble the prisons studied by Schrag, Garabedian, Wheeler, and Garrity. The Schrag-Garrity scheme is not easily applied to a department of corrections that comprises a number of institutions which house different types of offenders. In the Federal Bureau of Prisons, for example, prisoners are sorted out into reformatories, correctional institutions, medium security penitentiaries and maximum security penitentiaries, and special purpose institutions like the Medical Center according to criteria such as age, seriousness of criminal record, and prison behavior. Similar graded systems operate in Illinois, New York and, an example par excellence, California. Because of this assignment procedure, one might expect to find fewer square Johns at older, maximum security prisons for recidivists and escapees (for example, Leavenworth and Folsom), and fewer outlaws at new, minimum security institutions (for example, Chino and Seagoville). A higher proportion of right guys should be found as the security rating of the prison increases because of the increased criminal maturity of the population. Prison systems with separate facilities for emotionally disturbed inmates, for instance, the California Medical Facility and the Medical Center for Federal Prisoners, should siphon off a high proportion of dings and some outlaws. The California Department of Corrections screens inmates into types and allocates them to the separate institutions where men of a similar type are located.

To overcome some of the difficulties encountered in the Garrity model, we tried several of our own classification schemes. One of these efforts is illustrated in Figure 6.3, where we divided the sample into offender types and then applied additional identical attributes to each type. Again, the insufficient number of cases yielded by this classification discouraged its further use.

	Right Guy		Politician-Merchant		Outlaw Assaultive Drug		Square John	
	Criteria	Cases	Criteria	Cases	Criteria	Cases	Criteria	Cases
Psychiatric diagnosis	−	521	−	521	+	447	−	521
		↓		↓		↓		↓
Criminality in family	+	82	−	439	+	74	−	439
		↓		↓		↓		↓
Prior penal commitment	+	35	+	215	+	40	−	224
		↓		↓		↓		↓
Disciplinary reports	+	18	−	108	+	23	−	109
		↓		↓		↓		↓
Offense:	Robbery, burglary, narcotics	9	Grand theft, forgery, embezzlement	45	Assault	2	Homicide, abortion, sex other than rape	13

figure 6.3   Attrition in successive application of criteria in No. 2.

Other classification schemes that divided these and similar background variables into different types were tried and found unworkable. The chief difficulty continued to be the number of unclassifiable men. We then shifted our thinking to the consideration not of a set of types but of a set of value continuae or dimensions, on which one might locate any given degree of endorsement or indifference.

THE VALUE ORIENTATION BASIS OF INMATE TYPES

The four inmate types suggested by previous writers—right guy, square John, politician-merchant, and outlaw—seem to be the result of logically permuting two components of the inmates code: solidarity among inmates, and opposition to the staff. Thus, the norm-bearer right guy is defined as one who maintains opposition to guards and other staff and who maintains loyalty to the other inmates; the politician or merchant who peddles information or goods must minimize opposition to staff (to obtain these goods) but retains ties to other inmates; the outlaw stands against both staff and other inmates; and the square John is defined as the person who is more opposed to inmates than to staff. (The ding is on a different level of abstraction than the other types and seems more properly treated as a personality syndrome than as a role type.)

The inmate types based on distinctions between degrees of opposition to the staff and solidarity with the inmates may be represented as follows:

		High Opposition to Staff +	Low Opposition to Staff −
High Solidarity with Inmates	+	Right Guy	Politician-Merchant
Low Solidarity with Inmates	−	Outlaw	Square John

But our experience had led us not to expect clearly defined inmate types into which most men fit. If, indeed, the main axes were value orientations, it should be possible to study how differences in the endorsement of these value orientations are related to other aspects of prison conduct, including the response to treatment.

THE MEASUREMENT OF INMATE ATTITUDES AND NORMS

The inmate questionnaire discussed in Chapter V contained items adopted from several sociological definitions of the components of the inmate code.

The general prohibition of "ratting" places value on not providing information to the custodial authorities of the prison. The inmate should be able to take with a smile the pressure and sanctions imposed by the staff and not "cop out." The code also stipulates appropriate cynicism or suspicion concerning the norms of the "legit" world. The maxim is *Don't Be a Sucker.* On the other hand, the code urges altruism: inmates should share extra material goods with other inmates, and it asserts that if the inmates endeavor to stick together, it will lighten the burdens of doing time. Thus the two most general components of the code are a value on opposition to the prison staff and a value on collective solidarity among inmates. The following items were included to measure these components:

(a) Inmates Anderson and Baker, members of the same counseling group, have a serious dispute outside the group. Other group members notice the bad feeling between them and during a session ask Anderson what is wrong. Anderson says there is nothing wrong because he believes that if he tells the reason for the trouble at a group counseling session it would be like ratting on Baker.

How do you personally feel about Anderson's action?

(b) Inmate Dooley gets cut in a knife fight with another inmate. Dooley is called before the disciplinary committee. The committee asks him to tell them who he was fighting with. He refuses to name the other inmate.

How do you personally feel about Dooley's action?

(c) When the inmates stick together it is a lot easier to do time.

(d) If an inmate gets some important inside information, the right thing to do is to share it with his friends.

(e) In prison, a good rule to follow is to share any extra goods with your friends.

The significance of the concept of the inmate code is linked to the concept of socialization into the prison community's way of life, in which the code is functional for adjustment. The incoming novice quickly learns that many aspects of his civilian self are irrelevant to institution life. At time of reception at prison, many new admissions experience degradation and a corresponding need for ego support.[18] The inmate code exhibits the features of a protective ethos, counseling a collective stance that is functional amid the deprivations of institutional living, and drawing on elements of solidarity that also are valued in the playgrounds, neighborhoods, and gangs of preprison life as well. However, certain contradictions in the code and its actual implementation often serve to further frustrate the inmate. In his need for a substitute anchorage in the prison environment, the inmate seeks to apply the tenets of the code but is confronted with dual injunctions to "throw in his lot with his fellow inmates" yet "look out for himself" in an exploitative atmosphere. A full appreciation of the informal code of institutional living requires that this internal conflict be recognized. To some extent the myth of solidarity is espoused at the same time that the realities of prison life exhibit the character of "competition" for the good things the life affords. To the extent that it is endorsed, the inmate code may be thought of as acting like a brake on the unfettered exercise of force and cunning in the interaction of men in prison.

Thus, it has often been observed that, although inmate solidarity and a united front against the prison administration is a stated ideal of the inmate code, many inmates individually are wary and distrustful of other inmates, and they express a considerable sense of alienation and rootlessness in social relations in general.

Accordingly, a number of items posing questions about isolation and alienation were included in the questionnaire.

[18] See Goffman, op. cit., and Garfinkel, op. cit.

(a) In prison I keep pretty much to myself.

(b) There are very few inmates I really trust.

(c) There is really no group of men in this institution I am close with.

(d) There are basically just two kinds of people in the world, those in the know and those who are suckers.

(e) In general, police, judges, and prosecutors are about as crooked as the people they send to prison.

(f) These days a person doesn't really know whom he can count on.

Finally, in addition to questions to elicit responses about the inmate values and inmate feelings of individual isolation and alienation, we were interested in their opinion of the group counseling program at the prison. We, therefore, included items derived from statements, overheard in groups or in interviews, concerning the therapeutic impact of the group sessions, such as:

(a) Inmates in group counseling are less likely to violate parole than those who do not participate.

(b) Offenders in group counseling tend to break fewer prison rules than those who do not participate.

Questions about values, attitudes, the appropriate behavior of prison staff and inmates, and opinions concerning the treatment program brought the total number of items in the present analysis to 37 (see Table 6.1).

The interest at the outset was to determine if responses were patterned in a manner consistent with the a priori concepts listed above. Second, we wished to reduce the 37 scores to a much smaller number so that respondents could be cross classified on these and other variables without an excessively large number of tables to analyze.

Responses to the 37 items on the Inmate Questionnaire: Time 1 were intercorrelated, and the matrix factor analyzed, using the principal axis method. Thirteen factors were extracted before the eigenvalue was less than unity. Various numbers of factors were rotated via the verimax technique to obtain the best approximation to orthogonal simple structure. The six-factor solution was judged most satisfactory, accounting for 82 percent of the common factor variance.

On the Inmate Questionnaire: Time 2, administered six months after the first questionnaire, the identical items were cast into an intercorrelation matrix and factored. The first six factors accounted for 78 percent of the common factor variance and were retained for rotation.

Rotation of the second matrix was done independently of the first rotation. Although the order of the factors varied from Time 1 to Time

table 6.1   Thirty-Seven Items in the Factor Analysis

Var. 1   Inmates Anderson and Baker, members of the same counseling group, have a serious dispute outside the group. Other group members notice the bad feeling between them and during a session ask Anderson what is wrong. Anderson says there is nothing wrong because he believes that if he tells the reason for the trouble at a group counseling session it would be like ratting on Baker.

How do you personally feel about Anderson's action?

Var. 2   Inmate Dooley gets cut in a knife fight with another inmate. Dooley is called before the disciplinary committee. The committee asks him to tell them who he was fighting with. He refuses to name the other inmate.

How do you personally feel about Dooley's action?

Var. 3   If you reveal too much about yourself to any staff member, the information will probably be used against you.

Var. 4   Inmates Smith and Long are very good friends. Smith has contraband that was smuggled into the institution by a visitor. Smith tells Long he thinks the officers are suspicious, and asks Long to hide the contraband for him for a few days. Long takes it and hides it.

How do you personally feel about Long's action?

Var. 5   An inmate, without thinking, commits a minor rule infraction. He is given a "write-up" by a Correctional Officer who saw the violation. Later, three other inmates are talking to each other about it. Two of them criticize the officer. The third inmate, Sykes, defends the officer saying the officer was only doing his duty.

How do you personally feel about Sykes' action?

Var. 6   The best way to do time is to grin and bear it and not let the staff know that anything is getting you down.

Var. 7   If I have personal difficulties, the best people to talk them over with are staff.

Var. 8   Group counseling provides a lot of information to the staff which is used against the inmate.

Var. 9   An inmate, Smith, is generally believed to be an informer. Many inmates will have nothing to do with him. Smith signs up for a counseling group. Some of the group members resent his presence because they do not trust him and don't want to associate with him in any way. However, one member, inmate Jones, suggests the group express their feelings toward Smith and give Smith the opportunity to explain or defend himself.

How do you personally feel about Jones' suggestion?

table 6.1 (*continued*)

Var. 10	In dealing with staff, the inmate should stick up for what he feels is right and not let the staff set his standards or morals for him.
Var. 11	In prison I keep pretty much to myself.
Var. 12	There are very few inmates I really trust.
Var. 13	There is really no group of men in this institution I am close with.
Var. 14	I don't feel I have very much in common with other inmates here.
Var. 15	Most of the other inmates here are not loyal to each other when the chips are down.
Var. 16	The best way to do time is to mind your own business and have as little to do as possible with other inmates.
Var. 17	Inmates in group counseling are less likely to violate parole than those who do not participate.
Var. 18	Offenders in group counseling tend to break fewer prison rules than those who do not participate.
Var. 19	The group counseling program helps the inmate to better understand himself.
Var. 20	Group counseling brings about basic personality change in many offenders.
Var. 21	An officer who leads a counseling group is better able to understand an inmate's problems.
Var. 22	It's hardly fair to bring children into the world with the way things look for the future.
Var. 23	In spite of what some people say, the lot of the average man is getting worse, not better.
Var. 24	Nowadays, a person has to live pretty much for today and let tomorrow take care of itself.
Var. 25	There are basically just two kinds of people in the world, those in the know and those who are suckers.
Var. 26	In general, police, judges, and prosecutors are about as crooked as the people they send to prison.
Var. 27	These days a person doesn't really know whom he can count on.
Var. 28	Being with understanding fellow inmates gives a man a sense of not being totally alone.
Var. 29	I enjoy taking part in a good bull session with other inmates.
Var. 30	In prison, a good rule to follow is to share any extra goods with your friends.

table 6.1 (continued)

Var. 31   When the inmates stick together it is a lot easier to do time.

Var. 32   If an inmate gets some important inside information, the right thing to do is to share it with his friends.

Var. 33   In prison, generally, the only persons you really talk your personal problems over with are inmate friends.

Var. 34   The staff has made clear how they expect you to behave if you are to stay out of trouble.

Var. 35   Generally speaking, correctional officers are not competent to lead group counseling sessions.

Var. 36   Most men I know do *not* talk frankly and openly of their personal problems in group counseling.

Var. 37   There's a little larceny in everybody.

---

2 (a feature of the rotation procedure that is substantively irrelevant), the makeup of the factors was nearly identical. In each case the first five factors can be measured and interpreted with considerable clarity (see Table 6.2).

Factor A is determined by items that express the experience or desirability of solidarity among inmates, and it will be referred to as *Solidarity*. Factor B is formed by high loadings on items which state that the respondent feels separated, isolated, and distrustful of other inmates; it will be called *Isolation*. Factor C consists of items that express the therapeutic effects of counseling and is termed *Value of Counseling*. Factor D seems a measure of cynicism, anomie, and alienation, and it has been labeled *Alienation*. Factor E consists of items that express the value of opposition to staff, and keeping silent; it has been named *Opposition to Staff*. The last Factor (F) is, in both matrices, too vague to interpret.

Our interpretation of Factor A (Solidarity) and Factor E (Opposition) as measures of the inmate code is supported by a cross check with several facts that have been asserted in previous qualitative descriptions of prisons. It has been observed that prisonization—the process of taking on the values of the inmate community—is to some extent a function of early exposure to crime and arrest and time in prison, and that it serves to sanction continued illegal behavior. Scores on Opposition were significantly related to age at first arrest. Persons arrested early in their lives are more opposed to staff than men whose first arrest was late in their career (see Table 6.3).

The number of disciplinary reports recorded for an inmate is related to endorsement of opposition to staff. Men with no disciplinary reports are less apt to endorse that component of the inmate code, as is shown in Table 6.4.

This interpretation of the opposition factor is further strengthened by the correlation of differences in the endorsement of "opposition" and responses to open-end questions. When asked "what is the lowest form of inmate?" men gave a variety of answers, among which was "informer." Men high on opposition more often nominate the "informer" than men who reject this value (see Table 6.5). Similarly, when asked to state in their own words the "best kind of inmate," men endorsing the inmate code more often said the best kind of inmate is the man who does his own time (see Table 6.6).

The attitudes measured by the structured items are consistent with the replies expressed on the open-end question about the "main criticism of counseling." A tendency to perceive little value in counseling was significantly correlated with scores on the factor labeled *"value of counseling"* as well as related to scores on scales interpreted as *Isolation* from the *Inmate Community* (more isolated respondents more often expressing no criticism of counseling, less isolated seeing little value in counseling); *Alienation* (persons low on alienation being most critical of counseling leadership); and *Opposition* (men opposed to giving information to staff and who distrusted staff were more critical of the counseling program). All of these relationships were significantly above chance as measured by chi-square ($p < .01$).

TREATMENT RELATED DIFFERENCES IN ENDORSEMENT OF NORMS

One of the aims of the study design was to determine whether group counseling sessions lowered the endorsement of the norms of the inmate community. To the extent that counseling is successful, it should increase communication, should increase the candid disclosure of feeling states, and should call defenses and rationalizations into question. Thus it was hypothesized that in comparison with men in the control sample, (1) by broadening the basis of communication, counseling weakens adherence to the norm prescribing *opposition* to staff; (2) by increasing informal (status-suppressing) communication with the staff, and the discussion of individual weaknesses, counseling decreases collective *solidarity* among inmates; (3) because of the interaction in discussion of common personal problems, group counseling will result in the increased trust (reduced isolation) of the other inmates; and (4) by implication, espousing "legitimate values," counseling should result in lower *alienation* as measured by S role items. Finally, (5) to the extent that it is successful, counseling should result in more favorable attitudes toward the *value of counseling*.

table 6.2 Rotated Factor Matrices[a] of 37 Attitude Items at Time One (T_1) and Time Two (T_2)

Variable Number	Factor A, Solidarity		Factor B, Isolation		Factor C, Value of Counseling		Factor D, Alienation		Factor E, Opposition to Staff		Factor F (Not Interpretable)		H^2_1	H^2_2
	T_1	T_2	T_1	T_2	T_1	T_2	T_1	T_2	T_1	T_2	T_1	T_2		
28	.51	−.59	.02	.14	−.32	−.12	.04	.01	−.08	.05	.12	.08	.39	.39
29	.53	−.57	.23	−.23	−.12	−.03	−.12	.07	.24	−.04	.03	.01	.42	.39
30	.59	−.50	.04	−.13	.10	.01	.15	−.01	−.02	−.13	.06	−.03	.39	.28
31	.53	−.47	−.10	.03	.08	−.08	.17	−.21	.34	−.31	.03	−.15	.45	.39
32	.54	−.41	.15	−.16	.02	−.05	.08	−.11	−.04	−.18	−.05	−.25	.32	.31
33	.45	−.40	−.06	−.03	.09	.09	.04	−.07	.38	−.28	−.13	−.30	.37	.34
11	−.14	.15	−.56	.66	.02	−.05	.06	−.05	.16	−.08	−.06	−.04	.37	.47
12	−.04	−.03	−.68	.67	−.04	−.09	.06	.01	−.03	−.16	−.06	−.20	.47	.52
13	−.32	.18	−.43	.58	−.05	−.02	.18	−.10	.06	.07	.05	.08	.33	.39
14	−.30	.31	−.49	.53	.05	−.02	.19	−.15	−.20	.05	−.10	−.15	.42	.43
15	.01	−.13	−.53	.51	−.05	.11	−.02	.03	.05	.05	−.04	.10	.29	.30
16	−.15	.24	−.59	.50	.11	.00	.19	−.20	.14	−.29	.13	.20	.46	.47
17	−.01	.04	.03	.01	−.80	−.76	−.02	.04	−.13	.08	−.02	−.09	.65	.59
18	−.02	−.01	.02	−.03	−.72	−.73	.01	.07	−.13	.08	−.07	−.09	.55	.55
19	−.01	−.12	−.03	.07	−.55	−.59	−.14	.08	−.18	.27	.33	.28	.46	.52
20	.06	.00	.03	−.05	−.59	−.58	−.00	−.08	−.04	.15	.35	.26	.48	.43

160

Variable Number	Factor A, Solidarity		Factor B, Isolation		Factor C, Value of Counseling		Factor D, Alienation		Factor E, Opposition to Staff		Factor F (Not Interpretable)		H^2_1	H^2_2
	T_1	T_2	T_1	T_2	T_1	T_2	T_1	T_2	T_1	T_2	T_1	T_2		
22	.21	.03	-.10	-.01	.03	.03	.68	-.74	-.15	.05	-.04	-.14	.55	.58
23	.14	.06	-.22	.20	.01	.02	.65	-.71	-.10	.05	-.27	-.08	.57	.56
24	-.04	-.00	-.04	-.03	-.04	-.04	.65	-.69	.20	-.16	-.02	.02	.47	.50
25	-.02	-.10	.15	-.13	-.09	-.08	.62	-.51	.27	-.23	.08	.33	.49	.45
26	-.04	-.15	-.27	.20	.08	.20	.54	-.46	.26	-.25	.01	.12	.44	.39
27	.10	-.13	-.32	.40	.18	.04	.44	-.48	.26	-.19	.08	.02	.41	.44
1	-.00	.02	-.23	.10	.12	.07	.18	.00	.56	-.62	.11	.06	.43	.41
2	.22	-.11	-.19	.02	.07	.14	-.01	-.00	.58	-.56	-.05	.03	.43	.35
4	.06	-.16	.09	-.10	.09	-.00	.12	-.09	.51	-.51	-.25	-.17	.35	.33
5	.00	.11	-.00	.56	-.07	-.15	-.03	.00	-.52	.48	.34	.11	.39	.28
6	.03	-.08	-.25	.20	.00	.04	.21	-.20	.58	-.46	.08	-.03	.45	.30
7	.04	.05	.05	-.06	-.24	-.32	-.09	.09	-.50	.46	.26	.39	.38	.48
21	.08	-.11	-.02	-.01	-.13	-.48	-.04	-.01	-.15	.21	.60	.17	.41	.31
34	-.03	.06	-.28	.02	-.21	-.15	-.12	.03	.02	-.03	.33	.67	.25	.48
35	.02	-.22	-.35	.32	.03	.26	.04	.04	.17	-.19	-.54	-.31	.45	.35
3	.11	-.17	-.41	.26	.12	.12	.45	-.17	.39	-.53	-.07	.05	.55	.42
8	.10	-.08	-.13	.14	.23	.15	.43	-.35	.32	-.44	-.14	-.08	.40	.37
9	-.04	-.13	-.16	.17	-.21	-.11	-.18	.03	-.29	.37	-.22	-.09	.23	.21
10	-.09	-.25	-.37	.30	.03	.11	.21	-.01	.26	-.36	-.16	.08	.28	.30
36	.28	-.36	-.33	.36	.30	.25	-.01	-.04	.05	.08	-.16	.17	.30	.37
37	.24	-.28	-.37	.29	.15	.19	.09	-.17	.21	-.08	.12	.26	.29	.30

a Variables have been reordered to facilitate interpretation within factor and across time periods.

table 6.3 Opposition to Staff and Inmate Solidarity by Age at First Arrest (in Percent)

Factor Themes	Age at First Arrest			
	17 and younger ($N = 447$)	18–21 ($N = 174$)	22–25 ($N = 118$)	26+ ($N = 124$)
Opposition[a]				
Strongly reject	19	23	32	23
Reject	26	30	29	31
Endorse	32	30	22	33
Strongly endorse	23	17	17	13
Total	100	100	100	100
Solidarity[b]				
Strongly reject	14	23	24	26
Reject	26	24	22	20
Endorse	32	31	31	31
Strongly endorse	28	22	23	23
Total	100	100	100	100

[a] $\chi^2 = 18.56$, degrees of freedom = 9, p < .05, gamma = − .143.
[b] $\chi^2 = 15.91$, degrees of freedom = 9, not significant.

table 6.4 Number of Recorded Disciplinary Actions for Infractions of Prison Regulations ("Pink Slips") by Degree of Opposition to Staff (in Percent)

Opposition	Disciplinary Actions[a]		
	None	One	Two or More
Strongly reject	23	21	21
Reject	31	26	14
Endorse	31	29	31
Strongly endorse	15	24	34
Total	100	100	100
N	(536)	(224)	(88)

Table N = 848 (incomplete information = 23)
$\chi^2 = 26.70$
Degrees of freedom = 6
p < .001
Gamma = .174

[a] During current sentence only while at CMCE.

162

table 6.5 Opposition to Staff by Opinion: "What is worst kind of inmate?" (in Percent)

Worst Kind of Inmate

Opposition	Informer	Homo-sexual	Offensive Personal	Child Molest	Recidivist	Agitator	Thief	Other	Total	
Strongly reject	18	15	18	9	5	8	5	22	100	(142)
Reject	28	16	14	13	2	2	9	16	100	(163)
Endorse	40	11	15	9	1	5	9	10	100	(186)
Strongly endorse	49	14	12	10	1	3	5	6	100	(139)

Table $N = 630$ (no answers = 241)
$\chi^2 = 59.74$
Degrees of freedom = 21
$p < .001$
Gamma = $-.252$

163

table 6.6 Opposition to Staff by Opinion: "What is best kind of inmate?" (in Percent)

Best Kind of Inmate

Opposition	Does Own Time	Cooperates	Helps Self	Helps Other Inmates	Gets Out	Stable Personality	Other	Total	N
Strongly reject	24	9	24	12	4	18	9	100	(146)
Reject	35	9	15	9	4	20	8	100	(173)
Endorse	43	12	14	9	2	15	5	100	(200)
Strongly endorse	47	11	8	8	3	15	8	100	(130)

Table $N = 649$ (No answers = 222)
$\chi^2 = 32.85$
Degrees of freedom = 18
$p < .02$
Gamma = −.160

164

ARE VALUE ORIENTATIONS MODIFIED BY TREATMENT?

To test the effect of counseling on norms in the most direct way possible with data available, comparisons were made on a panel of inmates surveyed at a six-month interval. (A total of 554 respondents at time 1 were still in prison at time 2.) This period was one of peak activity at the prison, with all programs in full operation. Respondents were drawn from all categories of treatment and controls. The questions posed were: "Is there change in endorsement of norms in treatment groups, and is this change greater for treatment than for controls?"

Table 6.7 displays means and distributions of 20 items, grouped by the factor on which they are located. A comparison of each item, first at time 1 and then at time 2, reveals no overall significant changes. On items measuring *solidarity*, there is a slight shift in the direction of greater rejection of the items. This is also somewhat true of items in factor C (value of group counseling), with somewhat more optimism expressed at time 1 as compared with six months later. But the shifts are slight.

Table 6.8 shows the items summed into factor scores and cross tabulated in 2×2 tables. Dichotomized score means and standard deviations are shown, as well as chi square for change as suggested by Siegal.[19] There is no change greater than chance in any table; the one table showing a significant coefficient (*alienation*) seems due to the very skewed table, where most cases fall in one of the four cells.

Of course, it is possible that the effect of counseling groups is to reduce the endorsement of inmate norms for men in treatment. To determine if there is a differential shift in endorsement or a differential turnover for individuals in treatment and control categories, distributions, means, and turnover tables were computed within each treatment category. They are displayed in Tables 6.9 and 6.10. No main effects may be seen for treatment. There is a significant tendency for men in the mandatory controls category to become less isolated from other inmates, and for declared opposition to staff to be slightly lower at time 2 for the men in the large groups. But there is no evidence that treatment reduces the endorsement of inmate norms and beliefs as measured by these items.[20]

[19] Chi square for change is computed as $(A - D)^2/A + D$. It takes into account any change in either direction. See S. Siegal, *Non Parametric Statistics for the Behavioral Sciences*, pp. 63–67.

[20] Wilson and Snodgrass studied the relationship between a "therapeutic community" established in a maximum security institution and endorsement of the prison code, concluding that "the social organization of the therapeutic community is advantageous in opposing the prison code." The study did not, however, compare code endorsement by inmate types and did not involve comparisons of endorsement of the code by randomly

table 6.7   Twenty Items Stating Inmate Value Orientations: Differences Over a Six-Month Period

Factor Theme: Solidarity with Other Inmates

ITEM	TIME 1 Accept 1	2	Reject 3	4	Total	NA	TIME 2 Accept 1	2	Reject 3	4	Total	NA
In prison a good rule to follow is to share any extra goods with your friends	5 (27)	56 (299)	36 (189)	3 (15)	100 (530)	(24)	2 (13)	50 (263)	43 (230)	5 (28)	100 (534)	(20)
	Mean = 2.36		SD = .624				Mean = 2.51		SD = .635			
Being with understanding fellow inmates gives a man a sense of not being totally alone	10 (52)	79 (419)	10 (52)	1 (7)	100 (530)	(24)	11 (59)	71 (387)	16 (86)	2 (15)	100 (547)	(7)
	Mean = 2.03		SD = .498				Mean = 2.10		SD = .603			
If an inmate gets some important inside information the right thing to do is to share it with friends	1 (8)	40 (207)	53 (272)	6 (28)	100 (515)	(39)	2 (12)	35 (186)	54 (288)	9 (47)	100 (533)	(21)
	Mean = 2.62		SD = .612				Mean = 2.69		SD = .659			
I enjoy taking part in a good bull session with other inmates	4 (21)	62 (326)	30 (158)	4 (25)	100 (530)	(24)	3 (19)	64 (351)	28 (152)	5 (26)	100 (548)	(6)
	Mean = 2.35		SD = .634				Mean = 2.34		SD = .623			

table 6.7 (continued)

Factor Theme: Isolation from Other Inmates

ITEM	TIME 1 Accept		Reject		Total	NA	TIME 2 Accept		Reject		Total	NA
	1	2	3	4			1	2	3	4		
In prison I keep pretty much to myself	8 (44)	54 (282)	35 (185)	3 (16)	100 (527)	(27)	8 (47)	54 (294)	36 (197)	2 (11)	100 (549)	(5)
	Mean = 2.33		SD = .670				Mean = 2.31		SD = .653			
There are very few inmates I really trust	12 (66)	58 (311)	29 (153)	1 (9)	100 (539)	(15)	18 (97)	59 (320)	21 (113)	2 (10)	100 (540)	(14)
	Mean = 2.19		SD = .660				Mean = 2.07		SD = .677			
Most of the other inmates here are not loyal to each other when chips are down	14 (74)	59 (310)	25 (128)	2 (12)	100 (524)	(30)	13 (69)	60 (316)	25 (130)	2 (15)	100 (530)	(24)
	Mean = 2.15		SD = .675				Mean = 2.17		SD = .678			
The best way to do time is to mind your own business and have as little to do as possible with other inmates	16 (89)	49 (262)	30 (164)	5 (28)	100 (543)	(11)	10 (54)	49 (260)	39 (207)	2 (13)	100 (534)	(20)
	Mean = 2.24		SD = .784				Mean = 2.34		SD = .688			

table 6.7 Twenty Items Stating Inmate Value Orientations: Differences Over a Six-Month Period (continued)

Factor Theme: Value of Counseling

ITEM	TIME 1						TIME 2					
	Accept 1	2	Reject 3	4	Total	NA	Accept 1	2	Reject 3	4	Total	NA
The group counseling program helps the inmate to better understand himself	17 (92)	64 (337)	15 (80)	4 (20)	100 (529)	(25)	17 (88)	66 (345)	16 (86)	1 (9)	100 (528)	(26)
	Mean = 2.05		SD = .688				Mean = 2.03		SD = .630			
Offenders in group counseling tend to break fewer prison rules than those who do not participate	a†	58 (267)	42 (196)	a	100 (463)	(91)	a	49 (240)	51 (249)	a	100 (489)	(65)
	Mean = 2.42		SD = .494				Mean = 2.51		SD = .500			
Inmates in group counseling are less likely to violate parole than those who do not participate	a	51 (231)	49 (226)	a	100 (457)	(97)	a	49 (242)	51 (248)	a	100 (490)	(64)
	Mean = 2.49		SD = .500				Mean = 2.51		SD = .500			
Group counseling brings about basic personality changes in many offenders	a	77 (387)	23 (115)	a	100 (502)	(52)	a	76 (392)	24 (125)	a	100 (517)	(37)
	Mean = 2.23		SD = .420				Mean = 2.24		SD = .428			

table 6.7 (continued)

Factor Theme: Alienation from Conventional Beliefs

ITEM	TIME 1								TIME 2							
	Accept		Reject						Accept		Reject					
	1	2	3	4	Total	NA			1	2	3	4	Total	NA		
In general police, judges, and prosecutors are about as crooked as the people they send to prison	8 (41)	24 (126)	59 (309)	9 (46)	100 (522)	(32)	Mean = 2.69	SD = .740	7 (39)	23 (120)	60 (317)	10 (56)	100 (532)	(22)	Mean = 2.73	SD = .744
Nowadays a person has to live pretty much for today and let tomorrow take care of itself	2 (13)	18 (97)	65 (354)	15 (79)	100 (543)	(11)	Mean = 2.92	SD = .643	4 (21)	21 (112)	59 (319)	16 (86)	100 (538)	(16)	Mean = 2.87	SD = .713
In spite of what some people say the lot of the average man is getting worse not better	2 (13)	23 (127)	66 (356)	9 (46)	100 (542)	(12)	Mean = 2.80	SD = .613	3 (18)	21 (109)	66 (352)	10 (54)	100 (531)	(21)	Mean = 2.84	SD = .619
It's hardly fair to bring children into the world the way things look for the future	2 (13)	8 (44)	73 (396)	17 (91)	100 (544)	(10)	Mean = 3.04	SD = .585	2 (14)	12 (66)	66 (356)	20 (106)	100 (542)	(12)	Mean = 3.02	SD = .648

table 6.7 Twenty Items Stating Inmate Value Orientations: Differences Over a Six-Month Period (continued)

Factor Theme: Opposition to Staff

ITEM	TIME 1						TIME 2					
	Accept		Reject				Accept		Reject			
	1	2	3	4	Total	NA	1	2	3	4	Total	NA
Inmates Anderson and Baker, members of the same counseling group, have a serious dispute outside the group. During a session Anderson is asked what is wrong. He says nothing is wrong because he feels to do so would be ratting on Baker. How do you feel?	4 (23)	44 (232)	48 (249)	4 (23)	100 (527)	(27)	5 (29)	47 (251)	44 (235)	4 (21)	100 (536)	(18)
	Mean = 2.52		SD = .651				Mean = 2.46		SD = .660			
Inmate Dooley gets cut in a knife fight with another inmate. The discipline committee asks him to tell who he was fighting. He refuses. How do you feel?	19 (102)	57 (301)	19 (103)	5 (25)	100 (531)	(23)	14 (77)	59 (312)	23 (122)	4 (20)	100 (531)	(23)
	Mean = 2.10		SD = .752				Mean = 2.16		SD = .707			

Factor Theme: Opposition to Staff

ITEM	TIME 1 Accept........Reject						TIME 2 Accept........Reject					
	1	2	3	4	Total	NA	1	2	3	4	Total	NA
Inmates Smith and Long are good friends. Smith has smuggled contraband and asks Long to hide it. Long hides it. How do you feel about Long's action?	2 (13)	16 (87)	57 (298)	25 (131)	100 (529)	(25)	3 (18)	20 (106)	56 (295)	21 (111)	100 (530)	(24)
	Mean = 3.03		SD = .714				Mean = 2.94		SD = .736			
An inmate commits a minor rule infraction and is "written up" by an officer. Later three inmates are talking about it. Two criticize the officer. A third inmate, Sykes, defends the officer saying he was only doing his duty. How do you feel about Sykes?	6 (30)	63 (331)	25 (131)	6 (32)	100 (524)	(30)	6 (36)	65 (347)	24 (127)	5 (26)	100 (536)	(18)
	Mean = 2.31		SD = .673				Mean = 2.27		SD = .653			

* 1 = strongly agree, 2 = agree, 3 = disagree, 4 = strongly disagree.

† a = Agree and Disagree, only alternatives provided.

table 6.8 Change in Inmate Value Orientation over a Six-Month Period in Prison

Solidarity with Inmates

time 2	time 1 Accept	time 1 Reject
A	166	55
R	80	157

Sum = 458
x^2 change = 1.8

	time 1	time 2
$\bar{x}$:	1.52	1.46
σ:	.500	.499

Isolation from Other Inmates

time 2	time 1 Accept	time 1 Reject
A	213	69
R	59	115

Sum = 456
x^2 change = .79

	time 1	time 2
$\bar{x}$:	1.38	1.40
σ:	.486	.491

Value of Counseling

time 2	time 1 Accept	time 1 Reject
A	57	116
R	45	156

Sum = 374
x^2 change = 2.9

	time 1	time 2
$\bar{x}$:	1.46	1.42
σ:	.499	.493

Alienation from Conventional Beliefs

time 2	time 1 Accept	time 1 Reject
A	22	36
R	17	414

Sum = 489
x^2 change = 6.8[a]

	time 1	time 2
$\bar{x}$:	1.88	1.92
σ:	.323	.271

Opposition to Staff

time 2	time 1 Accept	time 1 Reject
A	102	77
R	63	222

Sum = 464
x^2 change = 1.39

	time 1	time 2
$\bar{x}$:	1.61	1.64
σ:	.487	.479

[a] There was a greater than chance turnover ($p < .01$) on alienation from conventional beliefs, but an inspection of the table shows most cases rejecting scale at both time 1 and time 2. Also see item distributions, Table 6.5.

table 6.9   Change in Values, in Treatment and Control Groups (in Percent)

		Time 1 Endorse ────→ Reject						Time 2 (6 months later) Endorse ────→ Reject							
		1	2	3	4	5	Σ	1	2	3	4	5	Σ	$\bar{x}_{t1}$	$\bar{x}_{t2}$
1	Voluntary small group	21	28	31	16	4	(164)	22	26	27	19	5	(170)	2.53	2.59
	Mandatory small group	26	32	26	12	4	(76)	21	28	30	17	4	(82)	2.36	2.55
	Mandatory large group	15	12	15	23	4	(26)	6	15	46	27	6	(33)	2.58	3.12
	Voluntary control	33	33	17	17	0	(42)	12	31	45	5	7	(42)	2.17	2.64
	Mandatory control	23	31	31	10	5	(174)	20	31	21	20	8	(185)	2.42	2.62
2	Voluntary small group	34	29	22	8	7	(163)	30	28	28	8	6	(169)	2.24	2.30
	Mandatory small group	34	31	20	12	3	(80)	30	34	22	10	4	(84)	2.19	2.23
	Mandatory large group	24	38	17	21	0	(29)	46	18	15	18	3	(33)	2.34	2.15
	Voluntary control	39	20	20	14	7	(41)	44	28	15	10	3	(39)	2.32	2.00
	Mandatory control	28	25	25	15	6	(177)	33	31	16	11	9	(174)	2.46	2.32
3	Voluntary small group	49	20	16	10	5	(152)	43	20	21	7	9	(149)	2.03	2.19
	Mandatory small group	32	22	16	17	13	(71)	31	19	29	12	9	(77)	2.55	2.48
	Mandatory large group	43	25	14	4	14	(28)	33	22	15	19	11	(27)	2.21	2.52
	Voluntary control	33	8	14	17	28	(36)	11	14	31	22	22	(36)	2.97	3.31
	Mandatory control	30	24	24	12	10	(148)	33	22	25	8	12	(162)	2.49	2.44

table 6.9 Change in Values, in Treatment and Control Groups (in Percent) (continued)

		Time 1 Endorse → Reject						Time 2 (6 months later) Endorse → Reject						$\bar{x}_{t1}$	$\bar{x}_{t2}$
		1	2	3	4	5	Σ	1	2	3	4	5	Σ		
4	Voluntary small group	4	7	15	30	44	(166)	6	7	16	25	46	(172)	4.01	3.97
	Mandatory small group	1	5	18	22	54	(82)	2	12	11	24	51	(84)	4.22	4.10
	Mandatory large group	0	3	13	30	53	(30)	0	6	15	42	36	(33)	4.33	4.09
	Voluntary control	2	2	22	24	49	(45)	0	7	21	12	60	(43)	4.16	4.26
	Mandatory control	3	4	14	32	48	(187)	4	7	11	29	50	(185)	4.17	4.13
5	Voluntary small group	6	32	42	18	2	(164)	9	29	40	19	3	(160)	2.79	2.76
	Mandatory small group	6	28	41	21	4	(78)	6	30	43	20	1	(80)	2.87	2.82
	Mandatory large group	6	16	36	39	3	(31)	10	35	31	21	3	(29)	3.16	2.72
	Voluntary control	9	40	33	13	4	(45)	11	32	36	21	0	(44)	2.64	2.66
	Mandatory control	2	30	39	25	4	(177)	5	32	35	26	2	(190)	3.00	2.88

1 = solidarity among inmates.
2 = isolation from other inmates.
3 = value of counseling.
4 = alienation from conventional beliefs.
5 = opposition to staff.

table 6.10   Change Over Six Months on Values within Each Treatment Category

	Solidarity with Inmates			Isolation from Other Inmates			Value of Counseling			Alienation from Conventional Beliefs			Opposition to Staff		
		Hi	Lo		Hi	Lo		Hi	Lo		Hi	Lo		Hi	Lo
Voluntary small group	H	54	21	H	71	19	H	70	13	H	9	13	H	29	27
	L	21	59	L	28	38	L	20	27	L	10	129	L	27	65
Mandatory small group	H	27	7	H	41	10	H	22	8	H	5	6	H	15	11
	L	15	24	L	11	17	L	10	21	L	0	70	L	12	37
Mandatory large group	H	5	0	H	15	4	H	12	1	H	1	1	H	6	7
	L	9	11	L	3	7	L	4	7	L	0	27	L	1	14[a]
Voluntary controls	H	15	3	H	18	6	H	5	1	H	1	2	H	15	3
	L	10	11	L	3	8	L	7	16[a]	L	1	38	L	5	19
Mandatory controls	H	64	24	H	68	30	H	52	17	H	6	13	H	36	29
	L	25	52	L	13	45[b]	L	15	45	L	6	150	L	18	87

Note. Number of subjects in each treatment category given; tables exclude cases which could not be scored because of nonresponse on some of the items, resulting in varying table totals.

[a] χ^2 for change = 4.5; $p < .05$.
[b] χ^2 for change = 6.7; $p < .01$.

SUMMARY

Our efforts to demonstrate clear, differentiated types of inmates (right guy, outlaw, and the like) were unsuccessful. Our observations at CMCE, have led us to question the extent to which such inmate types describe the bulk of the population of any institution in a departmental system of prison. However, we did adopt a dimensional mode of representing inmate values, derived from the factor analysis of questionnaire responses. We did not find that men in group counseling altered their endorsement of inmate values in a conformative (law-abiding) direction. Instead we found shifts toward greater dissatisfaction with treatment and much shifting and changing of views in both directions over a six-month period.

On the basis of these data, then, we must conclude that group counseling did not alter the endorsement of inmate norms, and correspondingly that to the extent that postrelease criminality is supported by continued endorsement of these values, group counseling in prison does not affect this source of parole violation.

selected experimental and control groups. See John M. Wilson and Jon D. Snodgrass, "The Prison Code in a Therapeutic Community," *The Journal of Criminal Law, Criminology and Police Science*, **60** (December 1969), pp. 472–478. Other reports of the relationship between inmate social organization and treatment programs include: Howard W. Polsky, *Cottage Six: The Social System of Delinquent Boys in Residential Treatment*, New York: Russell Sage Foundation, 1962; Elliot Studt, Sheldon L. Messinger, Thomas P. Wilson, *C-Unit: Search for Community in Prison*, op. cit.; David Street, Robert D. Vinter, and Charles Perrow, *Organization for Treatment*, New York: The Free Press, 1966; Charles R. Tittle and Drollene P. Tittle, "Structural Handicaps to Therapeutic Participation: A Case Study," *Social Problems*, **13** (Summer 1965), pp. 75–82.

‖‖‖

Parole: release from prison under conditions of minimum custody

(with Reneé E. Ward)

If the men from treatment and control varieties in the study design were discharged directly to a free civilian status, the follow-up phase of our research would be analogous to a clinical trial. That is, differences in survival rates would be cross tabulated with predischarge treatment exposure. However, almost all California prisoners are released from prison on parole, that is, they are released from prison before the completion of the maximum term of their prison sentence, subject to the rules governing parolee behavior laid down by the Department of Corrections. As the complete control of physical confinement gives way to the minimum custody conditions that are implied by parole to the community, the department transfers supervision responsibility to the Parole Division.

The purpose of this chapter is not to discuss parole per se but, instead, to examine the requirements, conditions, and restrictions imposed by the parole contract on the men in our study sample. Included are brief descriptions of the paroling procedure, the contractual relationship between the parolee and the state, the types of parole supervision, the factors affecting parole revocation, and the implications of the parole status for the civil rights of the ex-inmate.

The belief that the concept of parole is the best of any currently available alternative is asserted on a variety of grounds that include reducing the expense of penal confinement, helping to reestablish the offender in the community, and protecting society by a surveillance of recently released prisoners in the community.[1] Although most inmates prefer

[1] According to Sutherland and Cressey, there is "no well-known student of penology who is not wholeheartedly in favor of the principle of parole." Edwin H. Sutherland,

straight or "flat" discharge from prison to a release under any kind of supervision, parole is preferred to continued confinement in prison in order to complete long maximum terms which are a part of their indeterminate sentences. Parole in California is thus intended to be regarded as a routine procedure by both inmates and staff. More than 90 percent of Men's Colony—East inmates were released on parole in California, the other men being paroled to detainers in other states or in a few cases being deported to Canada or Mexico.

FORMAL ORGANIZATION OF THE PAROLE DIVISION[2]

The Chief of the Division of Adult Parole is directly responsible to the Director of the Department of Corrections. The five regional offices are geographically divided into more than 40 district offices, each of which constitutes a supervising unit (1 supervisor, 1 assistant supervisor, and 6 parole agents). Out-of-state parolees are the responsibility of an interstate unit located in departmental headquarters.

The Parole Agent series consists of four positions ranked I to IV, with IV representing the highest level. The regional director (Parole Agent IV) supervises the region and presents cases for review to the Adult Authority. The Parole Agent III administers the supervising unit or district office. The major responsibility for actual parole supervision is assigned to Parole Agents I and II.[3] The responsibilities of the latter are described in the departmental manual as follows:

> Responsible for parole supervision and treatment of a group of adult male felons, counseling them, their families, friends, employers as to their responsibilities and part in the parole program; arranging employment and home programs for prospective releases on parole; conferring with local

and Donald R. Cressey, *Principles of Criminology*, New York: J. B. Lippincott Co., 1960, p. 586.

2 The descriptive material given in this chapter obviously applies to the Parole Division during the period of our follow-up, that is, up to 1966. Several Officials of the Parole Division who read a preliminary draft of this chapter have contended that certain policies and practices are no longer followed. We would only refer the reader to the study of the parole division by Paul Takagi "Evaluation Systems and Deviations in a Parole Agency" unpublished Ph.D. dissertation, Stanford University, 1967, and to "Correctional Supervision: Some Persistent Problems" by Takagi, mimeographed paper, School of Criminology, University of California, Berkeley, 1967.

3 Blau and Scott have pointed out that clients with relatively little power are served by the *lowest* echelon in an organization—the persons with least tenure, experience, and authority. Correctional agencies are excellent examples of this phenomenon. More than 90 percent of our parole sample were supervised by Parole Agent I's. See Peter M. Blau and W. Richard Scott, *Formal Organizations* (San Francisco: Chandler Publishing Co., 1962), p. 60.

community agencies regarding parole programs and resources available to parolees and their families; recommending revocation or continuance on parole to Adult Authority.[4]

However, the first and last word concerning parole release and revocation does not rest with the Parole Division but, instead, with an independent administrative body known as the Adult Authority. This board consisted of eight full-time gubernatorial appointees employed for four-year terms. The Adult Authority was assisted by nine hearing representatives whose authority was limited to hearing cases and to making recommendations to be approved by the Adult Authority. In practice, the duties of an Adult Authority member and a hearing representative differed only in that the latter could not sign their names to the dispositions. Cases usually were reviewed by one member of the Adult Authority and by one representative.[5] (This constituted a quorum.) To validate an order, the representative's recommendations must be initialed by a second Adult Authority member.

According to the state penal code, Adult Authority appointees are to be persons with ". . . a broad background and ability for appraisal of law offenders and the circumstances of the offense for which convicted . . . a varied and sympathetic interest in corrections, sociology, law, law enforcement and education."[6] Most of the Adult Authority members had law enforcement or correctional work backgrounds. During the period of our study the board was composed of two police officials, one probation supervisor, and one parole supervisor (both with social welfare backgrounds), a prison warden, a union official, and a former member of the parole board for female offenders.

Operating under the state's indeterminate sentencing structure, the Adult Authority sets the length of prison term, determines parole eligibility, and fixes the discharge date for each inmate. (The board has the right to fix and refix terms for men both incarcerated and on parole.) Adult Authority panels and hearing representatives met monthly at each prison to review the eligible cases—inmates who had served the minimum time required by the sentence,[7] parole violators, and inmates whose parole had been previously denied. The outcome of a board appearance is based on factors such as criminal background, the type of offense, and

---

[4] California Department of Corrections, *Parole Agent's Manual*, Section 2-02.

[5] For certain offenders, for example, violence potential cases, the entire board will review the recommendations.

[6] California Penal Code, Section 5075.

[7] The date of an initial appearance before the board depends in large part on the offense, for example, 90 days is the minimum for crimes whose maximum sentence is less than 5 years, whereas a life termer may not have a hearing for 7 years.

prison behavior. Generally, parole decisions are influenced by negative factors such as number of prison terms, prior failure on parole, the public concern about certain types of offenses (for instance, narcotics sales, sex offenses, and homicide), by failure to participate in prison programs, and by the number of disciplinary reports received in prison.[8]

It is questionable how much participation in various treatment programs, such as vocational training, education, and group counseling, helps one to gain parole, but the absence of participation (an absence of visible criteria by which to measure changes in the "attitude" and behavior of an inmate) in these programs often is given as a reason for parole denial.

A second- or third-term check writer, for example, is more likely to receive an earlier parole date relative to his minimum-maximum terms than a first-term offender who has been convicted of homicide, even though the check writer is a poor parole risk. A reputation as a prison trouble-maker may be an obstacle to obtaining parole, but a record of no disciplinary difficulty does not necessarily mean preferential consideration.[9]

[8] Whatever criteria that the Adult Authority use have been found unsatisfactory by the Select Committee on the Administration of Justice of the California legislature. The median time served by male prisoners in California was 24 months in 1960, in 1967 it increased to 30 months, and in 1968 to 36 months. According to the Select Committee investigation, the contentions of the Adult Authority that inmates were ". . . more hostile, immature, prone to act out, and less motivated . . ." than those sent earlier or that there was an ". . . increasing number of felons in need of psychiatric care . . . (or) that a longer exposure to the prison treatment program would improve the response of paroled inmates," could *not* be supported. *Parole Board Reform in California,* Report of the Select Committee on the Administration of Justice, Assembly of the State of California, 1970, p. 13.

In 1968, the Assembly Committee concluded:

The timing of parole release for lesser offenders is determined by arbitrary and unscientific criteria that do not further the ends of justice, economy, or public safety.

Deterrent Effects of Criminal Sanctions, May 1968, p. 25. In 1970, the Select Committee on Administration of Justice recommended changes in the parole board structure which included the suggestion that the board "Develop clearly defined policy and operational procedures (including a Parole Readiness Index) for the parole of felon prisoners." *Parole Board Reform in California,* Op. cit., p. 15.

[9] Prisoners find parole board decisions inconsistent as evidenced by responses to our question: What is the most important thing to do to help you get parole as soon as possible?

—"Go along with the program. Might do one in one-hundred some good. I can't find a way out. Some go in 8 months, others not. I'm afraid to say anything."
—"Taking enough time. Some activities, but the board will ask if you have enough time. They think of some excuse other than time, but that's what they mean."
—"Keep your nose clean, and no beefs, at least, no serious ones. Just do your time, that's all."

An additional responsibility of the Adult Authority is to review Parole Division recommendations pertaining to parolee requests and actions. These matters may be as routine as the right to marry, or to sign a contract; or they may be as serious as the continuation, reinstatement, or termination of parole. In order to have the right to vote restored and the subsequent right to hold public office, it is necessary to receive a pardon, and the Adult Authority advises the governor in this matter of clemency.

When parole is granted, the Adult Authority usually specifies a release date. However, in some cases a man is released as soon as his parole program is approved.[10] If other special parole conditions are required, they are set at the time of the inmate's hearing in prison.

Once the inmate has received a definite date of release, he begins the transition from inmate to parolee status. Formally, he is given instruction about parole in pre-parole classes and by a parole agent. Attendance of at least one pre-parole class is officially required, but one third of the men in our sample never attended and one half attended only once. Almost every inmate met with a parole agent, although not usually his own agent, to discuss his release program (job, residence, child support, anticipated problems, and the like). Our interview material indicated that parole was not a frequent topic at group counseling sessions in prison.

Informally there are discussions with staff, and more significantly, "yard talk" with other inmates, many of whom are parole violators. It also should be borne in mind that many of the men in our sample were themselves recidivists whose correctional experiences included prior parole and probation experience (51 percent were serving, at least, their second term). Thus, the parolee's perception of parole reflects in the main his own experience and the experiences of his fellow inmates, experience which is negative by virtue of being once again in prison.[11]

—"I've got to show them I'm sincere in my actions as far as rehabilitation goes."
—"They don't give you any indication of what they want. You should bring them some church, I guess, cause they asked me if I went to church."
—"It depends—Quite a lot of counseling. They tell you to bring it to them. It doesn't seem right. It's supposed to be voluntary and they give you the juice."
—"It's really not known."
—"I don't know. Some guys do well and get nothing. I think the most important thing is what you did before you got in."
—"Nothing. I honestly feel that none of these programs have anything to do with getting out."

[10] In our parole sub-file sample of 650, 24 percent were released on approved parole plan (RUAPP). More than two thirds either received early release or were released on time. Only 3 percent were held more than 30 days over their parole date, and none were held over for more than 3 months.

[11] Skolnick has emphasized the importance of ascertaining the level of parole expecta-

Following release, the initial interview with the parole agent is designed to acquaint the parolee with his supervisor, to answer any questions he may have about parole, to provide him with any funds owed him by the state,[12] and to review the conditions of parole. In this section we review those conditions in terms of their practical implications for the parolee. In brief, parole in California includes the following conditions: the parolee must report to an approved program; must obtain approval before leaving the county or changing residence; must maintain steady employment; must submit monthly reports; must not consume alcohol in excess nor use narcotics nor carry, own, or sell any firearms nor associate with "disreputable" persons; must obtain approval to drive; must cooperate with the agent; must not commit unlawful acts; must obtain approval to marry and to conduct financial affairs; and must repay any Parole Division loans.

Most aspects of daily living, including all the important ones, are covered in the parole conditions.[13] Most free citizens would find it difficult to avoid violations of parole regulations if all were rigorously enforced. Nevertheless, the legality of conditions of the parole contract has been upheld in the courts:

> With parole defined as a conditional release, it follows that a parole authority may attach conditions to its grant of release. The only restriction placed upon it by the courts is that the condition must not be illegal, immoral, or impossible of performance. This restriction is based on the premise that a parole release creates a quasi-contract between the parolee and the state via its authorized agents. Therefore it has been held that because of this contractual quality of parole, a prisoner must accept the parole before it becomes operative. Once having accepted it, he is bound by all its terms, subject to the aforementioned restriction or limitation.

tion as a major factor in understanding parole outcome. Jerome Skolnick, "A Theory of Parole," *American Sociological Review*, 25, August 1960, p. 542–550.

[12] In the Release Program Study, a budget is decided on. The maximum ($60) is usually recommended. If the inmate has a trust fund, $60 is deducted from it. It is estimated that only about 1 in 7 have any additional money, and it is held in trust by the Department of Corrections. On appropriate petition specified amounts can be obtained. The inmate is given a portion of the release budget when he leaves the institution; the remainder is to be picked up at the initial interview with his agent. "This way it insures at least one visit to the parole office. It also insures that there will be enough money for room and board for a few days." If a man requires tools for his job, the agent can loan him the purchase price, if there are loan funds available.

[13] The conditions of parole which California uses are to be found in nearly every state's parole contract. Some states have additional requirements, such as child support, while others omit some California conditions. For a comparison of parole conditions state by state, see Nat R. Arluke, "Summary of Parole Rules," *National Probation and*

. . . It is upon this theory that courts have consistently upheld parole revocations for breach of conditions attached to the parole.[14]

Theoretically, a man may be returned to prison for failure to abide by any *one* of the obligations of the parole contract; in fact, this is not done. The conditions are regarded as a means to an end—supervision and control—enforcement is not an end in and of itself. Parole rules are enforced and violations are actionable depending on the features of individual cases and the degree of significance which seems to be attached to the various conditions by the California Parole Division.[15]

---

condition 1   Upon release from the institution you are to go directly to the program approved by the Division of Adult Paroles and shall report to the parole agent.

This condition attempts to structure the parolee's activities beginning with the first day of his release from the prison by requiring that he proceed directly to a specified parole office and by giving him only a portion of the funds allotted in his release budget. Inmates, generally, are not released on weekends in order to prevent problems that could arise from immediate contact with "undesirable persons" or from making mistakes connected with immediate financial problems, with the finding of work or housing without prior counseling by the parole agent who does not work on weekends. Finally, an immediate contact with the agent is designed to help establish "the influence" of the Parole Division in the mind of the parolee.

A designation of "Parolee at Large" is assigned to those who do not report in accordance with this condition. Although there are instances in which parolees abscond at the first moment of freedom, less than one percent of our sample failed to make this initial contact. In one such case, the bus on which the man was riding (from the prison) required repairs midway between the institution and the point of destination. Our parolee took this opportunity to go to a tavern where he proceeded to get drunk and was subsequently arrested.

---

condition 2   Only with approval of your parole agent may you change your residence or leave the county of your residence.

Parole Association Journal, **2**, January 1956, pp. 6–13. See also in the same issue Edward J. Hendrick, "Basic Concepts of Conditions and Violations."

[14] George Edwards, "Parole" in Sol Rubin (ed.), *The Law of Criminal Correction*, St. Paul: West Publishing Co., 1963, p. 556.

[15] Data for this analysis derive partly from interviews with parole agents but, mainly, from the review of several hundred parole files.

Failing to abide by this condition is cited in many violation reports submitted to the Adult Authority. It is one of those infractions that serves to buttress other violations rather than stand as a cause for revocation itself. According to the Parole Agent's Manual, "Failure to conscientiously adhere to this condition would probably not justify asking the Adult Authority to return the parolee to prison."[16] As a surveillance measure, it is, however, quite important.

---

condition 3   It is necessary for you to maintain gainful employment. Any change of employment must be reported to, and approved by, your parole agent.

The values underlying the philosophy of the Department of Corrections are especially evident in this condition. The Parole Division Manual notes that "Steady employment is a prerequisite for any satisfactory adjustment in life."[17] The importance placed on job stability (synonymous here with self-reliance) is revealed in this initial interview prognosis by the parole agent: "He seems sincere, but due to the fact that he has no meaningful ties with anyone in the area, prognosis for success on parole will depend on his ability to obtain and hold a job paying a reasonable wage."

The fact that a man is not supposed to be released on parole unless he has a job often results in job offers that fail to materialize or a job that takes advantage of the difficulty experienced by ex-inmates in finding employment.[18] The jobs that are available often offer the parolee substandard wages, poor working conditions, night and weekend work shifts, and the like. Consequently, many parolees are encouraged by the parole agent to get better jobs on their own. Only 20 percent of our sample were released to a job that lasted for longer than two months. Policy requires that the parolee inform his employer that he is on parole, but there are some differences among agents when it comes to how long a man is permitted to withhold this information. In such cases, it is felt that a

[16] California Department of Corrections, *Parole Agent's Manual*, Section 10-03.
[17] Ibid., Section 10-04.
[18] With respect to private employment, there are no antidiscriminatory measures that apply to persons with a criminal history. Public employment is usually denied a person with a criminal conviction, more often than not based on administrative discretion instead of statutory provision. In California, a man is eligible to apply for a civil service position after discharge from parole. Under the Landrum-Griffith Act, trade unions deny office to persons with a felony conviction. For further discussion of the legal foundations of job discrimination for the exconvict, see Sol Rubin (ed.), op. cit., Chapter 17, Sections 7-12, 21-23. For one discussion of the relationship between parole failure and unemployment, see Daniel Glaser, *The Effectiveness of a Prison and Parole System*, Indianapolis, Indiana: Bobbs-Merrill, 1964, pp. 311–361.

delay may help the parolee hold the job if he has become established in it.

The parole division places some restrictions on the type of employment a parolee may take. Tending bar and driving a taxi were two types of work most often rejected. There are, however, some exceptions. Employment in a "disreputable bar" was unsuitable for one man; instead the district supervisor suggested employment as a bartender in a "1st class bar." Another parole agent denied permission to a parolee who would have worked as a special deputy for a sheriff's office assisting in the transfer of prisoners; and still another agent felt that a particular homosexual parolee "should not be placed in a physical therapy position."

In addition to the implications of social stigma and the restrictions on type of work, there is for most parolees the fundamental question of job qualifications. A California Department of Corrections pamphlet describes the typical state prisoner as having "no trade skills."[19] Two-thirds of our sample were classified as being unskilled or having only semi-skilled employment before their prison sentence. Consequently, their employment tended to be sporadic, low paying, and uninteresting. (In addition, parolees include a disproportionately large number of Negroes and Mexican-Americans who are among the last to be hired and the first to be laid off.) A man's job history is an important factor in considering revocation or continuance on parole, and if technical revocation is at stake, job stability may be the strongest factor working in his favor. Steady employment, whatever the job, seems to be an advantage in contrast to those cases where vigorous but unsuccessful job-seeking efforts have been made or where the parolee has had more than one job with periods of unemployment.

---

condition 4   You must submit a written monthly report of your activities on forms supplied by the Division. . . . (It) shall be true, correct and complete in all respects.

A one-page monthly report of present residence and employment is required from all parolees. The manifest purpose of the monthly report is that it enables the parole division to know where to contact a parolee; that is, if a report does not come in or the parolee cannot be contacted at his reported residence or place of employment, it is necessary to determine whether he has left the area. In addition, failure to file a monthly report can be used as a second violation in cases where a man is returned to prison for committing a new crime. Failure to abide by this condition,

[19] A California Department of Corrections brochure, "Public Protection," 1963, cites employment problems for parolees.

as with others we have discussed, is used more often as a substantiating rather than a primary charge to revoke parole.

---

condition 5   The unwise use of alcoholic beverages and liquors causes more failures on parole than all other reasons combined. You shall not use alcoholic beverages or liquors to excess.

After stating that parolees are not a representative sample of citizens, the parole manual points out with regard to alcohol, that "these emotionally disturbed personalities (parolees) will probably not respond (to alcohol) in the same manner as the average citizenry."[20] Since it is recognized that alcohol will be consumed, it is *excessive use* that is prohibited for all parolees except those whose parole contract includes the special condition of total abstinence, in which case, *no* alcoholic beverage is to be consumed.[21] One type of offender for whom total abstinence was required was the sex offender (lewd and lascivious behavior, child molestation, rape). The presumption in these cases is that these crimes are more likely to occur under the influence of liquor. In other words, the question is the relative importance of the potential social consequences that may be associated with drinking. One parole official put it this way: "When a check writer gets drunk, he writes checks (a minor threat to society), but when a sex offender drinks, a child's safety is endangered."

The following case is a specific example of this point. The subject was arrested for being drunk in a parked vehicle. He was detained in custody by the parole division because 17 years earlier he had been convicted of assault with intent to commit rape. ("S's drinking to excess indicates a potential hazard to society.") When he was arrested for drunkenness a second time, the Parole Agent recommended revocation of parole. The Regional Administrator disagreed that the parolee in question was a "great potential threat" because the intent to commit rape had been the only entry of aggressive behavior on his record. According to the supervisor: "The resulting sentence (probation and some jail time) casts some doubt as to the viciousness of the assault." The Adult Authority in this case upheld the Regional Administrator.

Excessive drinking and/or frequent drunk arrests were the cause for technical violations for some men in our sample. One such revocation was explained by a district supervisor: "Although the subject has not been in-

---

[20] California Department of Corrections, *Parole Agent's Manual,* Section 10-06.

[21] It should be noted that a history of excessive drinking is not a justification per se for an absolute restriction because "many alcoholics are primarily a menace to themselves and do not represent a grave problem to the public." Ibid., Section 7-11.

volved in criminal activity while on parole, his completely uncontrolled drinking, and its suicidal overtones, constitutes a serious threat to himself, and it is felt that he is in need of a type of supervision and treatment [prison] that cannot be afforded on parole." In another case, the agent defined drinking as a negative but preferred behavior. "Relapse to alcohol is indicative of his weak nature, but it is an improvement over the past predilection for narcotics."

condition 6   You may not possess, use or traffic in, any narcotic drug in violation of the law. If you have ever been convicted of possession or use of narcotic drugs or become suspect of being a user of narcotic drugs and are paroled to a section of California where an Anti-Narcotic Program is, or becomes available, you hereby agree to participate in such programs. . . .

All persons with a history of opiate use were required to take the so-called "nalline test" five times a month—one scheduled test each week, and one surprise test—for the first six-month parole period. There were two testing centers in California—one in Los Angeles and one in San Francisco. The condition was waived for narcotic offenders paroled to areas without nalline offices.

An unexcused absence from a nalline test was interpreted as a resumption of narcotics use, and parolee status could be suspended. Evidence of narcotics use (positive nalline test and/or needle marks) called for immediate incarceration. The type and duration of confinement that followed a violation report (required in all cases involving resumption of narcotics use) depended on the type of parole supervision to which the prisoner was released. Narcotic Treatment Control Program parolees were assigned to special "treatment" units for 90 days. Parole could be reinstated on release without a loss in parole time. Men on regular parole generally were returned to prison for another year or more before becoming eligible again for parole. At the time of our study, parolees were not eligible for commitment to the civil commitment drug treatment center (California Rehabilitation Center), and they were not permitted to live at Synanon.

condition 7   You shall not own, possess, use, sell, nor have under your control any deadly weapons or firearms.

State law prohibits possession of weapons that can be concealed on the person by any citizen, but the parole condition extends to any firearm, including deactivated souvenirs. Hunting privileges can be granted.

Violation of this condition is quite serious in the light of the state's concern with the violence potential of any parolee. One parolee, for example, arrested on charges of robbery that were later dismissed, was held on a parole detainer while an investigation was made of the "gun" used in that offense—a "wooden toy rifle with no trigger arrangement, no chamber and no barrel."

---

condition 8   You must avoid association with former inmates of penal institutions unless specifically approved by your Parole Agent; and you must avoid association with individuals of bad reputation.

The parole division recognizes that contact does occur between parolees, but this condition is designed to prohibit establishing a relationship "which would cause the average individual to have just cause to suspect the motivating reasons."[22] The question naturally arises as to what the average man would consider suspect. The provision is manifestly aimed at persons with prison records, criminal backgrounds, or who are themselves the object of police attention. Sometimes, however, the interpretation can be broadened to include social distinctions of a noncriminal nature. The following examples indicate the problems which arise in the implementation of this ambiguous criterion.

> Due to a distance of travel from former residence to place of employment and being without transportation, subject moved to ———. . . . . This residence was with a Negro family where subject had a room. He was questioned regarding this type of residence which seemed to be satisfactory. It was clean. Subject had a room to himself. But a question of doubt still lingered in the agent's mind respective to this living with a family of Negroes. They seemed to be congenial and interested in him so no further action was taken regarding a request for subject to move.

There were no indications that the Negro family was involved in, or had a past record of illegal activities. The subject left this residence and shortly thereafter was charged with burglary in association with three Negroes (none were members of the family with whom he had lived). In the Adult Authority report that recommended the suspension of subject's parole, the parole agent reiterated his doubts: "The agent questioned the reason that subject, a Caucasian, would be residing with a Negro family."

Another instance where ethnicity seemed to enter into the evalua-

---

[22] *Ibid.*, Section 10-09.

tion of the "association" clause involved a parolee who had American Indian friends.

> Subject is running around with Indian girls again and is getting himself very dirty. He has a very low regard for himself and cannot feel comfortable in the company with anyone but Indians. . . . His dissolute action continued unabated with the keeping of late and unusual hours, association with drunk Indians, promiscuous sex activities with Indian girls. . . . He does not take advantage of or avail himself of the many fine opportunities for wholesome recreation in this area, nor of the religious or socially uplifting events. . . . His habits have become less acceptable socially. . . . He seldom bathes and has sex relations with girls of low status.

The significant element in the enforcement of this condition was the parole agent's judgment of the intent of the relationship. If an association was deemed a "healthy and helpful" one, it was approved. The kinds of relationships cited in violation reports included ex-crime partners, prostitutes, men currently in trouble with the police, and homosexuals.

During the course of the parole follow-up phase of this study, no parolees lived at Synanon, the private antidrug addiction organization which had received widespread acclaim from university criminologists and a number of correctional departments outside of California. Synanon units, for example, were introduced into the Nevada State Prison and the Federal Correctional Institution at Terminal Island, California during the course of our study. The California Department of Corrections, however, continued to maintain its opposition to Synanon, despite the disappointing results of its own drug treatment programs as well as the civil commitment program (to be discussed in greater detail in Chapter X). Men in our study sample were told that residence at Synanon would result in revocation based on the "association" clause of the parole contract. (Apparently, association with other parolees with drug use histories was not regarded as a problem for parolees attending group counseling sessions.) Shortly after our parole follow-up was completed, Synanon found a parolee who was willing to undergo revocation in order to get a court test of the Department of Correction ruling. In his book, *Synanon*, Guy Endore describes this case:

> In accordance with the rules of the parole system, Gil Faucette sent his parole officer a letter informing him that he had moved to new quarters. And that his address from now on would be the Synanon House in Santa Monica.
> In return he received a letter from his parole officer. The letter said:

"Pack your things. Bring all your personal belongings and report to your parole officer."

This was the turning point. Synanon's lawyer advised Gil not to reply. Instead Synanon filed a restraining order to prevent the department from forcibly removing Gil Faucette. . . .

. . . The basic argument offered by the parole officer against Faucette staying in Synanon was that it was four miles outside of this officer's officially assigned territory. . . . Two weeks after the hearing Judge Landis ruled in favor of Synanon. With the following comment charged with irony: "The suggested reason for requiring the petitioner to remove himself from Synanon House in favor of a hotel because it is closer to the office of his parole officer, does not appear of equal importance so far as the future welfare of the petitioner is concerned. . . ."[23]

The association clause also applied to illegal cohabitation. Common-law marriage is not legally recognized in California, therefore, the parole division could not condone the living together of unmarried persons. Homosexual relationships were similarly prohibited under this condition. However, there was considerable variation in the enforcement of these two kinds of association. One supervisor pointed out that, although these relationships may often be "constructive," casework services must "give way to departmental policy." The casework theory might give tacit approval by ignoring the situation, whereas the departmental policy, strictly interpreted, must move in the direction of either legalizing a union or of terminating it.

It is very difficult for men who have served a considerable portion of their lives in penal institutions to strictly abide by the prohibitions against association. Nearly one half of our sample came from families whose members had either committed a misdemeanor (16 percent) or a felony (25 percent). Approximately one half of the men were released to living situations with parents or siblings. In addition, a paradox exists between the general prohibition against "association" and the required interaction with former inmates at nalline centers, halfway houses, outpatient clinics, or group counseling sessions, which were approved and supervised by the Parole Division. In short, association is an ambiguous condition, useful in justifying a technical violation or in supporting a new felony conviction, but one that is frequently overlooked if parole adjustment is relatively trouble-free.[24]

[23] Guy Endore, *Synanon*, Garden City, New York: Doubleday & Company, Inc., 1967, pp. 303–304. Other books about Synanon are *Synanon: The Tunnel Back* by Lewis Yablonsky, Penguin Books, 1967, and *So Fair a House* by Daniel Casriel, Englewood Cliffs, New Jersey: Prentice-Hall, Inc., 1963.

[24] For further discussion of the problems encountered by probationers (parolees)

condition 9   Before operating any motor vehicle you must have permission from your Parole Agent and you must possess a valid operator's license.

If a parolee operates a car in violation of this condition, it generally becomes known to the agent only after the parolee has gotten into some difficulty associated with the vehicle such as a traffic violation or a drunk driving arrest. In most of California, and particularly in the Los Angeles area where public transportation is inadequate and great distances are covered in the course of normal activities, parolees have difficulty in coping with the restrictions imposed by this condition. Specifically, problems arose because parolees could not afford the mandatory liability insurance (required by California law), since often a history of alcohol, drugs, or motor vehicle violations placed them in a high premium category. Second, many parolees had great difficulty in obtaining a driver's license. For example, persons with a history of narcotics use who were assigned to regular parole could not get a driver's license until they had successfully completed six months of parole. (Parolees in the Narcotic Treatment Control Program, to be discussed, could get a license as soon as they were released.) Finally, the parolee had to have his parole agent's approval when purchasing a car if it required credit obligations.

The *Parole Agent's Manual* suggested that a "liberal interpretation" be made in connection with the failure to abide by this condition and, as is the case with some other charges, the absence of a driver's license occasionally was used as a supporting charge, but it was insufficient justification in itself to warrant revocation.

condition 10   At all times your cooperation with your agent, and your good behavior and attitude must justify the opportunity granted you by this parole.

In essence, any instruction with which the parolee does not comply could be regarded as a lack of cooperation. According to the manual:

On rare occasions, it may be necessary to resort to an authoritarian approach. . . . When such devices are resorted to the parolee has the

while living under the conditions imposed by probation (parole) departments, see Joel Bassett, "Discretionary Power and Procedural Rights in the Granting and Revoking of Probation," *Journal of Criminal Law, Criminology and Police Science*, **60**, December 1969, pp. 479–493.

responsibility of adhering to such conditions, and for failure to do so, the individual may be considered for return as a violator.[25]

The important phrase here is "may be considered for return." This is the blanket condition that can cover any behavior not specified in other conditions. Obviously, it could be used by agents desiring to remove obstreperous or nuisance cases from the community. Thus these recommendations were carefully reviewed by parole division supervisors and Adult Authority members and, in most cases, agents cited other technical violations in addition to a refusal to cooperate.

---

condition 11   You are to obey all municipal, county, state, and federal laws, ordinances, and orders, and you are to conduct yourself as a good citizen.

Violation of Condition 11 can be a sufficient reason for a return to prison, but the seriousness of any offense, the disposition of the case, and the circumstances surrounding the violation are all relevant. In the case of a felony conviction, the parolee is returned to prison. (However, he may not be returned to the prison from which he was paroled; his status would have changed to at least a second termer, and California prisons are graded according to the criminal history of the offender.) The new term may run concurrently with the term for which he was originally sentenced, or the court may specify a consecutive term, that is, one that can only be served after the completion of the former term. Revocation of parole on the basis of a new conviction is known as "return to prison with new term" (WNT).

Although parolees may be arrested for a felony, charges sometimes are dismissed, or if the case is tried, the parolee may be found not guilty. The Adult Authority, however, may return a man to prison as a technical violator despite these dispositions and precisely because of *alleged* involvement in the crime. Insufficient evidence for a court of law does not mean that the parole division necessarily accepts the man's claim of innocence. One parolee, a suspect in a burglary case, could not be located and his status became Parole Violator At Large. He turned himself in to the police, and the case was dismissed for lack of sufficient evidence. The parole agent, however, recommended that his parole be revoked because: "It is felt that sufficient information exists to establish that subject committed this offense beyond a reasonable doubt." The Adult Authority concurred and parole was revoked.

[25] California Department of Corrections, *Parole Agent's Manual*, Section 10-11.

A parolee also can be returned to finish term (TFT) for a number of other reasons. One of these is "returned to prison in lieu of prosecution." The manual requires that in order to justify revocation without a trial, the evidence must be "overwhelming" or an admission of guilt must have been obtained. Initiative for these dispositions must be taken by the district attorney. The manual cautions against this type of revocation in cases where the only evidence of involvement is the arrest and the charge. "The Parole Agent will explain to the local authorities the untenable position in which the Adult Authority is placed and encourage local prosecution."[26] It is always questionable outside of a court of law whether "overwhelming evidence" exists, but the revocation of parole for some men in our sample was accomplished in this manner.

Parolees also may be returned to prison (TFT) in lieu of serving a county jail term but only on request of the county officials. Our review of approximately 600 parolee files suggests that a felony arrest that is not followed by conviction seldom results in revocation. In one case, for example, no violation report was submitted on a man arrested on suspicion of robbery, forgery, and "possession of a gun by an ex-convict." He was found not guilty of the latter charge; the first two charges were dismissed. It does appear that, in most cases, after the second or third felony arrest, regardless of disposition, action is taken to revoke parole.

With respect to misdemeanor arrests or felony arrests reduced to misdemeanor charges (often if the defendant agrees to plead guilty), the response of the Parole Division seemed to depend primarily on the kind of adjustment that the parolee had made up to that point. Drunk arrests or traffic violations had little significance unless they occurred frequently. Confinement for petty theft and other short jail terms was usually followed by a continuation of parole. This is not to suggest that any law violations were regarded lightly by the Parole Division. All parolee behavior, including misdemeanor arrests, made up "parole adjustment" and could be cited at any time as justification for a return to prison for technical violation (see Figure 7.1).

Even when the parolee has been convicted of a new felony, that is, violation of Condition II, parole revocation recommendations specify additional violations of the parole contract. One reason for this is that if the conviction is successfully appealed (court's decision is overturned), the Adult Authority wants to be protected from the charge of returning the parolee to confinement without cause.

[26] Ibid., Section 8-02.

figure *7.1*   Parole behavior and the probability of return to prison

Parole Behavior	Retain on Parole	Return to Prison
Violations of Conditions 1 to 5, 7 to 10, 12 to 14	Usually	Rarely
		Parolee at large, once located often returned TFT
Violation of Condition 6 First detection of narcotics use	NTCP parolees placed in special confinement category	Rarely for NTCP parolees Often for regular parolees
Second detection	NTCP parolees seldom reconfined at special NTC Units	Usually for NTCP Certainly for regulars
Miscellaneous misbehavior though no crime is charged	Usually, though may be detained in jail on parole arrest	Seldom Suspicion of violence potential or "bizarre" actions may result in return TFT
		The need for medical or psychiatric treatment may also result in technical violation
Misdemeanor arrest or felony arrest reduced to misdemeanor charge: No conviction	Usually	Seldom
Conviction	Maybe	Seldom on first conviction but not infrequent after second or third misdemeanor arrest or conviction
		In lieu of county jail time
Felony arrest: No conviction	Especially if other parole behavior has been stable	Sometimes, especially if second time, if division is convinced of his guilt, or deal with prosecution was made, or if parolee had been violator at large (PVAL)
Conviction	Never	Automatic return with new term (WNT)

condition 12   Your Civil Rights have been suspended by law. You may not marry, engage in business nor sign contracts unless the Parole Agent recommends, and the Adult Authority approves, restoring such Civil Rights to you. . . . The following Civil Rights *only* are hereby restored to you at this time: You may make such purchases of clothing, food, transportation, household furnishings, tools, and rent such habitation as are necessary to maintain yourself and keep your employment. You shall not make any purchases relative to the above on credit except with the written approval of your Parole Agent. You are hereby restored all rights under any law, relating to employees such as rights under workmen's compensation, Unemployment Insurance laws, Social Security laws, etc.

In Condition 12 the Parole Division is primarily concerned with placing limitations on certain property rights, namely the ability to buy on credit.[27] The right to file a civil suit is *not* restored. This condition is designed to control the parolee's expenditures and indebtedness by placing an obstacle between him and credit buying. The parole agent must authorize any credit purchase, and Adult Authority approval must be sought for any purchase in excess of $1000. Some agents prohibited certain offenders—forgers, not sufficient-funds check writers, and embezzlers—from having a checking account. However, there is a question about whether the agent actually had the legal authority to support this prohibition.

Parolees must request restoration of the civil right to marry before the ceremony can take place. Permission, when granted, applies only to the woman in question. (These requests were regarded by many women as "engagement rings," this is, symbolic of a commitment on the part of the parolee; however, only the *right* to marry is involved, not necessarily the intention.)

condition 13   In time of actual need, as determined by your Parole Agent, you may be loaned cash assistance in the form of meal and hotel tickets. You hereby agree to repay this assistance. . . .

The usual loan consisted of chits redeemable at a local hotel or restaurant, though small amounts of cash (three to five dollars) were also

[27] For a complete listing of the types of contracts that do not require the permission of the Adult Authority or the parole agent, such as applications for patent or copyright, insurance forms, United States Defense Department papers, and the like, see ibid., Section 10-13.

given. Meal tickets were issued for each meal ($.78); hotel rooms were valued at approximately $10 a week. One agent informed us that "the institutions tell the men there is a parole (loan) fund. But frankly, it isn't so. The fund is whatever the agent has on him. The division allots each district office so much and our share is gone in no time." Refusal to repay these small loans could be considered an indication of "unsatisfactory adjustment."[28]

condition 14   *Special Conditions.* Registration with local police and participation in the Parole Outpatient Clinic (POC) represented the most frequently imposed special condition. Registration pertained to certain sex offenders, arsonists, and narcotic offenders. The parolee was required to report his registration number to his agent; departmental headquarters notified the agent if they did not receive notification of the parolee's registration. Failure to attend the Parole Outpatient Clinic could result in confinement in the county jail as a warning. Special conditions could be imposed by the Adult Authority during the parole period as well as prior to it.

Parole survival without due process rights

Parole is designed as a continuation of the overall custodial and correctional process. Actually, it is a special type of minimum custody. The parolee continues to serve the sentence imposed on him by the Adult Authority; even though he may reside outside of the prison setting, he is still subject to their surveillance and control. It should be emphasized that parole is legally regarded as an act of grace that can be withdrawn at any time the parole board believes that this action will serve the interests of the public or of the parolee.[29] The decision to revoke parole is administrative, not judicial. The legality of this principle has been upheld on two grounds: (1) the failure to comply with parole conditions is a violation of a legally binding contract, and (2) the granting of parole does not change the legal status of the prisoner who is subject to the supervision

[28] Ibid., Section 10-14.

[29] The parole agent is required to submit a violation report to the Adult Authority in the event of any arrest that involves criminal prosecution, parolee at large, serious parole violations, aggressive behavior, narcotics involvement, commercial or fraudulent schemes, and the like, ibid., Section 8-03. The agent recommends a course of action; his superiors concur or disagree; but the final decision is in the hands of the Adult Authority.

of the state. The legality of the parole contract combines with the offender's lack of civil rights to produce a status in which the question for the parolee is *survival* under conditions that are more severe than those of any civilian.

REMOVAL OF CIVIL RIGHTS

When a man is convicted of a crime he can be deprived of his life; more often he is deprived of his liberty. These deprivations are legally imposed according to due process of law. However, there are other rights of the offender, which are rarely specified in the sentence and often unspecified in the statute, that are automatically suspended.

Rubin notes that

> . . . despite considerable case law on the subject, the particular rights lost, the point at which they are lost, and the problems of restoring them are obscure both to convicted persons and to officials. Frequently the statutes refer generally to suspension of "civil rights" without specifying which rights are involved. As a result, "it is impossible," says one authority, "to state with certainty just what civil rights are lost by convicts generally. The statutes in the various states do not undertake to define in any inclusive manner the effect of criminal conviction upon civil and political status. . . ."[30]

There are three stages in the removal and restoration of rights for the California prisoner. First, on conviction he automatically loses certain property rights, and political and civil rights. Additional rights—mainly aspects of due process—are suspended when the man is paroled. Finally, at discharge from parole, there is a partial restoration of these rights.

On criminal conviction[31] an inmate's property rights are redefined, grounds for divorce are established, and his children may become adoptable. In cases where the penalty is death or life imprisonment, the prisoner can be deemed civilly dead.[32] His right to sue in court is suspended; busi-

---

[30] Rubin, op. cit., p. 623.

[31] A distinction should be made between *conviction* and *execution* of a sentence. In some states if the sentence is suspended, the man's rights are retained. Also, it is well to recall that what is not specifically removed by virtue of statute provision is retained.

[32] Civil death implies measures accorded in the case of natural death—nullification of the marriage, distribution of property, and the like—without the severing of duties, obligations, and liabilities (for example, responsibility for child support remains). Tappan describes civil death as consistent with the period of justice that included branding, mutilation, and the stocks and pillory, but as out of step with modern concepts of rehabilitation. Paul Tappan, "Loss and Restoration of Civil Rights of Offenders," *National Probation and Parole Assn. Journal*, **2**, January 1956, pp. 86–104. In addition to the death penalty and life imprisonment, the California prisoner becomes civilly dead

ness or professional licenses may be revoked;[33] and his rights to vote,[34] to hold public office and to act as trustee, are not merely suspended, but permanently forfeited.[35]

Men on parole in California are subject to search and seizure by parole agents who do not need a warrant; they can be arrested and held without a formal charge; they cannot be released on bail once a "hold" is placed by the Parole Division; in the event of a hearing revocation, they typically do not make a personal appearance and plea before the Adult Authority.[36] These measures have not been deemed a denial of due process but, instead, reflect the special status of the parolee, which does not entitle him to ordinary constitutional guarantees.[37]

during the period in which the death penalty is pending. See James Bentson, "Civil Death," *Southern California Law Review,* **26,** July 1953, pp. 425–434. See California Penal Code 2600.2601.

[33] California Penal Code 4853.

[34] California Constitution Amendment No. 2. ". . . no persons convicted of an infamous crime (a felony) may thereafter exercise the privilege of an elector." It is difficult to understand how such a prohibition protects society and rehabilitates the prisoner. This is not to suggest indignation on the part of those disenfranchised. Parole agents indicated that they rarely heard complaints about this issue. In 1960, the California electorate was given the opportunity to restore the franchise to ex-felons. The proposition to amend the State Constitution (Amendment 5) read as follows:

Change the prohibition of eligibility to vote from those convicted of infamous crime to those convicted of a felony *during punishment* and those convicted of treason or misappropriation of public funds (emphasis ours).

In other words, at discharge from parole, all but the specified offenders would automatically regain the franchise. The proposition was defeated: 2.3 million for, 2.9 million against. California Secretary of State, *Proposed Amendments to the Constitution and Statement of the Vote,* November 8, 1960.

[35] In other states, the right to serve on a jury or to act as a witness is denied to a parolee, but restored at discharge. Testimony generally is discredited on the basis of felony conviction. In California, only a pardon precludes impeachment as a witness. It should be noted that these forfeitures of civil rights do not derive from federal criminal statutes but, instead, are based on state or jurisdictional decisions. The right to vote is forfeited in three fourths of the states. For a general discussion, see Sol Rubin, op. cit., Chapter 17.

[36] California Department of Corrections, *Parole Agent's Manual,* Section 10-00.

[37] Although it cannot be assessed here, the stigma associated with a definition of exconvict must be acknowledged in terms of real and specific effects. It is a source of genuine strain to subsequent adjustment. "When he has paid his debt to society he neither receives a receipt nor is he free of his account." Tappan, op. cit., p. 86. Parolees find work difficult to obtain (licenses may be denied, they cannot be bonded, etc.), a parolee is regarded as an assigned risk for auto insurance purposes, and so forth. See Joseph Goldstein, "A Note on Stigma, Status Degradation and Status Elevation Ceremonies in the Criminal Process," *The Yale Law Journal,* **69,** 1960, pp. 590–592. Also see Harold Garfinkel, "Conditions of Successful Degradation Ceremonies," *American Journal of Sociology,* **61,** March 1956.

In California, a parole agent's police authority is limited in two major ways: (1) he has no jurisdiction over anyone who is not on parole, (2) he is not permitted to carry a gun. In most cases the parole agent makes an arrest accompanied by another agent. However, if resistance is anticipated, the agent may request that a policeman accompany him. Special state agents who are armed are assigned to transport parole violators.

In the areas of search and seizure and detention, however, an agent's police authority exceeds that of the usual police officer. (This power derives from the status of parolee; it does not represent a condition of parole.) For example, the agent is given blanket permission to search a man's premises without his consent and without probable cause.[38] An additional aspect of this same topic involves the efforts of some police officers to use the parole agent's power to search a person or place when they themselves are either unable or unwilling to get a warrant. The Parole Agent's Manual does caution against search "without real cause" and suggests that if a search is necessary, it be done in the presence of the parolee, accompanied by an explanation for the action.[39] Agents whom we interviewed indicated that this practice was rare, and they said that the police seldom asked for such "cooperation." When requests of this kind were made, they were, generally, in regard to narcotics cases.

Notice, significantly, that the power to arrest and to detain a civilian must involve, at least, a charge of probable cause that the civilian committed the violation of law. This is usually the case for a parolee, but it need not be. A parolee may be kept in jail without either a formal charge or the opportunity for bail. If the agent makes the arrest, a parole hold is automatically placed on the parolee which prohibits release without parole division approval. However, when the police make the arrest (presumably in connection with an alleged offense), the agent, generally, is notified that his parolee is being held. Often the parolee admits to the police that he is on parole, or he may already be known to the police. In addition, a special parole agent acts as liaison between the division and the local police. It is his job to place parole detainers on every parolee arrested.

On occasion, a parolee was released on bail (agents, in discussion with us, estimated "1 in 100") but only because he was *financially* able to post

---

[38] In the following case, the parolee contested the search of his apartment by agents who thought he was selling narcotics. The court denied the petitioner: "Granting of parole does not change the legal status of a prisoner; *in serving time outside of the prison he is constructively a prisoner of the state*, in the legal custody and under the control of the Adult Authority" (italics ours). *People v. Danne*, 141 Cal. App. 2d 499, 297 P. 2d 451 (1956).

[39] California Department of Corrections, *Parole Agents Manual*, Section 7-02.

bond immediately and because he knew or had an attorney who knew *how* release could be secured before a parole hold was placed. (Poor coordination between police and the Parole Division makes the quick release possible. Once a parolee is released on bail under these circumstances, he cannot be rearrested unless additional evidence is submitted. However, if it is felt that the parolee is either a "threat to society" or is likely to abscond, rearrest is possible under the general "good behavior" conditions of the parole contract.

The Parole Division seemed to be quite sensitive to prolonged detention, especially, when no prosecution was pending. Supervisors said that they encouraged their agents not to allow a man to remain in jail unnecessarily simply because they might not have had the time to investigate the case. However, large caseloads sometimes precluded immediate attention, and "temporary restraint," regarded as "a therapeutic device," involved confinement for several days or several weeks in some cases.[40] Some men also remained in jail for extended periods awaiting trial (because of parole detention and its implication for bail) even in instances where the maximum penalty for the crime is less time than they had already served.[41]

Parole may be contrasted with probation in this regard. When probation is revoked the probationer is present at the hearing; the parolee does not appear before the Adult Authority at the time that his violation report is being considered.[42] The question of whether the parolee has a constitutional right to a hearing has been consistently denied on

[40] One parolee's residence for one week was unknown. Even though no criminal activity was suspected, the agent arrested the man and by means of a parolee hold kept him in jail for seven weeks—a combination of temporary restraint and inadvertent detention.

[41] Time served generally applies to the sentence handed down by the court. In many cases the parolee is advised to enter a guilty plea to a lesser charge (or to plead guilty to the original charge) in order to obtain an earlier release.

[42] When asked whether this distinction between probation and parole was accurate, one district supervisor demurred. The interviewer restated the question: Does the parolee appear before the Adult Authority at a revocation hearing?

PA III. Yes, the parolee is present but not in person. The agent submits a violation report with his recommendations and the regional director [PA IV] takes this report to the board [Adult Authority]. The parolee has a chance to plead guilty or not guilty to the evidence presented in the report at the institutional hearing.

INTERVIEWER. You mean that after parole has been revoked and the parolee is re-institutionalized he appears before the Adult Authority to present his side of the case?

PA III. Yes, the Adult Authority may refix his term then [give him a new discharge date].

INTERVIEWER. Has there been an incident that you can recall where this hearing has made any difference to the parolee in terms of the consequences of the hearing?

PA III. Well, no, the board has already made up its mind.

the basis of the nature of the parole contract, the definition of parole as an act of grace, and the status of parolee that does not entitle the occupant to the usual constitutional guarantees.[43] In fact, this perspective represents the rationale for all the deprivations of due process discussed in this section.

These features of parole should be kept in mind in trying to understand accurately the experiences of our study subjects after their release from prison to the various programs of parole supervision.

Types of parole supervision

The variety of parole programs to which our study subjects were assigned was designed to take into account the special supervision needs and problems posed by a wide range of offender types. Frequency of contact with parole agents ranged from daily (as in the case of Halfway House residents) to a minimum of one visit every three months. Since the frequency and intensity of parolee-parole agent contact is positively related to the extent of misbehavior that can be detected, particularly technical violations, the frequency of contact is an important distinguishing feature of parole programs in California.[44]

REGULAR PAROLE

Most parolees were assigned to regular parole supervision. Regular caseloads averaged 72 parolees. A monthly report was required, and the agent was supposed to have, at least, one personal and one collateral contact

[43] For example, Holtzoff argues that a probationer is not entitled to the protection of the Fourth Amendment against search and seizure, and MacGregor states that although revocation must be for cause, due process does not apply to the hearing itself. Alexander Holtzoff, "Duties and Rights of Probationers," *Federal Probation*, **21**, July 1957; Helen MacGregor, "Adult Probation, Parole, and Pardon in California," *Texas Law Review*, **38**, 1960, pp. 887–915. For further discussions of the due process rights of probationers and parolees, particularly in regard to revocation, see Basset, op. cit., and Sanford H. Kadish, "The Advocate and the Expert-Counsel in the Peno-Correctional Process," **45**, 1961, pp. 803–841.

[44] In a comparison of the regular supervision of narcotic offenders with a special, more intensive type of supervision, drug use was detected more often among parolees in the latter parole program. California Department of Corrections, *Narcotics Treatment Control Program*, Report No. 19, 1963. See also Robert M. Martinson, Gene K. Kassebaum, David A. Ward, "A Critique of Research in Parole," *Federal Probation*, **28**, September 1964, pp. 34–38, for an elaboration of this point. Ohlin also has stated, "Improved parole supervision will increase the number of parolees returned for minor violations." Lloyd Ohlin, "The Routinizations of Correctional Change," *Journal of Criminal Law, Criminology, and Police Science*, **45**, November–December 1954, p. 403.

(conversation with a relative or employer) with the parolee every three months. Personal contact with the parolee, in most cases, came with an unscheduled visit to the parolee's residence. These visits generally lasted about 15 minutes. Although these short contacts may appear "meaningless" to the parolee (in terms of treatment), they actually are significant surveillance efforts.

A parolee serving a trouble-free parole may not see his agent more often than the required four times a year unless he initiates the contact. A man who has been in trouble with the local police, is unemployed, or is encountering some sort of personal problem will see more of his agent. In other words, on a regular parole basis, contacts with the agent increase with the amount of difficulty a parolee encounters.

INCREASED CORRECTIONAL EFFECTIVENESS (ICE)

During the 1960's the major research effort in the Adult Parole Division was the Special Intensive Parole Unit (SIPU) study which was designed to ascertain the effect of reduced caseloads compared with the average caseload.[45] In an operational outgrowth of this program, known as Increased Correctional Effectiveness (ICE), selected parole agents were assigned caseloads that numbered 30 men. Minimum contact in ICE units was a monthly, personal, unscheduled visit. Weekly group counseling sessions were mandatory.

The criterion for eligibility for the ICE program relied on the probability of successful parole as measured by the Base Expectancy Score—only the middle and upper one third were considered. The highly selective nature of this type of parole supervision is indicated by the exclusions. No inmate with a history of opiate addiction, extreme violence or "bizarre behavior," psychosis, or major sex deviance, was eligible. Also excluded were men who received a parole of more than 20 months and men whose vocational and academic deficiencies would make job placement difficult.

In keeping with the research design, no units that prepared men for the ICE program were operated at CMCE during the study. However, subsequent to their release, three men in our sample were assigned to small caseload ICE parole.

PAROLE SUPERVISION FOR NARCOTIC OFFENDERS

Regular. All offenders with a history of opiate use were given a five-year parole and, where location permitted, weekly nalline tests were also

---

[45] The best review of the SIPU program, the research conducted on SIPU and the consequences of the research findings (that reduced caseloads did *not* reduce recidivism) is to be found in Takagi, op. cit., 1967.

mandatory (see Condition 6). These men were assigned to agents with regular caseloads.

Nalline (N-allylnormorphine) is a synthetic opiate antinarcotic drug whose effects counteract the physiological responses to morphine derivations and thus permit the detection of drug use by a comparison of the size of pupil before and after subcutaneous injection. A decrease in pupil size indicates no use of an opiate drug in the last 48 hours. This is referred to as a negative test. Dilation of the pupil, on the other hand, is cause for immediate incarceration. There are situations less clearly defined than the positive or negative test. An intermediate reading referred to as "no change," evidence of needle marks even with a negative test, or an unexcused absence may result in a parolee being taken into custody and a board report being submitted. The agent is notified when a parolee is absent from testing. The parolee then has to be located and tested within 72 hours (later changed to 15 days) or his parole could be suspended and the status of Parolee at Large assigned to him. The consequences of a Nalline arrest (or suspension of parole) depended on the type of supervision involved. Return to prison was usually recommended for a parolee on regular parole.

NARCOTIC TREATMENT CONTROL PROGRAM (NTCP)

Compared with regular narcotics parole, the NTCP program featured "small caseload supervision, anti-narcotic testing (weekly) to detect return to drug use, and short-term confinement in treatment units for parolees returning to drug use."[46] Special agents were assigned 30 narcotics cases (other caseloads were 15 with counseling, or 45 without counseling), whereas regular agents, whose caseloads averaged 72, were given no more than five parolees with a narcotics history. Personal contacts were to be monthly instead of every three months. Parolees supervised by NTCP agents thus were subject to much closer control, consequently it was more likely that there would be more immediate investigation of an unexcused absence from testing. (Drug use was greater, that is, detected more often, among NTCP parolees.)

During the first year of NTCP operation, the agent was permitted considerable latitude in deciding what to do with the parolees whose resumption of narcotics was detected. After that year, however, discretion came to be mainly restricted in favor of uniform treatment—immediate arrest and short-term confinement. NTCP violators usually were transferred from the county jail to either of two Narcotic Treatment Control Units, located at the California Institution for Men at Chino or San

---

[46] *Narcotics Treatment Control Program, Report No. 19, op. cit.*

Quentin prison. This type of involuntary confinement for violating Condition 6 of the parole contract (narcotics use) replaced the more traditional approaches that were applied to addicts on regular parole—short-term jail, "dry out" or return to prison on technical grounds.[47]

Regarded as in-patient clinics, these units were completely separate from the main institutions and housed only parolees who had suffered a "relapse" or appeared to be in "imminent danger" of such a relapse, and who had not been involved in other criminal activities. Administrators sought a therapeutic community atmosphere by employing daily group counseling sessions. A first term at the "in-patient" clinic ranged from 70 to 90 days; a second admission required 180 days. Readmission was not automatic and was restricted to only the more promising cases.

HALFWAY HOUSE

A very special type of narcotics parole was the East Los Angeles Halfway House.[48] (This area had the highest incidence of narcotics arrests in the state and was the location of the only nalline testing center in Southern California.) Men scheduled for release to this area were randomly assigned to the project (2 percent of our parole sample were Halfway House parolees). They were expected to remain in residence for a minimum of 30 days, were encouraged to obtain employment, and were permitted to spend weekends with their families. Nalline test requirements and short-term confinement were the same as the ones described for other NTCP parolees. Being absent without official leave from the Halfway House resulted in a suspension of parole.

THE PAROLE OUTPATIENT CLINIC (POC)

There were three routes by which parolees could be involved in the Outpatient Clinic: the Adult Authority could require it, the parole agent could recommend it, or the parolee could volunteer for it. Attendance at the clinic was a special condition of parole for most sex offenders. Parole agents could recommend attendance at the POC because they were concerned about a man's behavior since his release from prison. If the recommendation was approved by the Adult Authority, the parolee was required

[47] Parole may be revoked and return to prison ordered for the resumption of narcotic use, but these actions do not usually occur in NTCP cases until the second detection. The prisoner in either case—a regular parolee returned for the first detection or an NTCP parolee returned for a second detection—is eligible for parole again in approximately 18 months.

[48] See Sethard Fisher, "A Community Correctional Residence for Rehabilitating Narcotics Offenders," paper presented at the annual meeting of the American Sociological Association, Los Angeles, California, August 1963, and Gilbert Geis, *The East Los Angeles Halfway House for Narcotic Addicts,* op. cit.

to attend. Termination of treatment was decided by the clinic psychiatrist.

Weekly attendance was recorded, and an unexcused absence generally was interpreted as a lack of sincere cooperation and a forerunner to the renewal of criminal activities. Consequently, the parole agent was notified immediately and was expected to take the appropriate action. Departmental regulations called for the clinic staff to inform the man's parole agent when information regarding the commission of a "serious" crime was revealed during therapy sessions. In other words, the relationship between the psychiatrist and his patient (the parolee) was not regarded as privileged in the way that ordinary therapeutic communication is defined. The power of the Department of Corrections to compel a therapist to divulge incriminating information has not actually been tested in a court of law, however. It seems a safe assumption that if therapeutic communication can be self-incriminating, then inmate confidence in treatment programs and personnel could be seriously inhibited (not to mention the difficulty of securing clinicians to work under "nonprofessional" conditions). Thus, apart from any rehabilitative function served, it would appear that the Parole Outpatient Clinic was intended to function as a mechanism to increase the control of the parolee. In the case of our study population, however, only 4 percent were involved in this program.

CONCLUSIONS

Despite the variety of parole programs, the great majority of Men's Colony—East inmates were released on regular parole. Those small groups of men who did go to the Halfway House or were assigned to the Outpatient Clinic, ICE, or the NTCP program were drawn from all treatment and control varieties, and our follow-up analysis was not confounded by having any one of our study groups assigned to a special parole program. Our purpose in providing these brief descriptions is mainly to point out the implications for parole survival that go with the assignment to some parole programs with special chemical testing for drug use or intense contact (surveillance) by parole agents. The incidence of parole violating behavior is in large part a function of the frequency with which the behavior is detected. Increase in grounds for parole violation thus may reflect nothing more than the initiation (termination) of new program, such as Increased Correctional Effectiveness and nalline testing. In Chapter X, we shall devote considerable attention to the problems that arise for correctional agencies when new treatment programs turn up *higher* recidivism rates.

We believe that the business of living as a parolee in the community should be viewed within the context of the legal bounds of the parole contract and the administration and bureaucratic decisions of the Parole

Division. Parolees are not free citizens and parole means, essentially, surveillance and control, not casework and counseling. Given the design and setting of this study—the prison and life in the community under the constraints of the parole contract—we now can present quantitative data dealing with some of the more important officially recorded aspects of the parole experiences of our study sample. Most important, we shall give follow-up data on the "success" or "failure" of men paroled from the various treatment conditions.

‖‖

Measurement of outcome: differences in parole survival of treatment and control groups

Does a program of group counseling conducted in prison have an effect on postrelease behavior that is different from the effect of imprisonment itself? This was the major research question of our study. Issues about the impact of imprisonment per se or about group counseling in a noninstitutional setting were not central to our purposes. Our data only incidentally show the extent to which being in prison changes the likelihood of committing another crime. For this, we would have needed a control group of comparable offenders who were not imprisoned. Recidivism rates cited in this study apply to prison inmates only.

In addition, our data cannot be interpreted to imply any evaluation of the relative merits of a "soft line" (group counseling) versus a "hard line" (no group counseling). There were no indications whatever that the program in C quad was any "harder" than the programs in the other quadrangles in which counseling took place.

It is important at the outset to describe clearly the research decisions made in connection with our efforts to conceptualize and to operationalize "outcome." The two main criteria used in evaluation studies are level of functioning—in the community, in one's personal life, on the job, and the like—and recidivism—whether the offender (patient) repeats the behavior which brought him to the "treatment" in the first place. It was conceivable that one way to approach the evaluation of the Men's Colony group treatment program would be to test whether, on release to civil society, participants carried out their activities or responsibilities more adequately or "got along" better than releasees with similar histories who had not been under treatment. Hence, the question to be asked would be: Do persons who have participated in group counseling function better in the community than persons who have not participated in group counseling? This, however, is *not* what we have done, and our data should not be construed as an answer to this question. Because it is in this area that we perceive the greatest likelihood for the misunderstanding or the misinterpretation of our findings, some further comments are necessary to specify reasons 'for not evaluating this program in terms of a level of general functioning.

The problems in evaluating level of functioning in the life situation are not peculiar to the study of crime. They pose similarly difficult issues for researchers in the field of medical care. Although (as we have stressed in Chapter I) there are many crucial distinctions between parolees and released medical or psychiatric patients, the problems encountered in the assessment of disability in medicine and psychiatry are instructive and applicable in penology. The term "disability" may be taken to refer to a person's incapacity to conduct his life in a manner that meets demands placed on him by his needs, aspirations, environment, and the expectations of others in relevant reference groups. Thus, the term may be very general in scope. In a post-hospitalization follow-up of patients, this incapacity might be a consequence of heart disease; in an exmental patient, it might be a consequence of unresolved psychoses; in a follow-up of prison inmates, it might be the consequence of continued criminal practices, of addiction to illegal drug use, of the stigma of being an exconvict, of unresolved aggressive tendencies, and the like.

In all of these populations, however, it is difficult to stipulate what is an adequate or optimal level of performance for most activities. There are few clear standards by which to compare incapacities and compensatory mechanisms, or by which to assess the relative degree of disability produced by various impairments. In short, although there are ways to measure organic or psychological impairment in laboratory, clinical, or test situations, there are few unambiguous, objective criteria for judging when a person is functionally disabled in conducting normal activities. For this reason, medical researchers cannot simply select a number of likely variables and construct an index from them that predicts an external criterion of disability. Instead, researchers must map out the components of functional impairment and level of performance and, then, must state the empirical relationship between the two. This requirement applies equally to sociological research.

It also is problematic to estimate the level of performance in normal life from measures of impairment per se. For example, Srole and his colleagues define mental health as, "freedom from psychiatric symptomatology and optimal functioning of the individual in his social setting."

The authors then remark that, ". . . some patients with (merely) a depression or an obsessive-compulsive reaction could be more functionally impaired than many ambulatory schizophrenics."[1] A given degree of organic or psychological impairment may result in different levels of performance depending on many factors, including the organization of a particular patient's personality, his previous level of functioning, his aspirations, and the amount of interpersonal support and social and economic resources at his command.[2]

[1] The Midtown Study outlines a number of criteria of positive mental health:

1. Ease of social interaction.
2. Capacity for pursuit of realistic goals.
3. Fulfillment of biological needs, such as childbearing and rearing.
4. Satisfying sense of social belonging: sensitivity to needs of others.
5. Feeling of adequacy in social roles, particularly sexual.
6. Optimal balance between independency-dependency, rigidity-plasticity needs.
7. Capacity for utilization of creative activity.
8. Capacity to accept deprivations and individual differences.
9. Conservative handling of hostilities and aggressions.
10. Identification with moral and ethical values.
11. Adaptability to stress (homeostasis).
12. Healthy acceptance of self (for example, body image and ego image).

Srole, Langner, Michael, Opler, and Rennie, op. cit., pp. 60, 63.

[2] Even the definitions of impairment may be different depending on the perspective. A well-known study of chronic illness in a rural area offers an example of this. Part of this useful research was a family survey conducted by lay interviewers. Respondents were asked to report disability "requiring either confinement to bed or house or at the very least, interruption of one's usual activities for seven days or more." Usual activities were interpreted as "working chores or household duties or going to school." With this procedure (lay interviewers), long-term disability was reported by 3 percent of the sample while medium-term disability accounted for another 12 percent. Thus the majority of the persons involved in the family interviews were classified as either having short-term or nondisabling illnesses or reported no illness at all. However, a similar sample was evaluated by a physician to determine medically disabling conditions which could appreciably affect the patient's well being or interfere with his social, economic or environmental activities. Using this criterion, only one person in seven was found to be free of current or potentially disabling disease. With such great disparity between respondents' reports of their performance and clinical estimates of their health, it would be difficult to estimate level of performance for most of the population from the recorded diagnosable medical problem. Roy E. Trussell and Jack Elinson, *Chronic Illness in Rural Area*, Boston: Harvard University Press, 1959, pp. 77, 151.

A survey of disability and chronic illness in Kansas City makes some analysis of the degree to which social roles are enacted and activity or health impaired. See Warren Peterson, "Metropolitan Area Health Survey," a report of *Community Studies, Inc.*, Kansas City, Missouri, June 1959.

The work of Allenstein on cardiac work capacity is promising in indicating the direction clinical assessment might take. Measurements in social situations outside the

With regard to correctional treatment outcome studies, it also is difficult to discern clearly any but gross differences in the manner in which individuals live after they leave prison. Unfortunately, base line studies of expectations, consumption standards, aspirations, strategies that utilize various levels of personal living resources, and skills and modes of coping with collective and individual stigma remain undone. Until these base line studies are available, it is risky to infer much about the adequacy of functioning for parolees from police and parole records.

In addition to this general difficulty of assessing the adequacy of postrelease adjustment, for studies evaluating correctional treatment, these assessments may be made from more than one perspective. The level of functioning may be viewed relative to local life space or relative to the dominant norms of society. Some ex-inmates may function "adequately" within a delinquent group or subculture. This type of adjustment, however, is regarded as unsatisfactory by the parole division.[3]

But aside from these empirical problems, it is a moot question whether level of functioning is really germane to the mission of correctional systems. As we stated earlier, we do not believe that men are imprisoned in order to improve their work skills, marital happiness, or emotional stability. It is true that within limitations set by budget, staffing, and custodial responsibilities, the California Department of Corrections makes an effort to influence the internal emotional states and the patterns of interpersonal relations of the inmates, with the hope that the prisoners will be discouraged from committing future illegal acts. However, the fact remains that this interest is incidental to the primary task of the department, which is to contain and to control convicted felons.[4]

---

examining room provide data on what actually happens to the heart when a man works in a steel mill. Allenstein's articles, however, arouse sociological interest in questions beyond the scope of his work. See Amafa B. Ford, Herman K. Allenstein, and David J. Turell, "Work and Heart Disease," *Circulation,* **20**, October 1959, pp. 537–548.

[3] "To the extent that crime is the byproduct of conflicting interpretations of what is proper conduct by different segments of a population, it is in no sense due to pathologies of the individuals involved, but to conditions peculiar to our social and political organizations. To that extent, crime is an aspect of political behavior, and those who hold the minority view must either change their behavior or find it regarded as criminal by the dominant majority." George Vold, "Some Basic Problems in Criminological Research," *Federal Probation,* **17**, 1953, p. 40.

[4] Quinney generalizes this point to include the entire apparatus of the law: "Criminal law may be regarded as an instrument of formal social control whereby an organized effort is made to regulate certain areas of behavior. As an instrument of social control, criminal law is most importantly characterized by its politicality. That is, (1) specific rules of conduct are created by a recognized legitimate authority, (2) designated officials interpret and enforce the rules, and (3) the code is binding on all persons within a given political unit." Richard Quinney, "Crime in Political Perspective," *American Behavioral Scientist,* December 1964, pp. 19–22.

The situation, if an oversimplification is allowed, is analogous to a manufacturing firm whose objective is to produce certain articles profitably. Because the prevailing theories of employee behavior stress the link between working conditions, morale, and rate of production, efforts are made to influence worker morale. These efforts, however, remain incidental to the primary purpose of the business, which is to make money.

In summary, we chose not to measure whether the personal lives of parolees were improved in some way by their involvement in group counseling. This measurement would be difficult in any case, but in the evaluation of prison treatment, for the reasons just stated, it seems to be somewhat beside the point. Thus, we have concentrated on criteria of treatment outcome that can be reliably measured, and which are directly germane to the primary responsibility of the Department of Corrections. We contend that the primary goals of correctional systems are to maintain secure, orderly inmate populations and to reduce recidivism. Hence, concepts of success and failure become operationalized in negative terms. *This study is, then, primarily concerned with the assessment of parole behavior in order to determine if exposure to a treatment program decreases the frequency with which the participants are returned to custody.*

MEASURES OF TREATMENT OUTCOME AS EFFECTED BY LENGTH OF FOLLOW-UP PERIOD

From the early stages of this project, several advocates of group counseling contended that the one-year follow-up provided for in our original study design was too short a period to demonstrate the "real" impact of the program. It was asserted, for example, that effects might be so subtle that they would not manifest themselves during the first year on parole, or that recidivism might not be reduced but that program participants might remain on parole longer or might commit less serious crimes than nonparticipants. Although we were inclined to think that one year would be an adequate test of the impact of group counseling experience, at least, insofar as recidivism was concerned, it soon became evident that one year would not be an adequate period, given the time lag involved between arrests and the final dispositions made by courts and the Adult Authority. As the initial data were gathered and analyzed, it became clear that a follow-up of at least 24 months was, indeed, indicated, and that 36 months would be preferable. For one thing, violation rates showed no signs of leveling off at the end of 12 months. Second, it required many more than 12 months to get 12-month parole information, both quantitative and qualitative. Many men who experienced trouble during their first year on parole did not turn up as parole violators until the second year because of the time required to process cases. Some revocations were related to the sheer passage of time during which a sufficient number of "minor" infractions or problems were accumulated, which exhausted the patience or resources of the parole agent. A one- or even two-year follow-up is an inadequate time period to measure treatment outcome, *not* because treatment effects are so subtle, but because it simply takes longer than that to gather evidence, judge, process, and record misbehavior.

Several published studies report the recidivism rate reaches a point of diminishing returns after 36 months. Glaser states: "*Apparently a three-year follow-up provides 90 percent of the probable future returns to prison data*"[5] (italics author). In 1965, Gottfredson and Ballard published results of an eight-year follow-up of 1810 California parolees which found that recidivism rates were a function of length of follow-up. "Difficulties occurred, though with decreasing rates, up to the end of the eight-year study period." However, 75 percent of all returns to prison did occur within 36 months from release. They concluded that a *two-year follow-up is not adequate* for program evaluation studies.[6]

Based on these results, we decided to extend the CMCE follow-up to three years. The decision has meant a considerable delay between the operation of the program and the publication of the results of its evaluation. However, our confidence in the accuracy of the study's conclusions has been greatly strengthened. Analyses testing major hypotheses used 36-month outcome data; some of the more specialized analyses, however, used 24-month data.

SOURCES OF FOLLOW-UP DATA ON PAROLE OUTCOME

As indicated earlier, an important feature of this longitudinal study is that departmental policy to parole men as soon as possible combined with the indeterminant sentencing structure makes for an unusually long period of

---

[5] To reach this conclusion, Glaser cites a follow-up study of California inmates released on parole in 1950. (At that time, 75 percent of male prisoners were released on parole.) Thirty-four and one half percent had been returned to prison within three years; by the sixth year, the figure had risen to 36.5 percent, and at the end of the eleventh year, recidivism had reached a total of 37 percent of the cohort. *Number of Men Paroled and Cumulative Percentage of Parolees Returned to Prison Each Year After Parole, 1950–61*, Research Division, California Department of Corrections, September 6, 1962. From Glaser, op. cit., p. 22.

A report of Federal releases followed for nine years found no appreciable increase in violations after the third year for either mandatory releases or parolees. *Statistical Report, 1966*, Department of Justice, Bureau of Prisons, Washington, D.C., pp. 82–83.

[6] In fact, they recommend a four- or five-year follow-up in order to determine the most accurate estimate of "unfavorable performance" (p. 35). Don M. Gottfredson and Kelley B. Ballard, Jr., *The Validity of Two Parole Prediction Scales: An Eight Year Follow Up Study*, Institute for the Study of Crime and Delinquency, Vacaville, California, 1965, p. 72. For a detailed discussion of this study, see footnote 26.

parole supervision for California parolees. Supervision, in turn, provides a mechanism for the systematic collection of certain kinds of follow-up data. These data were available from the Department of Corrections Research Division on every CMCE subject released under parole supervision.

The limitation of these data, of course, is the limitation of any source that relies on "officially reported" information. Law enforcement and correctional agencies do not have information about crimes committed by parolees that are not known to the police. Therefore, the number of cases of violations of the law (and of the conditions of parole) reported in this study does not represent the "true" violation rate for the study sample. An additional limitation is that our follow-up data were restricted to a relatively small number of quantifiable indices such as arrests and employment records. On the other hand, the Research Division made available parole agent and police reports which, for any independent research project involving a thousand subjects, would have been prohibitively costly to gather.

Organizational policies and operations, thus, make the scope of this longitudinal study possible, but it is also important to bear in mind that findings as to postrelease outcome that are given in this chapter and the next are based on data gathered by the organization under study.

PAROLE OUTCOME: OPERATIONALIZING THE CONCEPT

The Research Division of the California Department of Corrections has established a well-ordered operation to record the status of all releasees. This system brings together information sent by police departments to the California Criminal Identification and Intelligence Division, information submitted by parole agents and reports of actions taken by the Adult Authority. Hence, by providing the Research Division with a list of names and departmental identification numbers, we were able to obtain parole status information for all members of the sample at 6-, 12-, 24-, and 36-month intervals from date of release.

Most serious disposition known and whether the parolee had been *returned to prison* were the two items used to determine parole status (outcome) for our cohort. These designations were taken from the Research Division's 12-point scale for recording parole status. The items comprising the scale are as follows.

Minor Disposition

1. Returned to Narcotic Treatment Control Unit (both suspended or not suspended).
2. Arrest on technical charges only.
3. Parolee at Large with no known violation (PAL).

4. Arrest and release.

5. Trial and release.

6. Conviction with misdemeanor probation, with fine or bail forfeited, or with jail under 90 days.

Major Disposition

7. Parolee at large with a felony warrant (PVAL).
   Arrest on felony charge and release (guilt admitted and restitution provided) or arrest on felony charge and dismissed (guilt admitted in written statement and would be released if Adult Authority did not revoke parole in cooperation with District Attorney's wishes).
   Awaiting trial or sentence on felony charge.
   Death in commission of a crime or from drug overdose.

8. Ninety days to six months in jail.

9. Six months to nine months in jail.

10. Nine months or more in jail. Federal probation and/or suspended prison sentence.

11. Return to prison *in lieu of* new commitment, that is, arrest on felony charge more serious than in No. 7 above and would be prosecuted if Adult Authority did not revoke parole.

12. Return to prison anywhere with new commitment (WNT).

Since this category coded revocations, based only on new felony convictions (that is, it excluded technical revocations), it was necessary for us to check the second item—*return to prison*—to locate parolees recommitted for reasons *other* than a new crime. For example, a subject whose most serious disposition was drunkenness would be coded by the CDC (California Department of Corrections) as having received a minor disposition, *even though he might have been returned to prison* for excessive drinking. To obtain this latter information, it was necessary to combine the disposition code with the item "return to prison."

In sum, our classification was made as follows: parolees for whom no disposition was recorded were placed in the NO PROBLEMS category; those who received a minor disposition (Nos. 1 to 6) or a major disposition (Nos. 7 to 11) but were not returned to prison were placed in the MINOR PROBLEMS AND MAJOR PROBLEMS categories, respectively; men returned to prison either to finish term or with a new commitment were placed in the RETURN TO PRISON CATEGORY. NO PROBLEM and MINOR PROBLEM subjects were regarded as "successes"; MAJOR PROBLEM cases and men RETURNED TO

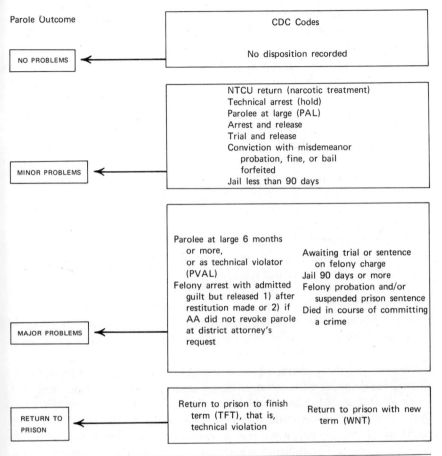

figure 8.1   Parole outcome classification, based on California Department of Corrections parole follow-up data.

PRISON were considered "failures." Figure 8.1 diagrams this classification scheme.

We feel reasonably confident that our measure of parole outcome is a valid summary of the parolee's legal status with police and parole authorities at various times during his parole. There is very little chance that a return to prison would go unrecorded, since that determination is made by the Department of Corrections. There were 273 men who successfully completed their paroles in periods of less than 36 months after release and, hence, they were discharged from parole supervision. Our data reflects the best information available to the Criminal Investigation Division concerning any involvement with California law enforcement agencies for these 273 men *subsequent* to their discharge, up to the 36-month cut off point for our sample. It was possible, therefore, to specify a 36-month outcome for every man in the sample regardless of whether he was in custody, still on parole, or discharged from parole.[7]

Two points concerning our outcome categories must be kept in mind. First, discrimination between adjacent categories—minor, major, and return to prison—is difficult, since placement may be, in part, a vagary of time and thus not entirely a characteristic of the inmate's behavior. That is, minor arrests, in sufficient numbers, can lead to parole revocation, and major arrests often are the prelude to court conviction or parole revocation. During one interval a parolee may be classified in the latest parole records as a major arrest, but his recommitment may be, in fact, already decided. If the return takes place after that interval, it will appear as a return to prison in the next interval; recommitments occurring more than 36 months after release were not reflected in our figures.

Second, the Research Division's method of recording parole status categorizes the parolee according to the most serious disposition that applies to him in the time period covered. In most cases this represents a realistic indication of his legal status, but for some men it undoubtedly masks improvement over time. For example, if a parolee was arrested on a drunk-and-disorderly charge in the first week of parole, but thereafter conducted his drinking with more prudence and discretion for thirty-five and three-quarter months, he would be carried in the MINOR PROBLEMS category. The same outcome designation would apply to the man who after many arrest-free months was arrested several times on drunk-and-disorderly conduct charges. The difficulties and expense of creating a separate record-keeping operation of our own to get independent monthly or quarterly ratings for each parolee outweighed the advantage of such profiles; hence, we have used the CDC classification system. The best we have been able to do in taking the time factor into account in recording parole experience is to note the length of time served on parole prior to revocation. Since the status of each parolee is recorded during the first, second, and third years of release, it is possible to make comparisons between study subjects who

---

[7] The State Criminal Identification and Investigation Division notifies the FBI of California parolees who are "at large" and receives information from them as to arrests and dispositions, which have been reported to the FBI, of California parolees in other states. Hence, arrests made outside of California for parolees in our study are included in the determination of parole status.

Data on *post-parole criminal behavior* that occurred outside of California may be lacking.

were returned to prison soon after release and men who stayed on parole longer.

The parole experience

It should be clear from the discussion of the parolees' legal status (Chapter VII) that their recidivism is not simply a matter of breaking the law, nor can it be viewed in the same way as one views felony convictions involving free citizens, that is, those members of the community enjoying full civil rights. Often legal dispositions did not accurately reflect the nature of the behavior that led to revocation. In fact, revocation is the end-result of a lengthy decision-making process that involves reviews of the parolee's behavior, his personality and past history, his agent's views, his agent's supervisor's views, and the views of the parole board, prosecutors, and the police. In other words, Parole Division policies, judgments, and administrative decisions play a critical role in determining the success or failure on parole.[8]

The following discussion illustrates general factors that must be taken into account in understanding the process of parole revocation. The cases cited were taken from parolee files and include parole agent narratives (transcriptions of interviews with the parolee), police reports, and Adult Authority dispositions. The materials were obtained from the Parole Division through the following procedure: precoded forms requesting copies of the above reports were sent to records officers in each parole district in the state for every man in our sample under supervision in that area. We made similar requests of records officers in California prisons to which some of the men had already been recommitted. (Both photocopy materials and records officers' time were paid for with project funds.) We were able to get photoduplicated copies of parolee records for 647 members of our follow-up sample who had been on parole for, at least, six

---

[8] Gottfredson, in commenting on this general topic, states: "Commonly used parole violation criteria, when a designation as a 'parole violator' is made on the basis not only of the parolee's behavior, but also on the response of the parole agent or the paroling authority provide . . . [a situation in which] an increase in 'parole violations' may reflect increased offending behavior by parolees, increased surveillance by parole agents, or changes in policy of the paroling authority." Don Gottfredson, "Assessment and Prediction Methods in Crime and Delinquency," *Task Force Report: Juvenile Delinquency and Youth Crime*, President's Commission on Law Enforcement and Administration of Justice, U.S. Government Printing Office, 1967, p. 173. In California, we know, for example, that at the time this study was conducted, the chances for remaining on parole if one violated technical conditions of parole were better if the inmate was released to the Southern Region than to the Northern Region. See Paul Takagi, *Evaluation Systems and Adaptations in a Formal Organization*, doctoral dissertation, University of California, Berkeley, 1967, Chapter 5.

months. The time from release ranged up to 24 months. These forms were returned to UCLA for coding and statistical analysis; they represent the parole subsample.

PAROLEE BEHAVIOR: INTERPRETATIONS FROM PAROLE AGENT REPORTS

Because he has both counseling and law enforcement responsibilities, the parole agent is the best source of officially recorded information about the experiences of ex-inmates in the community. Regulations and practices may vary over time and with jurisdiction, but during our study, at least, one personal interview was required every couple of months if the situation appeared to be nonproblematic; an interview was required more often if trouble was sensed or reported. Parole agents are responsible for making every effort to insure that the men under their supervision do not again violate the law. Consequently, they often are obliged to evaluate ambiguous situations with the aim of forestalling trouble. On the other hand, the Departments of Corrections do not expect revocation recommendations for every technical violation, and overly cautious parole supervision may result in reversals of agent recommendations by the paroling body. Nevertheless, considerable discretion is left to the agent and his supervisor. It is with these factors in mind that we give examples of how this discretion was exercised in cases of some of the CMCE parolees.

First, there are instances in which the Parole Division seemed to act in a lenient manner in applying the letter of the law. Extenuating circumstances seem to have led the Adult Authority to continue parole in the following two cases, even though parole conditions had been violated or a new crime had been committed.

G.W. was arrested for stealing two jars of instant coffee and sentenced to six months in jail. The parole agent recommended that the usual suspension of parole time while confined in jail not be invoked so that this man might be able to complete his parole while in the jail.

B.R. tried to commit suicide when he learned his mother was placed in a mental hospital. He had been listed as Parolee at Large (PAL) for failure to attend nalline tests and the outpatient clinic; he had also been arrested once on a drunk charge. The parole agent recommended continuance on parole after a psychiatrist's report indicated that B.R.'s suicide potential was "questionable." When released from police custody the parolee learned that his mother had died; he drank excessively, disappeared, and was listed again as PAL. Two weeks later, he turned himself in to the parole agent, who once again recommended reinstatement of parole and release to the Sheltered Live-In program of the Salvation Army and continue attending the outpatient clinic.

In another case, parole was revoked when the parolee threatened suicide, but a case involving assaultive behavior resulted in a decision to continue the man on parole.

W.L., an alcoholic, was returned to prison after three drunk arrests. The parole agent's supervisor had written in the Adult Authority report recommending revocation:

> Although Subject has not been involved in criminal activity while on parole, his completely uncontrolled drinking with expressed suicidal overtones, constitutes a serious threat to himself, and it is felt that he is in need of a type of supervision and treatment that cannot be afforded on parole.

R.J. was arrested and charged with assault with a deadly weapon. According to the victim (a young woman), subject forced his way into her hotel room, threatened her male friend with a knife and forced him to leave. He slashed the girl's forearm, cut the bedspread to pieces and stated he "had to leave for a minute to go to the rest room and warned her that if she attempted to leave, he would kill her." While he was in the rest room the girl hid the knife. When he came back she then excused herself to go to the bathroom but instead called the police. However, after arrest, the charge was reduced from assault with a deadly weapon to "maliciously destroying a bedspread."

Although there was no mention that R.J. was drunk, his behavior was not regarded as dangerous enough to create the view of him as having "violence potential"—a matter of great concern to the Parole Division.

Criteria other than criminal violations are sometimes the primary charges in revocation decisions. Some examples additional to those cited in Chapter IX include the following:

S.J. was involved in "completely unacceptable behavior" which was not, however, illegal. He was cited in the official record file as:

> Tardy, inattentive and lazy, exhibiting no ambition. Keeping company with married women; irresponsible job performance; unwilling to remain gainfully employed; clothes dirty; unkempt with several days growth of beard . . . his body emitted a very offensive odor noticeable from a distance. . . . He does not seem to be in the least interested in church, social organizations or community affairs. In view of the fact that subject shows no inclination whatever to accept responsibilities and obligations it is felt a violation report is in order.

One continuous and difficult area of parole decision making involves the question of what to do with men picked up or booked on several minor charges or in cases where the evidence of felony violation is not clear. Here are two such cases, each of which were ultimately resolved by revocation:

The parole agent was telephoned by G.C.'s estranged wife who charged that when "subject had assisted her in the transfer of their household goods, he had assaulted her and stolen her welfare money." Later, G.C. was arrested on a robbery charge and gave the following account. Subject asked a friend to make good on a NSF (nonsufficient funds) check he had signed to subject. When friend refused, G.C. proposed, as compensation, that the friend accompany him to a town in central California and beat up subject's estranged wife's current boyfriend. On the way the friend decided to rob a market and, in so doing, was shot and killed. G.C. was found asleep in the car in the parking lot, was arrested, denied knowledge of the robbery, but pled guilty. He was returned to prison with a new commitment because he had been found at the wheel of a get-away vehicle, as the agent put it, "even though asleep at the time the robbery occurred."

Subject G.H. was arrested for burglary, charge reduced to petty theft, and given ten days in jail. The agent noted: local police department reports they feel that the subject was not involved in petty theft till after the merchandise was stolen and he was in the car. At this time, he was informed of the theft. The police feel he was extremely uncooperative and at the time of arrest had much more information than he would give them. "It was because of this uncooperativeness that charges were filed. According to the sergeant, if subject had been cooperative, they would have dropped all charges."

In other cases, although the evidence of felony violation is unambiguous and guilt is admitted, revocation "to finish term" is recommended in lieu of prosecution. This may be done for parolees who "cooperate" with a district attorney.[9] For example, one parolee admitted to 19 burglaries but was not brought to trial for any of them. He was returned to prison as a parole violator to finish his current term because he was "cooperative."

---

[9] This type of accommodation to the legal system also occurs where civilians are involved. "Cooperation" with law enforcement agencies often results in dropping some charges or reducing the seriousness of the charge. See Donald J. Newman, "Pleading Guilty for Considerations: A Study of Bargain Justice," *Journal of Criminal Law, Criminology and Police Science*, 46, March-April, 1956, pp. 780-790, and by the same author, *Conviction: The Determination of Guilt or Innocence Without Trial*, Boston: Little Brown and Company, 1966, Part III.

It is difficult to generalize from these parole records which infractions (short of felony conviction) assure revocation and which call for continuation of parole. The parole contract provides the framework for revocation, but it is the parole agent, his supervisor, the regional parole administrator, and the Adult Authority who determine if a man who has violated the contract will be given another chance (or another and another) or whether he will be returned to prison to finish his term. (As was pointed out in one case, it is always possible for the Adult Authority to extend the present parole discharge date regardless of whether the man has been recommitted or continued on parole.) A conclusion, admittedly impressionistic, is that official actions are strongly influenced by a parolee's "demonstrated progress" to the point that this progress may outweigh the influence of law violations. Continued misbehavior or "inappropriate" or "unacceptable" conduct which may not include violations of the law, however, seems to set forces in motion that often lead to revocation. Parole decision-making is a complex process in which many kinds of information about parolee behavior are mixed with parole agent perceptions and hunches and the departmental policy to produce the actions that constitute the major measure of treatment outcome for this study. In the following section we present data that cast light on the question of which parolee actions are related to decisions to revoke or to continue parole.

THE DISPOSITIONS RECEIVED BY CMCE RELEASEES

By the end of 36 months, reports of some kind of disposition had been recorded by the Parole Division for all but 247 men (26 percent) in our study sample. Dispositions were divided between felonies (426 men) and misdemeanors or "technical" violations of parole (266 men). A few men received dispositions whose nature was unspecified (18) (see Table 8.1).

The next step was to determine how closely outcome was related to seriousness of violations reported. Table 8.2 shows that if a parolee had had any type of felony arrest, the chances for recommitment were substantial. Four out of five arrested at least once for a felony offense had been returned to prison, and decisions to return many of the additional 11 percent (classified *major problems*) had already been made. It is interesting to observe that more than one half of the men whose most serious disposition was a technical violation of parole of misdemeanor had also been recommitted. Notice also that 15 percent (38 men) of those with no recorded disposition had an outcome disposition recorded by us as something other than *no problems*. This does not indicate a discrepancy between the sources of outcome data but reflects the fact that we are reporting outcome for all men in our sample, including the ones whose police contacts came after discharge from parole.

table 8.1   Most Serious Disposition on Parole in Thirty-Six Months

	Cases	Percent of Total
Robbery and grand theft	32	3.3
Burglary	60	6.2
Forgery	41	4.2
Theft	105	10.9
Petty theft with prior shoplift 46		
Operate vehicle without owner's consent 34		
Fraud 4		
Receive stolen property 3		
Nonsufficient funds—checks 18		
Assaultive and sex related	27	2.8
Narcotics	52	5.4
Sale 14		
Possession 38		
Marijuana and dangerous drugs	27	2.8
Marijuana sale 7		
Marijuana possess 8		
Pills, acid 12		
Other felonies	84	8.7
Fail to provide 13		
Drunk drive 24		
Drive with license suspended 24		
Hit and run 3		
Possess gun 11		
Extortion 1		
Escape jail 1		
All other 7		
Misdemeanors	116	12.0
Battery, fighting, wife beating 18		
Contribute to delinquency of minor 2		
Reckless driving 6		
Disturbing the peace 11		

table 8.1   (continued)

	Cases	Percent of Total
Malicious mischief 1		
Drunk 49		
Vagrancy 7		
Tamper with auto 1		
All other 21		
Technical parole violations	170	17.6
Parolee at large only 77		
Technical violation 75		
Disposition not specified 18		
No recorded disposition	251	26.1
	965	100

table 8.2   Most Serious Disposition by Outcome at Thirty-Six Months (in Percent)

Outcome Measure	No Disposition	Misdemeanor Technical Parole Violation or Unspecified	Felony
No problems	85	—	—
Minor problem	11	32	10
Major problem	2	14	11
Return to prison	2	54	79
Total	100	100	100
	(247)	(284)	(426)

Treatment and control sample differences

Parole begins in prison. That is, the first steps associated with parole are taken inside prison walls. Initially, the Adult Authority grants a parole and sets a date for release. Then come preparole classes and the arrangements for job and residence. These prerelease factors are presumed to ease the transition from prison to community life and to predispose releasees toward patterns of living that are considered appropriate by the Department of Corrections. Other aspects of the parole situation, for instance, releasing a man to a community in which he has a criminal record, specifying special conditions or types of supervision (for example, nalline testing), and releasing a man who must assume child support obligations, are also thought to affect chances for successful "adjustment" in the outside world. Finally, factors such as levels of formal education and vocational training and inmate social type are reputed to be related to chances for parole success. We have made an effort to compare treatment and control categories (as we did in Chapter II with regard to pre-prison characteristics) to be certain that these extraneous factors would not bias outcome in favor of any one of the five groups. These data may be seen in Appendix G. In most cases we can also report on the empirical relationship between these variables and outcome.

OUTCOME PREDICTIONS

To be certain that differences between treatment and control subjects could not be attributed to differential parole prognosis, we compared them on a measure used by the California Department of Corrections—the Base Expectancy Score (BES). This is a weighted linear combination of 12 items taken from the inmate file, and it consists of the following components (in descending order of predictive weight): arrest-free period of five years or more, no history of opiate use, few jail commitments (two or less), present commitment based on offense other than checks or burglary, no family crime record, no alcohol involvement, first arrest for offense other than auto theft, one job held at least six months, no alias, present sentence on original commitment, favorable living arrangement (not transient), and two or fewer prior arrests.

On the basis of chi-square tests, there were no significant differences in BES between treatment categories.[10] The comparison presented in Table 8.3—a one-way analysis of variance—shows that though mean BES favors the control subjects, differences were not statistically significant.[11]

Notice that BES includes only information about the inmate's life *prior* to his commitment. In other words, neither in-prison experience nor the expectations about life on parole figure in the calculation of the score. We then compared subjects on several items of information collected from prison or parole records which reflect both prison life and conditions of release.

EDUCATIONAL LEVEL

At release significantly fewer men in voluntary controls had attended CMCE school (academic, not vocational) compared with men in other

---

[10] See Appendix A, Table A.5 for weighing of components and BES By Treatment Status in tabular form.

[11] For BES By Outcome see Tables 9.1, 9.2, and 9.3.

table 8.3   Analysis of Variance of Base Expectancy Differences by Treatment
Status

	Treatment Category				
	Mandatory Controls	Voluntary Controls	Mandatory Large Group Counseling	Mandatory Small Group Counseling	Voluntary Small Group Counseling
Number of cases	270	176	69	173	278
Means of BES	40.34	40.81	32.94	37.13	36.68
Standard deviation	30.93	31.64	29.05	28.07	30.30

	Sum of Squares	Degrees of Freedom	Mean-Square	F Ratio
Between	5183.05	4	1295.76	1.42
Within	879706.45	961	915.41	
Total	884889.50	965		Not significant

treatment-control categories.[12] However, there were no differences in categories in terms of years of school completed at release[13] (see Appendix G.4).

[12] Percentages of men in each category who attended prison school while confined at CMCE: Mandatory Controls—43; Voluntary Controls—25; Mandatory Large Group —43; Mandatory Small Group—40; and Voluntary Small Group—41. Neither prison school attendance nor vocational school attendance were significantly related to outcome.

[13] The last year of school completed at release was significantly related to outcome at 6, 12, and 24 months. Although the lowest return rate was among high school graduates who had taken additional work (but less than one year of college), about the same proportion of men with one or more years of college "failed" as men who had only a grammar school education. [Note. The number of men who attended any college was small (65).]

Classified Major Problems or Returned to Prison within Twenty-Four Months

Last Grade Completed	Percent	Number of Cases in Each Group
Fourth or less	69	48
Fifth and sixth	55	151

INMATE TYPES

In Chapter VI we described a typology of inmates based on attitude data. They were defined in terms of two elements often asserted to be related to postrelease behavior—opposition to staff and solidarity with inmates.[14] In connection with the comparability of treatment and control groups at release, we sought to determine whether any one type was overrepresented (or conversely, underrepresented) in one or more of these five groups. Treatment and controls contained about the same proportion of *Square Johns, Politicians, Right Guys* and *Outlaws* (Appendix G.5).

PREPAROLE CLASSES

Preparole class attendance was encouraged for all CMCE inmates whose parole dates had been set. These sessions, conducted by representatives of the Parole Division, were designed to discuss the terms of the parole contract, that is, to answer any questions inmates might have about the legal, occupational, personal, and social conditions of parole. Although most of the men in our sample (approximately two thirds) attended at least one session, significantly fewer nonparticipants in group counseling attended than participants (Appendix G.2). However, preparole class attendance was *not* related to parole success.

CRIMINAL RECORD IN RELEASE COMMUNITY

Another matter that concerns paroling authorities in regard to postrelease outcome is whether the inmate has a criminal record in the community to which he will be paroled.[15] Seventy percent of our sample were released

Seventh and eighth	54	257
Ninth	51	149
Tenth and eleventh	48	186
Twelfth	49	112
Less than one year college or post-high school courses	26	35
One year or more of college	57	30
N	(502)	(968)

$\chi^2 = 18.62$, df $= 7$, p $< .01$

[14] Although Square Johns were both less likely to have been returned to prison and more likely to have remained on parole without trouble than Right Guys, these differences did not attain an acceptable level of significance. In other words, men who expressed a low degree of inmate solidarity and were low in opposition to staff did not do significantly better on parole than men who were high in staff opposition and high in inmate solidarity (Table 9.7).

[15] Our data indicated that criminal record in the release community was significantly related to parole outcome.

to either Los Angeles or San Francisco, where most of the men had also been convicted, so that finding criminal records in the release community for two thirds of the parolees was not surprising. This was true for each of the treatment and control categories (see Appendix G.6).

PRISON ARRANGED JOBS

Underlying parole policy has been the assumption that men released without immediate employment are more likely to get into trouble than men who have a job to go to—thus, the requirement that every inmate[16] have a definite job or employer arrangements before he can be released. A review of records of the parole subsample revealed that many of the arrangements made to satisfy this requirement were vague, fictitious, or never materialized. In fact, less than one half of the men left prison to go to a definite job; the remainder were released to a trade union hiring hall or to the Salvation Army. Inmates participating in any one of the three kinds of group counseling were no more likely to have assured release employment than were nonparticipants. A higher proportion of men in mandatory small group counseling were released with definite employment although differences were not statistically significant (Appendix G.3).

CONDITIONS OF RELEASE

We thought that control subjects scheduled for parole might be detained in prison longer than treatment subjects, perhaps, to arrange a job or to clarify their living situation or to provide some other "assurance" of a safer prognosis. Or, perhaps, that controls might have been assigned more often to special programs of parole supervision that entailed more intensive surveillance.

Approximately two thirds of men in each treatment category were released within three days of the parole date specified by the Adult Authority. One type of parole did not specify a release date; instead, the inmate's release was based "upon approval on a parole plan" (RUAPP).

---

[16] Our data did not support this assumption—men released without jobs were no more likely to violate parole than were men released with a prearranged job. Recent data from a study of Minnesota parolees confirmed our findings. There were about the same proportion of men released to low-level jobs arranged by family or by friends merely to satisfy parole requirements ("out jobs"). After one year, there were no more parole violations for men released without employment than for men released to definite jobs. In addition, these data also indicated that men who got their jobs after release did as well, if not better, than men with prearranged jobs in terms of the kind (that is, quality) of employment, the ability to hold the job, and salary. William McRae, Bruce McManus, Roy Evans, and Nathan Mandel, "A Study in Community Parole Orientation," Department of Corrections, St. Paul, Minnesota (unpublished), 1968.

Again, nonparticipants were no more likely to have been given this kind of conditional release than the participants[17] (Appendix G.1).

During the years our study sample was paroled, the special parole situations to which assignment was possible included Increased Correctional Effectiveness (ICE), Special Intensive Parole Units (SIPU), Out-Patient Clinic (OPC), and Narcotic Parole (nalline testing). Approximately one in 20 men in our parole subsample were in one of these programs; nalline tests were required of an additional one in four. Men in control groups were assigned to these programs in the same ratio as the ones who had participated in group counseling.

We can now approach the issue of postrelease effects with greater confidence that the treatment groups were not significantly different from controls on parole prognosis, aspects of prison experience, or conditions of parole release.

TREATMENT EXPOSURE AND BEHAVIOR IN PRISON

We may begin our analysis of differences between men in treatment groups and in prison without treatment by examining data, such as there are, on the frequency of unwanted or disallowed behavior in prison. The only direct prison behavioral measure we have is the record of citations for infractions of inmate regulations which are routinely issued by the correctional officers. These written citations result in the inmate's appearance before the Disciplinary Committee. Thus it represents a conservative estimate of violations, since officers could not be presumed to note more than a fraction of this behavior. The citation (termed a Form 115) gave certain minimal description of the allegation as viewed by the staff. They were classified into four types of violations:

1. The actions involving rules pertaining to *persons* (chiefly fighting with other inmates).
2. The actions involving *inmate property* (theft and possession of contraband).
3. The actions involving prison *staff*—disrespect, disobedience.
4. The actions involving the *administration*, state property, being out of bounds, and the like.

Only about one half of the men in the evaluation study showed no viola-

[17] Men released prior to their specified parole date did significantly better on parole based on 12-month outcome than inmates released on time, after their date, or whose parole plan had been "approved" before date could be set. However, those released early accounted for less than 10 percent of the sample.

tion of a rule during their stay at CMC. The remainder were cited for a violation of one or more types of rules on one or more occasions. Table 8.4 shows that the differences on any given type—person, inmate property, staff, or administration—from one treatment category to another, amount to only a few percentage points. The frequency of citations varied by little more than 4 to 5 percent, with a difference of 10 percent being the largest. In these, as in the total summed across types of rule violation, the value of chi-square did not reach significance.

Treatment and parole performance

In this section we compare the treatment and control groups in terms of the problems each experienced on parole—problems including unemployment, financial dependence, alcohol and drug use, the number and seriousness of arrests, the length of confinement, and the type of parole offense—as well as parole outcome. These data are primarily based on analyses of parole file records representing a subsample ($N = 647$). The analyses of parole offenses and outcome make use of parole disposition data and thus involve the entire study sample.

EMPLOYMENT AND FINANCIAL DEPENDENCE

Considering the subsample for whom parole agent reports were available, approximately one in five of the men in each treatment category was unemployed within one month of release; over one half were working in some unskilled or semiskilled job; and between 10 and 20 percent had skilled white collar jobs. By eight months, about one in four men from each treatment and control group was in jail or prison. Mandatory controls were the least likely to have been unemployed during the time period covered in the parole narrative. Men from mandatory large groups and voluntary controls had the highest proportions of subjects unemployed. Differences were not significant, however. Men changed jobs to some extent within eight months, but fewer than one third of each treatment category had had more than three; about the same proportion of each group had one job only (see Table 8.5).

Again, based on subsample data, men from treatment groups were neither more nor less likely to have money available to them on release other than the funds provided by the Department of Corrections. They did not depend on others for financial support anymore than did the controls. Support tended to come from families instead of from official sources

table 8.4   Prison Rule Infractions by Treatment Status (in Percent)

	RULES ABOUT PERSON[a]			RULES ABOUT INMATE PROPERTY[b]			RULES ABOUT STAFF[c]			RULES ABOUT ADMINISTRATION[d]			TOTAL CASES
	None	One or More	Total	None	One or More	Total	None	One or More	Total	None	One or More	Total	N
Mandatory control	91	9	100	84	16	100	76	24	100	74	26	100	(269)
Voluntary control	88	12	100	81	19	100	77	23	100	74	26	100	(176)
Mandatory large group	87	13	100	78	22	100	71	29	100	70	30	100	(69)
Mandatory small group	86	14	100	83	17	100	82	18	100	64	36	100	(173)
Voluntary small group	90	10	100	82	18	100	76	24	100	65	35	100	(278)

[a] Table $N = 965$
$\chi^2 = 3.34$
df = 4
Not significant

[b] Table $N = 965$
$\chi^2 = 1.57$
df = 4
Not significant

[c] Table $N = 965$
$\chi^2 = 4.21$
df = 4
Not significant

[d] Table $N = 965$
$\chi^2 = 8.94$
df = 4
Not significant

TOTAL PRISON RULE INFRACTIONS[e]

	None	1 to 2	3 to 4	5 to 6	7 or more	Total	Total Cases (N)
Mandatory control	55	26	11	4	5	100	(269)
Voluntary control	51	31	10	3	5	100	(176)
Mandatory large group	46	32	13	7	2	100	(69)
Mandatory small group	47	36	9	3	5	100	(173)
Voluntary small group	47	31	11	6	5	100	(278)
Total	50	31	11	4	4	100	
N	(482)	(296)	(103)	(44)	(40)		

[e] Table $N = 965$
$\chi^2 = 13.12$
Degrees of freedom = 16
Not significant

table 8.5a   Employment at One Month and at Eight Months on Parole by Treatment Status (in Percent)

EMPLOYMENT

	One Month From Release[a]					Eight Months From Release[b]				
	Mandatory Controls	Voluntary Controls	Mandatory Large Group Counseling	Mandatory Small Group Counseling	Voluntary Small Group Counseling	Mandatory Controls	Voluntary Controls	Mandatory Large Group Counseling	Mandatory Small Group Counseling	Voluntary Small Group Counseling
Employed Unskilled, Semi-skilled	61	64	51	62	56	39	43	43	36	40
Skilled or White collar	18	10	21	14	21	18	9	14	15	16
Unemployed	18	19	25	19	20	22	24	7	24	18
In custody	3	7	5	5	3	21	24	36	25	26
Total	100	100	100	100	100	100	100	100	100	100
N	(150)	(131)	(44)	(114)	(170)	(130)	(120)	(28)	(97)	(141)

[a] Parole Subsample
Table N = 609
No information = 38
$\chi^2 = 19.54$; df = 16
Not significant

[b] Parole Subsample
Table N = 516
No information or not on parole eight months at the time the data was collected = 131
$\chi^2 = 18.34$; df = 16
Not significant

231

table 8.5b   Employment History on Parole for Men from Each Treatment Category (in Percent)

Treatment Category	Parole Employment			
	Employed All of the Time Since Release	Employed Some of the Time	Unemployed All or Most of the Time	Total (N)
Mandatory controls	40	51	9	100 (151)
Voluntary controls	38	45	17	100 (127)
Mandatory large group counseling	46	34	20	100 (41)
Mandatory small group counseling	46	41	13	100 (112)
Voluntary small group counseling	44	44	12	100 (170)

Parole Subsample
Table $N = 601$
No information $= 46$
$\chi^2 = 8.64$
Degrees of freedom $= 8$
Not significant

for about two thirds of the parolees considered "partially dependent"[18] (see Table 8.6).

DRUGS AND ALCOHOL

A history of the use of drugs or the excessive use of alcohol had several implications for postrelease behavior.[19] As we have stated, a drug history that included the use of heroin required periodic nalline tests to prove

[18] Sources of support were familial rather than official for about two thirds of the "partially dependent" men. Financial independence was significantly related to 12-month outcome. Twice as many men receiving aid from nonfamilial (that is, official) sources as men considered self-reliant were returned to prison within 12 months (36 percent versus 18 percent). Twenty-six percent of the men aided by their families were returned to prison within a year. $p < .01$.

[19] A preprison history of excessive use of alcohol was not related to outcome at 24 months; preprison history of drug use was significant at the .001 level.

table 8.6   Financial Independence and Dependence on Parole as Proportion
of Each Treatment Category (in Percent)

Treatment Category	Self-supporting	Dependent	Total (N)
	Financial Experience		
Mandatory controls	66	34	100 (149)
Voluntary controls	59	41	100 (126)
Mandatory large group counseling	73	27	100 (44)
Mandatory small group counseling	65	35	100 (111)
Voluntary small group counseling	72	28	100 (169)

Parole Subsample
Table N = 599
No information = 49
$\chi^2 = 6.28$
Degrees of freedom = 4
Not significant

nonuse; this had the effect of intensifying supervision. Rather than impose a special condition of abstinence for inmates who had had drinking problems (a condition whose violation could result in revocation), more commonly the agent was alerted that closer supervision might be required in these instances. Prison files revealed that about one out of three of our sample was classified as either a problem drinker or as an alcoholic, and a like proportion had a history of narcotics use. Parole subsample data indicates that the proportion was smaller than one in three: one in five had trouble associated with liquor; one in six had trouble associated with drugs.

Apparently, participation in group counseling did not reduce the likelihood of being cited for these problems. Differences between categories were not statistically significant (see Table 8.7).

ARRESTS AND JAIL CONFINEMENT

There were also no treatment or control group differences on the number of misdemeanor or felony arrests recorded in the parole records, no differences in total number of weeks spent in jail, and no differences in the most serious disposition received within three years after release. Notice that although differences were not significant, mandatory controls were less frequently arrested, especially for felony offenses, and less often confined in jail than men from any treatment category.

table 8.7 Problems on Parole with Alcohol or Drugs by Treatment Status (in Percent)

Treatment Categories	ALCOHOL[a]			DRUGS[b]		
	Percent Arrested on Parole for Drunkenness or Regarded as Problem Drinker	No Alcohol Problem	Total	Percent Known or Alleged to Use Drugs on Parole	No Drug Problem	Total
Mandatory controls (N = 163)	19	81	100	18	82	100
Voluntary controls (N = 138)	21	79	100	13	87	100
Mandatory large group counseling (N = 47)	17	83	100	17	83	100
Mandatory small group counseling (N = 120)	18	82	100	15	85	100
Voluntary small group counseling (N = 179)	20	80	100	18	82	100

[a] Parole Subsample
Table N = 647
$\chi^2 = .56$
Degrees of freedom = 4
Not significant

[b] Parole Subsample
Table N = 647
$\chi^2 = 2.09$
Degrees of freedom = 4
Not significant

table 8.8   Number of Misdemeanor and Felony Arrests by Treatment Status (in Percent)

Number of Arrests	Mandatory Controls	Voluntary Controls	Mandatory Large Group Counseling	Mandatory Small Group Counseling	Voluntary Small Group Counseling
			Treatment Category		
Misdemeanors[a]					
None	62	57	60	62	62
One	28	28	26	22	27
Two or more	11	15	15	17	12
Total	100	100	100	100	100
N	(163)	(138)	(47)	(120)	(179)
Felony[b]					
None	81	72	79	75	77
One or more	19	28	21	25	24
Total	100	100	100	100	100
N	(163)	(138)	(47)	(120)	(179)

[a] Parole Subsample
Table $N = 647$
$\chi^2 = 4.63$
Degrees of freedom = 8
Not significant

[b] Parole Subsample
Table $N = 647$
$\chi^2 = 3.84$
Degrees of freedom = 4
Not significant

PAROLE OUTCOME AT 36 MONTHS

The outcome index described earlier is a more systematic measure of parole outcome for the Men's Colony—East study sample. It distinguishes between men returned to prison, jailed for major trouble, jailed for minor trouble and, finally, those with no recorded arrests. Several versions of this measure of outcome at 36 months for treatment and control groups are presented in Tables 8.11 to 8.14. Data on the year of return to prison and on the seriousness of revocation also are given. All versions tell essentially the same story: *treatment and controls do not have significantly different outcomes.* That is, mandatory and voluntary control groups do about the same as their treatment counterparts. The exception was mandatory large group counseling that had the smallest proportion of no

table 8.9   Time Spent in Jail During Parole Period by Treatment Status
(in Percent)

Time Spent in Jail During Parole	Mandatory Controls	Voluntary Controls	Mandatory Large Group Counseling	Mandatory Small Group Counseling	Voluntary Small Group Counseling
			Treatment Category		
Not confined	53	42	45	43	47
Confined					
less than 1 week	6	10	9	8	9
1 to 2 weeks	5	10	2	5	9
3 to 4 weeks	6	5	13	15	9
5 to 8 weeks	8	12	13	13	6
9 to 16 weeks	17	18	18	16	17
17 to 52 weeks	4	3	—	1	3
Total	100	100	100	100	100
N	(157)	(136)	(45)	(120)	(177)

Parole Subsample
  Table $N = 635$
  No information $= 12$
  $\chi^2 = 28.28$
  Degrees of freedom $= 24$
  Not significant

problem cases and the largest proportion of men returned to prison (15 percent and 59 percent, respectively).

This conclusion was unchanged when we used the dichotomy employed by the California Department of Corrections, in which success equals no dispositions and only arrests or jail terms of less than 90 days, and failure refers to jail terms exceeding 90 days, federal probation or return to prison. A one-way analysis of variance (also using a dichotomized outcome) shows nearly identical means for the five categories of treatment status. F ratio of between group variance versus within group variance is not significant. (Notice the homogeneity between categories.)

Tables 8.13a and 8.13b compare treatment status on expanded versions of the outcome variable. One version distinguishes between repeats of trouble occurring on parole or following discharge; the other version indicates when revocation occurred. First, regarding successful completion of parole, although differences were not significant, mandatory contable 8.10   Most Serious Parole Disposition at Thirty-Six Months by Treatment Status[a] (in Percent)

Parole Disposition[b]	Mandatory Controls	Voluntary Controls	Mandatory Large Group Counseling	Mandatory Small Group Counseling	Voluntary Small Group Counseling
			Treatment Category		
Robbery	3	5	7	2	3
Burglary	6	7	10	5	6
Forgery	3	5	9	5	4
Theft	10	13	7	12	10
Assaultive and sex	4	4	2	3	2
Narcotic	5	5	9	5	6
Marijuana	2	4	2	4	3
Other felonies	11	7	12	5	9
Misdemeanor or technical	29	24	25	33	31
No disposition	27	26	17	26	25
Total	100	100	100	100	100
N	(270)	(175)	(69)	(173)	(276)

Table N = 963
No information = 5
$\chi^2 = 35.07$
Degrees of freedom = 36.
Not significant

[a] Unlike the regular outcome data, this source of disposition has not been updated to include actions taken against a man after discharge from parole, that is, completion of sentence.
[b] CDC classifications.

trols had the highest percentage of men discharged by the end of the three-year follow-up period; mandatory large group counseling had the lowest percentage. With the exception of this latter category, nearly 1 in 5 of the men in each of the other treatment categories had had no recorded arrests while on parole, had been discharged from parole supervision, and had had no subsequent contact with law enforcement agencies up to 36 months following their release from CMC—E.

Table 8.13a distinguishes between technical revocations and those that

table 8.11   Parole Outcome at Thirty-Six Months by Treatment Status (in Percent)

Parole Outcome at Thirty-Six Months	Treatment Category					
	Mandatory Controls (N = 269)	Voluntary Controls (N = 173)	Mandatory Large Group Counseling (N = 68)	Mandatory Small Group Counseling (N = 171)	Voluntary Small Group Counseling (N = 274)	Total[a] (N = 955)
Dichotomized*						
Success	42	34	30	43	40	39
Failure	58	66	70	57	60	61
Total	100	100	100	100	100	100
Four-Way**						
No problems	24	23	15	22	21	22
Minor problems	18	11	15	21	19	17
Major problems	10	10	11	7	10	10
Return to prison	48	56	59	50	50	51
Total	100	100	100	100	100	100

* $\chi^2 = 6.62$
Degrees of freedom = 4
Not significant

** $\chi^2 = 11.68$
Degrees of freedom = 12
Not significant

[a] By 36 months, 8 men of the 968 were dead, and information was incomplete on 5 others.

table 8.12   Analysis of Variance of Parole Outcome and Treatment Status

			Treatment Category		
	Mandatory Controls	Voluntary Controls	Mandatory Large Group Counseling	Mandatory Small Group Counseling	Voluntary Small Group Counseling
Number of cases	269	173	68	171	274
Means of outcome	1.41	1.33	1.29	1.42	1.40
Standard deviation	.49	.47	.46	.50	.49

	Sum Squares	Degrees of Freedom	Mean Squares	F Ratio
Between groups	1.53	4	.382	1.44
Within groups	225.79	950	.238	
Total	227.32	954		Not significant

reflect new convictions.[20] Mandatory large group counseling had a higher proportion of men convicted of new crimes than other groups, but the number of cases in this category is small. Revocations to finish term (technical violations) accounted for about two thirds of all returns within 36 months, and insofar as we could ascertain, once discharged from parole supervision, a man was rarely returned to prison during the follow-up period.

Table 8.13b considers only cases returned to prison. This analysis allows for the possibility that participation in group treatment might, at least, have delayed revocation. But, again, treatment and control cases had about the same experiences. The bulk of returns to prison occurred early in the follow-up period regardless of treatment status: 29, 28, and 26 percent of the three forms of group counseling, and 26 and 31 percent of the two control groups were revoked during the first year.

[20] Theoretically, a return with a new term (WNT) refers to a more serious violation than recommitment to finish term (TFT), which implies unsatisfactory parole performance but, as noted in Chapter VII, "cooperation" with police and judicial agencies makes this distinction, in practice, an unreliable indicator of the severity of behavior leading to revocation.

table 8.13a   Postrelease Status at Thirty-Six Months by Treatment Status
(in Percent)

			Treatment Category		
	Mandatory Controls	Voluntary Controls	Mandatory Large Group Counseling	Mandatory Small Group Counseling	Voluntary Small Group Counseling
Returned to Prison					
With new term	16	18	27	19	15
To finish term	31	37	29	31	35
After discharge from parole	1	1	3	—	—
Major Problems					
During parole	5	3	10	5	6
After discharge from parole	4	7	1	1	4
Minor Problems					
During parole	7	3	7	8	9
After discharge from parole	11	8	7	13	10
No Problems					
Still on parole	4	5	3	4	4
Discharged from parole	21	18	12	19	17
Total	100	100	100	100	100
N	(269)	(173)	(68)	(171)	(274)

Table $N = 955$
Dead $= 8$, incomplete information $= 5$
$\chi^2 = 36.19$
Degrees of freedom $= 32$
Not significant

GROUP TREATMENT AND PAROLE SUCCESS: THE NULL HYPOTHESIS IS SUPPORTED

Before proceeding further, the findings and analyses presented thus far should be summarized. The total sample of men released from prison during our study included some who were randomly assigned to living units where counseling was mandatory (one group was large, the others small)

table 8.13b Revocations by Treatment Status: First, Second, and Third Year from Prison Release (in Percent)

Returned to Prison	Treatment Category					
	Mandatory Controls	Voluntary Controls	Mandatory Large Group Counseling	Mandatory Small Group Counseling	Voluntary Small Group Counseling	Total
During first year	26	31	29	28	26	28
During second year	16	15	20	13	16	15
During third year	6	10	10	9	8	8
Total	48	56	59	50	50	51
N	(130)	(97)	(40)	(86)	(137)	(490)

$\chi^2 = 3.78$
Degrees of freedom = 8
Not significant

or to a quadrangle in which group counseling was not available (mandatory controls). The remainder of the sample contained men who were assigned to living units in which group counseling was available but where the inmates had the option to join (voluntary small groups) or not to join (voluntary controls).

The comparison on a variety of preparole items indicated that no one treatment-control category was favored in terms of having attended preparole classes, whether release was as scheduled or whether employment had been arranged prior to release. Each of the five catgories were equally likely to be comprised of men paroled with special conditions, and men with criminal records in the communities to which they were released. Each category contained, to about the same degree, the four inmate types. An analysis of variance established no significant difference in parole prognosis between treatment and control groups.

In addition to parole outcome at 36 months, experience of the study groups were compared for a subsample of parolees in terms of several additional indicators of problematic parole performance—unemployment, drug and alcohol use, jail terms, financial dependence, and the like. Although some small percentage differences were found (usually in favor of the voluntary control group), they were not of sufficient magnitude to allow us to reject the null hypothesis.

In short, parole performance, as measured by the specific criteria described above, was no different for the participants in group counseling than it was for nonparticipants. These findings were consistent at each follow-up interval. That is, there were no differences in parole outcome by treatment status measured at 6, 12, 24, and 36 months after release.

Although the main hypothesis under test in this study was stated in terms of *some treatment versus none*, we also can examine the impact on outcome of other facets of the counseling experience.[21] In the following section we consider some of these additional issues: Is the level of training of the group counseling leaders related to parole outcome? What is the significance of *requiring* a man to attend group counseling? Do men with attitudes favorable to group counseling fare better on parole? Do men who attend many counseling sessions differ on parole outcome from men who attended only a few? Do changes in group leader relate to parole success? Although none of these questions can be answered conclusively in this study because they were side issues to the primary hypothesis, available data does permit comparisons on postrelease out-

---

[21] To determine exactly how much of the variance could be explained by any aspect of treatment, using multivariate techniques, refer to the last section of this chapter.

come. Reinterpretation of data already presented and data from special analyses lends strength to the major conclusions of the study.

The implications for parole outcome of other aspects of the counseling experience

Additional conclusions about group counseling can be derived from data presented earlier in this chapter because the treatment varieties varied according to the level of training that the leaders received and because of the voluntary and mandatory aspects of the participation. We found, for example, that men from groups whose leaders were given regular departmental training did about the same on parole as men from groups whose leaders received special supplemental training.[22] The implications of this conclusion are particularly important for *future* group counseling programs. Negative outcome findings often are countered with the claim that the program (in this case group counseling) would have worked if the leaders had been better trained. Such an argument should be examined rather critically in light of these data.

By reanalyzing our data we could compare men required to participate with those for whom group counseling was not an option, as well as comparing men who chose to participate with men who chose not to. There were two mandatory treatment conditions—large and small; each is analyzed separately here. There were no significant differences in outcome at 36 months between volunteer groups; nor were there differences between the mandatory conditions. A comparison of volunteers with assigned men indicates somewhat poorer parole performance for men who were given the option, irrespective of which option they chose; but again, differences were not significant.

---

[22] In addition to the special training we provided for all mandatory small group counseling and mandatory large group counseling leaders, a higher percentage of them were members of the treatment staff. Twenty-three percent of the inmates in mandatory small groups and 12 percent of the men in voluntary small groups had leaders whose job classifications were caseworker, correctional counselor, school teacher, or program administrator. (Each of the three mandatory large groups had as a group leader a caseworker with a graduate degree in social work.) Fourteen percent of the men in voluntary small groups had vocational instructors as leaders, as compared with only 1 percent for mandatory small group counseling. The typical leader for men in both mandatory and voluntary small group counseling, however, was a member of the custody staff (61 percent in voluntary, 68 percent in mandatory). The remaining men had group leaders from more than one of these job categories. These differences were statistically significant.

table 8.14   Outcome at Thirty-Six Months for Optional Group Counseling Versus Optional Controls and Mandatory Counseling Versus Mandatory Controls (in Percent)

Optional Categories	Outcome					
	No Problem	Minor Problem	Major Problem	Return to Prison	Total	Number
[a]Voluntary small group counseling	21	19	10	50	100	(274)
Voluntary controls	23	11	10	56	100	(173)
Mandatory Categories						
[b]Mandatory large group counseling	15	15	11	59	100	(68)
Mandatory controls	23	18	10	49	100	(269)
[c]Mandatory small group counseling	22	21	7	50	100	(171)
Mandatory controls	23	18	10	49	100	(269)

[a] Table $N = 447$, $\chi^2 = 5.19$, degrees of freedom $= 3$, not significant.
[b] Table $N = 337$, $\chi^2 = 3.49$, degrees of freedom $= 3$, not significant.
[c] Table $N = 440$, $\chi^2 = 1.85$, degrees of freedom $= 3$, not significant.

ATTITUDES TOWARD COUNSELING

Systematic data concerning inmate values and attitudes were obtained by means of a questionnaire given to nearly 900 CMCE inmates of whom one third were included in the follow-up.[23] Of particular interest here are two factors derived from these data: opposition to staff and perceived value of group counseling. We dichotomized scores of these factors into HIGH and LOW and cross tabulated them separately with parole outcome at 36 months (see Table 8.15). These two factors then were combined with whether participation in counseling was voluntary or mandatory to make an index of "amenability to treatment" (see Table 8.16).

In this way we were trying to determine how inmates whose views were especially compatible with group counseling did on parole compared with men whose attitudes were less compatible. (Participation in group treatment was held constant.)

[23] See Chapter VI for details of this analysis and the sample used.

table 8.15   Staff Opposition and Value of Counseling Within Treatment and Control Groups* by Thirty-Six-Month Outcome (in Percent)

| | Opposition to Staff | | | | Value of Counseling | | | |
| | High[a] | | Low[b] | | High[c] | | Low[d] | |
Outcome	Treatment	Control	Treatment	Control	Treatment	Control	Treatment	Control
No problems	16	23	21	26	15	20	25	30
Minor problems	23	11	21	17	24	14	20	14
Major problems	5	6	5	8	5	10	5	5
Return to prison	56	60	53	49	57	56	50	51
Total	100	100	100	100	100	100	100	100
N	(77)	(52)	(80)	(72)	(101)	(61)	(56)	(63)

[a] Table N = 129
$\chi^2 = 3.37$, degrees of freedom = 3
Not significant

[b] Table N = 152
$\chi^2 = 1.59$, degrees of freedom = 3
Not significant

[c] Table N = 162
$\chi^2 = 3.38$, degrees of freedom = 3
Not significant

[d] Table N = 119
$\chi^2 = .82$, degrees of freedom = 3
Not significant

* Treatment includes voluntary and mandatory small group counseling and mandatory large group counseling. Control includes voluntary and mandatory controls.

table 8.16   Amenability to Treatment by Thirty-Six-Month Outcome (in Percent)

Outcome	Amenability		
	High	Not Known	Low
No problems	21	21	25
Minor problems	17	19	20
Major problems	9	6	5
Return to prison	53	54	50
Total	100	100	100
N	(34)	(228)	(20)

Table N = 282
$\chi^2 = .77$
Degrees of freedom = 6
Not significant

Findings did not support significant differences on outcome between treatment and controls on the factors "Opposition to Staff" and "Value of Counseling." On the one hand, Table 8.15 shows that whether or not respondents were in groups, men who scored low in opposition to staff had experienced less trouble on parole than men who scored high in opposition to staff. Yet, men whose view of counseling was low, regardless of their own involvement in the program, also did better after release. In addition, these data suggest that controls consistently had higher rates of success on both ends of the scales: more men with no reported problems and fewer returned to prison.

The "amenability" index goes one step further in that it compares outcome for group members whose views are not only conducive to parole success (according to the theory underlying group treatment) but whose *behavior* reflects these *views*, namely *voluntary* participation in the program. As we can see in Table 8.16, most respondents fall into the "mixed" category, many of whom were undoubtedly in the mandatory control condition. Nonetheless, only 54 men out of 282 satisfied all three criteria: 34 of whom represented men who could be thought of as "ideal" candidates for success, 20 as "ideal" candidates for failure. Again, no significant differences on outcome. In fact, men classified as being the least amenable tended to have slightly higher success rates.

STABILITY OF COUNSELING GROUPS

In a letter written to the authors at the termination of the data gathering phase of our project, the supervisor of group counseling for the California

Department of Corrections (Mr. Robert Harrison) predicted that although our data would show no relationship between treatment exposure and parole outcome, "stable" groups would do significantly better than controls and "unstable" groups. Specifically, he predicted that:

1. There will be no statistically significant findings that inmates exposed to unstable group counseling will do better in either institutional or parole adjustment than those with no group counseling.

2. If there are significant differences in parole outcome or institutional adjustment in 3 way comparisons of inmates with no group counseling, unstable group counseling and stable group counseling, these differences will not favor those with no group counseling of unstable group counseling.

   My guess is that subjects with stable group counseling will show a somewhat higher percent of favorable parole and institutional adjustment than subjects with no group counseling or unstable group counseling. If there is a large stable group counseling sample, my guess is that these differences will be significant.

These estimates were derived from the earlier "clue hunting" studies of group counseling conducted by Harrison and Mueller.[24] Based on this earlier research, significant differences in outcome were noted between "stable" groups (groups averaging no more than one member change per month and no leader change for, at least, one year) and "unstable" groups. This comparison, however, did not involve a control group; hence, no comparisons were made between men in stable groups and men who had had no group counseling participation. We believed that Harrison's findings about the superior performance of stable groups remained open to further empirical examination, since no control groups were used, but we found that we could not identify any groups at CMCE that met his criteria of stability. (The CMCE group counseling coordinator in regard to this issue glumly remarked, "We have a stable group if there's less than one leader change during a month.") Men moved in and out of groups frequently as their jobs or institutional activities required, as they stopped attending counseling sessions, as the leaders changed, and the like. No group had the same leader for an *entire year* because of changes in work shifts, job assignments, vacation and other absences, meetings, etc. Despite the fact that counseling groups at CMCE could not meet Harrison's criteria, we decided to undertake further analyses as a step

[24] See Paul F. Mueller, "Summary of Parole Outcome Findings in Stable Group Counseling," Research Division, California Department of Corrections, 1964.

in the direction of comparing stable and unstable groups with controls. This effort utilized data we collected about the number of group meetings that the men attended and the rate of leader change during their participation in the program.

To be included in the study samples a subject had to be at CMCE for at least six months, thus, theoretically, a man could have attended at least 25 sessions in the voluntary small group condition, as many as 50 if meetings were biweekly, as they were with mandatory small groups, and more than one hundred for the sessions in the community living units. No man who attended fewer than five group sessions was considered a counseling "participant." The median number of sessions attended was 35, the mean was 40, the range 5 to 129.[25] Attendance was dichotomized at the mean in HIGH and LOW. One half of the group members had the same leader for the duration of group counseling at CMCE; one in three had two leaders; the remainder had three or more leaders. Leader stability became NO CHANGE (1 leader) or CHANGE (2 or more leaders).

Since attendance was not always taken in large counseling groups, measures of central tendency did not include the 69 inmates in this treatment variety. However, their exposure was classified as HIGH because meetings were held daily for most of the study period and attendance was required.[26] Also participants in mandatory large groups were classified as

[25] As was the case for counseling sessions in mandatory large group counseling units, the original plan that mandatory small groups require attendance twice weekly had to be revised to require meetings once per week, again because of problems with leaders meeting their groups and the poor participation by group members. Still, attendance was significantly higher for men in mandatory small groups than in voluntary small groups ($p \leq .01$).

Meetings Attended	Mandatory Small Group	Voluntary Small Group
5 to 20	17 percent	28 percent
21 to 40	33 percent	33 percent
41 to 60	21 percent	23 percent
61+	29 percent	16 percent
N	(173)	(278)

[26] The mandatory large group leaders found that daily counseling sessions demanded too much of their time and that inmate participation was poor. Consequently, during the second year of the study, the sessions were reduced to twice weekly meetings. Data on satisfaction with counseling cited in Chapters V and VI indicated that participants in mandatory large group counseling were more dissatisfied than other group participants. Men who were tardy or refused to attend mandatory groups were eligible to receive "pink slips" (disciplinary actions) but, in fact, this infraction was reported only once to the prison Disciplinary Committee, which refused to take action.

table 8.17 Treatment Exposure and Leader Stability by Thirty-Six-Month Outcome (in Percent)

	Succeed	Fail	Total	N
Treatment Exposure[a]				
High attendance (more than 40 sessions)	43	57	100	(255)
Low attendance (5 to 40 sessions)	37	63	100	(258)
Controls	38	62	100	(442)
				(955)
Leader Stability[b]				
Stable (no leader change)	39	61	100	(273)
Unstable (at least one change)	41	59	100	(240)
Controls	38	62	100	(442)
				(955)

[a] $\chi^2 = 2.12$, degrees of freedom $= 2$, not significant.
[b] $\chi^2 = .449$, degrees of freedom $= 2$, not significant.

having had stable leadership because of the presence of multiple leaders, at least, one of whom remained with the group throughout.

Table 8.17 presents the first steps of this analysis: does high exposure or stable leadership affect outcome for all participants and controls? Men whose attendance was HIGH or whose group leader was the same throughout did not do significantly better on parole than the men who attended less than 40 sessions or who had had several group leaders. But, more important, they did no better than the controls.

When the two variables are combined (Table 8.18) into a four fold table for each treatment and control condition, we see that rates for men in small groups with high attendance ranged between 46 and 50 percent, regardless of leader change. However, men in the other high attendance treatment—community living—did about the same as low attendance participants and controls which had success rates between 35 and 40 percent. Again leader change seemed to have little bearing on outcome.

Mr. Harrison's hypothesis about the effects of stable group counseling was not supported when controls were included in the test. As indicated, we could not operationalize the "stability" of counseling groups just as he

table 8.18 Attendance and Stability of Leadership for Parole Success Cases at Thirty-Six Months for Each Treatment Category

	Mandatory Control			Voluntary Control			Mandatory Large Group			Mandatory Small Group			Voluntary Small Group		
	Percent Success	N	Total	Percent Success	N	Total	Percent Success	N	Total	Percent Success	N	Total	Percent Success	N	Total
High Attendance															
No leader change							35	(20)	68	50	(17)	34	46	(16)	35
Leader change										50	(25)	50	46	(31)	68
Low Attendance															
No leader change										37	(18)	49	40	(35)	87
Leader change										34	(13)	38	35	(29)	84
No Attendance	41	(111)	269	34	(58)	173									

250

specified, for no groups met those criteria. What we did do was to compare outcomes for men who had had more exposure to group counseling and who had the "benefit" of fewer leader changes. Post-release outcome was not significantly different irrespective of exposure to any type of group counseling program or stability of leadership.

||||||||||||||||||||||||||||||||||||||||||||||||||||||||||||||||||||||||||||||||||||||||||||||||||||||||||||||||||||||||||||||||||||||||||||||||||||||||||||||||||||||||||||||||||||||||||||

Measurement of outcome: an exploration of factors related to parole survival

(with John Vincent)

||

Variables related to parole success

We have described our measure of postrelease performance on parole and have argued that the parole violation rate reflects a complex of factors that involve much more than clear-cut violations of the criminal law. In the following section we present data that relate the chances of success-ful survival on parole to certain preprison experiences, demographic fac-tors, personality characteristics, and attitudes and values of our study sample.

BASE EXPECTANCY SCORE

The best parole predictor variables available to us were contained in the Department of Corrections' Base Expectancy Score (BES) formula, a weighted linear combination of twelve items taken from the inmate's prison record. The BES was originally developed by the Department of Corrections to maximize the correlation of precommitment information with parole performance, and it was chosen as the measure of prognosis because it was more accurate as a predictor of parole behavior than the other means of predicting success.[1] The fact that all but one of the items

---

[1] In a 1961 study, Gottfredson tested the utility of this index against predictions of parole success or failure through the use of interviews conducted with inmates by an associate superintendent of a prison and by clinical ratings. The superintendent states:

> I personally interviewed every man who was paroled from here for a period of a year some time during the last 30 days of the man's stay at the institution.

from inmate files that survived statistical analysis to form the scale were related to preprison experiences reflects the original aim of its developers to produce a scale using preprison data.[2]

The scores of CMCE releases on this index, divided into four intervals at half standard deviation points above and below the mean, were significantly related to outcome at 12, 24, and 36 months after release. Thirty-six-month outcome data are given in Table 9.1.

Of those with the highest BES (most favorable prognosis), 38 percent had no recorded problems; only 11 percent of those with the lowest BES (poorest prognosis) had no record of arrest. Conversely, rates for return to prison were 37 percent (high BES) and 64 percent (low BES).

A stepwise multiple regression of 29 variables on BES was computed to determine what other preprison and institutional experiences were highly correlated with it.[3] These data were derived from inmate records and are described in Table 9.2. The first twelve variables in the analysis (as shown in Table 9.3) reach a multiple correlation of .610; running the analysis through 29 variables increases the R only to .618. Notice that preprison data account for 10 items of the first 12 (having fewer months of prison time served and being released to regular parole supervision being the exception). However, number of months served is related to offense, and a history of narcotics use was the determining factor in whether special narcotics parole was imposed; hence, both these variables were strongly related to preprison factors.

This analysis suggests two things. First, that BES is well correlated with our total set of predictors, and second, that notwithstanding its value,

I reviewed the man's record briefly and paid particular attention to the man's psychiatric report; discussed the man's weakness with him and made a half page narrative report on his case setting forth the man's major problems. Finally, his success potential was estimated numerically on a scale from 0 to 10.

The clinical council report was a separate psychiatric summary prepared by a group of psychiatrists and psychologists before the inmate's release.

The definition of "favorable parole adjustment" was no major violation within 24 months of release to parole. A major violation meant the same as it does in our present study: 90 days or more in jail, or returned to prison or absconded. On a sample of 283 men, the correlation of Base Expectancy with parole adjustment was .48, while those of the superintendent's rating and clinical council rating were .20 and .21, respectively. In addition, either or both of the other ratings in a multiple index did not raise the accuracy of Base Expectancy further above .48. Don M. Gottfredson, "Comparing and Combining Subjective and Objective Parole Predictions," *Research Newsletter*, **3**, Vacaville, California Medical Facility, September–December, 1961.

[2] See Table 6, Appendix A for a list of components and exact weights applied to each variable.

[3] Although several of these variables are quite similar to the BES components, they were neither coded nor weighted in the same way.

table 9.1   Base Expectancy Scores by Outcome at Thirty-Six Months (in Percent)

Outcome	Base Expectancy Score				
	Very Low (0 to 23)	Medium Low (24 to 38)	Medium High (39 to 53)	Very High (54 to 98)	Total
No problems	11	16	19	38	(209)
Minor problems	17	19	23	14	(164)
Major problems	8	13	8	11	(94)
Return to prison	64	52	50	37	(490)
Total	100	100	100	100	
N	(384)	(138)	(124)	(311)	

Table $N = 957$
$\chi^2 = 93.27$
Degrees of freedom $= 9$
$p < .001$
Gamma $= .334$

there remains a substantial area of independence.[4] On this basis, we feel justified in including these other variables in multivariate analysis of outcome, despite the usefulness of BES as a summary measure of parole prognosis.

DEMOGRAPHIC CHARACTERISTICS AND COMMITMENT OFFENSE AS RELATED TO PAROLE SUCCESS

The younger a CMCE man was at the time of first arrest and at the time of his first commitment to prison, the greater were his chances of parole failure. For example, men arrested prior to their 19th birthday were returned to prison twice as often as men whose first arrest occurred after age 28 (see Table 9.4).

If a man was white he stood a better chance than a Mexican-American, and a black had less chance than either of them. Within two years of release, 34 percent of white, 22 percent of Mexican and 21 percent of black parolees had experienced no trouble, and conversely 39 percent, 45 percent, and 51 percent, respectively, had been returned to prison. After three years, the gap had widened for blacks and had narrowed for Mexican-

---

[4] The coefficient of alienation $(1 - r^2)$ on this equation exceeds .62; hence, more than 60 percent of the variance among the predictors is unexplained. Thus there is, at least, the possibility that treatment may effect parole survival and that these predictors, including treatment, may be related to outcome.

table 9.2   Variables Used in Computing the Multiple Regression of Twenty-
Nine Predictor Variables on Base Expectancy Score ($N = 957$)

Variable Number	Variable Entered	Means	Standard Deviation
1	Base Expectancy Score (00 to 99; 99 = good prognosis)	38.33	30.28
2	Criminal record in release community (1 to 2; 2 = Yes)	1.66	.47
3	Release job arranged in prison (1 to 2; 2 = Yes)	1.50	.50
4	Sentence (1 to 2; 2 = long, minimum of 2 years)	1.29	.46
5	Age at most recent prison admission (0 to 9; 9 = 50+)	3.95	1.68
6	Number of prison commitments (1 to 8; 8 = 8)	1.84	1.07
7	Months of prison time served (0 to 9; 9 = 121 months +)	4.89	2.18
8	Age at first arrest (0 to 8; 8 = 45 to 60)	2.18	1.94
9	Age at first commitment (0 to 8; 8 = 45 to 60)	3.86	2.07
10	Measured grade achievement (1 to 9; 9 = 11.5+)	5.85	1.99
11	Family members with felony record (1 to 2; 2 = felony)	1.16	.37
12	History excessive alcohol use (1 to 2; 2 = Yes)	1.46	.50
13	History of drug use (1 to 2; 2 = Yes)	1.43	.49
14	Psychiatric diagnosis (1 to 2; 2 = Yes)	1.47	.50
15	CMCE prison school (1 to 2; 2 = attended)	1.39	.49
16	Last grade school completed (0 to 9; 9 = college)	2.95	1.73
17	CMCE rule violations (0 to 4; 4 = 7+)	.83	1.07
18	Expect support minor child (1 to 2; 2 = Yes)	1.37	.48
19	Regular parole supervision (1 to 2; 2 = Yes)	1.87	.33
20	Voluntary small group participant (1 to 2; 2 = Yes)	1.29	.45
21	Mandatory small group participant (1 to 2; 2 = Yes)	1.18	.38

256   *Prison Treatment and Parole Survival*

table 9.2   (continued)

Variable Number	Variable Entered	Means	Standard Deviation
22	Mandatory large group participant (1 to 2; 2 = Yes)	1.07	.26
23	Attendance at group meetings (1 to 2; 2 = high exposure)	1.28	.45
24	Stability of group leadership (1 to 2; 2 = stable)	1.29	.45
25	Violent offense (1 to 2; 2 = violent crime)	1.17	.37
26	Burglary offense (1 to 2; 2 = burglary)	1.22	.42
27	Theft offense (1 to 2; 2 = theft)	1.28	.45
28	Drug offense (1 to 2; 2 = drug crime)	1.21	.41
29	Black (1 to 2; 2 = Black)	1.20	.40
30	Mexican-American (1 to 2; 2 = Mexican-American)	1.21	.41

Americans. The percentage of white parolees classified *no problems* was more than twice that of the black parolees and one and one half times that of the Mexican parolees. By three years, about 6 out of 10 parolees in both minority groups were back in prison[5] (see Table 9.5). We cannot say to what extent these differences reflect actual crimes committed or, perhaps, differential application (that is, enforcement) of parole rules and regulations. Nonetheless, 88 percent of the black parolees received some type of disposition other than *no problems* within 36 months following release, compared to 73 percent of the whites. These differences were statistically significant at the .001 level.

Table 9.6 correlates commitment offense with parole outcome. The

[5] Glaser and O'Leary conclude: "Negro parole violation rates are not higher than those of white parolees." The fact that they did not find racial differences was regarded as "puzzling." They suggest that differential paroling policy in prison may be responsible, but that, "evidence of its occurrence in prison is conflicting." Postrelease violation rates for one California group of parolees—3046 youth offenders—revealed higher rates for Negroes than for whites—49 percent versus 41 percent. Glaser and O'Leary, op. cit., p.19.

In his own study of federal correctional outcome Glaser found, once again, no differences between white and Negro parolees; 34.7 percent and 35.3 percent, respectively. Glaser, op. cit., p. 51.

table 9.3 Stepwise Multiple Regression Analysis: Twenty-nine Variables on Base Expectancy Score ($N = 957$)

Step Number	Variable Number	Multiple R	Multiple R^2	Increase in R^2	F Value at Entrance	Standard Error of Estimate	F Value to Remove at Step Number 29	Variable Name: Direction Toward Favorable Prognosis (High BES)
1	8	.3245	.1053	.1053	112.4214	28.6518	13.2263	Older when first arrested
2	26	.3883	.1508	.0454	51.0358	27.9295	32.7682	Offense not burglary
3	12	.4291	.1841	.0333	38.9453	27.3901	82.8898	No history excessive use alcohol
4	13	.4863	.2365	.0524	65.3443	26.5098	50.3675	No history drug use
5	27	.5328	.2839	.0474	62.9680	25.6870	20.6596	Offense not theft
6	7	.5617	.3155	.0316	43.8462	25.1272	24.8728	Fewer months of prison time served
7	19	.5773	.3333	.0178	25.3083	24.8147	21.7147	Regular parole supervision
8	11	.5929	.3515	.0182	26.6631	24.4829	24.2216	No history of felony arrest in family
9	9	.6011	.3614	.0098	14.5997	24.3092	10.3904	Older at first commitment
10	14	.6052	.3663	.0049	7.3707	24.2278	7.3654	Psychiatric diagnosis
11	10	.6083	.3700	.0037	5.5585	24.1696	4.9438	Measured grade achievement high
12	25	.6098	.3718	.0018	2.6921[a]	24.1480	2.2733	Some type violent offense

table 9.3 (continued)

Step Number	Variable Number	Multiple R	R²	Increase in R²	F Value at Entrance	Standard Error of Estimate	F Value to Remove at Step Number 29	Variable Name: Direction Toward Favorable Prognosis (High BES)
13	16	.6110	.3733	.0015	2.2810	24.1317	2.2704	Last grade completed high
14	2	.6119	.3744	.0011	1.6350	24.1235	1.0299	No crime record in community where paroled
15	4	.6126	.3753	.0009	1.3597	24.1189	1.4289	Long sentence
16	22	.6134	.3763	.0010	1.4599	24.1130	3.4778	Nonparticipant in mandatory large groups
17	3	.6141	.3771	.0009	1.3067	24.1091	1.1227	Had job arranged when paroled
18	18	.6146	.3778	.0006	.9476	24.1098b	.8941	Expected to support minor children
19	20	.6152	.3785	.0007	1.0436	24.1092	2.9119	Nonparticipant voluntary small groups
20	21	.6156	.3789	.0005	.6904	24.1132	1.8700	Nonparticipant mandatory small groups
21	24	.6162	.3797	.0008	1.2420	24.1101	1.5782	Unstable group leadership

table 9.3 (continued)

Step Number	Variable Number	Multiple R	R²	Increase in R²	F Value at Entrance	Standard Error of Estimate	F Value to Remove at Step Number 29	Variable Name: Direction Toward Favorable Prognosis (High BES)
22	28	.6165	.3801	.0003	.4855	24.1167	.6977	Drugs as commitment offense (no direction)
23	30	.6168	.3804	.0003	.5203	24.1229	.9840	Black or White, but not Mexican-American
24	29	.6173	.3811	.0007	1.0347	24.1225	.8673	Black (no direction)
25	6	.6176	.3814	.0003	.4094	24.1301	.5916	Few previous prison commitments
26	5	.6178	.3817	.0004	.5428	24.1360	.4974	Older at most recent prison admission
27	15	.6180	.3819	.0002	.2978	24.1452	.3423	Attended prison school (no direction)
28	23	.6182	.3822	.0002	.3490	24.1536	.3504	Attendance group counseling meetings low
29	17	.6182	.3822	.0000	.0200	24.1664	.0200	No violations of prison rules

[a] Point where F Value drops below .05 level of significance.
[b] Point where Standard Error of Estimate begins to increase.

259

table 9.4   Age at First Arrest by Thirty-Six-Month Outcome (in Percent)

Outcome	18 years or under	19 to 20	21 to 23	24 to 27	28 to 60
No problem	16	24	22	36	55
Minor problems	19	18	14	12	6
Major problems	10	10	8	8	13
Return to prison	55	48	56	44	26
Total	100	100	100	100	100
N	(592)	(122)	(101)	(73)	(66)

Total $N = 954$
$\chi^2 = 69.32$
Degrees of freedom $= 12$
$p < .001$
Gamma $= .2156$

table 9.5   Parole Outcome at Thirty-Six Months for White, Mexican, and Black Parolees (in Percent)

	Race		
Outcome	White	Mexican	Black
No problems	27	18	12
Minor problems	15	19	20
Major problems	12	6	9
Return to prison	46	57	59
Total[a]	100	100	100
	(544)	(200)	(189)

[a] Table $N = 933$ (excludes Indian and other minorities).
$\chi^2 = 29.46$.
Degrees of freedom $= 6$.
$p > .001$.

CMCE releasees originally committed for robbery, assault, and sex offenses fared better than the releasees for other categories of offenders.[6] (They were also less likely to repeat their offense on parole.) Narcotics offenders (not including marijuana cases), forgers, and burglars did poorest. (They were also more likely to have been cited on parole for their commitment offense.)[7]

THE QUESTION OF PERSONALITY AND PAROLE SUCCESS

A popular explanation for crime has been enduring or characteristic personality differences between "criminals" and noncriminals. However, efforts to demonstrate this proposition by using the empirical measure of personality structure have been unsuccessful thus far. Yet, the persuasiveness of the argument persists: that criminal tendencies stem from factors such as inadequate or inappropriate socialization, inner emotional disturbances, or fundamental anxieties about interpersonal relationships. Indeed, it is on assumptions like these that group counseling and other similar programs are built.

It was not our purpose to test these assertions; however, we were able to obtain psychological descriptions of our study sample from two sources—the diagnoses available in inmate files and the profiles from a personality inventory.

The prison records of many inmates include the accumulations of ratings, diagnoses, or classifications given them at various points in their criminal careers by psychiatrists, psychologists, or social workers. For all men released from our study population, 456 (47 percent) had received some kind of psychiatric diagnosis or notation. These men included all those committed for assaultive crimes. (There are also a large number of epithets phrased in psychiatric or psychoanalytic terms made by police officers, district attorneys, and judges; they were disregarded in our analysis.) Of those receiving ratings by qualified diagnosticians, 73 percent were referred to as "psychopathic," "antisocial," having "weak super-egos," "character disorders," or "emotionally unstable;" another 26 percent were in some state of psychosis; and 1 percent were said to have organic brain damage. *We found no significant association between the presence or ab-*

---

[6] For a detailed discussion of offense and recidivism, see Glaser, *op. cit.*, pp. 41–49; also see Glaser and O'Leary, *ibid.*, pp. 12–17.

[7] Regardless of the offense for which he was committed to prison, if a man was identified as having a history of narcotics use, he was not as likely to survive as men with no history of drug use (48 percent versus 38 percent at 24 months). It may be, however, that part of the reason for this is the nalline testing program, which increases the chances of detection for narcotics use, whereas other men's violations of the law cannot be verified by chemical means.

table 9.6 Commitment Offense by Thirty-Six-Month Outcome (in Percent)

Outcome	Homicide	Robbery	Assault	Burglary	Grand Theft, Forgery	Narcotics Sales	Narcotics Possession	Sex Crimes	Other
No problems	23	35	53	16	21	15	16	39	22
Minor problems	23	14	10	15	15	29	26	13	14
Major problems	—	11	5	11	12	7	4	9	11
Return to prison	54	40	32	58	52	49	54	39	53
Total	100	100	100	100	100	100	100	100	100
N	(13)	(109)	(19)	(215)	(271)	(68)	(133)	(44)	(85)

Total $N = 957$
$\chi^2 = 62.94$
Degrees of freedom $= 27$
$p < .001$

sence of these ratings and parole success or failure of the men so diagnosed.

Better information on the possible personality correlates of parole success was available from a general personality inventory, the California Psychological Inventory (CPI), taken by a subsample of inmates[8] to determine whether the postrelease outcome was higher for men whose scores on the CPI were "unusual." We cross tabulated parole status at six months with each of the CPI's 18 scales. Because no differences were found, a factor analysis was done from which four factors were derived, and they then were cross tabulated with 36-month outcome. The details of this analysis are given in Appendix E, which shows that *personality characteristics, as measured by the CPI, were not significantly related to parole success.*

ENDORSEMENT OF INMATE NORMS AND INMATE TYPES AS RELATED TO PAROLE
OUTCOME

In previous chapters, we discussed inmate value orientations and concluded that exposure to group counseling did not alter the endorsement of inmate norms. To the extent that postrelease criminality is supported by the continued endorsement of these values—opposition to staff, solidarity among inmates, alienation from conventional society, and isolation from others—group counseling participation would not lessen parole violation rates.[9] Here the question is whether the men who endorsed inmate norms were more likely to violate parole than the men who did not endorse them. About one third of the 870 men who filled out the questionnaires that measured inmate value orientations during the institutional data collection phase also were included in the follow-up study. Since this subsample did not differ in any important respect from the other men in the postrelease population, we felt justified in cross tabulating their scores on the four factorially constructed measures of inmates' values with their postrelease status at 36 months. (These data are given in Appendix F.)

We found a significant difference in parole outcome for those endorsing one of the four measures—alienation. The relationship was not in the expected direction. Men appearing most alienated did significantly better on parole than the men who were least alienated. Thirty-five percent of the former were classified no problems, compared with 16 percent of the latter. There were no differences on the remaining three measures of the inmate value system.

Permuting two of the four dimensions—opposition to staff and soli-

---

[8] The limitations on time and staff prevented giving the CPI to every inmate who left prison. It was administered and completed by 351 men in our sample (36 percent). We verified that the men who took the CPI did not differ from the other men either in prognosis (BES 61w) or in actual outcome on parole.

[9] See Chapter VI, p. 176.

darity among inmates—resulted in the four inmate types: Square John, Right Guy, Outlaw, and Politician.[10] These data permitted us to classify those men released, according to inmate type, and to compare them in terms of prognosis or parole success and actual outcome (see Table 9.7).

Notice that the prognosis was highest for prosocial and pseudosocial types and was lowest for the antisocial and asocial types. (The four-way classification of Base Expectancy Scores used in Table 9.1 would place scores of 40 and 42 at the medium high level and a score of 34 at the medium low level.)

Although there was a tendency for Square Johns to return to prison less often than Right Guys and, conversely, to have fewer reports of problems, these differences were not statistically significant.

Multivariate approaches to the assessment of treatment effects on parole outcome

In the light of the consistent findings presented thus far—no significant differences between treatment and control groups and outcome—we decided to extend the analysis one step further. A series of multivariate analyses was used to determine whether it was possible that a relationship between treatment and outcome was being obscured by the action of other variables that affected either one or the other or both simultaneously.[11]

One such variable was parole prognosis as measured by the Base Expectancy Score.[12] Earlier in this chapter we showed that BES means

[10] See Chapter VI, p. 152.

[11] Multivariate techniques involve assumptions about the model of the relationship under investigation, the sampling distribution, and the quality of the data at hand. Most standard books on multivariate methods describe assumptions implied in most of the techniques used. Principally, each technique tests a slightly different statistical model. Consequently, results obtained from one form of analysis are not directly comparable with those obtained from a different technique. Each analysis tells us something different about our data. See P. J. Rulon, "Distinctions Between Discriminant and Regression Analysis and a Geometric Interpretation of the Discriminant Function," *Harvard Educational Review*, **21**, pp. 80–90 (1951); T. W. Anderson, *Introduction to Multivariate Statistical Analysis*, John Wiley and Sons, New York (1958); William Cooley and Paul Lohnes, *Multivariate Procedures for Behavioral Sciences*, John Wiley and Sons, New York (1962); Raymond Cattell (ed.), *Handbook of Multivariate Experimental Psychology*, Rand McNally and Co., Chicago (1966); and Allen L. Edwards, *Experimental Design in Psychological Research*, Holt, Rinehart and Winston, Inc., New York (1968).

[12] BES was itself developed by means of multiple regression techniques using pre-prison and previous incarceration information; the criterion of parole success was nearly identical to the one used in this study.

table 9.7 Inmate Type by Parole Outcome at Thirty-Six Months (in Percent)

	Mean Base Expectancy Score	Outcome				Total
		No Problems	Minor Problems	Major Problems	Return to Prison	
Square John (prosocial)	42.49	32	16	6	46	100 (81)
Politician (pseudosocial)	40.46	14	23	7	56	100 (71)
Right Guy (antisocial)	34.26	17	19	5	60	100 (79)
Outlaw (asocial)	34.01	22	18	6	55	100 (51)

Table $N = 282$
$\chi^2 = 9.75$
Degrees of freedom = 9
Not significant

for the treatment and control groups were not significantly different. As a final step in establishing the argument that treatment-control differences in parole prognosis did not play a role in outcome, we computed an analysis of covariance for treatment and outcome, adjusting for initial differences in BES. Essentially this technique tests differences in group means that have been adjusted to discount the influence of a third variable. These data are shown in Table 9.8. Equalizing predisposition to succeed on parole across all treatment varieties did not result in any significant linear mean gain for treatment. In fact, the treatment category mean success scores (proportion succeeding on parole) were nearly identical.

Next we sought to determine whether or not variables other than the ones involved in the computation of BES might be related to either treatment and/or outcome, thereby obscuring the relationship between group counseling and parole performance. We have reported that the first twelve items in a stepwise linear regression of 29 items, from the prison record abstract, on BES produced a multiple of R of .60 (see Tables 9.2 and 9.3). In other words, we could not rule out the possibility that other variables were obscuring the relationship between treatment and outcome because 64 percent of the variance could not be explained by the twelve items in combination with BES.

These 30 preprison within prison and parole prognosis measures (including BES) were then run against a dichotomized parole outcome at 36 months. The results indicated that we could improve only slightly on the ability of the Base Expectancy Score, that is, we increased the multiple R from .24 to .34. The first five variables entered with sufficiently high F values to reach the .05 level of significance. Their contribution raised the multiple r to .30. The next eight variables raised the multiple r to .34. After this point, the standard error of estimate begins to increase, with negligible increase in r^2 (see Table 9.9). (Means and standard deviations of these 30 variables are shown in Table 9.2.)

Only two variables associated with group counseling appeared among the first thirteen: "high attendance" was step 9, and increased R^2 by .002. "Nonparticipant in mandatory large group counseling" was step 10. It enters after "high attendance" because all mandatory large group subjects were coded as *high exposure*, since men in this category met daily in 50-man groups. The order of entry of both items in the list of predictors developed in the computer analysis, however, is sufficiently far down the order to be accorded relatively low predictive power. Other treatment variables were even weaker. The variable "leader change" was step 21. The treatment variety "voluntary small group counseling" was step 25, and the variable "mandatory small group counseling" never met the

table 9.8   Analysis of Covariance: Treatment Status and Thirty-Six-Month Parole Outcome,[a] Covarying Base Expectancy Score

	TREATMENT CATEGORIES				
	Mandatory Control N = 269	Voluntary Control N = 173	Voluntary Small Group N = 274	Mandatory Small Group N = 171	Mandatory Large Group N = 68
Base expectancy $\bar{\chi}$[b]	40.1524	40.9653	36.5839	37.0643	33.4265
Raw outcome					
Unadjusted outcome $\bar{\chi}$	1.4126	1.3353	1.4051	1.4269	1.2941
Adjusted outcome $\bar{\chi}$	1.4052	1.3246	1.4116	1.4315	1.3130
Standard error of estimate of adjusted outcome	.0289	.0360	.0286	.0362	.0574

ANALYSIS OF COVARIANCE COMPONENTS

Source	DF	YY	Sum Squares (due)	Sum Squares (about)	DF	Mean-Square
Treatment (between)	4	1.5765	—	—	—	.2238
Error (within)	950	225.7387	13.3303	212.4084	949	—
Treatment and error	954	227.3152	13.2794	214.0358	953	—
Difference for testing adjusted treatment means				1.6273	4	.4068

Null Hypothesis (no difference among treatments after adjusting with covariate) $F_{(4,949)} = 1.818$ not significant

[a] Dichotomized 36-month outcome; where 2 = success and 1 = failure.
[b] BES means differ slightly from those reported elsewhere because of reduced 36-month N(955).

table 9.9   Stepwise Multiple Regression Analysis: Thirty Variables on Dichotomized Thirty-Six-Month Outcome
(N = 957)

Step Number	Variable Number	Multiple R	R²	Increase in R²	F Value at Entrance	Standard Error of Estimate	F Value to Remove at Step Number 26	Variable Name: Direction Toward Success on Parole Specified
1	1	.2387	.0570	.0570	57.6981	.4741	17.9094	High Base Expectancy score
2	9	.2627	.0690	.0121	12.3596	.4713	7.4132	Older at first commitment
3	16	.2790	.0779	.0088	9.1133	.4693	4.3637	Last grade completed high
4	15	.2925	.0856	.0077	8.0232	.4676	5.4557	Attended prison school
5	29	.3046	.0928	.0072	7.5671[a]	.4660	5.5812	White or Mexican-American, not black
6	18	.3097	.0959	.0031	3.3051	.4654	2.2576	Expected to support minor children
7	19	.3142	.0987	.0028	2.9119	.4650	2.8410	Regular parole supervision
8	27	.3189	.1017	.0030	3.1824	.4644	.4567	Offense not theft

table 9.9 (continued)

Step Number	Variable Number	Multiple R	R²	Increase in R²	F Value at Entrance	Standard Error of Estimate	F Value to Remove at Step Number 26	Variable Name: Direction Toward Success on Parole Specified
9	23	.3229	.1043	.0026	2.6978	.4640	6.0937	Attendance at group counseling meetings high
10	22	.3311	.1096	.0054	5.7177[b]	.4629	5.2035	Nonparticipant in mandatory large groups
11	17	.3329	.1108	.0012	1.2792	.4628	1.0694	No violations of prison rules
12	4	.3345	.1119	.0011	1.1303	.4628	.4126	Long sentence
13	13	.3358	.1127	.0008	.8750	.4628	1.7925	No history drug use
14	3	.3369	.1135	.0008	.8007	.4628[e]	.8648	Had job arranged when paroled
15	28	.3379	.1142	.0007	.7535	.4629	.9515	Drugs as commitment offense
16	25	.3389	.1149	.0007	.7102	.4630	.6147	Some type violent offense

269

table 9.9 (continued)

Step Number	Variable Number	Multiple R	R²	Increase in R²	F Value at Entrance	Standard Error of Estimate	F Value to Remove at Step Number 26	Variable Name: Direction Toward Success on Parole Specified
17	5	.3399	.1155	.0007	.7028	.4630	.2902	Older at most recent prison admission
18	7	.3402	.1157	.0002	.2335	.4632	.1978	Fewer months of prison time served
19	8	.3405	.1160	.0002	.2374	.4634	.2831	Older when first arrested
20	14	.3408	.1161	.0002	.1593	.4636	.1587	Psychiatric diagnosis (no direction)
21	24	.3409	.1162	.0001	.1359	.4638	.1806	Stability of group leadership (no direction)
22	2	.3411	.1163	.0001	.0843	.4641	.0960	No crime record in community where paroled
23	10	.3411	.1164	.0000	.0476	.4643	.0754	Measured grade achievement high
24	30	.3412	.1164	.0001	.0705	.4645	.0719	Black or white, but not Mexican-American

table 9.9 (continued)

Step Number	Variable Number	Multiple		Increase in R^2	F Value at Entrance	Standard Error of Estimate	F Value to Remove at Step Number 26	Variable Name: Direction Toward Success on Parole Specified
		R	R^2					
25	20	.3413	.1165	.0000	.0334	.4648	.0333	Voluntary small group participant
26	26	.3413	.1165	.0000	.0118	.4650	.0118	Offense not burglary
—	6[d]	—	—	—	—	—	.0092	Few previous prison commitments
—	21	—	—	—	—	—	.0035	Mandatory small group participant
—	12	—	—	—	—	—	.0014	History of excessive alcohol use (no direction)
—	11	—	—	—	—	—	.0006	No history of felony arrest in family

[a] Point where F value drops below .05.

[b] Nonparticipant in mandatory large group counseling enters after high attendance because all mandatory large group subjects were coded as "high exposure." Men in this treatment variety met daily in 50-man groups. The order of entry, however, is sufficiently far down in the list to be accorded relatively low predictive power. The negative direction is perplexing, yet this has been true consistently at other outcome time intervals.

[c] Point where standard error of estimate begins to increase.

[d] Values that follow are "F to enter," but did not reach the automatic program limit of .01 to enter for computation of r^2.

271

criteria for inclusion in the prediction equation. In other words, although we could improve on the ability of BES to predict parole outcome, *group treatment, defined along several dimensions—type, change of leader—did not enter the prediction equation until late in the analysis, or entered not at all adding no significant increase in predictive power.*[13] There is some indication that those men who attended most frequently did slightly better.

Notice that although none of the variables that were predictive of parole outcome in the bivariate case were associated with treatment status, there was still the possibility that some simultaneous combination of them would clarify the relationship. To use standard multiple regression, we had to dichotomize the outcome variable and, in so doing, we may have lost too much information. To make use of the four-group categorization of parole status, which was the best description that we could make with our data, we turned to discriminate analysis.

Multiple regression demands that *all* variables be interval, and we reasoned that the four outcome categories were, at best, ordinal in nature.[14] (Although mutually exclusive, it clearly was not sensible to assume that having minor problems was only half as bad as returning to prison, or that having major problems was as comparable to returning to prison as three is to four.) Discriminant analysis, on the other hand, demands that all *but* the criterion variable be interval. Thus, because it makes no assumptions about the criterion variable's numeric (scale) qualities, we were able to use our four-group measure of outcome.

Discriminant analysis aids in determining the contribution of prison group counseling to parole success or failure by computing the extent to

[13] As an exercise, we considered using the four-way classification of outcome (No Problems, Minor Problems, Major Problems, Return to Prison) as a continuous increasing variable, and computed the regression of variables on this measure of outcome. Here the value of R was .37. Although there is some alteration in the order of entry of predictor variables, it is evident that making the more powerful assumption regarding the outcome measure does not alter our conclusion about the role that treatment plays in its prediction.

[14] One of the primary virtues of analysis of variance (for the social scientist, at least) is that this type of multivariate technique does not make the assumption that all variables involved have the properties of interval scales. It does demand, however, that the criterion variable be interval. Parole outcome, as it is usually defined, is clearly not interval data; hence, the value of this feature of discriminant analysis for our study purposes. We dichotomized outcome for multiple regression analysis since this technique demands that all variables, including the criterion variable, be interval. The interval character of a dichotomy is easier to rationalize. With reference to binomial distributions, it can be shown that repeated samples drawn from a population of successes and failures soon approximate a normal curve. The point to be made here is that the problem of interval scale data did not arise when a dichotomized outcome was used for the one-way analysis of variance and multiple regression. See William L. Hays, *Statistics for Psychologists*, New York: Holt, Rinehart and Winston, 1963, p. 131, ff.

which treatment exposure emerges as a useful item of information in distinguishing success and failure cases. Unlike multiple regression, cases are designated as belonging to one of two or more groups. Here the question is approached in terms of the contribution of the treatment exposure variable to an index which assigns cases to one of the four outcome categories. That is, our interest in constructing an index which will distinguish between various categories of outcome is *not* primarily that of maximizing accuracy with a minimum of predictors; it is rather to determine if treatment status is among the variables that are useful *in distinguishing cases* in terms of outcome.[15]

Before presenting the findings of this approach, it is important to specify features of the discriminant analysis program used.[16] First is the virtue of ease of interpretability (extent of predictability) by providing a classification matrix, "U", and canonical correlation. Second is the stepwise feature of the program which indicates the relative influence of each variable to the overall assignment of cases to groups.

The classification matrix compares the group assignment made by the program to the actual assignment made by the researcher. In the case of two groups labeled A and B, the matrix consists of four cells that might be labeled true A, false A, true B, and false B. False A and B contain cases misclassified by the program. When these cells are compared to the marginals via percentages, it is readily apparent how effective a set of predictor variables was in assigning cases to groups.

"U" ranges from .9999 to .0000, where .9999 can be interpreted as no meaningful assignment. In the case of two groups, "U" is equivalent to $1 - R^2$ in a standard multiple regression analysis of the same predictor variables with a dichotomized criterion corresponding to the two "groups" in the discriminant analysis. Canonical correlations between the groups

---

[15] The stepwise analysis sought to locate the one variable that had the highest partial correlation with the dependent variable partialed on the variables already added (that is, the variable with the highest F value is added). It does not seek out combinations of variables, $X_1 X_2 X_3 \ldots X_n$, that might have had a greater predictive effect, thereby utilizing a variable in an earlier step than it would have been had it been taken singly. Since our primary interest was not to produce an index for parole prediction, this was not a crucial analytic omission. We wanted to show exactly how significant aspects of treatment were, *independent of other variables*, in distinguishing parole groups.

Of course, it is possible that treatment might only operate in combination with other variables, such as age at first arrest and type of offense. This type of analysis—a nonlinear model involving a boolian combination of variables—is discussed in the technical note at the close of this chapter.

[16] For a complete description of this program (BMDO7M) and other discriminant analysis programs, see W. J. Dixon (ed.), *Biomedical Computer Programs*, University of California Press, 1967, pp. 147–148; 214a–214u. (We used BMDO7M, version 9-1-65.)

and the predictor variables also are provided; there will be one less canonical correlation than there are groups. A correlation of 1.000 would indicate perfect assignment to groups. With two groups, the canonical correlation is identical with the multiple correlation coefficient "R" in a similar regression analysis.

The 30 variables, used in the multiple correlation, form the input to the discriminant analysis. Their "U" values and the order in which they were added appear in Table 9.10. The accuracy of the classification resulting from the index thus constructed is shown in Table 9.11. The first variable to be selected was *Base Expectancy*. [By itself it separates the extremes (no problems and returns to prison) fairly well, but on all four groups it can explain less than 10 percent of the variance.] The second variable added was *drug offense*, and the third variable added was *regular parole*—both indicators of parole vulnerability of narcotics users. The first treatment variable to enter the equation was high attendance (step 8). Like the univariate analyses presented earlier, it shows a weak tendency for men who attended 40 or more group counseling sessions to do better on parole than the men who attended fewer than 40 sessions or who were nonparticipants in the program. The absolute contribution of this item was very small. In fact, none of the variables specified, even BES, did a very effective job of independently predicting parole outcome.

Taken together, the 30 variables were able to successfully assign only 52 percent of the NO PROBLEMS, 47 percent of the MINOR PROBLEMS, 38 percent of the MAJOR PROBLEMS, and 41 percent of RETURN TO PRISON. Most of the explained variance is accounted for by BES plus a few additional items. Conversely, a very large amount of the variance of parole outcome is unaccounted for by prerelease information.

It should be reiterated that in these analyses we were less concerned with the total efficacy of prerelease variables in outcome prediction than we were concerned with assessing the specific contribution made by several treatment variables. And in this regard, we found that the weight of any item reflecting distinctions between participants in group counseling and nonparticipants was very slight. Even in combination with many other prisoner characteristics, treatment did not aid appreciably in accounting for parole success or failure.[17]

To conclude the empirical portion of this section and to further highlight the paucity of differences between treatment groups and their behavior on parole, we present an additional analysis: multivariate analysis

---

[17] Perhaps treatment would add to the prediction of parole outcome, but only in terms of an interaction with other variables, that is, in a nonlinear regression. For a detailed discussion of this issue, see the technical note in this chapter.

table 9.10   Stepwise Discriminate Analysis: Thirty Variables on Four Group Thirty-Six-Month Parole Outcome

Step Number	Variable Number	F Value on Entrance	F Value at Step No. 30	U Statistic	U Decrease
1	1	37.9063	11.6934	.8934	.1066
2	28	8.1864	1.9223	.8709	.0225
3	29	5.4340	3.8085	.8562	.0147
4	8	6.2745	7.0447	.8396	.0166
5[a]	9	4.9233	2.7498	.8267	.0129
6	15	3.3572	2.0026	.8181	.0086
7	16	2.9976	.8079	.8104	.0077
8	13	2.9196	7.0447	.8029	.0075
9	2	2.5350	2.0333	.7965	.0064
10	7	1.8890	.8079	.7918	.0047
11	10	1.7639	.0228	.7873	.0045
12	25	1.9733	.4833	.7824	.0049
13	23	1.5084	2.0730	.7787	.0037
14	22	2.0852	1.5995	.7735	.0052
15	6	1.3968	1.4947	.7701	.0034
16	18	1.2157	1.2332	.7671	.0030
17	19	1.0989	1.0341	.7644	.0027
18	17	.9816	.8646	.7620	.0024
19	30	.8971	.8074	.7598	.0022
20	27	.7578	.3304	.7580	.0018
21	3	.6259	.5758	.7565	.0015
22	4	.3942	1.5995	.7555	.0010
23	20	.3322	.3623	.7547	.0008
24	24	.2738	.2791	.7540	.0007
25	5	.2975	.2959	.7533	.0007
26	14	.2088	.1869	.7528	.0005
27	26	.0989	.1077	.7526	.0002
28	21	.0315	.0307	.7525	.0001
29	11	.0222	.0228	.7524	.0001
30	12	.0144	.0144	.7524	.0000

[a] Variables below do not reach .05 at entrance.

of variance. In this analysis the eight strongest predictors of parole outcome that were detected in the multiple regression results were included as covariates.

Inspection of the differences between the adjusted and unadjusted parole success means for each treatment classification (Table 9.12) reveals only slight changes. Mandatory controls and voluntary controls are decreased

table 9.11 Predicted Outcome Classification Using Thirty Variables in a Stepwise Discriminate Analysis Compared with Actual Four-Group Outcome at Thirty-Six Months

| Actual Designation | Predicted Assignment | | | | |
	No Recorded Problems	Minor Problems	Major Problems	Return to Prison	Total
No recorded problems	108	29	43	29	209
Minor problems	23	77	33	31	164
Major Problems	25	15	36	18	94
Return to prison	80	104	109	197	490
Total N	236	225	221	275	957

| Row Percentages | Predicted Assignment | | | | |
	No Recorded Problems	Minor Problems	Major Problems	Return to Prison	Total
No recorded problems	52	14	20	14	100
Minor problems	14	47	20	19	100
Major problems	27	16	38	19	100
Return to prison	16	21	22	41	100

| Column Percentages | Predicted Assignment | | | |
	No Recorded Problems	Minor Problems	Major Problems	Return to Prison
No recorded problems	46	13	20	11
Minor problems	9	34	15	11
Major problems	11	6	16	6
Return to prison	34	47	49	72
Total	100	100	100	100

slightly, and mandatory small group and mandatory large group participants are increased slightly.

Contrasting each treatment variety with the mandatory control classification (Table 9.13) yields impressive results. None of the p values achieve .05, with the exception of those due to the regression (covariates) or the Grand Mean. This is perhaps the strongest and most straightforward linear test, and the results are consistent with preceding analyses.

table 9.12 Multivariate Analysis of Variance, General Linear Hypothesis Model Group Counseling Status by Thirty-Six-Month Dichotomized Parole Outcome Using the Eight Strongest Predictors of Outcome as Covariates*
(Cell Means)

	Mandatory Controls	Self-Selected Controls	Voluntary Small Group	Mandatory Small Group	Mandatory Large Group
Unadjusted mean**	1.4126	1.3353	1.4051	1.4269	1.2941
Adjusted mean	1.3942	1.3459	1.4065	1.4351	1.3138

* These predictors are: Base Expectancy, age at first commitment, last grade in school completed, attendance at prison academic school, racial identification—black,[a] expected to support minor child upon release, regular parole supervision,[b] and theft as commitment offense.

[a] Dummy variables were created out of the nominal variable, black = 2, all others = 1.
[b] Not narcotic parole or a very few classified as some other special parole.

** Where success = 2 and failure = 1.

277

table 9.13   Multivariate Analysis of Variance, General Linear Hypothesis Model Group Counseling Status by Thirty-Six-Month Dichotomized Parole Outcome Using the Eight Strongest Predictors of Outcome as Covariates* (ANOVA)

	DF	Sum of Squares	Mean Squares	F Ratio	P Value
Anova error	950	225.73869	.23761967	—	—
Adjusted error	942	202.78492	.21527062	—	—
Regression	8	22.953770	2.8692213	13.328439	.00000000
Mandatory × Self-selected control	1	.22393756	.22393756	1.0402607	.30802272
Mandatory × Voluntary control small group	1	.15928877	.15928877	.73994666	.38989683
Mandatory × Mandatory control small group	1	.63416354	.63416354	2.9458899	.08642503
Mandatory × Mandatory control large group	1	.12938739	.12938739	.60104528	.43837405
Grand mean	1	11.318600	11.318600	52.578471	.00000000

* These predictors are: Base Expectancy, age at first commitment, last grade in school completed, attendance at prison academic school, racial identification—black;[a] expected to support minor child upon release, regular parole supervision,[b] and theft as commitment offense.

[a] Dummy variables were created out of the nominal variable, black = 2, all others = 1.

[b] Not narcotic parole or a very few classified as some other special parole.

In both univariate analysis and multivariate analysis we have evaluated the possibility that group counseling in the prison experience of inmates might induce fewer parole revocations. But we were unable to demonstrate any statistically reliable indications that group counseling had any direct impact on parole outcome for inmates who, voluntarily or involuntarily, participated in the treatment. All in all, the California Men's Colony study provides scant support for a program that represents a major component of the Department of Corrections' treatment effort. In the concluding chapter of this book, we examine the political implications that a study like ours has for the administrators and treatment program specialists of a public agency.

Technical note: Chapter IX

TECHNICAL NOTE ON METHODS OF ANALYSIS

To be reasonably confident that our failure to demonstrate the predicted association between treatment and parole outcome did not result from an oversimplified scheme of analysis, we extended the analysis to consider the linear assumptions that underlie standard multivariate analysis, nonlinear multiple regression analysis, alternative multivariate solutions, and multivariate outliers.

THE ASSUMPTION OF LINEARITY

Up to this point in the analysis of the data, no significant "main effect" of treatment on parole outcome has been demonstrated. It is still possible for some inmates to have gained from exposure to the types of group counseling conducted during the course of this study. Who might these inmates be, and how is it possible to detect them?

Since the implied general analytical model posits the possible operation of many variables (only some of which were or could have been measured), the number of logical combinations of just those variables measured becomes awesome. The classical solution to this problem would require a series of fully crossed factorial designs. It was simply not practical to implement such a design, let alone a series of these designs, in the prison under study. Indeed, it is unlikely that an elaborate and definitive research design of this kind will ever be implemented in any prison setting.

Given the design as it stands, classical statistical techniques could rigorously test only the main effects of treatment. To this end, the "main effects" contingency tables involved few assumptions about the "form" of the relationship under investigation.[18] All the multivariate analysis presented in this and the preceding chapters (one-way analysis of variance, stepwise multiple regression analysis, discriminate function analysis, and multivariate analysis of variance) involve the assumption of linearity to some degree.[19]

However, perhaps treatment is effective only if a set of nonadditive features are simultaneously considered.[20] This implies interaction or boolian qualification in the prediction of outcome. In other words, it is possible that more than just the *addition* of another variable is needed. Instead, the consideration of *levels* of variables and various *combinations* of *levels* of variables might be required.

For example, it may be possible for treatment to be effective with those men who have:

no history of drug usage,
but who have a drug-related commitment offense,
and who are over 30 at time of first commitment,
and who have a record of attending some college.

or, men who have:

a violence-related first offense,
and who are over 35 at age of first arrest,
and who do not have a criminal record in the community to which they
are released,
but who do have a history of excessive alcohol usage.

These qualifications would be decidedly nonlinear, involving boolian combinations of variables and levels of variables. Hopefully, they might (just might) also represent large enough portions of institutionalized populations to make these qualifications programatically important. Or, they also may indicate that some select groups are amenable to treatment and that, when exposed to this treatment, do indeed fare better on parole but, for the most part, the treatment employed simply has little effect on the great mass of inmates thus exposed.

---

[18] To this end, chi square as a measure of the existence of a "departure from expectation" is presented. Where appropriate, the statistical measure of "ordinal agreement," gamma, also is presented throughout the text.

[19] For a comparison of the underlying similarities between analysis of variance, regression analysis and analysis of covariance, see James Fennessey, "The General Linear Model: A New Perspective on Some Familiar Topics," *The American Journal of Sociology,* **74**, No. 1 (July 1968).

[20] The assumption of additivity basically implies that a constant given increment in any one of the predictor variables will be demonstrated by a given constant increment in the dependent variable. This means, for example, that the presence or level of one element has no enhancing or diminishing effect on the impact of another.

Nevertheless, given the design as it stands and the current state of statistical development, few other reconceptualizations of the problem or types of standard analyses were readily available, with one notable exception: nonlinear regression. As this technique seems to be relatively unknown, a discussion of it is appropriate.[21]

NONLINEAR MULTIPLE REGRESSION

One method of analyzing the effect of a number of predictor variables on a criterion variable is to plot the criterion values in hyperspace via coordinates given by the predictor variables. The resulting "swarm" of data points is difficult to conceptualize when there are more than three variables involved. Standard linear regression analysis attempts to develop a prediction equation that describes the criterion variable as a linear function of the predictor variables. A successful linear regression equation essentially describes a plane that floats through the data swarm in N-space. A multiple correlation coefficient of .999 indicates that nearly all the values of the criterion variable fall along a plane. Linear regression prediction equations typically involve a constant and coefficients (defining slope) times each predictor variable ($Y' = c + B_1X_1 \ldots B_kX_k$). Furthermore, simple algebra indicates that any polynomial having more than two terms can be represented as a sum of factored polynomials (equations). For example, $Y' = X^2_1 - X^2_2 + c$ can be represented as $Y'' = (X_1 - X_2)$ $(X_1 + X_2) + c$.

In the computer program used here, two or more prediction equations are incremented simultaneously. These equations then are multiplied together to describe a surface. Notice that each equation is itself linear; but, when two or more are multiplied together, nonlinear surfaces are described. In the simplest case, the criterion variable is approximated not by the value of a single expression but by the product of, at least, two linear expressions.

Three "orders" of solutions are illustrated here. On computer-generated problems where the form of the multivariate relationship is truly linear, the program generates a constant and coefficients in the first expression that

[21] Specific references to this technique are not readily available; however, the basic algorithms of this technique were presented by its developer, K. R. Wood, to the Western North American Region of the Biometric Society, at the University of California, Riverside, on June 22 and 23, 1965. An abstract of this presentation is available in *Biometrics*, Volume 21, No. 3, September 1965, p. 775, entitled "Nonlinear Discriminant and Principal Components Analysis." The program itself was developed by Mr. Wood and James Waddingham of the Health Sciences Computing Facility, financed by National Institute of Health, Grant FR3. Information about this program, Least-Squares Approximation by Products of Linear Forms, may be obtained by writing to the Health Sciences Computing Facility, University of California, Los Angeles, California.

meet the least-squares criterion. The second expression contains an extremely small but nonzero constant and coefficients that are very near unity. When the two expressions are multiplied together, the results are numerically identical to the values in a standard linear solution (there will be differences in nonsignificant digits due to the multiplication).

On computer-generated problems where the form of the multivariate relationship is truly parabolic, the program will generate a constant and coefficients in the first expression, as above, and will generate the same constant and coefficients in the second expression. When the two expressions are multiplied, the squared terms (and product terms) describe a plane that floats through N-space, the edges of which curve to form a trough.

On perfect third-degree computer-generated problems the program will generate constants and coefficients in three expressions. The N-space plane is not only brought up at the edges but bent in the middle (the so-called saddle shape or flying diaper).

SEQUENCE OF OPERATIONS

In practice the program starts with one form, in one expression, in one polynomial, partialing out the effects of all other variables and producing a table of stored increments for each variable and the resulting increase in r^2. It then searches this table for the one increment for the one variable that will maximally increase r^2, and it makes that increment. Then it holds all other variables constant and starts anew. It continues in this iterative manner until no single change in a single variable in a single form will markedly change the r^2. At the same time it makes a comparison with changes in increments of variables in a second or third linear form. Eventually, the program generates a fully general polynomial expression that is the sum of many factored polynomials.

LINEARIZED NONLINEAR SOLUTIONS

If a simple nonlinear relationship between treatment and outcome was posited, it would be possible to linearize either the treatment or the outcome measure and to compute a standard linear regression on the transformed variables. Since the argument includes the notion that other variables besides treatment are operative, it would be necessary to transform many variables. If a simple second-degree model were posited, it would be necessary to input the original variables, their squares, and the resultant product terms. Since the linear multivariate analyses presented in the text involved 30 variables and the number of possible product terms is $N(N-1)/2$, close to 500 variables would have been needed just to test the second-degree model.

If a general third-degree model was posited and tested via the transformation process outlined above, several thousand variables would be involved. Even if the 500 variables were successfully generated and inputed, interpreting the results would have been nearly impossible. If the third-degree solution were attempted, the number of variables would have exceeded the number of cases, even in the relatively large sample employed in this study. When the number of variables exceeds the number of cases, matrix singularity occurs, invalidating the analysis. The output tends to consist of pages of solid numeric characters; the volume is dependent solely on the leniency of the monitoring system. In short, although the second-degree solution would have been nearly uninterpretable, the third-degree solution would have been unintelligible.

Three different "orders" of solutions have been illustrated. The program is currently written with the capability for seventh-degree solutions. As an aid to interpretation, the program is constrained to economize on both the number of variables per form and the number of forms. In essence, the program attempts to build a model that best characterizes the data, nonlinear if it must be, linear if possible, and efficient.

ALTERNATIVE SOLUTIONS

The second major consideration introduced by this note was that of alternative solutions. One of the sacred cows of classical statistical analysis is that any regression algorithm worth its salt must be "unique." A traditional criterion for uniqueness is that the equation be a "least-squares solution." In theory, solutions that are even slightly less than "least squares" are not unique; although in practice there are often several different "solutions," involving different variables or different weightings of the same variables, that may be much more interpretable to the researcher.

The nonlinear regression program used had the additional feature of attempting alternative solutions, using different variables, or the same variables, with different weights in either linear, nonlinear, or a combination of both. The program was constrained so that each "polynomial" was essentially orthogonal to the previous forms. Consequently, it was possible to explore the notion that treatment might be a prominent variable in predicting outcome in an alternative or slightly less than least-squares regression equation.

THE PROBLEM OF MULTIVARIATE OUTLIERS

Another problematic feature of linear regression analyses, which has received little attention, is the detection of outliers or cases with atypical values. When this problem is raised, it is acknowledged that the presence of outliers will distort a solution; the value of the resulting r^2 may be either artificially increased or decreased. Solutions to this problem usually entail diligent cleaning of the data prior to submission.

But "cleaning" usually implies that a researcher has examined the data, variable by variable, making a determination that suspiciously high or low values are legitimate (not categories for missing information, no response, inapplicable codes, and the like). Routine coding checks and coder reliability tests are supposed to eliminate errors *within* the range of legitimate values. However, it is possible for cases to be coded correctly, to be free of extreme values, and still be extremely atypical of the rest of the sample.

Some standard multiple regression programs have the option of preening out "residuals" on a case-by-case basis. If the researcher scans this list and notices those cases with suspiciously large residual values, errant cases may be spotted. But they would be errant within the context of linear solutions. The program used here prints out residuals, but they reflect nonlinear abnormalities if the solution was of a higher degree.

In addition, during the course of analysis, the nonlinear program alternately excludes and returns cases that dramatically increase or decrease the value of r^2. The results of the two iterations can be compared. If during subsequent iterations the same cases appear and if at the end of the analysis these same cases have large residual values, it is fairly certain that these cases are typical of the rest.

SUMMARY

The attempt to show that treatment in a prison setting affected behavior on parole from a linear model was not successful. An attempt was made to determine if, in fact, the linear model applied. A nonlinear form of multiple regression that is capable of fitting more complex surfaces was employed. Fortunately, for interpretation purposes[22] the analysis indicated that going to relatively more sophisticated attempts to approximate or to build up a model that would allow treatment to operate in higher-degree forms *did not* appreciably aid in the prediction of parole outcome. Consequently, only the linear results are presented.

In summation, the nonlinear statistical analysis found no significant multivariate outliers in the data (either linearly or nonlinearly defined), no significant nonlinear relationships directly or indirectly involving treatment as a variable, nor any alternative linear or nonlinear solutions involving treatment.

---

[22] There is a limit to the interpretability of very complex surfaces, since it is possible to describe an extremely contorted surface if there are enough variables, enough coefficients, and enough freedom in the model.

||||||||||||||||||||||||||||||||||||||||||||||||||||||||||||||||||||||||||||||||||||||||||||||||||||||||||||||||||||||||||||||||||||||||||||||||||||

Why group counseling does not reduce parole violation and what of it

||||||||||||||||||||||||||||||||||||||||||||||||||||||||||||||||||||||||||||||||||||||||||||||||||||||||||||||||||||||||||||||||||||||||||||||||||||||||||||||||||||||||||

The data that we have just presented do not confirm the expectations expressed by many persons at the outset of this study. Recall that members of the Adult Authority initially objected to our requirement of a control sample of men who would be "denied" the opportunity to participate in group counseling. These officials believed enough of the rhetoric of group treatment to raise serious question before they reluctantly consented to this condition for 600 inmates. There was also some concern about the possible political repercussions attendant to "denying" treatment to inmates who later violated parole, another assumption of treatment effectiveness. Now, having given data on the relationship between parole survival and treatment exposure, we shall discuss what we consider to be the main reasons that group counseling did not show the effects predicted by departmental personnel, and we shall examine some of the implications of our study for correctional administrators, treatment professionals, and the prospects of continuing evaluative research in public agencies.

In considering these matters, we shall address ourselves to several related issues. First, the rates of return to prison are relatively high, with over one half of the men back in prison at the end of three years. How does this compare with other statistics on parole failure?

Second, if group counseling has no demonstrable effects on inmate attitudes or subsequent behavior, is it because the influence of the inmate "community" negated the influence of the group experience? In other words, is the "failure" of group counseling to be found in the solidarity of the inmate social system?

A third area of concern pertains to the implications of the findings of this study for the agency administrators and the treatment professionals.

And finally, did this evaluative study have any impact on the program or the agency after the preliminary report was delivered?

Recidivism: national figures compared with California data

First, it is appropriate to comment on the overall parole violation rate observed in the three-year follow-up.

Figure 10.1 shows the flow of cases from one year to the next for a

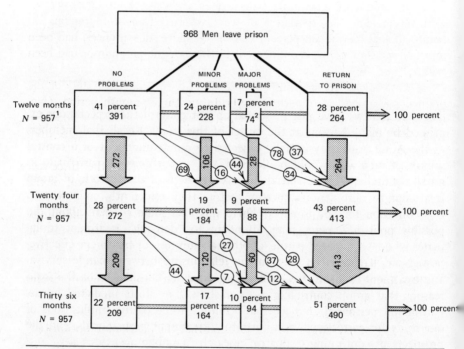

[1] At the 36-month outcome, eight men had died and the classification of three men was unknown.

[2] Nine men reclassified to minor problems.

figure 10.1   The movement of class through three years of post-release experience

36-month period. Recall that in the nature of record keeping, cases can move only from a lesser to a greater difficulty; they do not move the other way. That is, the record at any given point in time shows the most serious disposition since release from prison. The tendency is for about one half of those men who had no reported trouble during the first year to continue to avoid trouble to the end of the 36-month period. For the rest of the initially troublefree men, there was a tendency to move to minor arrests or short jail stays. For men who experienced minor problems during the first year, there was a greater chance of continuing in that outcome category than there was of moving to the "failure" categories. For men who were arrested on serious charges or who received long jail sentences during the first year, there was a high probability of their subsequent return to prison.

By the end of 36 months, 51 percent of the original cohort of releases were back in prison: two thirds had been returned to-finish-term, and the remainder had been recommitted on new convictions.[1] Another 10 percent were serving long jail sentences or were awaiting trial or sentencing on felony charges. Seventeen percent had served short jail sentences, had been returned for short-term reconfinement in the narcotic program or had been arrested and, in some cases, convicted for a misdemeanor, or had been arrested on felony charges but released. Twenty-two percent (209) of the original cohort had no reported arrests during the 36-month period. (Notice that this figure excludes 38 men who did not receive a disposition while on parole but who were arrested subsequent to discharge from parole up to the end of the 36 months.)

In all, 272 men were discharged from parole within the three-year follow-up period: four out of five *no problems* cases, over one half of the men classified as *minor problems*, and slightly over one third of the *major problems* cases. The majority of these men remained in the community without being arrested, but 104 (40 percent) did encounter some trouble with law enforcement agencies, including seven men who were convicted of felony crimes.

The figures from our study do not agree with the recidivism figures reported for the United States Bureau of Prisons. Based on his review of several studies of federal recidivism, one parole official concludes in a report to the United States Attorney General that the "outlook is optimistic." The most "optimistic" of the studies cited, and the one on which this positive conclusion rests, was a three-year projection of adults released and adults receiving "warrants" (revocation dispositions) in any one year from 1955 to 1963. These failure rates ranged from 13 to 18 percent.[2] Another study involving three-year follow-up periods for all federal releases (including some youth cases) in the period 1955 to 1963 reported

---

[1] Another California study had a reverse distribution of TFT and WNT revocations after 36 months: one third as technical violators and two thirds for major new offenses. Gottfredson and Ballard, op. cit., p. 27.

[2] Zeigel W. Neff, "Report of the Acting Chairman of the Board of Parole," in *Annual Report to the Attorney General*, United States Department of Justice, 1966, p. 489.

failure rates between 22 to 29 percent.[3]

In a study widely quoted by prison administrators, Daniel Glaser reports:

> . . . of 1015 cases constituting a random sample of adult male pris-
> oners released from federal prisons in 1956, a total of about 31 percent
> were found to be reimprisoned:
>
> 26.6 percent on new felony sentences;
> 1.7 percent as parole or conditional release violators, when suspected
> of new felonies;
> 2.8 percent as parole violators with no felonies alleged.
>
> An additional 3.9 percent received non-prison sentences for felony-
> like offenses (e.g., petty larceny, carrying concealed weapons). Including
> the latter, we arrived at what we call a total "failure rate" of 35 percent.[4]

Glaser supports his estimate of a 35 percent *failure rate* with data on California parolees released between 1950 and 1961: thirty-six and one-half percent had been returned to prison within six years.[5] These rates obviously represent a marked contrast to our figure (51 percent *returned to prison within three years*). They also are lower than recidivism data from two other recent studies.[6] One of these studies, conducted by Gottfredson and Ballard, involved an *eight-year* follow-up of 1810 men released to California parole in 1956. Their analyses showed an overall return rate of 46 percent by the third year: thirty percent were returned with "major new offenses" and 16 percent were returned as technical violators. (By the end of the study, 57 percent had been returned to prison—two thirds for new felony convictions.) With time adjusted, their three-year data were nearly identical with ours (see Table 10.1).

The second study reporting recidivism at 24 months after release for California parolees compared more closely with our 24-month outcome (43 percent) than with the outcome for federal releasees at 60 months (31 percent return to prison): for men paroled in each of four years, 1961 to 1964, return to prison rates within 24 months were 44 percent, 47 percent, 45 percent, and 41 percent, respectively.

Although Glaser contends that only about one *third of all men re-*

[3] Ibid., p. 488.

[4] See Daniel Glaser, *The Effectiveness of a Prison and Parole System*, Indianapolis: Bobbs-Merrill Company, Inc., 1964, p. 20.

[5] Glaser, op. cit., pp. 21–22.

[6] Gottfredson and Ballard, op. cit., data adopted from Table VI, p. 27; and "Parole Outcome for 6 Years of Felon Releases to California Parole, 1961–66," Research Division, Department of Corrections, Sacramento, California. These data excluded men supervised on parole outside of California but included outside prison commitments.

table 10.1   Comparison of Recidivism Rates of Two California Parole Follow-up Studies

Percent Returned to Prison	California Men's Colony Sample (N = 968)	Gottfredson-Ballard 1965 Parolees (N = 1810)
During first year	28	22
During second year	15	15
During third year	8	9
THIRTY-SIX MONTH TOTAL	51 Percent	46 Percent

leased from an entire prison system are returned to prison, he recognizes that differences between systems do occur, and he accounts for these differences primarily in terms of organizational policies. Presumably he would account for the higher rate of recidivism in California, when compared to the federal system, with the following arguments.

The proportion of releasees returned to prison tends to be higher

(a) where probation is used extensively so that only the worst risks go to prison;

(b) where parole is used extensively so that many poor-risk parolees are released on a trial basis;

(c) where a large proportion of parolees are returned to prison when they have violated parole but have not been charged with or convicted of new felonies;

(d) where there is a high over-all crime rate in the communities to which prisoners are released, so that there is high prospect of the releasee coming from and going to highly criminogenic circumstances.[7]

We cannot compare California and federal figures on all of these points, but some comments are in order because of the publicity given to Glaser's recidivism figures by correctional officials. More California felons are placed on probation than was the case in the federal system in 1964, 1965, and 1966: 51 percent, 51 percent, and 52 percent compared with 44 percent, 37 percent, and 38 percent, respectively.[8] It seems relevant, how-

[7] Glaser, op. cit., pp. 24–27.

[8] For these years, number of cases convicted felons were as follows:

	California	Federal
1964	27830	26773
1965	30840	28757
1966	32000	27314

ever, to raise questions about the nature of "poor risks"—not only about poor risks who are denied probation but about poor risks who are denied parole.

It is the case that more California prisoners than federal prisoners are conditionally released. That does not mean, however, that all other federal prisoners, including the presumably poorer parole risks, leave prison without supervision at the expiration of their terms. The federal system employs an intermediate procedure between parole and expiration of sentence called "mandatory release" (formerly called "conditional" release).

> Where the applicant is denied parole on his original hearing and there is no subsequent change in the Parole Board's order of denial, he is released by operation of law. Such mandatory release will occur at the end of the sentence . . . less such good time . . . as he may have earned through his behavior at the institution. He is released as *though on parole, with supervision* until the expiration of the maximum term or terms for which he is sentenced less one hundred and eighty days. Insofar as possible release plans are completed before the release of such prisoner and he is continued under supervision for any period longer than one hundred and eighty days remaining on his term, under the conditions established by the Board. . . .

> If a parolee or mandatory releasee does not demonstrate capacity and willingness to fulfill the obligations of a law abiding citizen or if continuance in the community becomes detrimental to the integrity of the parole system or incompatible with the welfare of society, he may be reimprisoned. . . .[9]

Mandatory releasees, unlike parolees, may have but are not required to have jobs and housing arranged as a condition of release, but they are under the supervision of federal parole officers and are subject to the conditions of the parole agreement. Parolee and mandatory releasee categories, then, can be combined in the sense that return to prison for both groups can be for technical parole violations, and in the sense that parole supervision means the routine collections of data on postrelease experience. Thus, California and federal prison recidivism studies do not involve such disparate "risk" populations as might appear—if one compares California parolees with federal parole and mandatory release populations. It seems

---

Crime and Delinquency in California, 1966, Department of Justice, Sacramento, California, p. 37; *Statistical Abstracts of the United States*, 1964, 1965, 1966, p. 152, 155, and 158, respectively.

[9] *Rules of the United States Board of Parole*, Department of Justice, Washington, D.C., 1958, p. 15.

to us that this feature of Glaser's argument for explaining the higher recidivism rates of California over federal releasees is not as viable an explanation as the following two factors.

The first point to be made is that, in 1951, parole was not used for all California prisoner releasees, presumably least in the case of "poor risks." During the time of our study, 90 percent or more of California's releasees went out on parole.[10] Is the higher failure rate for Men's Colony —East in recent years the result of this change in paroling practice? To answer this question we must first try to determine the "poor risks" who in earlier days would not have been as frequently paroled or would have been paroled only after serving more of their sentences. Here a distinction must be drawn between empirically established parole risks and ones that are established for reasons related to the tactics of organizational survival. For example, most parole boards regard men convicted of homicide, assault, and sex offenses as poor risks. These cases in California call for special diagnostic examinations by the prison psychiatrist so that the Adult Authority may assess "violence potential" in making their decisions about parole. These offenders are regarded as poor risks because their crimes are the kinds that arouse the greatest public concern and that are most likely to bring forth public condemnation of parole and prison officials if the men commit offenses after they are paroled. The risk factor here, then, is not to be measured in terms of statistics which indicate that men who commit crimes of violence will repeat their offenses. In fact, the opposite is the case. Studies of criminal careers indicate that burglars, forgers, and thieves are most likely to repeat their offenses and to violate parole, yet they are paroled more readily than men convicted of assaultive crimes for which there is greater public aversion. These general points apply to the Men's Colony study sample.

Table 10.2 shows the extent of felony involvement on parole by each CMCE commitment offense category. Narcotics and burglary offenders showed the greatest persistence in criminal activity: more than one half

---

[10] There has been a steady increase in the use of parole in California for the last 20 years. Seventy-five percent of male felons released from all California institutions were released to parole supervision in 1950; in 1960, the figure was 85 percent; and in 1965, 89 percent. Presently the figure exceeds 90 percent.

Federal use of parole has not been as extensive. For example, in 1965, of all male federal releasees (conditional and unconditional), parole accounted for 34 percent, mandatory release 24 percent, and the remainder (42 percent) were released unconditionally. This figure—56 percent conditional release—is somewhat less than in 1950, when 62 percent were released under some type of supervision. *California Prisoners, 1960*, Department of Corrections, Sacramento, California, p. 49, and *National Prisoner Statistics*, Department of Justice, Bureau of Prisons, Washington, D.C., Bulletin No. 40, November, 1966, pp. 12, 15, and 27.

of the men in each category received dispositions for some type of felony while on parole. Narcotic offenders on parole were more often cited for the same violation than were other categories of offenders. "Violent" offenders were less likely than all other offender types to have been associated with any type of felony activity or to have been cited for a "violent" offense.[11]

The point of this argument is that a more restrictive parole policy in California in the early 1950's does not necessarily mean that the men most likely to violate parole were the "poor risks" who were kept in prison. It is more likely that the men who served longer terms and were less readily paroled included the empirically established "good risks." The actual risks for offender categories should be kept in mind in looking at the recidivism rates of CMCE inmates. It is worth noting that only about 8 percent of our parolee cohort was comprised of men committed for homicide (12), assault (18), and sex offenses (47)—offender types that represent, from a statistical perspective, "good risks" but who, from a policy perspective, represent "poor risks."

A second, and very significant, difference between California and fed-

---

[11] Our data on repeated crime are fairly consistent with a Pennsylvania report of recidivism for 29,000 parolees released between 1946 to 1961.

	Repeated Crimes (in Percent)
Burglary	11.1
Forgery	10.2
Narcotics (includes marijuana)	10.1
Sex offenders, Homicide and Assault	6.9
Larceny (Theft)	6.4
Robbery	5.1
Other	10.2

Similarities between these data and ours as presented in Table 10.2 should be noted, as must the disparate findings; narcotics 10 percent versus 30 percent; theft 6 percent versus 18 percent; and the "violent" crimes 7 percent versus 11 percent. Although the categories undoubtedly include a somewhat different grouping of offenses than ours, and while they represent "crimes committed" rather than "dispositions received" (which do not necessarily involve conviction), there is yet another factor that more adequately might explain these differences, especially in regard to the narcotic and sex offenders. That factor is increased surveillance implied by the required visits to nalline centers for men with a narcotics history and required out-patient clinic attendance for the sex offenders. Pennsylvania Board of Parole, "A Comparison of Releases and Recidivists from June 1, 1946 to May 31, 1961," December 20, 1961, cited by Daniel Glaser and Vincent O'Leary in *Personal Characteristics and Parole Outcome*, United States Department of Health, Education and Welfare, 1966, p. 17.

table 10.2   Felony Offenses Cited on Parole within 36 Months of Release by
the Offense for which Committed
(in percent)

	Parole Offense		
Commitment Offense	Same as Commit- ment Offense	Some Other Felony Offense	Cited for any Type of Felony Offense
Narcotics ($N = 117$)	21	34	55
Burglary ($N = 221$)	15	36	51
Forgery ($N = 108$)	10	37	47
Theft ($N = 138$)	18	27	45
Marijuana and dangerous drugs ($N = 99$)	9	32	41
Robbery ($N = 145$)	6	32	38
Homicide, assault and sex related ($N = 77$)	11	10	21
Others[a] ($N = 60$)	10	32	42

[a] This is a CDC classification and, among other offenses, includes escape, kidnapping, arson, possession of weapons in prison, and conspiracy.

eral correctional systems (not mentioned by Glaser), is the indeterminate sentencing structure used by many states, including California. The use of this policy has two important consequences: first, maximum terms are longer and second, the *proportion of term served on parole is greater.*[12]

Since parole supervision means the collection of information about parolees, including activities that prompt returns to prison in lieu of prosecution, and activities that constitute technical violations of parole, the longer the parole period (and more intensive the supervision), the greater the chances for a man to be returned to prison. Federal prisoners are released sooner from the correctional apparatus and this decreases their chances of being returned for technical reasons. *Differences in recidivism rates may be artifacts of organizational policy such as increased use of parole rather than a pure measure of criminal activity.*

In regard to returning men to prison for technical violations of parole

[12] More specifically, (1) the indeterminate ". . . maximum [length of sentence] was *twice the length of the definite term*" (emphasis ours) and (2) "releasees with definite sentences served about 40 percent of their term, while releasees with indeterminate sentences served about 27 percent of the maximum." *National Prisoner Statistics: Characteristics of State Prisoners, 1960,* Department of Justice, Federal Bureau of Prisons, Washington, D.C., pp. 18, 29.

and the revocation of parole because of new felony convictions—Glaser's third qualification—there seem to be substantial differences between federal and California policies. This comparison, however, is made difficult because Glaser's figures reflect return to federal prison for all releasees, and California figures reflect return to prison for parolees only. In the federal system, men released at expiration of sentence obviously cannot be returned for violating conditional release agreements. Most of Glaser's 35 percent "failure rate" consisted of new felony commitments (26.6 percent). Only four and one half percent were returned as technical parole violators, including suspicion of felonies.[13] Eighteen percent of our study sample were returned with new convictions and 33 percent were returned as parole violators to finish their original term. A better contrast here would be drawn between recidivism rates for federal and California parolees.

Finally, with respect to Glaser's fourth qualification of his general propositions concerning recidivism rates, we have no way of estimating the "criminogenic potential" for the communities to which CMCE men were released. Glaser's study, however, also lacks this information, we presume, since we are not aware of any tests or measures of "criminogenic potential" that have been established for American cities.

Glaser's argument, it should be noted, applies to prison *systems*, not to individual prisons. Logically, one would expect differences in recidivism figures between maximum and minimum security prisons, with medium security prisons about in the middle. Although our data pertain to one prison, CMCE is a medium security institution with its population an almost perfect representation of modal departmental prisoner characteristics; its recidivism rate is slightly more than 50 percent within three years after release. Furthermore, another 10 percent of the study population was in serious trouble for felony violations not yet completely processed by the criminal justice system. (In some of these cases the men were returned to

---

[13] We are also not optimistic about Glaser's suggestion of tabulating whether a parolee was returned to prison on a "new" felony commitment. The administrative return of parolees in lieu of new prosecution according to due process of law is a commonplace occurrence in any parole system. Without inspection of the particular case, one cannot reliably conclude whether in a given instance a parole is revoked because the parolee did not adhere to the contract requirements or because the police are of the opinion he is "noncooperative" when they wish to use him as an informer (often the case with narcotics users), or because the district attorney accepts a plea of guilty to a misdemeanor instead of trying for a felony conviction, or because the police or prosecutor prevails on the parole division to revoke parole in lieu of a criminal prosecution in court.

prison but were not included in our statistics because the actions taken against them came after the 36-month follow-up period.)

Because we are reporting recidivism figures for a medium security prison population in one of the nation's best correctional systems, and because it seems to us that correctional systems will make even greater use of probation, parole, and indeterminate sentencing practices in the future, we are not inclined to agree with Glaser's general estimate that only about one-third of the men released from prison are returned—particularly if this is intended as a prediction.

Because Gottfredson and Ballard's "difficulty rate" was nearly identical year by year for three years with our outcome findings, it seems reasonable to estimate that a like proportion (70 percent) of our cohort would have absconded, been in jail at least 60 days, or have been returned to prison by the eighth year if we were able to extend the CMCE follow-up for that period. This is twice the "failure rate" of the federal correctional study.[14]

[14] Our study and Glaser's study measured recidivism in terms of the proportion of a group of men returned to prison during a specified period (1, 2, 3, 4, 5 years, etc.) from an original cohort of releasees. (Technical and felony recommitments were considered separately.) Gottfredson and Ballard's study of 1810 California parolees used this method and another for measuring recidivism.

First, employing the more commonly used measure (percent in trouble of a cohort), they found 1272 men (70 percent) had been confined for at least 60 days in jail, had absconded, or were back in prison within 8 years from release (p. 24). "Difficulties" break down as follows:

	Percent
Minor Convictions (one or more convictions of at least 60 days confinement but not more than one year)	12
Absconding	1
Return to Prison	
Violator no convictions	12
Violator minor convictions	4
Major offense (California) felony	35
Major offense (Elsewhere) felony	6
TOTAL	70

The other way of considering recidivism involves the percentage of men revocated (TFT or WNT) as a proportion of "surviving parolees," that is, men still exposed to the risk of difficulty. Gottfredson and Ballard used this technique to test two common assumptions: (1) that "parole violation occurs soon after parole" and its corollary, "the longer a man goes without difficulty after parole, the greater is the likelihood that he will not be in further difficulty," and (2) a two-year follow-up is adequate for program evaluation studies.

As far as the state of California is concerned, a more accurate estimate would seem to be that at least 50 percent of parolees will return within a three-year period with minor increases likely as the follow-up period is extended.[15]

Men with Various Types of Difficulty and No Difficulty as Percents of Parolees Remaining with No Difficulty and Exposed to Risk of Difficulty (p. 31)

Year after Parole	Number of Men with No Difficulty in Prior Year	No Difficulty (includes up to 60 days in jail)	Minor Conviction or Absconding	Parole Violators No Major Offense	Parole Violators Major New Offense
1	1810	75.08	2.43	7.29	15.19
2	1359	76.16	3.53	8.02	12.29
3	1035	82.51	3.67	4.35	9.47
4	854	87.82	3.16	.82	8.20
5	750	90.40	2.80	.40	6.40
6	678	91.30	3.24	—	5.46
7	619	92.08	3.23	—	4.68
8	570	94.39	4.74	—	.88
TOTAL	1810	29.72	13.65	16.35	40.28

Gottfredson and Ballard conclude that these data support the first assumption but not the second.

> If a parolee has survived the first year after parole without difficulty [i.e., with less than 60 days jail sentences] is he less likely to be in difficulty during the next year? The data [above] give little support to this contention, since the percent with no difficulty in the second year (among those exposed to the risk of difficulty) is little different from the percent with no difficulty during the first year [75 percent and 76 percent respectively]. Thereafter, however, the proportions with no difficulty tend to increase, so that there is less likelihood of difficulty the longer the man has been in the community without difficulty (*minor convictions expected*) (emphasis ours) (p. 30).

Although it is true that most parole violation occurred early, it is worth noting that "difficulties" continued to occur up to the end of the study. There was a fairly constant increment of men in the minor conviction column. (Bear in mind that minor convictions are defined as one or more convictions with sentences of at least 60 days confinement but not more than one year.) There was also a steady accumulation of men convicted of felony offenses. (The average felony offense and prison return occurred *more than two years* after release from prison) (p. 35). The possibilities for technical violation naturally decrease as men are discharged from parole supervision.

[15] The conclusion is not consistent with recent statements of California correctional officials. One popular magazine article states that "The 'repeater' rate among released convicts, which to run close to 50 percent as it does in most states, has been reduced to 32 percent." "The California Plan—How One State is Salvaging its Convicts," *U.S. News and World Report*, August 24, 1970, p. 44.

A revised view of the prison community

After a review of the substantial literature dealing with the social organization of inmate social systems, we approached the problem of evaluating the effect of group counseling on parole behavior by asking whether a widespread counseling program in prison would constitute a communication alternative to the restricted channels of information exchange maintained by the informal inmate social system. The norms and roles of such a system were viewed as being, at least in part, a reaction to the pains of imprisonment. Some of these norms sanctioned continued criminal activity and supported criminal self-conceptions, and thereby represented forces that resist the intended reformative effects of the various prison programs. If it were possible to get inmates and staff members to come together in small groups where there would be a frank confrontation of both the institutional and personal problems of the participants, perhaps the effect would be to reduce the social distance between the two groups and to increase the understanding of each for the other's needs and interests. This, in turn, would challenge important tenets of the inmate code, such as the categorical injunctions to avoid information exchange with staff and to maintain solidarity among inmates.

As indicated previously, we thus hypothesized that exposure to group counseling would result in the decreased endorsement of the inmate code, would undermine traditional inmate role types and would be associated with increased success on parole. In our effort to empirically validate this hypothesis, we soon encountered problems. The conception of the inmate community as composed of certain groups of identifiable inmate types appeared to have severe limitations. We found that we could assign very few men to inmate "types" either through the classification schemes of others or through our own efforts. The best that we were able to do was to assign inmates to "factor types." Even this procedure, however, did not increase our predictive power in terms of parole performance. Furthermore, we do not feel that the values held by inmates are adequately understood by considering them simply as organized compensatory reactions to the pains of imprisonment. At the time of our study, the inmates did not seem to be a well-organized community solidified in their resistance to an oppressive prison regime. They seemed to be a collection of men who defined themselves as being faced with a combination of surveillance, control, and manipulation in which they viewed the counseling program as either a benign or a sinister part. Being in a counseling group and not being in a counseling group did not appear to affect the way inmates evaluated their relations with staff members. These difficulties, which are reported in

Chapter VI, prompted us to turn to considerations of theory and then to a modification of the view of the prison community reported in previous prison studies.

The prison has been viewed as a "closed" social system in which there are a variety of severe deprivations which generate a code that helps inmates adjust to these deprivations. It seems to us that these aspects of the current theory are analytic rather than strictly empirical distinctions, and we suggest that it may be more useful to examine prisons from a different point of view. The principal features of this proposed view are:

1. Many prisons are not self-contained and isolated systems but are relatively permeable units in larger systems called departments of correction.

2. Because of differences in the conditions of imprisonment between departments of correction and between prisons of higher or lower security ratings within the same department, inmates in prisons throughout the United States are reacting to very different combinations of material, social, and psychological deprivations.

3. The preprison backgrounds of inmates influence the kinds of adaptations that are made to combat the pains of imprisonment.

THE PRISON AS A CLOSED SOCIAL SYSTEM

The study of the prison as a closed system, like the study of the mental hospital as a small society, or the factory as a social system, adopts a theoretical view that focuses on interaction within the organization and minimizes attention to interaction with the world surrounding the organization.[16] It is altogether proper to do this, since for many purposes the behavior of the members of the organization is conditioned by the fact of membership and the constraints directly imposed by that system. However, with this frame of reference it becomes difficult to see external factors that influence behavior within the system. For example, to analyze the hospital as a small social system provides valuable data, but it is unlikely to shed much light on other problems such as, say, the role of a Municipal Commission of Charities, the efforts of the Teamsters to organize the nonprofessional personnel, the significance of the Outpatient Clinic bud-

---

[16] See William Caudill, *The Psychiatric Hospital as a Small Society*, Cambridge: Harvard University Press, 1958; Ivan Belknap, *Human Problems of a State Mental Hospital*, New York: McGraw-Hill, 1956; Alfred H. Stanton and Morris S. Schwartz, *The Mental Hospital*, New York: Basic Books, 1954; W. Lloyd Warner, and J. O. Low, *The Social System of the Modern Factory*, New Haven: Yale University Press, 1947; and F. J. Roethlisberger and W. J. Dickson, *Management and the Worker*, Cambridge: Harvard University Press, 1939.

get to the city councilmen, and the pattern of patient recruitment which distinguishes it from another hospital on the other side of town. In this connection, Etzioni has observed that the hospital is, strictly speaking, not a small society at all—because societies have functional autonomy and hospitals do not.[17] Similarly, the study of the *prison* as a closed community can lead to ignoring a myriad of relations between the prison and the larger society. Whether one or the other of these perspectives is more fundamental will not be debated here; it is enough to regard both as legitimate so long as the level of system reference is made explicit in the analysis.[18] The historical facts indicate, however, that the study of the prison as a unit of a larger social organization has been neglected.

Most studies of prison communities have stressed that the prison constitutes a *closed social system* with definite organizational and physical boundaries within which inmates are confined, under close surveillance, and regulated by a set of rules that restrict their contact with the outside world. Prisons have been shown to exhibit many features characteristic of isolated communities, including distinctive forms of slang and argot, social conventions, statuses, roles, and a stratification system.[19] However, we submit that these features are also characteristic of other more open collectivities such as universities, factories, hospitals, and military establishments. These features are also characteristic of social movements, such as religious sects, and occupational aggregates, such as carnivals and circuses.

THE DEPARTMENT OF CORRECTIONS AS AN INCLUSIVE SYSTEM

The relative isolation of prison inmates should not obscure the many important connections between the prison and the surrounding society in general and the statewide Department of Corrections in particular. There are many ways in which the prison is not an insulated community.

Directives and policies flow from departmental headquarters to the prison. The prison must provide daily or monthly reports on various aspects of its operations to headquarters. The most important matters involved in this exchange are the allocations of funds for state programs, physical plant, job quotas, and inmate population.

Personnel are transferred from one prison to another and from various divisions of the Department of Corrections. In addition to transfers of

[17] Amitai Etzioni, "Interpersonal and Structural Factors in the Study of Mental Hospitals," *Psychiatry*, **23** (February 1960), p. 17.

[18] See the cautionary remarks in Talcott Parsons and Edward Shils, *Toward a General Theory of Action*, Cambridge: Harvard University Press, 1954.

[19] See, for example, Erving Goffman, *Asylums*, Garden City: Anchor Books, 1961, p. 4; Lloyd E. Ohlin, *Sociology and the Field of Corrections*, New York: Russell Sage Foundation, 1956.

personnel, training programs and meetings bring some personnel from all institutions to central training sites.

Many specific decisions that affect prison operation are made outside its walls. Inmates are received in reception-guidance centers where decisions are made regarding the type of institution in which to confine the offender, and about the type of program recommended for him within the limits of institutional facilities and custodial considerations. At the other end, since the use of indeterminate sentencing and parole has replaced "flat" terms, the Adult Authority conducts hearings and sets release dates for inmates. This body also indirectly affects inmate programs by making known its concern that certain inmates participate in certain treatment programs.

Inmates are transferred from one prison to another during a given sentence. One of the more regularly observed attributes of large organizations or departments is that problems are often met locally by physically moving the troublemaker from one place (prison, cell block, hospital ward, dormitory, school) to another (so-called "bus therapy"). There are also institutions for well-behaved prisoners. In addition, parole violators are often returned to a prison other than the releasing institution because the fact of parole violation has changed their status in terms of "rehabilitation potential." The size of the California Department of Corrections makes for a greater variety of institutions and programs and, hence, a potentially larger number of places to which inmates can be recommitted or transferred. In addition to having 10 prisons that differ in architecture, custody classification, and type of inmate populations, the department includes a myriad of other installations such as conservation and forestry camps, narcotic treatment units, halfway houses, and parole offices.

We obtained a rough indication of the extent of the transfer process by tabulating the proportions of a random sample of San Quentin inmates who served their current sentence in more than one prison. All California prisoners start their terms in a reception center and then move on to a prison, but approximately 40 percent of San Quentin inmates had served time in two or more prisons in addition to the reception center on one sentence.

The frequency of intra-departmental transfer of inmates and the large number of prisons in a Department of Corrections, which makes possible numerous transfers and differentiated types of prisons, is a feature of contemporary penology that must be presumed to have implications for inmate norms and role types.

The transfer of inmates from one kind of facility to another means that the prison population is constantly changing and that friendship ties and the informal organization required to encourage support of the tenets of the inmate code are continually being disrupted. Although the reaction of any inmate is to one prison at a time, regardless of the total number in which the sentence is served, his mode of adjustment has implications for the likelihood that he will serve part of his term elsewhere. If he becomes a tough guy or an operator or a model prisoner, he may be transferred accordingly. In large prison systems, such as in California, New York, Illinois and the federal government, inmate behavior is rarely a reaction to confinement in one institution. Most of the earlier studies by Clemmer, Sykes, Schrag, McCleery, Cloward, McCorkle and Korn, Wheeler, Garabedian, and others[20] concern inmate reaction to confinement in a single prison—in most cases a maximum security prison. In addition, most of these studies were conducted in states with departments of corrections that had only one or two institutions for adult male felons. This is not to suggest that other investigators have not observed the possibility or even the likelihood that inmate roles may vary according to type of prison,[21] but studies of prisons as parts of a system are not part of the current sociological literature.

To summarize this part of our argument, many of the prisons in the United States are most appropriately studied as functioning subsystems within a larger bureaucratic organization, incorporating elements from this larger department. Significant events within the prison walls cannot be understood without an examination of their relevance to the chain of command in the department or bureau, and of their implications for other institutions and agencies with which the prison maintains exchange relations.

THE INMATE CODE AS A REACTION TO THE PAINS OF IMPRISONMENT

A second feature stressed by the conception of the prison as a community is the relative deprivation of satisfactions and resources and the loss of status that inmates held in the outside community. These deprivations

[20] Clemmer, op. cit.; Gresham M. Sykes, *Society of Captives*, Princeton: Princeton University Press, 1958; Clarence Schrag, op. cit., pp. 342-356; Richard H. McCleery, *Policy Change in Prison Management*, East Lansing: Michigan State University, 1957; Richard A. Cloward, "Social Control in the Prison," in *Theoretical Studies in Social Organization of the Prison*, op. cit., pp. 20–48; Lloyd W. McCorkle and Richard Korn, "Resocialization Within Walls," *The Annals*, **293** (May 1954), pp. 88–98; Stanton Wheeler, "Role Conflict in Correctional Communities," in Donald R. Cressey (ed.), *The Prison*, op. cit., pp. 229–259; and Peter G. Garabedian, "Socialization in the Prison Community," op. cit.

[21] Garrity, for example, has asserted that the description of the culture and social structure becomes less relevant as the number of institutions increases and as inmates are selectively committed to institutions organized around specialized concepts. Donald L. Garrity, "The Prison as a Rehabilitative Agency," in Donald R. Cressey (ed.), *The Prison*, op. cit., p. 361.

make for a process of deculturation in terms of ability to function according to the expectations of the free community, and they promote the internalization of norms and values that are a part of the inmate culture of the prison community. The character of these norms and values of the inmate culture—the Inmate Code—is said to derive from the qualities of institutional life and the total control of behavior attempted there. Inmate conduct, as we have indicated earlier, is guided by the inmate code, and a deviance from it is supposed to be punished by ostracism and, in some instances, by physical abuse.

The actual extent of support of the inmate code in the prisons studied earlier must remain matters of informal impression and conjecture, since no quantitative survey data on this question were obtained. It should be noted, however, that the studies we cite as beginning the trend of analyses of the prison as a community included Clemmer's effort to empirically validate the assertions about inmate loyalty that had been made by earlier observers of prison life. Clemmer found that a majority of the inmates in the prison he studied were not engaged in primary group relationships with other inmates, and that almost 40 percent of the population could be classified as solitary or semisolitary persons.[22] Sykes also found in a study of the extent of loyalty among inmates in a maximum security prison that 41 percent of the sample informed on their fellow inmates.[23] At CMCE, we found that the degree of endorsement of the basic tenets of the inmate code was considerably lower than we originally expected.

Our findings have prompted us to question the extent to which inmates internalize criminal norms as a result of prison confinement, and the extent to which this is a factor in recidivism. It has been argued by Clemmer that the process of "prisonization" increases from the beginning to the end of the sentence.[24] In the study of federal prisons by Glaser,[25] and of the Washington prison by Wheeler,[26] a curvilinear relationship was found with the highest endorsement of conventional norms at the beginning and end of the prison term. We might have found a curvilinear relationship between length of time in prison and support of inmate norms had we attempted to measure them at early, middle, and late periods of current

22 Clemmer, op. cit., p. 119.

23 Gresham M. Sykes, "Men, Merchants, and Toughs: A Study of Reaction to Imprisonment," *Social Problems*, 4 (October 1956), p. 134.

24 See Donald Clemmer, "Imprisonment as a Source of Criminality," *Journal of Criminal Law, Criminology, and Police Science*, **41** (September–October, 1950), pp. 311–319.

25 Daniel Glaser and John R. Stratton, "Measuring Inmate Change in Prison," in Donald R. Cressey (ed.), *The Prison*, op. cit., pp. 388–390.

26 Stanton Wheeler, "Socialization in Correctional Communities," op. cit., *American Sociological Review*, **26** (October 1961), pp. 697–712.

sentence on each prisoner. Aggregate data from our own study, however, turned up no evidence of a curvilinear relationship in the endorsement of inmate norms and the time served in prison, nor did we find a correlation between the endorsement of inmate norms and the number of terms of confinement.

We would expect to find more solidarity among inmates and more traditional prison inmate types in a correctional system with only one institution for adult felons and where that institution is characterized by more severe material and social-psychological deprivations. Endorsement of prisoner norms and role configurations at a maximum security prison in California, for example, should reflect the criminal history of the population, the severity and range of deprivations, and the fact of being an "end of the road" institution where it is possible for troublemakers and recidivists to accumulate, and where mean length of sentence is longer because of these same factors.

In conclusion, the difficulties in measuring inmate types in the prisoner community that we encountered forced us to reconsider our conception of the bases for prisoner types and behavior.[27] We were led to speculate that some prisons might have a lower probability of housing certain inmate types than other prisons. The possible differences between prison communities in small and large departments of correction can be highlighted in two conceptual models. The first model assumes one prison for the confinement of all or most of the adult felons in a state, a low-level of material satisfactions, the frequent use of physical punishment and restraint, a minimum of free expression of inmates, and a strong prohibition of interaction between staff and inmates except in highly structured contexts. The second model assumes many prisons in a department of corrections, inmate populations to some degree selected according to different criteria for various institutions, a high proportion of inmates serving their sentence in two, three, or more institutions, a minimal amount of material deprivation, and a more open communication network among inmates and between staff and inmates.

We would expect that strong endorsement of the inmate code would be found to a lesser degree in the second situation. Cliques and cabals, which reinforce the code, and long years of association, out of which differentiated roles emerge, are likely to be disrupted by transfers of inmates, particularly inmates who are identified as troublesome. The effect of transfers is twofold: it increases both the homogeneity and the turnover of

---

[27] Sheldon Messinger has also noted the need for an updated view of the inmate community in his article "Issues in the Study of the Social System of Prison Inmates," *Issues in Criminology*, **4** (Fall, 1969), pp. 133–141.

separate prison populations, thus reducing both the raw material and the time required for highly differentiated roles in the inmate social structure.

When strong endorsement of the code does occur, however, it would have greater significance in minimum and medium security prisons in which there is more emphasis on treatment goals. The inmate code can be accommodated to by a staff that is primarily oriented along traditional custody lines. The old cons, politicians, and stool pigeons could be used to help maintain an orderly and relatively calm inmate population. To oversimplify, given the objectives of custody, utilization of the con boss and inmate organization to achieve those ends would seem to fall in the category of the calculated risk for the traditional prison. On the other hand, if the goal is inducing change in behavior or attitude, such collusion is inimical to those ends in the treatment-oriented prison.[28]

Evaluations of correctional treatment: some implications of negative findings

It is not difficult to make a strong case for the systematic assessment of organizational activities with a view toward increased efficiency, lower costs, and the more effective utilization of personnel and facilities. Nor is it difficult to find departments of correction or prison officials who endorse the principle of evaluation. It is difficult, however, to find many prison systems where the principle has been implemented in terms of the establishment of research divisions that do more than actuarial data collection or so-called "human bookkeeping." Even smaller is the number of published studies of correctional program evaluations reported either by research divisions or by independent investigators. In fact, the majority of these studies have been conducted in just two prison systems: the Federal Bureau of Prisons and the California Department of Corrections.[29] In addition to developing most of the innovations in correctional treatment, most

---

[28] A psychiatrist, well-known for his innovative work in the therapeutic community concept in mental hospitals and corrections, comments: ". . . in correctional systems, one is dealing with the norms of the prison system on the one hand, and of the inmate system on the other. The goals of the two systems are incompatible." Maxwell Jones, *Social Psychiatry: In the Community, in Hospitals, and in Prisons*, Springfield, Illinois: Charles C. Thomas, 1962, pp. 90–91.

[29] Robert H. Fosen and Jay Campbell, Jr., "Common Sense and Correctional Science," *The Journal of Research in Crime and Delinquency*, 2, 1966. Fosen and Campbell report that a survey of 48 correctional systems in the United States indicated that only 19 reported some kind of research operation. Of the total annual budget for adult correction in the United States, one third of one percent is devoted to self-study. Two systems, California and New York, account for more than one half of the total investment in research, p. 75.

of what we now know of programs that do *not* work has come from studies undertaken in these two systems. But the very fact that a public agency has cooperated in an evaluation study implies that the data are not innocuous, especially if they indicate that programs are not achieving publicly stated goals. For organizations supported by public funds, arguments for budgets are often linked to plans for program development or expansion, and in the scrutiny of budget committees, research findings may acquire a political import.

Only in recent years has the evaluation of action programs occupied the attention of social scientists. A look back over the past several decades indicates that research in the field of penology has proceeded in three phases.

The first phase consisted of early empirical studies of prisons as social organizations. Stemming from these investigations, and carried forward by the burgeoning influence of psychological theories of criminal behavior, the next phase consisted of the formulation and development of new treatment and approaches. During the third—and current—phase, a major portion of research funds and effort have been devoted to the evaluation of the programs developed in phase two.

The starting point for a brief history of systematic research in corrections is difficult to establish, but beginning with Donald Clemmer's study, published in 1940, sociologists began to pay attention to prisons as social organizations. These studies were analyses of inmate roles and types, guard-inmate interaction, the culture of the prison community, and the patterns of inmate behavior. Although prison treatment programs were also described, these descriptions were peripheral to the examination of inmate social systems. Aside from the usual references to the limitations of educational and vocational programs, and casework and psychiatric services, little effort was made to measure their impact on institutional or postrelease behavior. These early studies explored issues of interest to sociologists, and from the viewpoint of prison officials, these inquiries did not disturb the inmates or staff members nor did they disrupt the daily operations of the prison. Furthermore, the studies often suggested new and interesting ways of looking at the prison experience, and they focused on problems related to the "adjustment" of inmates to the prison life—a topic of considerable relevance to those charged with maintaining peace and quiet behind the walls.

By the mid-1950's, however, juvenile delinquency and crime rates became a matter of public concern. Corrections departments found that legislators, the press, and the public expected their organizations to "do something" about the rising crime rate not only by punishing the guilty, deterring the criminally-inclined, and by securely confining those convicted, but also by "rehabilitating" criminals before they were returned to the com-

306 Prison Treatment and Parole Survival

munity. Thus a period of intensive interest in correctional treatment programs began with an enlargement of prison staffs to include men with training in a variety of special fields that were related to changing the personality (and presumably the behavior) of the criminal. The influence of psychodynamic (Freudian) psychology and of psychiatric explanations of criminal behavior was evident in the criminological literature as well as in the increased recruitment of social workers, psychologists, and psychiatrists for work in prisons and probation and parole departments; in the reformulation of prison "treatment" concepts to include the efforts to change inmates in addition to providing them with educational and vocational skills; and in the change of nomenclature surrounding every aspect of imprisonment. Prisons came to be termed correctional institutions; inmates were called residents; isolation and segregation units became "adjustment centers." New programs such as group counseling, group therapy, the therapeutic community, community living, and guided group interaction based on the earlier studies of the social structure of inmate communities were initiated. This phase in the recent history of corrections might be called *the period of the promise of treatment.*

But promises, particularly promises made about problems of public concern, can be taken on faith or hope for only a limited time. When the postrelease behavior of prisoners toward whom these treatment efforts were directed seemed to show few changes for the better, legislators, as representatives of the public interest, began to ask for evidence of the actual impact of expensive treatment programs. Thus, another phase in correctional research was begun—the period of *treatment program evaluation.* The reverberations of this shift are being felt today in all quarters. The evaluation of treatment programs has implications not only for agency and institute heads but also for treatment staff and, ultimately, for the theories underlying the programs. Although the theories of behavior and programs for treatment by social workers and clinicians characterized the second phase, this third phase has been engineered in the main by sociologists who learned that government funds and the computer made possible bigger and better evaluative studies, and that some important persons in the correctional establishment were interested (in fact anxious) to have sociologists do studies of something beside inmate types and the role of the prison guard. In addition, because sociology is a research discipline and is not principally concerned with the clinical treatment of clients or patients, the evaluations of treatment efforts could be undertaken, in most cases, by researchers who did not have theoretical or ideological investments in the programs.

Not everywhere, but in a sufficient number of places so that the trend is clear, professionally conducted evaluation research has become a part of correctional and parole departments. The increased sophistication of scientific research methods and data analysis techniques, and the increased availability of both public and private sources of funds to finance research projects have enabled correctional administrators to chart the problems and progress and the failure and success of treatment programs by calling on departmental research divisions in some cases and, in others, by seeking the services of university researchers.

However, sociologists, clinicians, custody staffs, and prison administrators have discovered that, although the incorporation of treatment programs and research projects into the day-to-day business of running a prison can be justified, in practice it poses some problems of "adjustment" for the prison staff. Correctional officers and nonclinical treatment staff members no sooner became accustomed to the theories, techniques, and jargon of the clinician than they were confronted with the additional task of adapting to the theories, techniques, and jargon of the sociologist. Reconciling these two perspectives poses problems for all, but particularly for prison administrators who often feel themselves in the middle between the clinicians and social workers on the one hand (regarded as tender-minded, impractical people who see in every inmate a patient) and, on the other hand, the sociologists and statisticians (regarded as tough-minded, impractical people who see in every inmate an IBM card). Corrections department officials thus find themselves facing not only the problem of how to resolve competing philosophies which assert that punishment or treatment will "protect society" but also the problem of carrying out the mandate to evaluate their own programs in a manner that is satisfactory to legislators, to the treatment specialists, and to the researchers. Heads of departments of corrections and wardens have had several decades, experience in trying to deal with the custody-treatment dilemma, but only during the past few years have the problems associated with evaluative research become prominent.

IMPLICATIONS OF NEGATIVE FINDINGS FOR CORRECTIONAL ADMINISTRATORS

Several correctional programs thought to be "rehabilitative" were evaluated in Daniel Glaser's study of the federal prison and parole system, in which matched samples of "successes" and "returned violators" were compared to determine the impact of prison education and prison work experience on recidivism. Correlational analysis indicated that, although approximately twice as many successes as violators reported the use of prison training on postrelease jobs, the proportion of either successes or failures using training was never more than one fifth. Academic education was no more effective than vocational training. In fact, inmates who had enrolled in the prison school had higher failure rates than those who did not participate in the educational program. Glaser qualified this finding by pointing out that, among other things, a disproportionate number of inmates with less than an eighth grade education were enrolled in prison classes; these men may have represented poorer risks for postrelease success. However, he goes on to make the interesting observation that prison education may, in some cases, actually be dysfunctional for postrelease adjustment by inspiring unrealistic aspirations or by substituting education for other prison programs that might have provided a more useful preparation for the postrelease period.

The correctional version of therapeutic community and group counseling approaches in a "halfway house" for narcotics parolees in California was studied by Geis.[30] Again, there were no significant differences in the number of new criminal convictions between the experimental and control groups. Other studies reporting no differences between treatment and control groups include the careful evaluation of social casework and group therapy applied to delinquent girls by Meyer, Borgatta, and Jones,[31] the experimental Guided Group Interaction program at Boys Republic in California reported by Empey, Newland, and Lubeck,[32] the Special Intensive Parole Unit projects in California reported by Havel[33] and the California Civil Commitment Program for Drug Addicts.[34] Even the Community Treatment Project, held out by the California Youth Authority as the one successful correctional program, has now had the validity of its findings seriously challenged.[35] Robert Martinson, a former member of our project

[30] Gilbert Geis, *The East Los Angeles Halfway House for Narcotic Addicts*, Institute for the Study of Crime and Delinquency, Sacramento, California, 1966.

[31] Henry Meyer, Edgar Borgatta, and Wyatt Jones, *Girls at Vocational High*, Russell Sage Foundation, New York, 1965.

[32] LaMar Empey, G. E. Newland, and Steven Lubeck, *The Silverlake Experiment: A Community Study in Delinquency Rehabilitation*, University of Southern California, 1965. (Mimeo)

[33] *Special Intensive Parole Unit Reports, Phases I, II, III, and IV*, Research Division, California Department of Corrections.

[34] *Report on Civil Commitment Program for Narcotics Users*, Research Division, California Department of Corrections, 1967.

[35] For a description of the Community Treatment Project see Marguerite Q. Warren, Virginia V. Neto, Theodore B. Palmer, and James K. Turner, *Community Treatment Project: An Evaluation of Community Treatment for Delinquents*, Research Report No. 7, California Youth Authority, August 1966; and Marguerite Q. Warren, "The Community Treatment Project: History and Prospects," in S. A. Yefsky (ed.), *Law Enforcement Science and Technology*, Washington, D.C.: Thompson Book Co., 1967, pp. 191–200. Paul Lerman's reanalysis of C.T.P. reports led him to conclude that the positive results in favor of the experimental group over the control group reflected not differences in the delinquent behavior of the boys, but differences in the parole-revoking behavior of the parole agents. See Paul Lerman, "Evaluative Studies of Institutions for Delinquents: Implications for Research and Social Policy," *Social Work*, 13 (July 1968), pp. 55–64.

staff, recently completed an exhaustive study of the entire literature on correctional treatment. In a personal communique to the authors he reports:

> The Treatment Evaluation Survey (tentative title) has been almost four years in the making and should be published in 1971 under the auspices of the Office of Crime Control Planning of the State of New York. This work was designed to be a critical summary of all studies published since 1945 evaluating the effect of any type of treatment applied to convicted offenders. A six month search uncovered 231 studies which met the criteria for inclusion. The studies were individually annotated, arranged into convenient sub-categories, and critically analyzed.

> Although the overall conclusions of a work of this magnitude and complexity are difficult to convey in a few words, I think it is fair to say that there is very little evidence in these studies that any prevailing mode of correctional treatment has a decisive effect in reducing the recidivism of convicted offenders.

The generally disappointing outcomes of correctional treatment program evaluations are not atypical or unusual. Negative findings on treatment outcome have been the rule rather than the exception since the Cambridge-Somerville youth study published in 1955.[36] They have, however, been appearing in increasing numbers in the last five years, reflecting the increased pressure put on correctional administrators by legislators to provide "evidence" of the effect of treatment programs. Now, so many studies have reported no significant differences between experimental and control samples that the very departments which have submitted their treatment programs to evaluation find themselves running a greater risk of public criticism than do the less innovative departments. In many cases, treatment innovation has represented change that had been pushed through by progressive forces against the inertia of tradition, and evaluation has been undertaken with the expectation that programs will be proven to be successful. Peter Rossi has described this situation, which is becoming a common experience for social science researchers.

> Although as social scientists we can expect the new social programs to show marginal effects, the practitioner does not ordinarily share our pessimism—at least, not when he faces the Congressional Appropriating Committee. Hence, the claims made in public for the programs are ordinarily pitched much higher, in terms of expectation of benefits, than we could realistically expect with the worst of research and much better than we could expect with the best of research. Thus it turns out that

[36] Edwin Powers and Helen Witmer, *An Experiment in the Prevention of Delinquency,* New York: Columbia University Press, 1951.

one of the major obstacles to evaluation research is the interests in the maintenance of a program held by its administrators. Their ambivalence is born of a two horned dilemma: On the one hand, research is needed to demonstrate that the program has an effect; on the other hand, research might find that effects are negligible or nonexistent. . . .

The will to believe that their programs are effective is understandably strong among the practitioners who administer them. After all, they are committing their energies, careers and ideologies to programs of action and it is difficult, under such circumstances, to take a tentative position concerning outcomes. Hence, most evaluation researches which are undertaken at the behest of the administrators of the programs involved are expected to come out with results indicating that the program is effective. As long as the results are positive (or at least not negative) relationships between practitioners and researchers are cordial and sometimes even effusively friendly. But, what happens when it comes out the other way?[37]

In more and more instances it appears that correctional agencies have begun to feel that perhaps the liberal, forward-looking, modern, scientific, and experimental stance so applauded a few years ago is ultimately repaid by sour faces and blue pencilings from legislative committees and budget analysts when negative findings are the result of program assessments. Prison administrators who once said, "Come on in and do your research, we have nothing to hide," may now be starting to feel that, after all, they do have something to hide. Because the most innovative departments have often argued their case for "treatment" funds by appealing to the pragmatic criteria of recidivism reduction, they find it difficult to continue such urging in the light of negative results. For an organization whose output is not a tangible product, the use of systematic evaluation is a more acceptable basis on which to judge the success or failure of a program or policy than are impressions. In other words, scientific investigations are increasingly being used to justify next year's budget. This subjects the organization to cross-pressures. On the one hand, there is an intellectual commitment to the rules of science, objectivity, reliability, and comprehensiveness—but, on the other, there is a realistic need to use statistical material as a rationale for action and as a technique of persuasion when seeking legislative support on fiscal matters. In sum, an inherent conflict exists between the norm that evaluation is a necessary corrective to the tendencies of organizations to proceed uncritically—especially where the public's money is concerned—and the organization's need to present an efficient face to those

[37] Peter H. Rossi, "Boobytraps and Pitfalls in the Evaluation of Social Action Programs," N.O.R.C. Reprint from the 1966 Social Statistics Section, Proceedings of the American Statistical Association, p. 128.

who look upon it. It is thus only an apparent paradox that the strong proponents of modern correctional methods have become sensitive to the fiscal implications latent in every research proposal that bears on the question of treatment evaluation. The indications are that the open-door policy may one day give way to a more selective hospitality toward outside researchers, or to a more selective presentation of the findings of program evaluations since, as the research reports come in, there is a dearth of good tidings for both the treatment specialists and for the program administrators.

Paul Takagi has provided an excellent example of what happened in the Parole Division of the California Department of Corrections when the results of the evaluation of the Work-Unit Program were presented to the agency. This report compared the performances of parolees under parole agents who had 35-man caseloads with parolees under parole agents who had 70-man caseloads.

> The report was issued on December 22, 1965, and had a devastating effect on the parole agency. In short, there was no difference in parolee recidivism rates between the two types of supervision. The findings were devastating because: The 1964 legislature appropriated funds to initiate ". . . a small-caseload program, so that: (1) sufficient time be available to the agents to accomplish tasks required of them; (2) the problem of violence be attacked . . . ; (3) the needs of society be protected; and (4) there be differentiated treatment of all parolees" (Agency Document, "Work Unit Evaluation," Dec. 22, 1965, p. 1). The expectations were that the parolees under small caseloads would have favorable outcomes. In response to these discouraging findings, the chief of the parole agency brought together the regional administrators and the district supervisors responsible for the small-caseload program. (The 35-man-caseload agents constituted homogeneous district units.) The meeting began with the observation that the small caseloads were not producing favorable results. Charts and tables were presented comparing relative performances at the regional and district office levels. I interviewed one of the members who attended the meeting.
>
> > The logic they (headquarters) presented was that agents supervising small caseloads have more time and should therefore get more mileage out of these cases. The small-caseload agent is supposed to develop community resources so he can continue to handle these marginal parolee cases in the community.
>
> The chief of the agency stated that henceforth the units in the agency will compete against one another to see who can produce the lowest technical violation rate. In order to reduce the technical violation rates

among the small-caseload agents, the supervisors will be required to hold a detailed case conference with the agent recommending a technical violation and explore what alternatives are available in the community so a parolee need not be returned to prison. If the supervisor agrees with the agent's recommendations to return the client to prison, then the supervisor must state in writing a justification for the recommendation. Such a case, however, will then be reviewed by the regional administrator with the view toward disagreeing with the field recommendations. If the regional administrator should agree with the return recommendations, then he, too, must state why he agrees.

The further requirement was made that copies of such reports will be forwarded to headquarters for review and training purposes and that the material will be utilized to evaluate the performances in the field. The chief of the agency added one final note. All future promotions will be considered in terms of how well the district supervisors and the regional administrators have provided leadership in reducing the technical violation rates. At this juncture in the meeting, my informant indicated one of the participants at the meeting responded to these unwritten policy requirements with an exclamatory: "Bullshit!" The chief of the agency turned to the man and said: "Mr. C―――, you hold a responsible position in this organization; and, if that is the way you feel, perhaps you should not be in that position."

Headquarters' pressures upon the regional administrators and the small-caseload supervisors served effectively to reduce the technical violation rates in the subsequent months. It is noteworthy that on December 30, 1966, one year later, a report on the small-caseload program was prepared for the members of the Joint Legislative Budget Committee. The cover-letter to the report reads as follows:

> The (small-caseload program) originally funded by the 1964 Legislature and placed into effect in early 1965, represents a major breakthrough in its having provided parole service for community protection . . . .

> As can be seen from the results described in the summary, program outcome has been decidedly positive, with a significant impact having been made *on reduction of felons returned to prison.* During 1965, this program also made possible major savings in institution costs previous to release on parole, accompanied by a higher parole success rate.

> In economic terms, the approximate 1¼ million dollars annual cost has virtually been offset by more than one million dollars in savings.

In addition, there are a number of hidden savings represented in fewer crimes, reduced law enforcement and court costs which are attributable to the program . . . (Memorandum to Members of the Joint Legislative Budget Committee, Dec. 30, 1966).

Favorable outcome suddenly became an issue in the parole agency, not because of interest in promoting professionalism, nor in effecting administrative efficiency. Rather, the agency's interest in reducing the technical violation rate was in response to pressures from the state legislature to show results in a field where results are difficult to demonstrate. This pressure was the 1¼ million dollars allocated to the parole agency to place one-half of the parolee population in small caseloads, and the legislature wanted to know what services and results were produced for this amount of money. The arguments for small caseload have an intuitive logic similar to the arguments for reducing classroom size, that the professional will have more time to devote to individual client needs and, in this way, be able to achieve the objectives of rehabilitation or educational achievement. When favorable results—in this case, lower technical violation rates—could not be demonstrated, the objectives of the emergency task were re-defined by administrative fiat.[38]

Takagi's report is useful not only in illustrating the problems evaluative research poses for administrators but it also illustrates how fluctuations in recidivism rates, "failure" or "difficulty" rates, or any measures of parolee survival may reflect changes in agency policy, not changes in parolee behavior.

SOME IMPLICATIONS OF NEGATIVE OUTCOME FOR TREATMENT PROFESSIONALS

It is not only the administrators of departments of corrections who are becoming concerned about the findings of studies of correctional effectiveness; the same studies are beginning to cause uncomfortable pressures for many treatment professionals. In some institutions, resistance to research on program effectiveness is expressed, not by the custody staff, but by the treatment staff. This resistance is openly expressed by some treatment specialists, usually social workers, who contend that "we are dealing with *people*, not statistics here." But most treatment professionals are aware that they must appear ready to accept "hard" or "objective" evaluations of their efforts and that more subtle means of dealing with the negative findings of outcome studies must be found. Some of the defenses they have

---

[38] Paul Takagi, "Evaluation Systems and Adaptations in a Formal Organization," unpublished Doctoral Dissertation, Stanford University, 1967, pp. 158–161. Reprinted with permission.

raised have been described by Donald Cressey as a "vocabulary of adjustment" by which staff members can justify whatever they are doing as "corrective." Cressey's illustration of this point is so good and the arguments so likely to be heard by evaluators of social action programs that it warrants reproducing.

> . . . let us assume that a state has passed a law requiring all its parole agents to be registered psychiatrists who will use professional psychiatric techniques for rehabilitating parolees. Let us assume further that the required number of psychiatrists is found and that after ten years, a research study indicates that introduction of psychiatric techniques has had no statistically significant effect on recidivism rates—the rates are essentially the same as they were ten years earlier. The following are ten kinds of overlapping themes which are likely to be popular among the personnel with personal interests in continuing the program.

1. "You can't use rates as a basis of comparison—if only one man was saved from a life of crime the money spent on the program is justified."

2. "Even the New York Yankees don't expect to win all their ball games; the program certainly *contributed* to the rehabilitation of *some* of the clients."

3. "Recidivism is not a good criterion of efficiency; 'clinical observation' indicates that the criminals handled psychiatrically are 'better adjusted' than were the criminals going out of the system ten years ago and that even the repeaters are 'less serious' repeaters than were those of a decade ago."

4. "Psychiatric techniques for rehabilitation never were tried; the deplorable working conditions made success impossible—there was not enough time, case loads were too big, and salaries were so low that only the poorest psychiatrists could be recruited."

5. "You can't expect any system in which the criminal is seen for only a few hours a week to significantly change personalities which have been in the making for the whole period of the individual's life and which are characterized by deeply-hidden, unconscious problems; we can only keep chipping away."

6. "For administrative reasons, the program was changed in mid-stream; good progress was being made at first, but the program was sabotaged by the new administrator (governor, legislature)."

7. "The technique was effective enough, but the kind of criminals placed on parole changed; ten years ago the proportion of criminals amenable to change was much greater than at present."

8. "Had the technique not been introduced, the recidivism rates would be much higher than at present; the fact that there is no difference really indicates that the technique has been very effective."

9. "There are too many complex variables which were not controlled in the study; a depression (prosperity) came along and affected the recidivism rate; the newspapers gave so much publicity to a few cases of recidivism that parole was revoked even in many cases where genuine progress toward rehabilitation was being made."

10. "The study is invalid because it used no control group, but it has pointed up the need for *really* scientific research on psychiatric techniques; we must continue the program and set up a ten-year experimental study which will reassess our potential, locate some of the transactional variables in the patient-therapist relationship, determine whether some therapists have what we may term 'treatment-potent personalities' and others have what we are tentatively calling 'recidivistic creativity,' identify whether the catalystically-oriented therapeutic climate is self-defeating when occupied by reagent-reacting patients, and measure the adverse effects of post-therapeutic family-warmth variables on favorably-prognosticated and emotionally-mature dischargees. . . ."[39]

In addition to several of the above arguments, we add others that were raised by treatment professionals in their efforts to cast doubt on the validity of the findings of our study:

1. "What goes on between the group leader and the group members (the 'therapeutic' relationship) cannot be measured by statistics."

2. "The impact of the group experience may not be felt for, perhaps, 10 years after the man leaves prison."

3. "The presence of outsiders (the research staff) disturbs the normal conduct of the program or the group or the session."

4. "Even though they may come back to prison, the inmates are better adjusted (or happier or more emotionally stable) people for having participated in the program."

Perhaps the most popular defense, outside of arguing that since the program failed its resources should be doubled, is the advancement of post hoc goals that are the ends for which the researchers should have been testing in the first place.[40] This particular practice, in fact, has been identified by

[39] Donald R. Cressey, "The Nature and Effectiveness of Correctional Techniques," *Law and Contemporary Problems*, Duke University School of Law, 23 (August 1958), pp. 761–762. Reprinted with permission.

[40] See Rossi, op. cit., p. 129.

Joseph Eaton and called "scientific newism."[41] Scientific newism calls for a succession of programs each of which is evaluated, found wanting, but then is reported to be replaced by an "improved model."

This vocabulary reflects an area of real difference between correctional treatment workers and researchers. The criterion by which some social workers and clinicians judge their efforts reflects, in turn, professional training in schools that eschew "the numbers game" in favor of "clinical" assessments of treatment outcome. Despite the fact that evaluative studies based on caseworkers or clinician's "feelings" and/or "experience" have been found to be less reliable than statistical prediction based on comparisons of matched treatment and control groups, there are some staff members who continue to deny that statistical assessments have any "real" meaning.[42]

In his discussion of the conflict between researchers and treatment personnel in regard to evaluative research, Rabow has pointed to several underlying issues such as the emphasis of the treatment staff on "here and now" problems of organizing and implementing programs, while researchers are primarily concerned with trying to establish research designs that ultimately expedite some kind of empirical assessment of the programs. Furthermore, treatment personnel are part of the correctional system, while researchers, as members of university faculties or independent research organizations, have little or no commitment to the organizations they study. Rabow characterizes the positions of the treatment staff and the researchers with respect to program evaluation as similar to the positions taken by debaters and scientists:

> . . . clinicians, administrators and board members concentrate more upon lending credence to already accepted methods than to an objective, unbiased appraisal of the techniques used. This approach is analogous to the debater who seeks mainly for evidence to support his previously accepted proposition rather than to the scientist who refrains from making a conclusion until he examines both sides of a question. The debater presents only those data which support his viewpoint and discards the remainder. The scientist must draw his conclusion from the total mass of data.[43]

The problem for treatment personnel, as noted previously, is that a "nonscientific" stance in regard to program evaluation is impolitic at the present time. Since the arguments that the treatment "saved one man" or

[41] Joseph W. Eaton, *Stone Walls Not a Prison Make*, Springfield, Illinois: Charles C. Thomas Publishers, 1962, pp. 35–41.

[42] See Paul E. Meehl, *Clinical vs. Statistical Prediction*, Minneapolis: University of Minnesota Press, 1954.

[43] Jerome Rabow, "Research and Rehabilitation: The Conflict of Scientific and Treatment Roles in Correction," *The Journal of Research in Crime and Delinquency*, 1 (January 1964), p. 75.

that the negative outcome due to treatment only shows that twice as much money, personnel, or effort should go into the program are not apt to be accepted, a more subtle defense mechanism has been adopted—the *rhetorical research question*. In contrast to *analytic* questions (which deal with questions of. how certain variables cluster and interrelate, or whether null hypotheses or substantive, "if A, then B" hypotheses are supported) and *evaluative* questions (which are concerned with the extent to which a goal has been achieved as measured by certain specified criteria), rhetorical questions about treatment "effectiveness" are designed to raise issues but not to provide answers. These questions are typically formulated when there is pressure by outsiders for an assessment of a program that has not been empirically evaluated, when negative findings indicate that the program is not achieving its "present" goals, or in ceremonial contexts as one of a series of steps to a foregone conclusion. The important point about rhetorical research questions, as Cressey has observed, is that they are set up so that they cannot be resolved.[44]

The rhetorical research question, examples of which are given above, has come into increasing use by treatment professionals—and for different reasons by correctional administrators—as negative results accumulate. For both groups, however, the basic purpose of those questions is to accommodate to evaluative research findings or to minimize the impact of anticipated negative answers to evaluative research questions. For example, one may question whether an evaluation was appropriate in the first place.

> . . . the impact of group counseling on the correctional apparatus cannot be appraised until some models can be set up for test. The task now is not to prove that group counseling works. Eager advocates of research must be patient with an era of experimentation in group counseling. Nothing will be settled in any massive study which could conceivably be executed now. Dozens of small issues must be resolved before group counselors can be adequately trained. In the meantime, the gains which the correctional apparatus makes from the mere existence of this practice within its gates should sufficiently reward its tolerance.[45]

Implication of the Men's Colony study for sociology and penology

LIMITATIONS OF SOCIOLOGICAL STUDIES OF PAROLE

Difficulties in interpreting parole success and failure rates seem partly a result of the tendency to study parole from the relatively narrow focus of

[44] See Cressey, op. cit., pp. 758–761.

[45] John P. Conrad, *Crime and Its Correction*, Berkeley: University of California Press, 1965, pp. 246–247.

parole *prediction*. Parole outcome has been regarded implicitly as simply a function of the behavior of the parolee; this view has resulted in the neglect of the study of the parole officer as a decision maker. Moreover, the parole division has not been studied as a complex social organization. Thus we are led to the awareness that our data on parole success and failure do not provide a clear indicator of postrelease behavior, since we do not fully understand the nature of the parole experience. What is clear is that parole outcome is not related to exposure to counseling programs.

If it is reasonably accurate to suggest that emphasis on the prison as a closed, total institution has distracted sociological attention to the wider organization of the department of corrections, it is doubly warranted to note that the organized character of postrelease life for the parolee is poorly understood by sociology.

Parole has mainly served as either an independent variable for sociologists and criminologists interested in predictive recidivism with a regression equation of background characteristics of parolees, or else has served as a criterion of program success or failure. Yet, close acquaintance with the routine workings of a modern parole division quickly reveals the complex nature of parole supervisions and the range of discretion and judgment exercised by the parole agency.[46]

What is clearly needed is a study of the organization of parole, the nature of parole supervision, the interaction of parolee and agent, and the life situation of the parolee. Until we know more about the basis of parole decisions in continuing or revoking parole, we are not likely to be able to determine how to reduce parole violation rates—unless one wishes to reduce the amount of information the parole officer has about the parolee and/or to reduce the range of parolee actions that may be used by parole agents to justify "revocation." The introduction of "due process" considerations into the parole supervision mechanism would probably do just that. The larger questions still remain: what methods of controlling antisocial behavior can be used with justice?[47]

THE NATURE OF THE POSTRELEASE PERIOD

As we have stressed in previous chapters, the parole period represents not the release from prisoner status to free civil status, but the extension of

[46] For exceptions see Takagi, op. cit.; Martinson, Kassebaum, and Ward, op. cit.; Don M. Gottfredson and Kelly B. Ballard, Jr., "Differences in Parole Decisions Associated with Decision-Makers," *Journal of Research in Crime and Delinquency*, **3** (July 1966), pp. 112–119; and James Robison and Paul Takagi, "The Parole Violator as an Organization Reject," in Robert M. Carter and Leslie T. Wilkins, *Probation and Parole: Selected Readings*, New York: John Wiley and Sons, Inc., 1970, pp. 233–254.

[47] *Parole Board Reform in California*, Assembly of the State of California, 1970.

correctional control to the community. The task of the parolee is to conform to the expectations and regulations of the parole division. The legal
status and truncated civil rights of the parolee, the surveillance to which
he may legitimately be subject, and the procedures that are provided for
his speedy administrative return to custody place his behavior under a set
of interpretations different from those normally applied to civilian behavior. In the peculiar status of parolee, there are a set of poorly understood contingencies that may be fairly closely related to the interaction of
parolee, parole division, and community, and that can best be understood
in terms of the matrix of demands and sanctions that define the parolee's
life situations.

We suggest, therefore, following the works of Lemert, Becker, Goffman, Kitsuse, Scheff, Turk and others, that prison and parole might be
approached from the standpoint of a correctional career.[48] Such an approach would examine the nature of the prison intake of representative
types of inmates—that is, make designations on the basis of how the commitment conviction was obtained by the state; it would seek to determine
the salient stages and contingencies for entering and exiting along a career
line in which the individual is linked progressively more closely with the
state's law enforcement agencies. It would explore the ways in which the
information and impressions of various personnel counseling the prisoner
are acquired or assembled; the manner in which the record file is updated
and used by various persons fateful to the career of the inmate.

This approach would study the total set of expectations about inmate
life articulated in the prison and would seek to extend this understanding
to the activities of the parole division in the community at large. It would
endeavor to discover the actual bases of crucial parole agency decisions
about the released prisoner, and the various stratagems employed by parolees to minimize their vulnerability to return to custody. It would collect
longitudinal data on men through several cycles of arrest-conviction-incar-
ceration-parole and would endeavor to construct a model of the career lines

---

[48] See Edwin M. Lemert, "Deviation as a Process," *Human Deviance, Social Problems and Social Control*, Englewood Cliffs, New Jersey: Prentice-Hall, Inc., 1967, pp.
3–64; Howard S. Becker, *Outsiders: Studies in the Sociology of Deviance*, New York:
The Macmillan Company, 1963, especially pp. 19–58; Erving Goffman, "The Moral
Career of the Mental Patient," *Asylums*, Garden City, New York: Anchor Books, Inc.,
pp. 127–169; John I. Kitsuse, "Societal Reaction to Deviant Behavior: Problems of
Theory and Method," in Howard S. Becker, *The Other Side: Perspectives on Deviance*,
New York: The Macmillan Company, 1964, pp. 87–102; Thomas J. Scheff, *Being
Mentally Ill: A Sociological Theory*, Chicago: Aldine Publishing Company, 1966; Aus-
tin T. Turk, *Criminality and Legal Order*, Chicago: Rand McNally and Company,
1969; and an excellent new book tracing the career of the felon, *The Felon* by John
Irwin, Englewood Cliffs, New Jersey: Prentice-Hall, Inc., 1970.

that maintain an individual in a certain continuous connection with law enforcement unless and until some exit point is reached. We strongly suspect that, until sociologists have collected better data on this whole process, we may be making assumptions about the nature of criminality that may not be supportable by evidence.

ASSUMPTIONS OF PRISON TREATMENT

For the sociologist, there are theoretical problems posed by the steady accumulation of evaluation studies that fail to confirm positive expectations about psychological treatment programs. Interesting ideas about behavior change that results from the manipulation of interpersonal relations, or the impact of group counseling or the advantages of smaller parole case loads, have all been easier to discuss in project proposals than in final reports. At the conclusion of our research, we feel the responsibility for speculation on what might be fruitful lines of further inquiry into treatment programs. The most fundamental requirement for further research on the effectiveness of prison and parole programs would seem to us to be a frank recognition that psychological treatment programs involve assumptions about the causes of crime, the informal and formal organization of the prison and parole, and the nature of the postrelease experience, all of which may be quite unrealistic when applied to actual existing conditions.

CAUSES OF CRIME

A recent article summarizes, with considerable force and clarity, the problem to which we refer. Austin Turk points out that theories about criminal behavior conceptualize the phenomenon of crime in various ways. They include:

1. Criminal behavior as an indicator of conflict within the person . . . .

2. Criminal behavior as the expression of participation by the offender in a criminogenic subculture . . . .

3. The occurrence of criminal behavior where the offender, because of having been socialized in a different culture, either does not know or does not accept certain legal norms.

4. The violation of laws by essentially normal persons in the course of realistic conflicts of interest . . . to satisfy the demand for illicit goods and services, . . . to utilize illegal means to control and profit from legitimate economic activity, [the] resistance by vested interests to legal restraints . . . of legitimate economic activity, an inequitable and unstable economic structure . . . [and] conflict between those who

seek to preserve a given authority structure and those who are trying to modify or destroy it.[49]

Turk goes on to state:

. . . efforts have been characterized by a lack of careful and consistent distinctions between (a) the stigmatization of deviants, persons who are in some way offensive to others, and criminalization, the processes by which certain persons are officially defined as criminals, violators of legal norms; (b) realistic or normal as opposed to unrealistic or pathological behavior and conflict situation; (c) legal and non-legal norms. Most criminologists have, moreover, assumed for research purposes, that arrest is tantamount to guilt and that arrest and conviction categories are equivalent to homogenous behavior categories. Variations in legislative, judicial, and enforcement behavior have seldom been treated other than as sources of error in estimating rates of deviance.[50]

To the extent that prison holds a heterogenous collection of persons, including men who have been labeled criminal without possessing abnormal emotional or personality attributes, the manipulation of such attributes, even if successful, will not affect the probability that men from prison will be again labeled criminal subsequent to their release from custody.

OBEDIENCE AND INSIGHT

Treatment programs of a psychological derivation, for instance, group counseling, set forth therapeutic goals such as the acquisition of greater insight and self-responsibility. By contrast, the regulations and procedures in the prison are, openly and obviously, aimed at instilling habits of obedience and docility in inmates, both while confined and later in the outside world. The presumption of the legitimacy of the existing order, and the desirability of conformity to the regulations of the institutional and societal status quo are not seriously called into question. Thus, for example, we were sometimes impressed with staff members' efforts to convince a Mexican or black-American that his grievances over racial discrimination in the outside community were merely attempts to rationalize his own antisocial behavior; when this psychological argument failed to produce assent (particularly when it provoked the inmate to angry words), the staff member would remind him that, anyway, the inmate's behavior led to

---

49 Austin T. Turk, "Conflict and Criminality," *American Sociological Review*, 31, June, 1966, pp. 338–339.
50 Turk, op. cit., p. 340.

his being in prison, so that, for pragmatic reasons, he had better learn to "change his ways." To the extent that obedience is the goal of correctional efforts, attempts to implement a treatment program that seeks insight into emotional determination of conduct and increase in the sense of individual responsibility may be perceived by both staff and inmates as somewhat beside the point.

Implications of the Men's Colony Study for the California Department of Corrections

Our efforts to adhere to the research design were greatly aided by the high degree of support and cooperation we received from the California Department of Corrections. To begin with, the department agreed to every major condition required in the design (not always a convenience to the institution); it did not go back on its original commitment throughout the five-year period of data collection.

We tried to anticipate many of the questions about adverse findings which might be plausibly raised by the department and by treatment professionals, and we attempted to cope with them in the research design. As a first step, every effort was made to obtain a fair test of the program. The research was done in a prison system that is directed by some of the best men in the field of corrections. The inmates studied were neither the more intractable offenders confined in maximum security prisons, nor were they the good treatment potential men more likely to be found in first term, minimum security facilities. The study subjects are representative of the "average" inmate population in a correctional system. Furthermore, they are confined in the most up-to-date prison in the department in terms of physical plant and staffing. In addition, a sufficiently large study population was used to permit adequate statistical analysis; random assignment of subjects was made to the various treatment and control conditions; contamination of the sample groups was kept at a minimum because of the physical structure of the institution. Also evaluated was a group counseling condition, especially included for this study, in which group leaders were given training beyond that which the present resources of the Department of Corrections could afford. The follow-up was extended for an unusually long period of time (three years) to take into consideration the long-term effects of treatment.

In a department that has now made group counseling and community living programs a part of the program of every prison in the department, has made inmate participation in the programs compulsory in some institutions, and has made participation in postrelease group counseling mandatory for every parolee in the state, have our negative findings had any appreciable impact? The group counseling program is still the major psychologically based treatment effort in the California Department of Corrections. The Research Division of the California Legislature, however, included a rather careful review and summary of our research in a report, *The California Prison, Parole and Probation System*, presented to the Assembly. The study was undertaken in an effort to find "evidence that correctional programming provides effective rehabilitation."

The findings support the following conclusions:

I. There is no evidence to support claims that one correctional program has more rehabilitative effectiveness than another.

II. Statistics on recidivism exaggerate the extent to which convicted offenders return to serious crime.

III. The likelihood of a citizen being subjected to personal injury or property loss can be only infinitesimally lessened by the field of Corrections.

IV. The increase in public protection gained by the imprisonment of large numbers of offenders, of whom few are dangerous, is outweighed by the public costs involved.

The above conclusions form the basis of the single recommendation: that no more funds be provided for the construction of state prison facilities.[51]

Even this strong statement and a legislature that is becoming doubtful of the ability of prisons to "rehabilitate" may not markedly diminish the utility of the treatment approach as a *rationale* for incarceration. Precisely because the concept and connotations of psychological treatment provide a suitable imagery with which to depict imprisonment, it is unlikely that studies which fail to confirm such treatment's effects will lead to the abandonment of the treatment ideology. The assumptions of the treatment-oriented correctional system, namely that criminal behavior stems from a disturbed emotional state and that the work of a correctional system is to change or to constrain this emotional behavior, combine to provide a broad mandate for the use of power in a diffuse manner. It is a basis for proceeding against behavior that is regarded as "dangerous." For example, several years ago the United States Supreme Court ruled that it was unconstitutional to hold, as California did, drug addiction per se to

[51] James Robison assisted by Carol Sanders and Suellen Stalder, *The California Prison, Parole and Probation System*, Technical Supplement No. 2, A Special Report to the California Assembly, 1970. For making available this and other reports developed by the California Assembly Office of Research, the authors thank Robin Lamson.

be a crime. Quite so, responded the state, drug addiction is a disease . . . and the best place to "treat" it is in an institution operated by the Department of Corrections. Since then, "civil commitment" of narcotics users has sufficed to place hundreds of persons in involuntary long-term custody and parole. Given that the role of agencies of law enforcement is to apply sanctions against persons who are regarded as not conforming to certain rules, it may be expected that various tactics will be employed in an effort to further the objectives of maintaining order. It seems likely that both the flexibility and the benign visage of treatment will continue to be of value to social control agencies.

appendixes

appendix A   Comparability of Respondents in Treatment and Control Varieties

table A.1   Treatment Status by Primary Offense (in Percent)

OFFENSE

TREATMENT STATUS	Murder, Manslaughter, Negligent Homicide	Robbery-First, Second, or Attempted, Assault with Intent To Rob	Assault, Attempted Assault, ADW, Wife/Child Beating, Murder	Burglary—First, Second or Attempted	Grand Theft, Embezzlement, Forgery, NSF, Auto Theft	Rape, Assault with Intent to, or Attempted Rape	Other Sex—Pandering, Pimping, L and L, Sex Perversion, Incest	Narcotics Sales, Marijuana, and Dangerous Drug Sale	Narcotics Possession	Other[a]	Total
Voluntary small group counseling	1	11	2	23	30	1	3	7	14	9	100 (265)
Mandatory small group counseling	2	15	3	21	26	1	3	7	15	7	100 (170)
Mandatory large group counseling	—	10	1	32	22	3	3	9	18	1	100 (65)
Voluntary controls	1	11	2	22	32	3	2	8	9	9	100 (169)
Mandatory controls	2	10	2	22	29	2	2	5	15	12	100 (258)

Table $N = 966$
NA = 2
Sample = 968

$\chi^2 = 33.78$
Degrees of freedom = 36
Not significant

[a] Includes arson, kidnapping, abortion, and extortion.

table A.2   Treatment Status by Type of Prior Commitment (in Percent)

Treatment Status	Type of Prior Commitment									
	None	Arrests or Fines Only	Jail, Farm Workhouse, Detention House or Other (Maximum Sentence Less Than One Year)	Probation or Supervision Only or with Fines	Training Reform or Industrial School	Probation and Jail	Reformatory	Penitentiary Only	Penitentiary and Other Commitments	Total
Voluntary small group counseling	3	5	10	4	1	19	14	6	38	100 (278)
Mandatory small group counseling	2	7	12	1	1	22	19	5	31	100 (173)
Mandatory large group counseling	3	5	12	—	—	32	10	6	32	100 (69)
Voluntary controls	4	8	7	3	2	23	12	3	38	100 (176)
Mandatory controls	6	7	10	4	1	24	10	4	24	100 (270)

Table N = 966
NA = 2
Sample N = 968

χ^2 = 32.54
Degrees of freedom = 32
Not significant

table A.3   Treatment Status by Race (in Percent)

Treatment Status	Race					Total
	White	Mexican	Negro	Indian	Other	
Voluntary small group counseling	56	23	18	1	3	100 (278)
Mandatory small group counseling	56	24	19	—	1	100 (173)
Mandatory large group counseling	51	17	29	—	3	100 (69)
Voluntary controls	61	18	19	—	2	100 (176)
Mandatory controls	58	20	20	—	2	100 (270)

Table N = 966 χ^2 = 9.67
NA = 2   Degrees of freedom = 16
Sample = 968   Not significant

table A.4   Treatment Status by Intelligence (in Percent)

Treatment Status	Very Superior or Superior (120+)	High Average (110 to 119)	Normal (90 to 109)	Dull Normal (80 to 89)	Borderline and Defective (79-under)	Total
Voluntary small group counseling	6	24	45	20	5	100 (277)
Mandatory small group counseling	4	23	49	19	5	100 (169)
Mandatory large group counseling	3	14	44	31	8	100 (69)
Voluntary controls	7	22	51	17	3	100 (175)
Mandatory controls	7	23	45	21	4	100 (265)

Table N = 955
NA = 13
Sample = 968

$\chi^2 = 22.32$
Degrees of freedom = 24
Not significant

table A.5   Treatment Status by Base Expectancy (Prognosis) Standard Scores (in Percent)

Base Expectancy
Standard Scores

Treatment Status	Very Low (0 to 23)	Low (24 to 38)	High (39 to 53)	Very High (54 to 98)	Total
Voluntary small group counseling	44	13	13	30	100 (278)
Mandatory small group counseling	39	18	13	30	100 (173)
Mandatory large group counseling	46	16	16	22	100 (69)
Voluntary controls	38	12	14	36	100 (176)
Mandatory controls	37	14	12	37	100 (270)

Table $N = 966$ $\chi^2 = 11.51$
NA $= 2$ Degrees of freedom $= 12$
Sample $N = 968$ Not significant

COMPONENTS AND WEIGHT: BASE EXPECTANCY (PROGNOSIS)

	Variable	Weight
A.	Arrest-free period of five or more years	12
B.	No history of any opiate use	9
C.	Few jail commitments (none, one or two)	8
D.	Not checks or burglary for present commitment	7
E.	No family criminal record	6
F.	No alcohol involvement	6
G.	Not first arrested for auto theft	5
H.	Six months or more in any one job	5
I.	No aliases	5
J.	Original commitment	5
K.	Favorable living arrangement	4
L.	Few prior arrests (none, one or two)	4

appendix B Characteristics of Adult Felon Population in California State Institutions[1]

I.   Offense

II. Ethnic Group

III. Age

IV. Parole Status

V.   Prior Commitment Record

VI. Escape Record

[1] See Chapter II.

Characteristics of Adult Felon Population in California State Prisons by Institution as of December 31, 1963 (in Percent)

Characteristics	Total Males (N = 20669)	CMCE (N = 2333)	Correctional Training Facility (N = 3149)	California Institution for Men (N = 1445)	CIM Branch at Tehachapi (N = 609)	California Medical Facility (N = 1202)	CMCW (N = 1436)	Deuel Vocational Institution (N = 807)	Folsom (N = 2522)	San Quentin (N = 4686)
I. Offense										
Homicide	7.8	6.7	4.2	5.9	3.0	12.4	12.4	8.8	7.3	12.3
Robbery	22.4	21.2	24.4	26.7	20.4	23.5	6.8	30.4	26.6	22.7
Assault	3.9	3.8	3.7	3.5	2.3	5.7	4.5	4.0	3.4	5.4
Burglary	17.3	16.3	19.7	22.4	20.0	15.3	10.7	18.5	15.3	13.5
Thefts except auto	4.1	2.8	3.9	6.6	5.6	3.2	7.1	2.5	3.3	2.8
Auto theft	2.5	2.9	3.2	3.5	2.8	2.4	1.8	3.8	1.7	1.5
Forgery and checks	11.4	8.1	9.2	17.0	15.3	10.1	18.7	10.0	6.9	7.6
Rape	3.0	4.4	3.5	1.3	1.1	4.8	1.3	3.6	1.9	4.5
Other sex	5.2	7.6	2.4	1.0	1.1	7.7	21.2	2.3	4.6	5.7
Narcotics and dangerous drugs	16.3	19.4	20.7	8.9	26.3	7.9	10.0	10.3	17.0	17.3
Escape	2.3	3.0	3.0	0.1	0.6	1.4	0.3	2.6	4.8	3.0
Habitual criminal	0.5	0.4	—	—	—	0.6	1.3	0.1	2.4	0.2
All other	3.3	3.4	2.1	3.1	1.5	5.0	3.9	3.1	4.8	3.5
II. Ethnic group										
White	55.5	56.6	49.8	55.1	49.1	74.4	72.4	62.2	52.9	50.0
Mexican descent	16.7	18.0	23.6	10.6	20.5	8.8	6.0	16.4	16.7	18.6
Negro	26.0	23.4	25.4	32.9	30.2	14.8	18.7	20.2	28.1	29.5
Other	1.8	2.0	1.2	1.4	0.2	2.0	2.9	1.2	2.3	1.9

Characteristics of Adult Felon Population in California State Prisons by Institution as of December 31, 1963 (in Percent) continued

Characteristics	Total Males (N = 20669)	CMCE (N = 2233)	Correctional Training Facility (N = 3149)	California Institution for Men (N = 1445)	CIM Branch at Tehachapi (N = 609)	California Medical Facility (N = 1202)	CMCW (N = 1436)	Deuel Vocational Institution (N = 807)	Folsom (N = 2522)	San Quentin (N = 4686)
III. Age										
Under 20	0.6	—	1.3	0.3	—	0.7	—	7.8	—	0.1
20 to 24	16.5	19.1	36.6	26.0	13.1	17.1	—	56.2	0.4	9.2
25 to 29	23.4	29.3	30.4	30.2	33.2	23.7	0.2	17.5	8.3	29.6
30 to 34	19.6	20.9	15.7	21.3	26.4	18.4	1.0	4.7	22.7	26.0
35 to 39	16.1	14.2	9.0	12.3	14.5	17.5	2.9	5.1	28.4	18.5
40 to 44	9.7	6.7	4.8	6.6	8.7	10.5	9.2	4.1	17.8	9.3
45 to 49	5.7	4.0	1.3	2.1	2.8	6.8	20.9	2.1	10.6	4.0
50 to 54	3.8	2.1	0.7	0.9	0.8	3.0	22.9	1.6	6.8	2.0
55 to 59	2.2	1.6	0.2	0.3	0.3	1.3	18.5	0.5	3.1	0.8
60 and over	2.4	2.1	—	—	0.2	1.0	24.4	0.4	1.9	0.5
IV. Parole status										
Not paroled since committed	66.2	74.5	74.2	78.1	59.1	71.7	69.4	84.7	55.8	60.8
Paroled and returned once as violator	23.5	20.4	19.8	16.1	27.4	19.2	19.9	11.9	27.8	27.8
Paroled and returned twice as violator	7.9	4.2	5.3	5.0	10.2	6.7	7.8	2.5	12.0	8.9
Paroled and returned three times or more as violator	2.4	0.9	0.7	0.8	3.3	2.4	2.9	0.9	4.4	2.5

Characteristics of Adult Felon Population in California State Prisons by Institution as of December 31, 1963 (in Percent) continued

Characteristics	Total Males (N = 20669)	CMCE (N = 2233)	Correctional Training Facility (N = 3149)	California Institution for Men (N = 1445)	CIM Branch at Tehachapi (N = 609)	California Medical Facility (N = 1202)	CMCW (N = 1436)	Deuel Vocational Institution (N = 807)	Folsom (N = 2522)	San Quentin (N = 4686)
V. Prior commitment record										
No prior commitments	10.8	12.0	9.4	20.4	10.0	17.5	17.0	15.9	2.2	11.2
Prior jail or juvenile only	41.0	48.6	59.2	50.9	45.5	37.4	22.3	64.2	13.4	42.4
1 prior prison commitment	25.0	24.4	21.1	19.7	28.9	21.6	20.5	11.0	30.8	28.7
2 prior prison commitments	12.1	9.0	6.5	5.8	10.2	11.8	12.7	5.2	24.8	11.4
3 prior prison commitments	5.9	3.2	2.5	2.2	3.4	6.0	10.0	2.1	15.1	4.2
4 or more prison commitments	5.2	2.8	1.3	1.0	2.0	5.7	17.5	1.6	13.7	2.1
VI. Escape record										
No record of escape	78.1	75.7	76.7	92.4	83.5	76.4	89.6	73.7	62.1	76.2
Record of escape from:										
Jail	16.0	18.7	19.7	7.1	15.3	16.9	5.9	22.8	19.2	17.8
Prior prison commitment	2.3	2.0	0.9	0.3	0.6	2.2	3.8	0.9	7.3	1.9
Present commitment	3.6	3.6	2.7	0.2	0.6	4.5	0.7	2.6	11.4	4.1

appendix C Underlying Assumptions of Special Group Leader Training Program

//

The terms and assumptions of this brief description reflect the point of view of the trainer, William Schutz. We present this approach to provide an understanding of the orientation of the program. We do not have adequate measures of the actual operating differences of the counseling leaders in their groups. However, the lengthy excerpts of tape recorded group training sessions give data on the behavior of, at least, some of the group leaders. (See Chapter VI.)

Counseling theory

In formulating the objective of the supplemental training program, it was assumed that counselors should be competent to do the following:

1. Enable groups to explore and discuss different problem areas at sufficient depth so that significant issues are worked through, thus leading to more long-range benefit to participants.
2. Handle any emotional distress group members may encounter.

To accomplish these aims, the training program for group leaders attempted to cover these areas:

1. Experience with theory and practice of group counseling.
2. Experiences that will lead to insight about group processes.
3. Experiences that will lead to heightened insight about the counselor himself, his own needs and defenses, and his impact on other people.

There are many approaches to group counseling. The one used in the present situation reflects the orientations of the trainer. In order to make clear the approach used to train the counselors, a brief description of the method follows; a short statement of the theoretical basis of the approach has been published elsewhere (Schutz, 1961).

The point of view of the training seminar

The primary contribution of the group counseling situation is the presentation to group members of personal and interpersonal reality. Having a small group of people meeting together intensively with no ostensible task provides an opportunity for learning about one's self and others in a way that is difficult to attain in most other settings. The quality of the reality obtained by the group members depends primarily on two factors:

1. *Honesty and openness*. If group members cannot express their true feelings, then there can be but limited benefit from a counseling group. To present to each other the veneer usually used for daily contact and not to allow a look into the feelings beneath it means that the counseling experience has no advantage over normal human contacts. Honesty and openness refers to a person's willingness to tell others how he really feels. This readiness depends primarily on trust in other people, the ability to be aware of one's feelings, and on the avoidance of self-deception.

2. *Variety and depth*. If the counseling experience is a bland, casual one devoid of personal involvement and strong, significant feelings, there is but a limited opportunity for learning. No matter how honest and open group members are with each other, if they are simply not experiencing any strong feelings, or if their more important feelings are not brought out within the group, then there is no opportunity to learn about these significant feelings.

Becoming more aware of reality is useful for both personal growth and intellectual learning. The counseling group experience can lead to an improvement in a person's productivity and happiness as a person and in the various roles he plays, to increased intellectual knowledge about individual and group processes, and to a more effective coping with the problems of life.

The group leader as completer

These aims provide direction for the behavior displayed by the group leader. (The term group leader will be used here as a more neutral term than counselor, therapist, trainer, or other possibilities. "Counselor" conveys giving advice of counsel, behavior not always consistent with the present training approach.)

The group leader must help to create a situation in which a wide variety of feelings are aroused, discussed, and worked through, and must provide intellectual tools for conceptualizing what the participants have experienced so that it is easier to comprehend and generalize.

The function of the leader is to be a "completer." He must have a knowledge of what functions must be fulfilled in the group in order for it to accomplish its goals; he must be sensitive to the situation when some of these
functions are not being fulfilled; and he must be able to act in a way that
facilitates their accomplishment. The facilitation may be accomplished through
direct action by the leader, or he may utilize group members to help accomplish the desired result. Knowing which group members can be helpful in a
given situation requires the ability to assess their qualities accurately.

The group leader is effective to the degree that he has a repertoire of methods for dealing with various group situations, and the ability to know when a
particular method is appropriate. He is in the position of making guesses or
hypotheses about what is happening in the group. His hypothesis directs his
behavior. An enumeration of some of these group leader methods follows.

1. Silence. In general, the more activity the group initiates on its own,
the better. By taking a relatively passive role, especially at the beginning of
the group's life, the leader is communicating to the group that he is not the
source of all knowledge nor should they look to him to initiate behavior.
The leader is attempting to convey to the group members the belief that they
have resources themselves, and they are encouraged to develop and use them.
Usually to reinforce this idea, the leader must deal effectively with direct
questions from group members. Often group members may be oriented to him
as they are used to being oriented toward officers, teachers, or bosses. By
turning back the question or by refusing to answer, the leader can reinforce
the group-centered nature of the interaction. The leader should make it evident that he thinks that the members are capable of effective group interaction.
The knowledge that someone in authority has respect for their abilities helps
to keep them from depending on the group leader for guidance and aids in
an examination of their own resources.

Silence also is appropriate when the group is working effectively. An inex-
perienced group leader frequently feels that he must demonstrate his influence
and knowledge in the group by maintaining a central role at all times. Usually
this will satisfy the leader's needs, but it interferes with the progress of the
group. A group leader's insight into the workings of the group often will occur
to a group member soon after it occurs to the leader.

In a sense, a group leader is successful to the degree that he is unnecessary.
If the group operates in the same manner with the leader as without him,
then he has contributed all he can to the group.

Abdication of the active leadership role often elicits feelings of hostility
toward the group leader. Along with the hostility usually comes a defense of
the leader by other members. Ordinarily this is a very desirable situation because it exposes various attitudes toward authority and then leads to an
exploration of these attitudes. It is important to remember that the leader's

main job is not to remain likeable and respected at all times. (These attitudes may be primarily the leader's needs.) An important part of his role is to act in such a way as to evoke important feelings from group members and to help them understand these feelings. Inevitably, some of these feelings will be directed toward the leader, but defensive behavior on his part is often inhibiting to the group.

Another value of leader silence is to present an ambiguous authority figure. By not revealing much of himself to the group the leader allows group members to project on to him whatever attributes they feel he has or want him to have. This can lead to learning in two ways: (1) by comparing the different perceptions of the leader held by various members, much can be learned about how each person tends to see authority figures; and (2) as the leader begins to reveal himself more, the way in which he emerges as a person also may be compared with members' original perceptions of him, and the reasons for their distortions explored.

In summary, silence can be a useful device for a leader, (1) to establish the group, instead of leader-centered interaction, (2) to avoid interfering with work being done by the group, and (3) to encourage projections onto the leader figure to be used for learning about members' responses to authority.

2. Here and Now.   The primary focus in small group interaction is on the current experiences that happen within the group. Examination of these experiences gives the group its unique advantage over other types of learning situations. If group members bring in incidents from their past or from aspects of their life that are unrelated to the group, there is little the group can do but give advice or, perhaps, support. The strength of the group is best utilized when group members can react to behavior that they have experienced directly. The objective of the group leader is to assist the group to focus on that aspect of the behavior which is a common experience of the group.

The behavior a group member exhibits in the group context has an important relation to behavior expressed outside the group and, therefore, an understanding of this behavior should be of general value and application. Furthermore, this is the behavior that the group members have experienced directly and can respond to most adequately. For example, if a group member begins to talk about troubles with his wife, the most useful way for the leader to handle the problem is to focus the group on the member's behavior in the group. The individual alone, or with the group's help, can make the connection to his relationship to his wife. For the group to comment on his wife's behavior or on the events in his marriage as he relates them would have minimal value, since the group members' information about these events is only second-hand from a nonobjective reporter. This advice would be of limited value.

The here-and-now rule cannot be adhered to inflexibly. Sometimes a beginning group needs some material to use in order to get to know each other and the here-and-now material is too unfamiliar to allow the group to function effectively toward this end. In this case they must use other content to talk about. The second situation in which outside talk is useful is that which begins with here-and-now. For instance, in the example above, after the group discusses the person's here-and-now behavior, it can be of value in helping him explore his behavior outside of the group in relation to that observed by all. Group members can help him perceive the relationship between his behavior in and out of the group.

Influencing group members to discuss current experiences and attitudes can be done in several ways. In some groups it can be done directly by making an explicit rule at the beginning of the group meetings. For groups that feel more comfortable with rules, this is sometimes very effective. In other cases, the rule can be introduced more gradually by group-leader interventions that will ultimately be recognized by the group.

3. *Feelings.* The most useful area of group exploration is the members' feelings. It is, however, very difficult for many people to identify their feelings, since they have been taught that it is wrong to feel jealous, weak, or hostile. However, with concentration on these feelings, it is possible for people to become more aware of these aspects of their personalities and of the impact of such feelings on their attitudes and behavior.

The following are some examples of how the group can make use of feelings in their day-to-day work. The examples refer to inmate groups, but they apply more generally.

(a) Inmates frequently complain about the guards. Instead of defending the actions of the guards, the group leader can focus the group on the feelings toward the guards that they are expressing in the group at that moment. Once the inmates are focused on the feelings they are expressing, they may relate these to general attitudes toward authority, and then perhaps to feelings that they have toward authority "on the outside." They can examine a present feeling to discover its basis. Thus, a complaint session may be turned into a useful exploration of vital issues for inmates.

(b) When a new member enters a group, there can be a number of reactions experienced by both new and old members. An exploration of those immediate feelings can lead to a discussion of issues that are related to group membership and marginality. Sometimes the newcomer, or an old member identifying with the newcomer, will experience a familiar feeling of not belonging to an already established group, of "barging in where he's not wanted," or that nobody really cares about him or will help him.

These feelings can often lead to an exploration of similar feelings one experiences as a child and the behavior that resulted from these feelings. From this can come insight into the basis of some of these feelings and more understanding of how people really do feel about the newcomer. This comes from a discussion by the group members of their feelings toward him. He then can see how much of the feeling is determined by attitudes toward any newcomer and how much is determined by reaction to him as a person.

Many other issues can be illuminated by this situation—for example, the feelings of the old members about the newcomer in terms of distrust, competition, fear, and the like. Again, all of these very important issues can evolve from the here-and-now feelings about the newcomer.

(c) In most inmate groups, there are one or more withdrawn members. An examination of the group's feelings toward the withdrawn member, and of the feelings of the member himself, usually uncovers another set of significant problems. Frequently, the withdrawn member will speak of or exhibit an inability to express his feelings directly, causing him to feel frustrated. Or, the withdrawn person may express the feeling that no one cares about what he has to say, or the feeling that he will demonstrate how stupid he is if he talks, or that, perhaps, he will say something that will cause people to react hostilely. In any case, he has expressed an important feeling and one that can be pursued into other areas of life with the prospect of obtaining insight and of experiencing catharsis.

The feelings of the other group members toward the withdrawn person often involve distrust. Someone who will not talk frequently may draw much hostility, as people feel he is watching and judging them. These feelings also can be explored profitably.

Thus, it is not necessary to bring in events from the outside in order to elicit strong feelings. Most of the significant emotions that are important in understanding personal and interpersonal dynamics exist within the group setting. The use of these feelings as the basis for group interaction usually leads to an experience with greater impact, involvement, and opportunity for positive change.

4. Facilitation. There are many techniques a group leader must utilize to facilitate the group's accomplishment of its goals. The challenge to the leader, in part, is knowing when to use each technique.

Many people are inhibited and reluctant to express themselves openly and honestly. There are a wide variety of reasons for their difficulty, but a number of methods exist for dealing with it. Some of them are as follows.

Some people need only to be asked to express their feelings and to be given the prospect of support from the group leader, in particular, as well as from the group itself. With others, this method is not as effective because their defenses are such that this kind of support will permit them to continue to hide or to evade. For example, intellectualizers—people who manage their anxious feelings by talking about the situation in intellectual terms—often are unaffected by support. They frequently need to be challenged or attacked by the leader, or need to have their defense pointed out to them in order to begin to break through to the point where they can express feelings. More active participation by the group leader is required to get these people to feel things instead of just talking about them. Acting-out techniques as in Gestalt therapy are often effective. For example, if a person is acting as if he were superior to the other members of the group, the leader may ask him to stand up and actually be above them physically and to report how he feels. Or if the group members are trying to help him and he is rejecting their attempts, he may be asked to actually push someone away physically and to examine how the experience affects him. These methods are often dramatically effective.

Another method for "uncorking" people with difficulty in expressing their feelings calls for the group leader to demonstrate the type of behavior he wishes the group members to express. For example, he can express his own actual feelings at any given moment, especially feelings of inadequacy as when he is confused as to what is happening in the group. This often makes him more human, and demonstrates that one may feel this way without great personal injury or deflation. This method does require considerable security on the part of the group leader.

Another method for helping a group obtain its goals involves the assessment of particular types of group members. Frequently in a group the focus of discussion is on one member, and an entire session is devoted to a discussion with and about him. Group leaders and group members often feel this is unfortunate because that person "dominates" the group. However, a member may be permitted to dominate the discussion if he is expressing feelings that are shared, at least in part, by other members of the group. They may "use" him in a constructive way by comparing him and his behavior to their own. Their questions often really mean, "How much are you like me?" If the focus of attention is not related to feelings shared by other group members, it will rarely remain the focus for very long.

Usually, people who occupy this focal position are able to express their feelings more easily than other group members. They may also be more dogmatic or may represent one pole of a dilemma very clearly, which permits the other members to see it more clearly. The group leader should try to identify these people and to facilitate their participation. This often helps a group make progress and makes use of one person to free others.

5. Leadership Style. The methods used by any particular group leader must be based on the type of person he is. It is very important for a group leader to know himself well and to know the impact that he makes on others. Knowledge of this impact can be used to make his participation more effective. For example, if the group leader is viewed as very strong and elicits competitive feelings in men, he can be aware of this and can help group members to identify feelings of competition.

The method adopted by a group leader should fit his personality. If he tends to be taciturn and quiet, he will probably be most effective as a group leader if his style of leadership is built around that type of behavior. On the other hand, if he tends to be more gregarious and informal, then a style built around this type of interaction will be best for him. If a leader predisposed to one style tries to take on the role of the other, the falseness of his behavior will be apparent to group members and his usefulness may be diminished. In short, the leader can help the group most if he acts naturally. Since he is asking group members to be open and honest, and to avoid self-deception, it is important that he provide a model of that type of behavior himself.

6. Content. Although the content of the group discussion varies greatly from one group to another (see Schutz, 1958), there are particular interpersonal and personal issues that people hold in common, and the more these issues can be brought to the surface for discussion, and the deeper the discussion goes, the more likely that beneficial change will take place in group members.

One set of issues revolves around the problems of contact with others in terms of wanting to be included in group activities on the one hand, and in being allowed privacy on the other. Related to this are feelings of isolation and loneliness, and the search for one's identity. Often these issues are reflected in discussions of religion where the search for one's place in the world is an issue, or in racial issues where the question of marginality enters. Trying to determine one's identity and what people really want are crucial problems that can often be dealt with very profitably in a group if these concerns can find expression.

Another set of issues concerns the question of power, control, and authority. Feelings of competition, rebellion, and dependency are related, and at a deeper level these problems become issues of masculinity, strength, and competence. Problems regarding one's own sexual competence and feelings about homosexual encounters fall into this area. They are often difficult to elicit in a group because of cultural taboos, but they are extremely valuable for the group to try to work through. Also involved here are issues of expressing hostility and destruction and the ability to control these impulses. Inmates especially are concerned with this.

Issues related to affection usually occur later in the group life. They have to do with establishing close, personal relations with people and with expressing warm feelings to others. Discussions of heterosexual relationships enter at this point with the problems of jealousy, rejection, and love usually prominent in the discussion. Also of concern are the clashes between the norms of society and one's impulses as, for example, when a married person is attracted to someone else, or the difficulty in becoming close to someone of the same sex because of homosexual implications.

To the degree that a group of staff members can work through issues like these in a meaningful way, it has had an experience with the possibility that profitable changes will occur within the inmate members of groups that they will subsequently lead.

appendix D Group Opinion Inventory: Dimensions of Satisfaction and Dissatisfaction in the Groups[1]

Early in the project, we assembled a preliminary questionnaire to measure satisfaction in groups. For a pretest of the suitability of items at CMCE, 26 items were adopted from a questionnaire developed at Harvard University.[2] In addition, 34 new items were written to present language and situations more directly related to the prison setting. This version was administered to inmate members of seven counseling groups at CMCE. Out of 95 subjects, only one did not return a usable questionnaire.

In the initial inspection, 16 of the original 60 items showed less than 15 percent endorsement on either side of the neutral point and were removed from further correlational analysis. Responses to the remaining 44 items were inter-correlated.

The abundance of correlations significant at greater than .01 level justified a factor analysis of the matrix. A factor analysis by means of the principal axis technique extracted 12 factors of which the first six factors accounted for 68

[1] See Chapter V.

[2] The items were derived from a general questionnaire developed at the Laboratory of Social Relations at Harvard by Arthur Couch and Robert F. Bales. In their study of a sample of Harvard underclassmen in five-man groups, a 50-item factor analysis yielded four orthogonal factors, named as follows:

    I.   *Interpersonal Satisfaction.* The degree to which group members feel that interpersonal consideration was shown for the feelings of others, giving a freedom from dominance and an equal opportunity for participation in the discussion.

    II.   *Satisfaction with Goal Attainment.* The degree to which group members feel that they were able to arrive at the group goal with high task efficiency and attain a realistic solution to their instrumental problem.

    III.   *Rejection of the Task.* The degree to which the members indicate a lack of involvement in the group task and place the blame for their rejection on the unacceptable nature of the task itself.

    IV.   *Identification with the Group.* The degree to which the members indicate an acceptance of the other group members as involved contributors to the group goal.

347

percent of the total common factor variance. These six factors were rotated to orthogonal simple structure by means of the verimax solution. From the content of these high loading items, six factors were tentatively interpreted as follows: task accomplishment, therapeutic effects, respondent participation, level of group activity, members' likability, and distrust. The pretest items that best measured these factors were selected for inclusion in the Group Opinion Inventory. This revised version was administered to the members of approximately two thirds (50) of the counseling groups under study—sample size, 490.

From the best items of the pretest and with the addition of several new items that asked about inmate trust or distrust in the confidentiality of the group sessions, a 24-variable matrix was selected for factor analysis. These items appear in Table D.1. Rather than rotate to the criteria of the small pretest, we again used the mathematical criterion of simple structure to govern rotation. The correlations, eigenvalues, and rotated loadings are shown in Tables D.2 and D.3. Although the order is different, the content of the six factors replicated the pretest.

The highest and purest loadings for Factor I are on variables 1 ("In this group not enough people take responsibility for keeping discussion going"), 15 ("There is too much silence in this group"), and 11 ("The group tries to do the best it can in group counseling"). It also has high but shared loadings on 2 ("Most members do not seem to know what to do in the group"), and 4 ("This group does not accomplish as much as it should"). Factor I was termed *Active Task Accomplishment of Group*.

Factor II has only three items that are highly loaded; they refer to the respondent's participation: 7 ("I enjoy talking in this group"), 9 ("I seldom have anything to say in the group"), and 10 ("I am fairly active in group sessions").

Factor III is composed of the items that express liking for or likability of other members: 17 ("Most men in this group are well thought of by other inmates"), 18 ("I have several friends in this group"), and 19 ("The friendly spirit of joking is one of the best things about this group").

The new items that assert inmate fears about the use of his group statements for custodial purposes or inmate gossip comprise the basis of Factor IV. Two of the five items contained in this factor are: 20 ("I'm afraid what I say in group counseling sessions may go into my record jacket"), and 24 ("Most men in the group hesitate to say anything bad about themselves because it may be reported to the Adult Authority").

Respondent views of the therapeutic effects of counseling on him are expressed in items 3, 5, 6, and 8, which comprise the fifth factor. Included are: "In most group meetings I don't think our conclusions were detailed enough to be realistic," and "I do not think this group is able to help me."

The last factor contains two items, 13 and 14, asserting or denying the

table D.1   Group Opinion Inventory: Twenty-Four Variables

Matrix Number	Item
1	In this group not enough people take responsibility for keeping discussion going.
2	Most members do not seem to know what to do in group.
3	In most of our group meetings, I don't think our conclusions were detailed enough to be realistic.
4	This group does not accomplish as much as it should.
5	I do not think this group is able to help me.
6	I am bored most of the time with discussion in this group.
7	I enjoy talking in this group.
8	I do not feel I have a problem this group can help.
9	I seldom have anything to say in group.
10	I am fairly active in group discussion.
11	Group tries to do best it can in group counseling
12	Members' reasoning usually clear and logical.
13	Some people in group talk too much.
14	Nobody tries to dominate discussion in my group.
15	There is too much silence in this group.
16	Usually everyone talks a fairly equal amount in my group.
17	Most men in this group are well thought of by other inmates.
18	I have several friends in this group.
19	Friendly spirit and joking is one of the best things about this group.
20	I am afraid what I say in group counseling session may go into my record jacket.
21	Members in this group talk about meetings to other inmates.
22	Men in this group cannot be trusted to keep confidential what is said in group.
23	Few people are really interested in what is being said in group.
24	Most men in group hesitate to say anything bad about themselves because it may be reported to Adult Authority.

table D.2   Group Opinion Inventory: Satisfaction Items, Zero-Order Correlations (Decimal Points Omitted)

Variable Number	1	2	3	4	5	6	7	8	9	10	11	12	13	14	15	16	17	18	19	20	21	22	23	24
1	*	53	34	44	24	27	-16	22	14	-06	-38	-34	13	-10	40	-34	-30	-03	-05	20	13	26	31	26
2		*	43	50	29	33	-25	21	26	-10	-35	-40	17	-13	33	-23	-29	-06	-08	30	08	30	38	37
3			*	47	42	44	-24	35	31	-06	-28	-30	17	-06	18	-14	-19	-03	-11	29	-04	32	36	34
4				*	44	46	-31	32	29	-15	-43	-35	12	-14	29	-33	-21	-10	-10	22	04	35	39	25
5					*	66	-44	61	49	-28	-29	-30	26	-04	14	-18	-15	-12	-01	34	-04	30	36	25
6						*	-51	47	50	-31	-29	-29	26	-10	22	-21	-25	-16	-05	35	-06	33	40	28
7							*	37	-60	49	39	34	23	14	16	29	15	21	16	37	08	-25	-29	-23
8								*	40	-19	39	34	31	-01	11	-13	-10	-04	07	27	00	25	33	30
9									*	-48	-22	-13	31	-19	18	-24	-01	16	-04	23	-06	25	29	27
10										*	21	-21	25	-11	21	14	-18	-04	-14	38	00	28	29	27
11											*	26	21	06	-16	30	16	16	06	-23	-01	-14	-12	-10
12												*	-08	15	-30	32	25	12	13	-19	-04	-31	-29	-24
13													*	-03	-15	-18	37	10	24	-19	-03	-33	-29	26
14														*	-27	21	-22	-04	-07	23	01	-32	-14	-07
15															*	-09	15	09	07	-02	-09	10	-05	22
16																*	27	16	21	-33	14	-29	-14	-18
17																	*	29	24	-09	14	-32	17	22
18																		*	24	14	-08	10	-05	-05
19																			*	13	-14	10	-20	-16
20																				*	09	27	17	48
21																					*	29	08	15
22																						*	37	41
23																							*	33
24																								*

table D.3   Group Opinion Inventory of Satisfaction Items: Rotated Orthogonal Factor Matrix[a]

Variable Number	Active Task Accomplishment FI	Respondent Participation FII	Likeability of Members FIII	Members' Distrust FIV	Treatment Effects on Respondent FV	Group Participation FVI	h^2
1	−72	−07	00	−14	−21	−07	60
15	−66	16	−15	−17	02	−07	52
11	62	−22	−21	00	14	−05	51
2	−61	−04	09	−20	−36	−01	55
4	−59	05	08	02	−46	−02	57
10	10	−82	−07	06	00	−02	69
7	06	−70	−13	00	32	09	65
9	−07	67	03	−16	−42	−12	67
19	02	07	−73	10	01	−04	55
17	27	−09	−56	21	05	20	49
18	00	−25	−56	−25	03	10	45
21	−16	−01	−13	−67	26	−16	58
24	−16	04	21	−64	−38	02	63
20	−06	33	−03	−56	−39	11	59
22	−25	09	35	−53	−28	−13	56
5	−15	33	−01	01	−72	−05	65
8	−04	21	−08	−09	−71	−12	58
6	−24	39	09	−01	−68	−09	69
3	−34	−08	12	−11	−66	08	59
14	18	−04	−07	−03	−03	78	65
13	10	04	09	−22	−41	−67	69
12	51	−20	−39	05	13	07	48
16	50	−21	−21	04	−03	35	47
23	−34	−01	18	−18	−47	−12	41

[a] Variables have been reordered for ease of interpretation.

table D.4 Satisfaction and Dissatisfaction of Members of Each Type of Counseling Group (Percent "Agree")

FACTOR I ACTIVE TASK ACCOMPLISHMENT (PERCENT "AGREE")

Item	All Groups	Mandatory Large Groups	Mandatory Small Groups	Voluntary Small Groups	x^2 (3 × 4 Table)	P
1. In this group not enough people take responsibility in keeping discussion going.	52	78	53	42	43.29	p < .01
2. Most members do not seem to know what to do.	49	65	52	41	19.05	p < .01
4. The group does not accomplish as much as it should.	56	81	61	43	43.30	p < .01
11. This group tries to do the best it can on group counseling.	74	47	79	83	55.10	p < .01
12. Members' reasoning usually clear and logical.	60	36	65	65	26.00	p < .01
15. There is too much silence in this group.	25	59	25	13	74.00	p < .01
16. Usually everyone talks a fairly equal amount in my group.	52	20	45	68	63.30	p < .01

table D.4 (continued)

FACTOR II RESPONDENT'S PARTICIPATION (PERCENT "AGREE")

Item	All Groups	Mandatory Large Groups	Mandatory Small Groups	Voluntary Small Groups	x^2 (3 × 4 Table)	P
7. I enjoy talking in this group.	72	47	69	84	51.60	p < .01
9. I seldom have anything to say in the group.	32	57	36	19	47.40	p < .01
10. I am fairly active in group discussions.	78	56	76	87	47.50	p < .01

FACTOR III LIKABILITY OF MEMBERS (PERCENT "AGREE")

Item	All Groups	Mandatory Large Groups	Mandatory Small Groups	Voluntary Small Groups	x^2 (3 × 4 Table)	P
17. Most of the men in this group are well thought of by other inmates.	75	59	77	82	18.7	p < .01
18. I have several friends in this group.	77	84	74	76	3.5	Not significant
19. The friendly spirit and joking is one of the best things about this group.	44	24	50	49	28.9	p < .01

table *D.4* (continued)

FACTOR IV MEMBERS' DISTRUST (PERCENT "AGREE")

Item	All Groups	Mandatory Large Groups	Mandatory Small Groups	Voluntary Small Groups	x^2 (3 × 4 Table)	P
20. I am afraid what I say in group counseling sessions may go into my record jacket.	20	35	17	18	18.9	p < .01
21. Members in this group talk about meetings to other inmates.	57	83	48	53	36.3	p < .01
22. The men in this group cannot be trusted to keep confidential what is said in the group.	43	71	43	32	40.3	p < .01
23. Few people are really interested in what is being said in the group.	45	73	47	32	49.5	p < .01
24. Most men in this group hesitate to say anything bad about themselves because it may be reported to the Adult Authority.	38	61	41	29	35.4	p < .01

table D.4   (continued)

FACTOR V   TREATMENT EFFECT ON RESPONDENT (PERCENT "AGREE")

Item	All Groups	Mandatory Large Groups	Mandatory Small Groups	Voluntary Small Groups	x^2 (3 × 4 Table)	P
3. In most of our group meetings, I don't think our conclusions were detailed enough to be realistic.	43	59	46	35	22.9	p < .01
5. I do not think this group is able to help me.	26	42	32	18	28.2	p < .01
6. I am bored most of the time by discussion.	27	45	33	15	45.1	p < .01
8. I do not feel I have a problem this group can help.	35	50	40	26	23.5	p < .01

FACTOR VI   GROUP LEVEL OF PARTICIPATION (PERCENT "AGREE")

Item	All Groups	Mandatory Large Groups	Mandatory Small Groups	Voluntary Small Groups	x^2 (3 × 4 Table)	P
13. Some people in the group talk too much.	42	47	49	36	9.6	Not significant
14. Nobody tries to dominate discussion in my group.	62	59	59	65	5.0	Not significant

opportunity of equal verbal participation: "Some people in the group talk too much" and "Nobody tries to dominate the discussion in my group."

To summarize, the six factors were termed:

I. Active Task Accomplishment of Group (The group makes progress.)
II. Respondent's Participation (In this group I am active.)
III. Likability of Members (Men in this group are liked.)
IV. Members' Distrust (What is said is not kept confidential.)
V. Treatment Effects for Respondent (The group helps me.)
VI. Group Participation Level (The group is active.)

Table D.4 presents data on satisfaction and dissatisfaction. Across all groups, findings can be summarized as follows: (1) one half felt that the group was accomplishing something and that members were trying—the other one half disagreed; (2) three fourths claimed to be active participants; (3) the majority agreed that other group members were active too; (4) few groups were characterized by joking and friendliness, although most members were well thought of by the other group members; (5) there was an optimistic perception of group counseling's therapeutic impact; and (6) considerable dissatisfaction was expressed (although not by a majority) in regard to members' distrust of the privacy of the group.

However, the more interesting consequence of this analysis was the difference *between* mandatory large groups (daily), mandatory small groups (weekly), and voluntary small groups (weekly). Compared to respondents in these latter two counseling varieties, respondents in the mandatory large groups were significantly (1) *more critical* of their group's performance, (2) *less optimistic* concerning the therapeutic effects of the programs, (3) *more distrusting* of fellow inmates and staff, (4) *less active* participants in group sessions, (5) *less favorably* disposed to members of the group and (6) *less likely* to regard their group's spirit as friendly. On one dimension—group activity level—treatment conditions did not vary.

ROLE DIFFERENTIATION

Laboratory studies of small groups call attention to two primary functional problems that characterize groups like the ones under study. These problems are the *task focus* (working toward a group goal) and the *integrative or expressive focus* (expressing and reducing tensions in interpersonal relations). That is, the first is concerned with "getting the job done," the second is concerned with how the members "get along with one another."[3] Davis developed two subtypes

[3] See Robert Bales, *Interaction Process Analysis*, Cambridge: Addison Wesley, 1950;

within each area and formulated a simple measure for each.[4] Within task-related acts the distinction is made between initiating and coordinating behavior; the integrative function is divided into positive expressive (tact) and negative expressive (joking).

We adapted Davis' items to apply to the prison groups. The items below were used as indicators of the task and expressive foci of behavior.

In many groups, some persons tend to one kind of talking more than others. On the questions below, check how you think you are.

Task Initiative

1. (a) I often get the discussion going by introducing ideas and opinions for the rest of the group to talk about. Yes_____ No_____

   (b) How many other men in the group often do this? _____

Task Coordinating

2. (a) In group sessions, I often try to clear things up and keep the discussion on the track. Yes_____ No_____

   (b) How many other men in the group often do this? _____

Expressive Positive

3. (a) I often make comments to heal hurt feelings of other members in the group when the discussion gets rough. Yes_____ No_____

   (b) How many other men in the group often do this? _____

Expressive Negative

4. (a) I often make jokes in the discussion to get a laugh out of the group. Yes_____ No_____.

   (b) How many other men in the group often do this? _____

On both measures of task prominence, and on one measure of integrative behavior, men in mandatory large groups less often reported that they were active than either of the small group counseling conditions. (Of course, this may reflect the fact that the opportunity for participation is more limited in a group of 50, compared with a group of ten or twelve members.) On task coordination, activity was highest for the small, voluntary groups. Similar differences were observed between the three treatment conditions in the responses estimating "how many other men" did a given type of behavior.

and Talcott Parsons, Robert Bales and Edward Shils, "Dimensions of Action Space," in Working Papers in the Theory of Action, Glencoe: The Free Press, 1953.

[4] James A. Davis, Great Books and Small Groups, Glencoe: The Free Press, 1961, pp. 71–72.

table D.5   Task and Expressive Prominence by Type of Counseling
(in percent)

		Mandatory Large	Mandatory Small	Voluntary Small
Task Item A	YES	41	55	72
	NO	59	45	28
	Total (N)	(85)	(154)	(226)
Task Item B	YES	28	51	58
	NO	72	49	42
	Total (N)	(86)	(156)	(232)
Expressive Item A	YES	22	39	39
	NO	78	61	61
	Total (N)	(84)	(153)	(129)
Expressive Item B	YES	17	14	18
	NO	83	86	82
	Total (N)	(89)	(157)	(233)

Task Item A.   In group sessions, I often try to clear things up and keep the discussion on the track. $\chi^2 = 27.94$, df $= 2$, $p \le .01$.

Task Item B.   I often get the discussion going by introducing ideas and opinions for the rest of the group to talk about. $\chi^2 = 23.03$, df $= 2$, $p \le .01$.

Expressive Item A.   I often make comments to heal hurt feelings of other members in the group when the discussion gets rough. $\chi^2 = 8.76$, df $= 2$, $p \le .02$.

Expressive Item B.   I often make jokes in the discussion to get a laugh out of the group. $\chi^2 = 1.11$, df $= 2$, not significant.

Thus, on a variety of measures, satisfaction and activity appeared lowest in Community Living sessions and highest in small, voluntary groups.

appendix E Personality Differences and Parole Outcome[1]

⁣⁣⁣

The California Psychological Inventory (CPI) is a well-known, widely used test intended for use on nonpsychiatric respondents.[2] It consists of 480 simple self-descriptive statements. Its author, Dr. Harrison Gough, developed 18 scales by item analysis to assess nonneurotic, nonpsychopathic components of personality. We calculated these scales but, in a preliminary analysis, did not show any differences between any of the 18-scale—scores and parole success or failure six months after release.

We also were impressed with the need to condense this fairly sizable number of separate scales to a smaller number that would be more economical to use and somewhat easier to conceptualize. Data published by Gough and others show considerable real and artifactual (item-overlap) intercorrelation among the scales. Moreover, the four groupings suggested by Gough are based on the similarity of scale interpretation, in turn, related to item discriminability on criterion groups, and not on correlation clustering. These two facts suggested that fewer and more meaningful scores could be obtained by the factor analysis of the 18-scale—scores when the test was administered to a subsample of 380 inmates prior to their release from CMC. Four factors were extracted by using the principal axis technique. Verimax rotation to simple structure produced the factor matrix shown in Table E.1. The rotation was not wholly successful in locating variables clearly on one factor, but interpretation of the four rotated factors is possible.

Factor I is determined by scales indicating responsibility (Re), Socialization (So), Self-control (Sc), Tolerance (To), Good impression (Gi), and Achievement via conformance (Ac). It shares high loading with Factor IV on Well-being (Wb) and with Factor II on Intellectual efficiency (Ie). The emphasis of these components is on being responsive and on conforming to social expectation. The term *Conventional adjustment* is suggestive of one pole of this factor.

Factor II consists of items measuring outgoing, self-assured activity orienta-

---

[1] See Chapter VIII.

[2] Gough, Harrison, *Manual for the California Psychological Inventory*, Consult. Psych. Press, Palo Alto, 1957.

table E.1   Rotated Factors of the CPI (380 Prison Inmates)

Factor I	Conventional Adjustment				h^2	Gough's Terms
Wb	.68	.21	−.31	−.48	.83	Measures of social-
Re	.76	.37	.03	−.14	.74	ization, maturity and
So	.76	.10	.21	−.00	.63	responsibility.
Sc	.87	−.17	−.27	.11	.88	
To	.64	.30	−.57	−.19	.86	
Gi	.77	.09	−.23	.31	.75	Achievement poten-
Ac	.80	.39	−.15	−.14	.83	tial and intellectual
Ie	.54	.47	−.38	−.42	.84	efficiency.

Factor II	Extroverted Assertiveness				h^2	Gough's Terms
Do	.18	.84	.04	.05	.74	Measures of poise,
Cs	.38	.71	−.37	−.04	.78	ascendancy and self-
Sy	.32	.81	−.08	−.17	.79	assurance.
Sp	−.02	.62	−.52	−.33	.77	
Sa	−.09	.89	.01	−.08	.80	

Factor III	Independent Rationalism				h^2	Gough's Terms
Ai	.42	.20	−.69	−.20	.73	Achievement via in-
Py	.42	.16	−.57	.14	.54	dependence and in-
Fx	−.16	−.08	−.84	.11	.75	tellectual mode.

Factor IV	Feminine Deviance				h^2	Gough's Terms
Cm	.30	.19	.28	−.76	.78	Interest mode.
Fe	.28	−.01	.12	.57	.41	

tion. Scales measuring dominance (Do), Capacity for status (Cs), Sociability (Sy), Social presence (Sp) and Self-acceptance (Sa) show high loadings on this factor, for which the term *Extroverted assertiveness* is suggested.

Factors III and IV are neither statistically nor semantically as clear as the first two dimensions. Factor III is defined on the positive pole by measures of Achievement via independence (Ai), Psychological mindedness (Py), and Flexibility (Fx). The term *Independent rationalism* is advanced to designate this factor.

Factor IV contains only two scales that have high loadings on this dimension. One scale is Femininity (Fm), which loads on the negative end of the factor. On the opposite pole is Communality. Keeping in mind that the sample is male inmates, the term *Feminine deviance* is tentatively advanced for this factor.

The results obtained in this analysis are closely similar to a factor analysis of the CPI published in 1960 by Mitchell and Pierce-Jones, despite differences in sex and type of respondent.[3] The earlier work used a sample containing 213 female and 45 male students in a teacher training curriculum. Four factors resulted, which the authors titled Adjustment via social conformity, Social poise or extroversion, Superego strength, and Capacity for independent thought and action. The loadings obtained by Mitchell and Pierce-Jones are found in Table E.2. The first two factors are almost identical to our analysis. Their fourth factor is somewhat like the third factor in the present report. Their third factor contains scales better located on our Factor I.

Both analyses are consistent with a suggestion by Kassebaum, Couch, and Slater (in an analysis of the MMPI) that the two major factors to emerge in any large personality inventory would be adjustment-maladjustment and extroversion-introversion.[4] Notice that their earlier study contained some of the same scales.

Because of the scale intercorrelations, and the similarity of our factor analysis with previous work, we decided to score the CPI as four dimensions of response, rather than 18 separate scores.

By using the Thompson's pooling squares technique described fully elsewhere,[5] we constructed a scale to measure each factor. This technique allows the investigator to estimate the extent to which each factorial measure is correlated with the other factors, and to add or to subtract variables to increase factorial purity. We were only moderately successful in this effort, as is indicated in Table E.3, showing the degree to which the four scales are associated. Factors II and III are significantly correlated; we were unable to construct a purer measure, possibly because of the amount of item overlap in the component scales.

Scores on Factors I and II were consistent with certain traits of the respondents. Factor I (conventional adjustment) was lower for men with a large number of prior commitments, with men who had done more prison time, and who were first arrested and jailed at an early age. It was also inversely related to favorable parole prognosis, but not significantly. Extroverted assertiveness was positively correlated with grade achievement, intelligence, and father's occupational status. We were particularly curious to learn if these factors or any of the other CPI dimensions would be related to the adjustment of the parolee to the demands of his parole obligations.

We cross tabulated the CPI factor scores with parole adjustment as of

[3] Mitchell, J., and Pierce-Jones, J., "A Factor Analysis of Gough's California Psychological Inventory," *J. Consult. Psychol.*, 1960, **24:5**, pp. 453–456.

[4] Kassebaum, G., Couch, A., and Slater, P., "Factorial Dimensions of the MMPI," *J. Consult. Psychol.*, 1959, **23:3**.

[5] Thompson, Godfrey, *Factorial Analysis of Human Ability* (fifth edition), London: University of London Press, 1951, Chapter IX.

table E.2   Mitchell and Pierce-Jones 1960 Analysis: Rotated Factor-Matrix for the California Psychological Inventory

CPI Scales	I	II	III	IV	h²
Class I measures of poise, ascendancy, and self-assurance					
1. Dominance	.18	.76	.04	−.09	.61
2. Capacity for status	.21	.59	.04	.50	.64
3. Sociability	.27	.78	.04	.15	.71
4. Social presence	−.01	.62	−.23	.51	.70
5. Self-acceptance	−.17	.77	.08	.05	.63
6. Sense of well-being	.79	.16	.05	.23	.70
Class II measures of socialization, maturity, and responsibility					
7. Responsibility	.58	.09	.44	.21	.58
8. Socialization	.43	.02	.57	−.06	.51
9. Self-control	.92	−.19	.08	−.01	.77
10. Tolerance	.67	.11	.15	.54	.78
11. Good impression	.83	.08	−.08	−.06	.71
12. Communality	.02	.06	.58	−.02	.34
Class III measures of achievement potential and intellectual efficiency					
13. Achievement by conformance	.80	.25	.23	.08	.77
14. Achievement by independence	.47	.02	.11	.67	.69
15. Intellectual efficiency	.46	.24	.16	.53	.58
Class IV measures of intellectual and interest modes					
16. Psychological mindedness	.47	.22	−.16	.32	.40
17. Flexibility	−.12	.02	−.25	.56	.39
18. Femininity	−.02	−.02	.45	−.04	.21
Percentage of total variance	26%	15%	7%	12%	

36 months postrelease (see Tables E.4 to E.7). There was a slight tendency for more conventional individuals to be returned less often to prison than low scorers on I, but the difference was not significantly greater than chance. Factor II is also in this direction but, again, the difference is slight and not significant. We are forced to conclude that personality characteristics, at least as measured by the CPI, are not directly related to parole success or failure.

table E.3   Correlation of Factor Loadings and CPI Scale Scores

The Scale Scores Measuring Each Factor	Correlation Coefficients			
	I	II	III	IV
I Conventional adjustment	.98	.08	.04	.00
II Extrovertive assertiveness	.05	.98	−.06	.02
III Independent rationality	−.29	.12	−.90	.02
IV Feminine deviance	−.01	−.15	−.12	.99

table E.4   Factor I Conventional Adjustment (in percent)

Thirty-Six- Month Outcome	Low	Medium	Medium-High	High
No problems	22	21	22	25
Minor problems	15	19	18	18
Major problems	11	9	8	12
Return to prison	52	51	52	45
Total	100	100	100	100
N	(65)	(104)	(123)	(51)

Table N = 343
$\chi^2 = 1.75$
Degrees of freedom = 9
Not significant

table E.5   Factor II Extroverted Assertiveness (in percent)

Thirty-Six- Month Outcome	Low	Medium	Medium-High	High
No problems	23	25	18	25
Minor problems	16	19	16	23
Major problems	3	11	11	8
Return to prison	58	45	55	44
Total	100	100	100	100
N	(61)	(113)	(120)	(49)

Table N = 343
$\chi^2 = 7.56$
Degrees of freedom = 9
Not significant

table E.6   Factor III Independent Rationalism (in percent)

Thirty-Six-Month Outcome	Low	Medium	Medium-High	High
No problems	22	23	25	14
Minor problems	14	16	20	22
Major problems	12	9	7	12
Return to prison	52	52	48	52
Total	100	100	100	100
N	(50)	(128)	(115)	(50)

Table $N = 343$
$\chi^2 = 5.31$
Degrees of freedom = 9
Not significant

table E.7   Factor IV Feminine Deviance (in percent)

Thirty-Six Month Outcome	Low	Medium	Medium-High	High
No problems	24	15	14	12
Minor problems	18	24	10	0
Major problems	9	9	10	12
Return to prison	49	52	66	76
Total	100	100	100	100
N	(281)	(33)	(21)	(8)

Table $N = 343$
$\chi^2 = 7.33$
Degrees of freedom = 9
Not significant

appendix F   Endorsement of Inmate Values by Parole Outcome at Thirty-Six Months[1]

Table 1   Opposition to Staff
Table 2   Solidarity
Table 3   Isolation
Table 4   Alienation
Table 5   Value of Counseling

table F.1   Opposition to Staff by Parole Outcome at Thirty-Six Months (in Percent)

Opposition to Staff	Parole Outcome				Total
	No Problems	Minor Problems	Major Problems	Return to Prison	
Very high	26	21	2	51	100 (57)
High	22	18	10	50	100 (95)
Moderate	17	20	6	57	100 (70)
Low	20	17	5	58	100 (60)
	(60)	(53)	(17)	(152)	

Table N = 282
$\chi^2 = 6.08$
Degrees of freedom = 9
Not significant

[1] See Chapter VIII.

table F.2   Solidarity by Parole Outcome at Thirty-Six Months (in Percent)

Solidarity	No Problems	Minor Problems	Major Problems	Return to Prison	Total
Very high	27	16	5	52	100 (58)
High	28	18	7	47	100 (74)
Moderate	9	26	6	59	100 (78)
Low	22	15	6	57	100 (72)
	(60)	(53)	(17)	(152)	

Table N = 282
$\chi^2 = 12.55$
Degrees of freedom = 9
Not significant

table F.3   Isolation by Parole Outcome at Thirty-Six Months (in Percent)

Isolation	No Problems	Minor Problems	Major Problems	Return to Prison	Total
Very high	17	17	11	55	100 (54)
High	24	24	—	52	100 (94)
Moderate	21	17	6	56	100 (84)
Low	22	14	12	52	100 (50)
	(60)	(53)	(17)	(152)	

Table N = 282
$\chi^2 = 14.43$
Degrees of freedom = 9
Not significant

table F.4   Alienation by Parole Outcome at Thirty-Six Months (in Percent)

	Parole Outcome				
Alienation	No Problems	Minor Problems	Major Problems	Return to Prison	Total
Very High	35	5	5	55	100 (54)
High	22	26	4	48	100 (105)
Moderate	13	15	5	67	100 (55)
Low	16	22	10	52	100 (68)
	(60)	(53)	(17)	(152)	

Table N = 282
$\chi^2 = 21.69$
Degrees of freedom = 9
P ≤ .01
Gamma = .111

table F.5   Value of Counseling by Parole Outcome at Thirty-Six Months (in Percent)

	Parole Outcome				
Value of Counseling	No Problems	Minor Problems	Major Problems	Return to Prison	Total
Very High	34	10	5	51	100 (59)
High	21	23	5	51	100 (61)
Moderate	15	24	7	54	100 (75)
Low	18	17	7	58	100 (87)
	(60)	(53)	(17)	(152)	

Table N = 282
$\chi^2 = 11.18$
Degrees of freedom = 9
Not significant

appendix G Prison Experience and Postrelease Experience[1]

Table 1 Days Following Parole Date Spent in the Institution Awaiting Release
Table 2 Pre-Parole Class Attendance
Table 3 Pre-Parole Employment
Table 4 Last Year of School Completed when Paroled
Table 5 Inmate Type
Table 6 Evidence of a Criminal Record in the Community to which Parolee was Released

[1] See Chapter VIII.

table G.1   Days Following Parole Date Spent in the Institution Awaiting Release by Treatment Status (in Percent)

Days Awaiting Release	Treatment Category				
	Mandatory Control	Voluntary Control	Mandatory Large Group	Mandatory Small Group	Voluntary Small Group
Release prior to parole date	10	5	2	8	8
Within 3 days	55	61	60	58	55
More than 3 days	11	8	17	16	9
No exact date specified, to be released when parole plan was approved	24	26	21	18	28
Total	100	100	100	100	100
N	(163)	(138)	(47)	(120)	(179)

Parole Subsample
Table N = 647
$\chi^2 = 13.63$
Degrees of freedom = 12
Not significant

table G.2   Pre-Parole Class Attendance by Treatment Status (in Percent)

			Treatment Category		
Number of Preparole Classes Attended	Mandatory Control	Voluntary Control	Mandatory Large Group	Mandatory Small Group	Voluntary Small Group
None	38	35	17	25	29
One	48	42	73	51	50
Two or more	14	23	10	24	21
Total	100	100	100	100	100
N	(141)	(125)	(41)	(111)	(169)

Parole Subsample
Table $N = 587$ (no information $= 60$)
$\chi^2 = 18.91$
Degrees of freedom $= 8$
$p \leq .05$
Gamma $= .097$

table G.3   Prerelease Employment by Treatment Status (in Percent)

			Treatment Category		
Prerelease Employment	Mandatory Control	Voluntary Control	Mandatory Large Group	Mandatory Small Group	Voluntary Small Group
Definite job	46	45	41	57	43
Salvation Army, job did not materialize, Union hiring hall, released without a job	54	55	59	43	57
Total	100	100	100	100	100
N	(156)	(136)	(44)	(115)	(172)

Parole Subsample
Table $N = 623$ (no information $= 24$)
$\chi^2 = 7.01$
Degrees of freedom $= 4$
Not significant

table G.4 Last Year of School Completed when Paroled by Treatment Status (in Percent)

Last Year of School Completed	Mandatory Control	Voluntary Control	Mandatory Large Group	Mandatory Small Group	Voluntary Small Group	Total
Fourth or less	4.0	2.2	7.2	5.7	6.4	4.9 (48)
Fifth or sixth	13.7	22.7	15.9	13.2	14.3	15.6 (151)
Seventh or eighth	25.9	25.5	28.9	28.3	25.8	26.5 (256)
Ninth	16.6	17.6	13.0	15.6	13.3	15.4 (149)
Tenth or eleventh	19.6	16.4	21.7	17.3	20.8	19.1 (185)
Twelfth	12.2	10.7	10.1	13.8	10.4	11.5 (112)
Less than one year college or post high school courses	2.9	2.2	2.8	5.2	4.3	3.6 (35)
One year college	2.9	.5	—	—	2.8	1.7 (17)
Two or more years college but no graduation or degree	1.1	1.7	—	.5	.7	.9 (9)
College graduation or degree	.7	—	—	—	.7	.4 (4)
Total	100.0	100.0	100.0	100.0	100.0	100.0
N	(270)	(176)	(69)	(173)	(278)	

Parole Follow-up Sample
Table N = 966 (no information = 2)
$\chi^2 = 35.90$
Degrees of freedom = 36
Not significant

table G.5   Inmate Type of Treatment Status (in Percent)

Type	Mandatory Control	Voluntary Control	Mandatory Large Group	Mandatory Small Group	Voluntary Small Group	Total	
Square John	36	27	29	24	26	29	(82)
Politician	25	27	24	22	26	25	(72)
Right Guy	21	33	33	30	30	28	(81)
Outlaw	18	13	14	24	18	18	(51)
Total	100	100	100	100	100	100	
N	(79)	(45)	(21)	(54)	(87)		

Sample for Inmate Typology
Table N = 286 (no information = 1)
$\chi^2 = 6.01$
Degrees of freedom = 12
Not signifcant

table G.6 Evidence of a Criminal Record in the Community to which Parolee was Released by Treatment Status (in Percent)

Evidence of a Criminal Record	Treatment Category					
	Mandatory Control	Voluntary Control	Mandatory Large Group	Mandatory Small Group	Voluntary Small Group	Total
Yes	70	65	65	64	65	66 (629)
No	30	35	35	36	35	34 (337)
Total	100	100	100	100	100	100
N	(270)	(176)	(69)	(173)	(278)	

Parole Follow-up Sample
Table N = 966 (no information = 2)
$\chi^2 = 2.8$
Degrees of freedom = 4
Not significant

374

Author Index

Subject Index